Beginning Portable Shell Scripting

From Novice to Professional

Peter Seebach

Apress®

Lead Editor: Frank Pohlmann
Technical Reviewer: Gary V. Vaughan
Editorial Board: Clay Andres, Steve Anglin, Ewan Buckingham, Tony Campbell, Gary Cornell,
    Jonathan Gennick, Michelle Lowman, Matthew Moodie, Jeffrey Pepper, Frank Pohlmann,
    Ben Renow-Clarke, Dominic Shakeshaft, Matt Wade, Tom Welsh
Project Manager: Richard Dal Porto
Copy Editor: Kim Benbow
Associate Production Director: Kari Brooks-Copony
Production Editor: Katie Stence
Compositor: Linda Weidemann, Wolf Creek Press
Proofreader: Dan Shaw
Indexer: Broccoli Information Management
Cover Designer: Kurt Krames
Manufacturing Director: Tom Debolski

Distributed to the book trade worldwide by Springer-Verlag New York, Inc., 233 Spring Street, 6th Floor, New York, NY 10013. Phone 1-800-SPRINGER, fax 201-348-4505, e-mail orders-ny@springer-sbm.com, or visit http://www.springeronline.com.

For information on translations, please contact Apress directly at 2855 Telegraph Avenue, Suite 600, Berkeley, CA 94705. Phone 510-549-5930, fax 510-549-5939, e-mail info@apress.com, or visit http://www.apress.com.

Apress and friends of ED books may be purchased in bulk for academic, corporate, or promotional use. eBook versions and licenses are also available for most titles. For more information, reference our Special Bulk Sales–eBook Licensing web page at http://www.apress.com/info/bulksales.

The source code for this book is available to readers at http://www.apress.com. You may need to answer questions pertaining to this book in order to successfully download the code.

For Nora, who believed.

Contents at a Glance

Contents

APPENDIX B   **The *sh* Utility** 297

About the Author

PETER SEEBACH is a programmer who writes or, possibly, a writer who programs. He enjoys writing on topics from C standardization to operating system internals; he programs in C, Ruby, Lua, and shell by preference and several other languages when absolutely necessary. He lives in Northfield, Minnesota, and owns cats (who cannot program and do not write).

About the Technical Reviewer

GARY V. VAUGHAN, in his own words:

```
: ${This='sed -n'} #ightly:
$This 1s,^,not\ ,p<<rose
obsfuscated!
With red pen wielded
every page will be a
rose

: A perpetual traveler with no
time `for sight_seeing in earnest. I
do sleep ${when-1} # am
done`; juggling=100 pet=projects...

# but somehow,
in_the_end () { I=always return "to mending libtool"; }
```

(You get extra credit if you can predict what this would do if you ran it.)

Acknowledgments

The idea for this book came from Frank Pohlmann, who also edited it and provided a great deal of guidance in making sense of my disjointed ramblings on the topic. Gary V. Vaughan's technical advice and broad experience were invaluable throughout. I am particularly indebted to Sven Mascheck's excellent pages of information about historical shells, as well as the guide to shell portability included in the autoconf documentation. Many other developers contributed tidbits, interesting trivia, or feedback on proposed code; there are too many to list, I'm afraid. This book (and everything else I do) would not have been possible without support from my beloved spouse, Jesse.

## CHAPTER 1

Introduction to Shell Scripting

The UNIX command-line interface has been criticized for complexity and a steep learning curve, but no one disputes that it is one of the most flexible and programmable user interfaces ever developed. The core of the UNIX command-line interface is the *shell*, a program that interprets and executes user commands. The shell can take commands from a keyboard or stored in files; the syntax and commands are the same either way. A file containing shell commands is called a *shell script*. Many systems offer shells that are arguably programmable; the UNIX shell environment is actually good at it. As a result, thousands upon thousands of programs have been implemented as shell scripts. This book treats the shell as a serious programming language and introduces the practice of *portable* shell scripting—the development of scripts that can be expected to run on a variety of host systems or even different shells on the same system. What systems, you ask? Anything that looks reasonably like UNIX, whether it's Solaris, Linux, NetBSD, OS X, or even environments such as Cygwin, which provides UNIX-like behavior under Windows. Don't mistake this for an exhaustive list; I don't have the space to include one; and furthermore, new systems that are released may well comply with the same standards.

Not everyone thinks highly of portability as a goal. Linus Torvalds once said, "Portability is for people who cannot write new programs." As a great fan of portability, I am inclined to nearly agree. I prefer, "Portability is for people who are too busy to write new programs." Users often imagine that portability is a gigantic nightmare requiring a huge amount of additional work; however, in the vast majority of cases, writing portable code takes little extra time, and pays for itself quickly. Portability usually does not mean writing completely different versions of the same program for every system; rather, it means writing a single version that is correct everywhere.

About This Book

This book is about programming in the Bourne shell and its derivatives; the Korn shell, the Bourne-again shell, and the POSIX shell are among the most obvious relatives. This book does not cover the many other UNIX and UNIX-like shells, such as Plan 9's rc, or the Berkeley csh. It does cover a number of common UNIX commands, as well as a few somewhat less common commands, and briefly looks into some common utilities, such as sed and awk, which have historically been used heavily in shell scripting. While even further divergent things, such as AppleScript, the Tcl shell, or even graphical shells like the Mac OS X Finder, are technically shells, this book ignores them entirely, and hereafter uses the term *shell* to refer to the UNIX Bourne shell family.

The audience for this book is UNIX users who wish to write shell scripts. The focus on portability offers a better investment in future utility, but the material should be useful even to users who only plan to work on a single system. Portability is not restricted to running on different variants of UNIX; it also applies to running on future releases of the same variant or on different shells. This book is not intended as a complete or comprehensive reference to the shell or to UNIX commands. Instead, it offers information on the shell language, with a focus on areas where shells or utilities vary. Since the shell is not just a single language but a family of related languages, this book also talks about how you decide what shells to use and how to adapt to other shells. Furthermore, this book covers the basics of effective shell programming and effective use of other peoples' shell programs. You may be asked to run a nonportable script on a new system; this book helps you do that. It is never too late to begin thinking about portability.

It is assumed that the reader has some familiarity with UNIX shell conventions and syntax, as well as common UNIX commands. For instance, I do not explain what echo or rm does. However, a novice user should be able to understand the material with a little extra time spent playing with the examples.

Conventions

This book uses a number of typographical conventions for clarity. As you have probably already noticed, code fragments, such as the names of programs like grep in the main text, are represented in monospaced text. Longer code fragments are illustrated as follows:

```
#!/bin/sh
# hello.sh, version 6.23.7: greet the reader
echo "hello, world!"
```

When the results of a code fragment are displayed, they are shown in a separate listing, like this:

```
hello, world!
```

References to UNIX manual pages use the conventional *program(section)* usage; for instance, ls(1) refers to the ls program in section 1 of the UNIX manual. In cases where user input is included in a code listing, user input is in **bold**. Italicized text is used to indicate key definitions of technical terms; a *technical term* is a word you already know being used to refer to a specific technical feature of the shell (or of this book). Italics are also used to identify placeholder names. The rm *file* command removes *file*.

Shell scripts are rich with punctuation, and conventions are adopted for this as well. When first referring to punctuation, I generally use the most common name (and occasionally common alternatives, especially when they are more common for a particular usage) and illustrate the symbol in parentheses. Fonts and displays vary widely, so the symbols you see on your computer may look a bit different. For instance, the vertical bar character (|) is a solid bar on some systems, and on other systems may look nearly the same as a colon (:). The character with the most names is probably the symbol called variously octothorpe, sharp, hash, or pound (#). The name octothorpe is my favorite because people are completely consistent in not having any idea what I'm talking about, but in this book I use sharp, which is originally musical terminology for the symbol. If you have never studied music, this is a great excuse to start now. Further references to a symbol may use a common name or just the symbol inline in the code format for brevity.

What Shell Scripting Is

For purposes of this book, the term *shell script*, or just *script*, is used to refer to any program written in the Bourne shell language (Bourne shell is the traditional UNIX /bin/sh) or its derivatives. The UNIX shell is not just the primary user interface of a traditional UNIX system; it is also a full-featured programming language. Shell scripts are simply sets of shell commands, just like those entered on the command line. Indeed, experienced shell programmers often type simple scripts directly on the command line, rather than storing them in a file.

Although any shell can be used interactively or for scripting, there are often differences between a good scripting shell and a good interactive shell. An interactive shell should nearly always have rich command editing and history facilities; these are useless in scripting. A good scripting shell should be fast and ideally small for performance reasons; this weighs against it being the best choice for a command-line shell. Some users do prefer the more advanced feature sets of the bigger shells, even for scripting, but those features make scripts less portable.

The word "scripting" reflects a historical assumption about shell programming; the majority of shell programs are automations of tasks humans can, or used to, perform. The computing world is full of horror stories about some huge task that someone spent hours (or days) performing manually. The horror in these stories comes not just from the large amount of time spent, but rather, from the understanding that the time was *wasted*. However, in modern usage, scripting usually refers more to a language implementation choice; a scripting language is one in which code is parsed at runtime, rather than a compiled language (such as C). In this book, the term *script* is usually used to refer to a shell program.

Scripting is not restricted in scope to major defined projects with written requirements. Shell programs tend to be small, quickly written, and astonishingly powerful for their size. Common, daily tasks are frequently automated by shell users. Even users who do not consider themselves programmers often take advantage of some of the more familiar "cookbook" shell scripting features. Experienced users will write simple programs "on the fly," typing them directly at the prompt without bothering to create a file to hold the code. Larger shell programs are somewhat rarer, but they have their place as well. Most noticeably, the configure scripts shipped with thousands of free software packages are actually shell scripts, and very complicated (and surprisingly portable) ones at that.

Used well, the shell can perform in a variety of roles. In general, the shell is used to manipulate things. Three things shell programs often manipulate are

- Data
- Files
- Other programs

Manipulating Data

A huge number of shell scripts revolve around the large variety of line-oriented utilities for manipulating textual data that have been provided with UNIX systems. Not every data stream is easily or naturally represented as a series of lines of text. However, an astounding variety of data can be represented this way, and doing so provides access to a wealth of flexible utilities to solve any number of complicated problems.

The exceptionally rich selection of data-manipulation utilities provided by UNIX-like systems owes a great deal to the huge problem space that line-oriented data lends itself well to. Furthermore, line-oriented data are often exceptionally friendly to human users, who can immediately see whether results are roughly as expected; this has led to using a lot of simple line-oriented data streams in prototyping and development phases.

A number of UNIX utilities build on this by providing translations from other data sources to line-oriented data, which can then be massaged easily through simple shell scripts to produce detailed reports. The existence of a convenient "glue" language to let utilities cooperate encourages the development of small, specialized programs that work together effectively to accomplish virtually any computing task. Such programs may be slower than custom-coded applications for a particular job, but they take a fraction of the development effort to produce.

For the cases where line-oriented textual representations of data are inappropriate, the shell can still provide an excellent glue language. Archive utilities, graphics utilities, and others have been built around the flexibility inherent in the shell. Users coming from a non-UNIX background are often shocked that the most common native archive utilities on UNIX do not perform any compression; their archives contain the included files unmodified. The wisdom of this is revealed when you look at the space savings of replacing the classic compress program with the newer gzip, and later of replacing gzip with bzip2 or even the newer lzma. In each case, the archive programs (most notably tar) could be used with a new compression or decompression algorithm without any modifications at all. Likewise, a change from one archiver to another can be handled nearly transparently.

Manipulating Files

Sometimes, what matters isn't the content of files, but manipulating the files themselves or the directories containing them. Thus far, the shell is simply unequaled in this field; indeed, the most technically impressive graphical applications are so far from the power and flexibility of the shell that it is hard to think of them as competition at all. On some desktop systems, a program to tell you how much space each directory on your system takes up, and perhaps help you clean it, might be successfully sold as commercial software. In the UNIX shell, a fairly detailed report—even coupled with automatic archiving of rarely used large files—is a simple matter of typing a few lines of code.

However, file manipulation code is easy to get wrong, especially with files with unusual names, such as those using special characters or spaces. There are many shell idioms that simply cannot be made to function when interacting with file names containing new lines; avoid these like the plague. Other special characters can be less painful, but spaces in file names trigger an astounding variety of bugs, even in long-used scripts written by experienced programmers. Unfortunately, you cannot always control the names files are given by users.

A great deal of shell programming revolves around file manipulation, and this has led to an astonishingly rich variety of file-related tools on most UNIX systems. Some of these tools are a little opaque to users; in many cases, this is because they are designed first as building blocks to use in shell scripts and only secondly as programs to be used directly by users.

Installation utilities can be written as shell scripts, taking advantage of the portability and flexibility of the shell, as well as its ability to embed other data. A once-common example was "shell archive" (or shar) files, which consisted of simple shell programs to reproduce a series of files portably on remote systems. These fell into relative disuse due to the security problems implicit in using execution of code generated on another system as an archive format and the widespread availability of substantially more robust archive utilities. On the other hand, the GNU tar utility source code is available as a shell script because users who have no archive utilities have to start somewhere. (Similarly, GNU make has a shell script build procedure available.)

Manipulating Programs

Scripts are used heavily in nearly every phase of a UNIX system's life. With the exception of Mac OS X's launchd, virtually every UNIX system's service startup is handled through a maze of shell scripts. From the System V init scripts (reproduced, loosely, in many Linux systems) to NetBSD's very different rc.d subsystem, shell programs are excellently suited to the task of identifying configuration state and running programs appropriately. I have met many programmers who are not system administrators, but I've never met a successful UNIX system administrator who couldn't program in shell.

Shell programs have been heavily used in bootstrapping the builds of programs in other languages, such as C. The GNU autoconf suite builds huge (and impressively robust) shell scripts that run reliably across hundreds of platforms. The portability of carefully written shell code often makes it easier to develop robust tests and automate common build processes; anyone who has had to manually edit header files to configure for a local UNIX-like system's quirks will be familiar with the disadvantages of the manual process. Shell scripts are often more portable than features of other programs; for instance, using a shell script to build a makefile for use with the make utility may be easier than writing a makefile that works with all the common variants.

This kind of usage is often called "glue" code; it is the code that holds things together. UNIX utilities and programs are often designed with the assumption that, if you really need to automate a function, you will write a program to do so. The shell is one of the primary languages used to do this.

What Shell Scripting Isn't

Shell scripts are not a complete replacement for programs in other languages. One issue is that the shell is almost always slower than a compiled language, or even than many interpreted languages, but there are additional limitations. Many of the utility programs scripts are ill-equipped to handle arbitrary binary data, or data where the primary unit of operation isn't a single line of text. The shell itself is virtually useless as a language; the real power and flexibility come from the huge variety of utility programs the shell can use to perform common tasks. Paying attention to portability can restrict your options further, even as it gives you the chance of running on a wider variety of targets.

Scripts are not usually high-performance. Programs that are computationally intensive are unlikely to be written in shell in the first place; a ray-tracer in shell would be more of an installation artwork than a programming project.

Shell scripts are usually portable only between UNIX-like environments. With the introduction of Mac OS X, that has come to include the Macintosh desktop environment, as well as the traditional UNIX-like servers (and desktops). Windows users with the Cygwin environment, or commercial products like the MKS Toolkit, may also take advantage of shell scripting, but shell techniques usually don't translate well to an unmodified Windows system.

With specialized exceptions, shell scripts are essentially free of graphical interfaces. There are a few add-ons or specialized utilities to allow some graphical work, but they are not portable. Furthermore, they don't seem to fit well with the underlying philosophy of the shell; you're usually better off switching to a more general language at that point.

Performance Issues

Shell scripts generally don't perform very quickly. Many of the most fundamental actions in a script involve the spawning of a completely separate program to actually do the work. In fact, the amount of work going on behind the scenes in shell scripts is huge; it is a major influence on the very low tolerance that UNIX-like systems have for high-process startup costs. Shell scripts are at their best when the computational or I/O requirements of their tasks exceed the cost of spawning additional processes. Writers expecting their scripts to run on emulated UNIX-like environments on systems like Windows have to exercise caution.

In many cases, a script with performance issues becomes an invitation to develop a well-considered utility program. Sometimes writing even a simple small C program can dramatically improve the performance of a script, but the development time cost tends to reserve this for the rare case when a script's performance is primarily shell-bound.

Expansion Options

The shell has either the most astoundingly flexible plug-in architecture ever seen in a programming language, or no plug-in architecture at all. I lean toward the latter view. You can implement anything you want as a tool usable in shell scripts, as long as it maps well onto line-oriented textual data. Support for manipulation of binary streams is decent but much more limited; you cannot expect to use grep effectively on them, for instance. The language simply doesn't provide for the sorts of plug-ins and extensions that you see in languages like C, Perl, or Ruby. While some shells offer frameworks to allow new features to be plugged in, the language specification doesn't provide for this at all. This can be a disadvantage. Well-designed glue utilities can help some, but there are limits to what you can express cleanly enough to justify the effort.

Why Shell?

After this discussion of the limitations and weaknesses of the shell, you may wonder why shell scripting matters. The answer is simple; while there are things the shell isn't good at, for the things shell is good at, there is very little better. Very few languages are as widely available. There are hundreds of thousands of devices running UNIX-like systems these days, and they may not come with a compiler, but they very often include a shell and some core functional commands. Even if you do not intend to write many shell scripts, the commands in a UNIX makefile are shell commands; and many things that are too complicated for make to handle are trivial in the shell. Of course, this makes it possible that your makefile, rather than your C code, will be the limiting factor on where your code is portable.

The shell is a powerful and expressive language. The huge library of existing filters and tools is a great starting point. Furthermore, shell programming makes it easy to build new filters from existing filters. Familiarity with the shell can also make it easier to solve programming tasks that require work in other languages; often, the shell's amazing flexibility as glue code to combine things allows a couple of small, simple programs to give you a very powerful program.

Furthermore, shell programming pays dividends in daily use if you work on a UNIX-like system. Being able to write small scripts to handle common tasks (or even one-off tasks that would take hours to do by hand) justifies a little time spent learning a new language.

In the end, the UNIX shell is one of the most durable programming languages in use today. While there have been extensions and developments in shell programming over the past 30 years, many shell programs written in the 1970s are still usable today. While competing languages have found some traction, they primarily target tasks the shell isn't good at, leaving the shell's primary domain largely unchallenged.

The Bourne Shell Family

This book focuses on shells derived from the classic Bourne shell distributed with early UNIX, and, in particular, on the standard POSIX shell. There are a number of shells in this family, and this book covers some of the common (or unique, but interesting anyway) extensions they offer over the base shell language. The shells covered are the following:

- *Bourne shell (old* sh*)*: The shell that started it all. The Bourne shell was the standard system shell in early AT&T UNIX, and most modern shells are moderately compatible with it. While this is the baseline, early Bourne shells lacked some features now universally provided. For most users, this shell is of marginal relevance, as nearly all major systems now provide a POSIX shell; only a few do not provide a POSIX shell as /bin/sh. More information on getting into a more modern shell is provided in Chapter 7.

- *POSIX shell (*sh*)*: This is the baseline shell. Users familiar with older UNIX systems will note that many of the features described for the POSIX shell are innovations (many of them inherited or acquired from variant shells). While an occasional reference is made to some of the limitations of earlier shells, the modern landscape is consistent in providing reasonably stable and full-featured POSIX shells. Furthermore, even on systems lacking such a shell, it is usually practical to acquire one of the other variants. In most cases, *portable* in this book means "running on the POSIX shell without modification."

- *Almquist shell (*ash*)*: The Almquist shell was developed as a reasonably compatible independent re-implementation of the POSIX shell included with SVR4 UNIX. It was distributed originally primarily with BSD variants. This shell is much smaller than some of the other variants, but maintains (in its original form) POSIX compatibility. The Almquist shell is familiar to many users as the Busybox shell.

- *Bourne-again shell (*bash*)*: The GNU Bourne-again shell is the largest, and arguably most complete, shell. It has a history of aggressive feature adoption, and can run nearly anything, although early versions had some compatibility quirks. Many Linux systems ship with bash as the default /bin/sh, as does current Mac OS X. Scripts developed for bash, and using its extensions, may not run on other shells. Many users dislike the performance costs of bash. A number of scripts for Linux systems (such as the quilt patch manager) assume that the shell is bash, which has caused portability problems. Don't do that.

- *Debian Almquist shell* (dash): This is a derivative of the Almquist shell used in Debian and derived systems, such as Ubuntu. It has been installed as the default shell on some Debian variants for a while now, exposing a number of scripts that erroneously depended on bash-only extensions. This shell exists as a small, fast implementation of the basic portable shell.

- *Korn shell* (ksh): Developed by David G. Korn at AT&T, ksh was one of the first Bourne shell derivatives to add many of the features now adopted elsewhere as standard. There are multiple versions: historic ksh, the 1988 revision (ksh88), and the 1993 revision (ksh93). The current versions are available as source from AT&T.

- *Public-domain Korn shell* (pdksh): Before the Korn shell became free software, a public domain clone of it was written. While there are a few noticeable compatibility differences, for the most part, pdksh and ksh88 are compatible implementations. A number of systems have used pdksh as a shortcut to getting a reasonably full-featured POSIX shell. More modern systems often replace pdksh with ksh93.

- *Z shell* (zsh): The Z shell is probably by far the most divergent of those listed here from the historical Bourne shell. However, zsh can be configured to perform as a fairly solid POSIX shell, and on some systems it may be the only shell available that can be made to execute POSIX shell code at all. (For more information on encouraging zsh to behave like a POSIX shell, see Chapter 7.)

Nearly every example in this book (except those used to illustrate differences between these shells) will run identically on all of these except the pre-POSIX Bourne shell. This diversity of options is certainly one of the reasons to favor shell-derived languages for programming.

Why Portable?

Portable code is more useful. If your scripts are portable, they will survive changes in your platform. This offers two key benefits. First, you can freely switch platforms whenever you want. Second, you can use a broader range of platforms.

There is no perfect system. Every system you might use has flaws. You will want to change systems from time to time. You may find that your best choices for different systems are different operating systems, running on different hardware. Portability lets you share code between things. People, and companies, have been known to get trapped on a platform because they wrote unportable code that makes it too expensive to migrate. In the long run, writing portable code saves you work.

Furthermore, the cost of portability is often greatly overestimated. People look at the pages and pages of output of a typical configure script and assume that there are dozens or hundreds of things they need to check for and write alternative code for. In general, this is not the case. Writing unportable code for two systems, as well as code to distinguish between them, is not generally the first strategy to take when pursuing portability. Programs taking that approach, whether in shell or any other language, in general become quickly unmaintainable.

The best way to write portable code is to understand the language and tools you are working with. A lot of unportable code results from people who don't understand a chunk of code, copying it and modifying it until it seems to work. Don't do that! It is fine to copy a chunk of code you do not understand; however, study it and experiment until you understand it before you use it. Often, much of the code in a large and poorly maintained project is irrelevant and unneeded, and it is present only because someone saw it done and didn't understand why.

As developers throughout the open source world have learned, and documented, in many cases there is no real difference between writing code well and writing it portably. Well-organized code that isolates its assumptions (see the discussion on this in Chapters 7 and 8) tends to be easy to maintain on any platform, as well as easy to port. Furthermore, as soon as you give some attention to the assumptions you have made about your environment, you are likely to realize that you do not need to make those assumptions. Fixing the assumptions creates code that is not only more portable, but also simpler and thus easier to maintain.

Many programming books encourage you to try experiments to see what happens. This often leads to horribly unportable code. Portable code behaves predictably on multiple systems. Unportable code doesn't necessarily behave badly; it may, in fact, do exactly what you were hoping for on the machine you were on when you tried it. Knowing that something "works" on a single machine is no substitute for knowing how it works and being able to predict what it will do on another machine.

Does this mean you shouldn't perform experiments? Of course not! It means you should perform your experiments several times on a variety of computers and shells. Don't be too quick to trust vague memories, either of what is or what is not portable. (For a concrete example, see the sidebar "Checking Your Assumptions" later in this chapter.)

Why Not?

This book focuses on the Bourne shell, with a little discussion of the major derivatives. I don't talk about the C shell (csh) much, even though this is a book on shell scripting. There are several reasons for this, but they all come down to the C shell being a pretty decent interactive shell, though not nearly as good as a programming shell. Tom Christiansen's seminal article "Csh Programming Considered Harmful" has stood the test of time, and this representative quote is as true today as it was when it was first written:

> *While some vendors have fixed some of the csh's bugs (the tcsh also does much better here), many have added new ones. Most of its problems can never be solved because they're not actually bugs per se, but rather the direct consequences of braindead design decisions. It's inherently flawed.*

> —Tom Christiansen, www.faqs.org/faqs/unix-faq/shell/csh-whynot/

The C shell is not a compatible relative of the Bourne shell; past the simplest one-liner scripts, the two are simply incompatible. The C shell and its variants (most noticeably tcsh) are popular for interactive use but have little to offer for portable shell programming. Their most significant features are related to elaborate (and extremely powerful) command history. The job control features that motivated many users to switch to the C shell are now widely available in Bourne shell derivatives. Perhaps more importantly for the purposes of this book, these features have essentially no impact on noninteractive use in scripts.

Other UNIX-like shells, such as Plan 9's excellent rc, are omitted, not because they are ill-suited to development, but because they are not as consistently installed on as broad a base of systems as the Bourne shell family and offer very different language features. Any UNIX-like machine you use will have a shell that is similar enough to the Bourne shell for programming purposes; many will not have the other shells installed. While it is often easy to install these shells, you may not always have the permissions needed to install them globally, and needing to do so is one more thing that can go wrong. More generally, non-shell scripting languages, such as Tcl or Perl, are too far afield to mix well, even though some of them provide shell-like interfaces; Tcl's wish and Ruby's irb, while interesting and useful, are better approached in the context of those languages, rather than as though they were "shell variants."

The only languages other than shell discussed at any length are sed and awk, which are often used for stream editing and processing within shell scripts. Note, though, that the shell is a very friendly language and loves to cooperate. You can generally use other scripting languages easily from shell.

Beyond Portability: Cleanliness and Good Living

This book talks a lot about portability concerns. It also talks about how to write clean code. Cleanliness in code is a somewhat fuzzy concept, and programmers argue over it for hours. You might wonder why this book discusses style, defensive programming, and common conventions, which have no functional impact on the shell itself. There are good reasons.

If you are interested in portable code, it is because you want your code to work on multiple platforms. Code that is broken identically on ten platforms is of no use to you. Established shell conventions make it easier for other people to read your code, make it easier for you to read other peoples' code, and usually have sound engineering principles behind them. Similarly, learning to program defensively is essential to making good use of the shell. Because the shell runs with no sandbox, and with all of the caller's privileges and access to the file system, it is extremely dangerous to run badly written shell code.

Writing clear, clean code makes it easier for you to see what is happening and why. Clean code is more likely to be portable, easier to port when needed, and more likely to be useful enough to be worth the bother of porting. In short, to borrow the words of C.A.R. Hoare:

> There are two ways of constructing a software design: One way is to make it so simple that there are obviously no deficiencies, and the other way is to make it so complicated that there are no obvious deficiencies. The first method is far more difficult.

> —C.A.R. Hoare, 1980 Turing Award Lecture

Writing clean code saves you time. It saves you time porting, it saves you time debugging, and it generally saves you time even during initial development. If you are sharing source with other users or developers, clean code will get more contributions and more useful feedback. If you are prototyping and revising your design as you go, clean code will be easier to maintain and update. Of the code I wrote ten and 15 years ago, the clean code has stayed with me and adapted quickly to new systems; the badly written code has not survived and has often been too much work to update.

Do not write carelessly or poorly, even for small one-off scripts. Sloppy work is habit-forming.

What's in This Book

The next section offers a very quick overview of the shell, without going into great detail on the formal syntax or semantics of shell scripting. If you've used the shell before, you may be able to skip it and get into the more detailed material in the following chapters. The next chapter gives a detailed look at the various ways in which the shell performs pattern-matching. Following this are four chapters of detailed discussion of shell features, explaining their specifications more precisely, and showing how to make effective use of them. After this are chapters on portability of shell language constructs and utilities commonly used in shell programming, and then on shell script design and interactions with other languages. If you encounter unfamiliar terminology, look in related sections; I have tried to define terms when I first use them.

Introducing the Shell

This section gives a quick tour of shell usage, starting with basic usage and display conventions, and then moving on to the basics of quoting and variables. There are some generalizations to which you will later learn exceptions, but it gives a quick basic grounding in what the shell does. This overview should make it easier to see where each of the following chapters fits in. Throughout this, you may find yourself asking questions that start out "but what happens if . . . ?" which are not answered in this chapter. As mentioned in the previous discussion on portability, go ahead and try them, but be aware that the results may sometimes vary between shells.

Whether being used interactively or from a script, the shell's basic operation is the same. It reads lines of input, which it breaks into words (usually around spaces), performs substitutions and expansions, and finally executes commands. Much of the shell's power comes from the fact that the shell has rules for modifying the words it is given to generate commands. This section gives a brief overview of these rules, and the ways to keep the shell from performing these modifications inappropriately.

Most of the material in this section is covered in more detail (indeed, with a particular attention to fiddly little details) later in the book.

Interactive and Noninteractive Usage

In interactive usage, the shell indicates readiness for input by displaying a string called a prompt Generally, the default prompt is a dollar sign ($). If the shell is expecting a continuation of previous input, the prompt changes to a greater-than sign (>). In interactive usage, the shell usually shows the output of each command before printing the next prompt. For instance, the following interactive session shows both of these prompts:

```
$ echo 'hello
> there'
hello
there
```

In the preceding example, the shell gives the first prompt ($) and waits for input. The user enters the text `echo 'hello`. The apostrophe, or single quote, begins a quoted string; in a quoted string, the shell does not break words around spaces or new lines, and the string is not complete until the other quote is seen (this is explained a bit more in the section "Introducing Quoting" later in this chapter). The shell cannot execute this command yet because the string isn't complete. The shell knows there must be more input; it displays the secondary prompt (>), and waits for more input. The user enters the text **there'**. The second apostrophe ends the string. Unlike some languages, the shell uses pairs of identical apostrophes for strings, rather than using left and right quotes. With the string complete, the shell now returns to looking for the ends of words or commands. It sees a new line (from the user hitting return), and this ends the command.

The shell runs the command, passing the quoted string to the echo command, which displays its arguments. Note that the new line within the quoted string becomes part of the argument to echo, and the result has a new line in the same place. The same continuation prompt is used when a shell syntax structure (such as if-then) is incomplete.

When the shell is running a command provided to it from a noninteractive source, no prompts are displayed. To run these examples noninteractively, save them in a file, then run your shell of choice on the file; for instance, if you have saved an example as hello, you can invoke it with the command sh hello. Another option is to create an executable shell script. To do this, add a line to the beginning of the file indicating that it is a shell script:

```
#!/bin/sh
```

This line is often called a *shebang* (short for *sharp-bang*, the nicknames of the first two characters on the line.) A file starting with this, and marked as executable, is treated as a script for the named program. Some users prefer to put a space after the exclamation mark (!), but it is not needed (the notion that it might be on some systems is a very persistent portability myth). To mark a script executable, change its mode:

```
$ chmod +x hello
```

Once you have done this, you no longer need to specify the shell interpreter, although you will usually need to specify the path to a program in the current directory to use it:

```
$ ./hello
```

Prompts vary from shell to shell, and many systems change the default shell prompt. While not all shells support this, some can interpolate things (such as the current directory) into the shell prompt. Some shells, on hardware that supports it, will even colorize the prompt.

The biggest difference between interactive and script usage is in the interleaving of output and input. When you work interactively, each command's output is displayed before the shell offers you a new prompt. When you run a script, commands are run in sequence without pauses. While this book typically uses chunks of shell code without prompts to illustrate points, the same code entered at a prompt would generally have the same effect, despite the formatting differences.

Simple Commands

A *simple command* is just a command (such as echo or ls) and its arguments. In the absence of special characters (called *metacharacters*) or words that have special meaning to the shell (called *keywords*), a series of words followed by a new line are a simple command. Control flow constructs (such as if statements, discussed in Chapter 3) are not simple commands.

The shell breaks each line of input into sequences of characters called *words*, usually around spaces and tabs, although there are other ways to separate words. The process of splitting text into words is called *word splitting*. It does not matter how many spaces (or tabs) you place between the words. A line beginning with a sharp (#) is a comment and is ignored by the shell. The first word on a line (which may be the only word) is the command (usually an external program) to run; the following words are passed to it as parameters, called *arguments*. The echo command displays its arguments, separated by spaces if there's more than one argument, and followed by a new line. (This is usually the case; however, the echo command is full of nonportable special cases discussed in Chapter 8.) Each of the following commands produces the same output:

```
$ echo hello, world
hello, world
$ echo hello,      world
hello, world
$ echo      hello,     world
hello, world
```

As you can see, the shell modifies input text before executing it. In this case, for instance, the spaces between words are not counted or recorded; rather, the shell just uses them to detect word boundaries. A quick way to get some insight into how your commands are being modified is to put the shell into trace mode, by issuing the command set -x. This will cause the shell to show you each simple command before executing it. To turn this off, issue the command set +x. Each simple command, as finally executed, is echoed back with a plus sign (+) in front of it before the shell executes that command. For more information on trace mode, including the circumstances where it displays something other than the plus sign, see Chapter 6. Be aware that the exact format of the message may vary from one shell to another. Regardless, tracing is usually quite helpful in understanding the shell. For instance, the following transcript shows that the commands executed by the shell have had strings of spaces replaced by single spaces:

```
$ set -x
$ echo hello, world
+ echo hello, world
hello, world
$ echo hello,      world
+ echo hello, world
hello, world
$ echo      hello,     world
+ echo hello, world
hello, world
$ set +x
+ set +x
```

If you are experimenting with the trace feature on the command line, do not forget to turn it off with a final set +x. However, in the pursuit of brevity, the set +x is omitted in future examples.

You can enter several simple commands on a line by separating them with semicolons (;). Semicolons are a good example of a *metacharacter*, a character that has special meaning to the shell even when it is not separated from other text by spaces:

```
$ echo hello;echo world
hello
world
```

The semicolon breaks this into two commands. The second command is executed immediately after the first, and the user is not prompted between them.

Introducing Variables

Variables are named storage that can hold values. The shell expands a variable when the variable's name occurs after a dollar sign ($), replacing the dollar sign and variable name with the contents of the variable. This is called variable *expansion*, or *substitution*, or occasionally *replacement* or even *interpolation*. Of these terms, expansion is used most often in documentation, but substitution is probably the clearest. Variables are assigned using an equals sign (=) with no spaces around it:

```
$ name=John
$ echo hello, $name
hello, John
```

Unlike most other programming languages, the shell uses different syntax when referring to a variable than when assigning a value to it. Variable names start with a letter or underscore, followed by zero or more letters, numbers, and underscores. Some shell programmers use all capitalized names for variables by convention, but in this book, I use all capitalized names only for environment variables or special predefined shell variables (such as $IFS, which is explained in Chapter 4). Do not use mixed case; it works, but it is not idiomatic for the shell.

If a variable has not been set, it expands to an empty string; there is no warning (usually) for trying to use an unset variable, which can make it hard to detect simple typos. Variables in shell are always strings; the shell does not distinguish between strings, integers, or other data types. The shell is generally considered a typeless language.

If you want to obtain a value from the user, you can do so using the read command to read a line of input and store it in a variable, as in the following example:

```
$ echo Please enter your name. ; read name
Please enter your name.
Dave
$ echo Hello, $name.
Hello, Dave.
```

If you try to assign a value including spaces to a variable, you will discover that the shell splits the line into words before trying to assign variables. Thus, this doesn't work:

```
$ name=John Smith
sh: Smith: command not found
$ echo hello, $name
hello,
```

A brief explanation of what went wrong follows in the next section; a full explanation of what went wrong is found in Chapter 3. For now, the key lesson is that the assignment doesn't work, and you need a way to prevent the shell from splitting words.

Introducing Quoting

The separation of input into words is generally very useful, but it is occasionally desirable to prevent it. For instance, if someone created a file named hey you, trying to remove it might prove frustrating:

```
$ rm hey you
rm: hey: No such file or directory
rm: you: No such file or directory
```

To overcome this, you must tell the shell that, rather than being a special character that separates words, the space is just a literal character with no special meaning. This is called *quoting*, and the most common way to do it is by enclosing material in quotes. Quotes can be single quotes or double quotes; in both cases, the shell does not use distinct left and right quotes, but uses the same quotes on both sides. [On a slightly related note, text surrounded by back quotes (`) is not being quoted; that is one of the syntaxes used for embedding the output of shell commands, much as variables are substituted. Command substitution is explained in Chapter 5.] Most commonly, you simply enclose a string in single quotes (') to prevent the shell from modifying it. Here's a review of the hello world example, using quoting:

```
$ set -x
$ echo 'hello, world'
+ echo hello, world
hello, world
$ echo 'hello,      world'
+ echo hello,      world
hello,      world
$ echo '      hello,      world'
+ echo       hello,      world
      hello,      world
```

Single quotes prevent the shell from modifying input, including word splitting. The quote marks themselves are removed. While this is useful for arguments, it is important not to quote things that you do want the shell to split. For instance, the following script doesn't do what the user probably wanted:

```
$ set -x
$ 'echo hello, world'
+ echo hello, world
sh: echo hello, world: command not found
```

With all the spaces quoted, the shell has no way of knowing the user meant to invoke the echo command; instead, it obligingly looks for a command named echo hello, world. Since there isn't one, the shell prints an error message.

> **Note** Error messages may vary between shells. Do not worry if you try an example and get an error message in a slightly different format. Also, the display of an error message may depend on whether the shell was executing a script. For a syntax error or other shell error, the shell usually gives the name of the script and the line number it was executing. This does not mean you should not run examples and try them out for yourself; it does mean that it is not always a good idea to depend on the exact contents of an error message.

You can now pursue the previous example of trying to assign a full name, including a space, to a variable:

```
$ name='John Smith'
$ echo hello, $name
hello, John Smith
```

The quotes allow you to assign a value containing spaces to a variable. When the variable is substituted, the space is included. Try to figure out the next example before you run it:

```
$ command='echo hello, world'
$ $command
```

There are two ways you might reasonably expect this to play out. One is that the shell will respond with hello, world. The other is that it will respond with an error message, such as sh: echo hello, world: command not found. Since word splitting happens before variable expansion, you might reasonably expect the error message, but in fact the shell greets you. The reason for this is that the outputs of variable substitution are usually subject to word splitting again. (The results are not then subject to variable substitution.) In this case, that's very useful. But consider what happens if you are trying to preserve spaces, not just include them:

```
$ name='Smith,     John'
$ echo $name
Smith, John
```

No problem; you know how to protect spaces, right?

```
$ name='Smith,     John'
$ echo '$name'
$name
```

You need a way to ask the shell to expand variables but not perform word splitting. Conveniently, the shell has multiple quoting mechanisms. If you want some special characters, but you still want to quote spaces, you can use double quotes. The shell substitutes variables in double-quoted strings:

```
$ set -x
$ name='Smith,     John'
+ name=Smith,     John
$ echo $name
+ echo Smith, John
Smith, John
```

```
$ echo '$name'
+ echo $name
$name
$ echo "$name"
+ echo Smith,      John
hello, Smith,      John
```

The text $name is substituted both when unquoted and when in double quotes; it is not substituted when in single quotes. When unquoted, the substituted value is subject to field splitting (much like word splitting, but see the in-depth discussion in Chapter 4); inside double quotes, it is not. If you have used other scripting languages, you may have seen this distinction between single and double quotes before; it is very useful to be able to distinguish between a purely literal string and one in which you want variables to be substituted, and the shell syntax is familiar to many users. Single quotes are the easiest to understand; a single-quoted string lasts until the next single quote. No other characters have any special meaning within single quotes. Of course, this makes it hard to get a literal string including a single quote; to do that, use double quotes. This allows an expansion on an earlier example:

```
echo 'What is your name? '
read name
echo "I'm sorry, $name, but I can't let you do that."
```

```
What is your name?
Dave
I'm sorry, Dave, but I can't let you do that.
```

Note the use of double quotes to protect the spaces and other punctuation, including single quotes. Try to guess what the following code will produce before running it:

```
echo "What is your name?"
read name
echo I'm sorry, $name, I can't let you do that.
```

In this version, because the single quotes were not themselves quoted, they defined a quoted string. This has two effects: The first is to prevent $name from being expanded, and the second is the removal of the apostrophes, which the shell interprets as single quotes. For this reason, shell programmers often use double quotes around strings passed to echo even when no obvious need to is in evidence. It is easy to forget that a harmless apostrophe is actually a sinister and dire single quote, plotting ambush and mayhem from its lair between "n" and "t." Having the quotes there is a good example of defensive programming. The use of double quotes to get literal single quotes (and single quotes to get literal double quotes) is easy enough once you are used to it, but it can be a bit surprising at first.

As you have probably noticed, the quote characters themselves are not included in the strings they quote. Quoted strings are considered to be part of the same word as anything they are adjacent to. It is a common misconception that the quoted material is itself a "word" to the shell, and that a pair of adjacent quotes are treated as separate words. This is not so, and this leads to the way to get single quotes into a string that is single-quoted when you want an apostrophe but do not want any expansion:

```
$ echo '$name is a variable, now, isn'"'"'t it?'
$name is a variable, now, isn't it?
```

The two single-quoted strings are adjacent to a double-quoted string containing only an apostrophe; when the quotes are removed, these become a single shell word. The echo command receives only one argument. As this example illustrates, there are a great number of subtleties to the interactions of these features, but this quick tour should prepare you to follow along with code even if you haven't used any of these features before.

The printf Command

The printf command was introduced some years back, but many users are unaware of it. It mostly emulates the behavior of a C function by the same name, used to format output. The first argument to printf is called a *format string*, and describes an output format. Certain special characters in the format string need to be filled in with data; these data are taken from the other arguments, in order. This is easier to show than to describe:

```
$ name="John"
$ printf "Hello, %s!\n" "$NAME"
Hello, John!
```

CHECKING YOUR ASSUMPTIONS

When I originally drafted this text, I used echo in all of the examples because it was the only portable command for displaying text. It is problematic in many ways (it gets its own section in Chapter 8), but there's nothing else. The wonderful and expressive printf utility is unfortunately not portable. After all, it's only found on BSD systems and Linux systems and built-in to bash and ksh93. Actually, it looks like Solaris has it. In fact, I searched among something around 30 systems, and the only system I could find that anyone had still running in which printf did not work in /bin/sh was a SunOS box (not Solaris) a friend of mine had still running, even though it was officially unsupported due to unfixed Y2K bugs.

I did some informal polling. Every experienced shell programmer I talked to "knew" that the shell command printf was a new feature (or had never even heard of it). No one thought it was portable, but it turns out to be substantially more portable than many features I have been taking for granted for ten years. While it is true that it is a new change, it is a change specified by the current UNIX standards, and one that appears to have become essentially universal. So, even if you are pretty sure you know that something isn't portable (or that it is), check your assumptions!

The special sequence %s indicates that a string should be displayed; the next argument is interpreted as a string and replaces the %s. The character determining what kind of object to print (such as a string or a number) is called a *format character*, and the whole character sequence is called a *format specification*. Other common formats are % (print a percent sign), d (print a number), o (print a number in octal), x (print a number in hexadecimal), and f (print a floating-point value). The other thing printf does is interpret backslashes followed by special characters; these combinations are called *escape sequences*. The most important one to know about is \n, which represents a new line. Unlike echo, printf does not automatically finish its output with a new line character:

```
$ echo "Hello!" ; echo "Goodbye!"
Hello!
Goodbye!
$ printf "Hello!" ; printf "Goodbye!"
Hello!Goodbye!$
```

In fact, even the shell's prompt can end up on the same line as the output from a printf command. This can be a bit of a surprise to new users, and even experienced users will get it wrong occasionally. However, it is also extremely useful in some cases. If you wish to display a prompt and then request input from the user, being able to omit the new line is quite handy. (There is no portable way to do this with echo, although there are several nonportable ways that may work on individual systems.)

The other thing printf is good at is formatting—not just displaying output, but display-ing it according to particular rules. There are three key concepts in displaying fields. The first is *width*, or how many characters to display at a minimum. Width, given as a number between the % and the format character, is used to format output so it lines up nicely:

```
$ printf "%3d: lined\n%3d: up\n" 1 100
  1: lined
100: up
```

The width of 3 causes the printf command to display at least three characters, even if it does not need that many. But what if there are more? There is also a way to limit the number of characters printed; this is called *precision*, and is written as a number following a period, once again between the % and the format character. Precision limits the total number of characters printed for strings; for floating-point numbers, it limits the number of characters printed after the decimal point.

```
$ printf "%.5s\n%.5s\n" John Samantha
John
Saman
```

You can specify both width and precision; if you do this, the precision is used to deter-mine what to print, and the width then influences whether the shell pads the output. Padding can be controlled a little. The two most common ways to control padding are to specify flags, which are put before the width. (If there is no width, there is no padding, and there is no point to specifying flags.) The two common flags are left justification (-), and zero padding (0). Zero padding applies only to numeric values. Idiomatically, the pattern %02x is used to express byte values in hexadecimal:

```
$ printf "%02x\n" 197 198
c5
c6
```

This example also illustrates another feature: If you provide additional arguments, printf recycles its format string, starting over at the beginning. Format specifications without argu-ments are treated as though the argument was a 0 (for numeric formats) or an empty string (for string formats).

There is only one significant flaw in the printf command, which is that you cannot easily use it to display arbitrary characters. The C language printf function has a %c format specifier, which prints a numeric value as a raw character; for instance, on an ASCII-based machine, the C code printf("%c", 64); prints an at sign (@). In the shell command, %c is equivalent to %.1s; it prints the first character of its argument, which is treated as a string. So, for instance, printf '%c\n' 64 prints 6. However, you can print characters using an escape sequence; a backslash followed by three octal digits is printed as the character in question, so printf '\100\n' prints @. In later chapters, you'll see how you could use printf to create a format string containing arbitrary characters as octal escape sequences.

Some implementations of printf take additional options (starting with hyphens) before the format string. In portable code, never start a format string with a hyphen. If you want to display a hyphen, use %s:

```
$ printf '%sv' -
-v
```

Be very careful with parameter substitution in printf format strings. The translation of format specifiers into arguments happens after parameter substitution; if you substitute a parameter containing % characters into a format string, those % characters may become format specifiers. If you wish to include the value of a parameter in your displayed output, always use a suitable format (usually %s) and provide the parameter as a double-quoted argument:

```
$ password="xfzy%dNo"
$ printf "Your password is $password.\n"
Your password is xfzyONo.
$ printf "Your password is %s.\n" "$password"
Your password is xfzy%dNo.
```

In general, I recommend using single-quoted strings as printf format strings; this ensures that the calling shell will not do something unexpected with any backslash escape sequences you used (behavior of backslashes inside double-quoted strings is not always 100% portable), and that no parameter substitution occurs; this allows you to be sure you know what your format string is.

Some implementations of printf have difficulties with particularly long formats; for example, the Solaris printf aborts when given the format string %05000d. Exercise caution with large formats.

What's Next?

This whirlwind introduction covers enough so that, even if you've never tried to use the shell before, you can follow along with the examples used to illustrate various points of shell architecture and design. The next chapter talks about patterns and regular expressions; if you're familiar with those already, you can skip ahead, but you might like the quick refresher. Now, on to the fiddly little details!

■ ■ ■

## CHAPTER 2

Patterns and Regular Expressions

This chapter is a bit of a digression; if you are comfortable with patterns and regular expressions, you can just skip ahead to Chapter 3, where I begin the discussion of shell syntax. However, if you are unfamiliar with patterns and regular expressions, this material turns out to be very important for understanding and illustrating the coming examples. Furthermore, you will have to learn it to be an effective shell programmer, so if you haven't learned it before, start early.

Shell programming is heavily dependent on string processing. The term *string* is used generically to refer to any sequence of characters; typical examples of strings might be a line of input or a single argument to a command. Users enter responses to prompts, file names are generated, and commands produce output. Recurring throughout this is the need to determine whether a given string conforms to a given pattern; this process is called *pattern matching*. The shell has a fair amount of built-in pattern matching functionality (especially if you are comfortable with relying on POSIX shell features). Pattern matching is not unique to the shell; other programs, such as find, use the same pattern-matching rules. A special variant of shell pattern matching, called *globbing*, is used to expand file name patterns into groups of matching names. The distinction between globbing and pattern matching is a bit vague; many people call all patterns globs and use the term *file globbing* for the special case of matching file names. The shell manual pages, however, tend to call pathname expansion globbing.

Furthermore, many common UNIX utilities, such as grep or sed, provide features for pattern matching. These programs usually use a more powerful kind of pattern matching, called *regular expressions*. Regular expressions, while different from shell patterns, are crucial to most effective shell scripting. While there is no portable regular expression support built into the shell itself, shell programs rely heavily on external utilities, many of which use regular expressions.

Shell Patterns

Shell patterns are used in a number of contexts. The most common usage is in the case statement (see Chapter 3 for more information). Given two shell variables string and pattern, the following code determines whether text matches pattern:

```
case $string in
  $pattern) echo "Match" ;;
  *) echo "No match";;
esac
```

If $string matches $pattern, the shell echoes "Match" and leaves the case statement. Otherwise, it checks to see whether $string matches *. Since * matches anything in a shell pattern, the shell prints "No match" when there was not a match against $pattern. (The case statement only executes one branch, even if more than one pattern matches.)

For exploring pattern matching, you might find it useful to create a shell script based on this. The following self-contained script performs matching tests of a number of words against a pattern:

```
#!/bin/sh
pattern="$1"
shift
echo "Matching against '$pattern':"
for string
do
  case $string in
  $pattern) echo "$string: Match." ;;
  *) echo "$string: No match." ;;
  esac
done
```

Save this script to a file named pattern, make it executable (chmod a+x pattern), and you can use it to perform your own tests:

```
$ ./pattern '*' 'hello'
Matching against '*':
hello: Match.
$ ./pattern 'hello*' 'hello' 'hello, there' 'well, hello'
Matching against 'hello*':
hello: Match.
hello, there: Match.
well, hello: No match.
```

Remember to use single quotes around the arguments. An unquoted word containing pattern characters such as the asterisk (*) is subject to globbing (sometimes called *file name expansion*), where the shell replaces such words with any files with names matching the pattern. This can produce misleading results for tests like this. File name patterns are discussed in more detail in the next section.

Pattern-Matching Basics

In a pattern, most characters match themselves, and only themselves. The word hello is a perfectly valid pattern; it matches the word hello, and nothing else. A pattern that matches only part of a string is not considered to have matched that string. The word hello does not match the text hello, world. For a pattern to match a string, two things must be true:

- Every character in the pattern must match the string.
- Every character in the string must match the pattern.

Now, if this were all there were to patterns, a pattern would be another way of describing string comparison, and the rest of this chapter would consist of filler text like "a . . . consists of sequences of nonblank characters separated by blanks," or possibly some wonderful cookie recipes. Sadly, this is not so. Instead, there are some characters in a pattern that have special meaning and can match something other than themselves. Characters that have special meaning in a pattern are called *wildcards* or *metacharacters*. Some users prefer to restrict the term wildcard to refer only to the special characters that can match anything. In talking about patterns, I prefer to call them all wildcards to avoid confusion with characters that have special meaning to the shell. Wildcards make those two simple rules much more complicated; a single character in a pattern could match a very long string, or a group of characters in the pattern might match only one character or even none at all. What matters is that there are no mismatches and nothing left over of the string after the match.

The most common wildcards are the question mark (?), which matches any character, and the asterisk (*), which matches anything at all, even an empty string. (If this sounds very wrong, and you think they modify previous characters, you are thinking of regular expressions. Regular expressions, discussed in detail in the "Regular Expressions" section of this chapter, are much more expressive and somewhat more complicated.)

The ? is easy to use in patterns; you use it when you know there will be exactly one character, but you are not sure exactly what it will be. For instance, if you are not sure what accent the user will greet you in, you might use the pattern h?llo, in case your user prefers to write hallo, or hullo. This leaves you with two problems. The first is that users are typically verbose, and write things like hello, there, or hello little computer, or possibly even hello how do i send email. If you just want to verify that you are getting something that sounds a bit like a greeting, you need a way to say "this, or this plus any other stuff on the end."

That is what * is for. Because * matches anything, the pattern hello* matches anything starting with hello, or even just hello with nothing after it. However, that pattern doesn't match the string well, hello because there is nothing in the pattern that can match characters before the word hello. A common idiom when you want to match a word if it is present at all is to use asterisks on both sides of a pattern: *hello* matches a broad range of greetings.

If you want to match something, but you are not sure what it is or how long it will be, you can combine these. The pattern hello ?* matches hello world but does not match hello alone. However, this pattern introduces a new problem. The space character is not special in a pattern, but it is special in the shell. This leads to a bit of a dilemma. If you do not quote the pattern, the shell splits it into multiple words, and it does not match what you expected. If you do quote it, the shell ignores the wildcards. There are two solutions available; the first is to quote spaces, the second is to unquote wildcards. So, you could write hello" "?*, or you could write "hello "?*.

In the contexts where the shell performs pattern matching (such as case statements), you do not need to worry about spaces resulting from variable substitution; the shell doesn't perform splitting on variable substitutions in those contexts. (A disclaimer is in order: zsh's behavior differs here, unless it is running in sh emulation mode. See Chapter 7 for more information.)

Character Classes

The h?llo pattern has another flaw, which is that it is too permissive. While your friends who type with a thick accent will doubtless appreciate your consideration, you might reasonably draw the line at hzllo, h!llo, or hXllo. The shell provides a mechanism for more restrictive matches, called a *character class*. A character class matches any one of a set of characters, but nothing else; it is like ?, only more restrictive. A character class is surrounded in square brackets ([]), and looks like [characters]. The greeting described previously could be written using a character class as h[aeu]llo. A character class matches exactly one of the characters in it; it never matches more than one character.

Character classes may specify ranges of characters. A typical usage would be to match any digit, with [0-9]. In a range, two characters separated by a hyphen are treated as every character between them in the character set; mostly, this is used for letters and numbers. Patterns are case sensitive; if you want to match all standard ASCII letters, use [a-zA-Z]. The behavior of a range where the second character comes before the first in the character set is not predictable; do not do that. Sometimes, rather than knowing what you do want, you know what you don't want; you can invert a character class by using an exclamation mark (!) as its first character. The character class [!0-9] matches any character that is not a digit. When a character class is inverted, it matches any character not in the range, not just any reasonable or common character; if you write [!aeiou] hoping to get consonants, you will also match punctuation or control characters. Wildcards do not have special meaning in a character class; [?*] matches a question mark or an asterisk, but not anything else.

Character classes are one of the most complicated aspects of shell pattern matching. Left and right square brackets ([]), hyphens (-), and exclamation marks (!) are all special to them. A hyphen can easily be included in a class by specifying it as the last character of the class, with no following character. An exclamation mark can be included by specifying it as any character but the first. (What if there are no other characters? Then you are specifying only one character and probably don't need a character class.) The left bracket is actually easy; include it anywhere, it won't matter. The right bracket (]) is special; if you want a right bracket, put it either at the very beginning of the list or immediately after the ! for a negated class. Otherwise, the shell might think that the right bracket was intended to close the character class. Even apart from the intended feature set, be aware that some shells have plain and simple bugs having to do with right brackets in character classes; avoid them if you can.

If you want to match any left or right bracket, exclamation mark, or hyphen, but no other characters, here is a way to do it:

```
[][!-]
```

The first left bracket begins the definition of the class. The first right bracket does not close the class because there is nothing in it yet; it is taken as a plain literal right bracket. The second left bracket and the exclamation mark have no special meaning; neither is in a position where it would have any. Finally, the hyphen is not between two other characters in the class because the right square bracket ends the definition of the character class, so the hyphen must be a plain character.

Many users have the habit of using a caret (^) instead of ! in shell character classes. This is not portable, but it is a common extension some shells offer because habitual users of regular expressions may be more used to it. This can create an occasional surprise if you have never seen it used, and want to match a caret in a class.

Table 2-1 explains the behavior of a number of characters that may have special meaning within a character class, as well as how to include them literally in a class when you want to.

Table 2-1. *Special Characters in Character Classes*

Character	Meaning	Portability	How to Include It
]	End of class	Universal	Put at the beginning of the class (or first after the negation character)
[	Beginning of class	Universal	Put it anywhere in the class
^	Inversion	Common	Put after some other character
!	Inversion	Universal	Put after some other character
-	Range	Universal	Put at the beginning or end of the class

Ranges have an additional portability problem that is often overlooked, especially by English speakers. There is no guarantee that the range [a-z] matches every lowercase letter, and strictly speaking there is not even a guarantee that it matches only lowercase letters. The problem is that most people assume the ASCII character set, which defines only unaccented characters. In ASCII, the uppercase letters are contiguous, and the lowercase letters are also contiguous (but there are characters between them; [A-z] matches a few punctuation characters). However, there are UNIX-like systems on which either or both of these assumptions may be wrong. In practice, it is very nearly portable to assume that [a-z] matches 26 lowercase letters. However, accented variants of lowercase letters do not match this pattern. There is no generally portable way to match additional characters, or even to find out what they are. Scripts may be run in different environments with different character sets.

Some shells also support additional character class notations; these were introduced by POSIX but so far are rare outside of ksh (not pdksh) and bash. The notation is [[:*class*:]], where *class* is a word like digit, alpha, or punct. This matches any character for which the corresponding C is*class*() function would return true. For example, [[:digit:]] is equivalent to [0-9]. These classes may be combined with other characters; [[:digit:][:alpha:]_] matches any letter or number or an underscore (_). Additional similar rules use [.*name*.] to match a special collating symbol. (For instance, some languages might have a special rule for matching and sorting certain combinations of letters, so a ch might sort differently from a c followed by an h) and [=*name*=] to match equivalence classes, such as a lowercase letter and any accented variant of it.) These rules are particularly useful for internationalized scripts but not sufficiently widely available to be used in portable scripts yet. To avoid any possible misunderstandings, avoid using a left bracket followed immediately by a period (.), equals sign (=), or colon (:) in a character class. Note that this applies only to a left bracket within the character class, not the initial bracket that opens the class; [.] matches a period. (This is more significant in regular expressions, where a period would otherwise have special meaning.)

Character classes are, as you can see, substantially more complicated than the rest of the shell pattern matching rules. Table 2-2 shows the full set.

Table 2-2. *Shell Pattern Characters*

Pattern	Meaning
?	Any character
*	Any string (even an empty one)
[...]	One character from a class
Anything else	Itself

Using Shell Patterns

Shell patterns are quite powerful, but they have a number of limitations. There is no way to specify repetition of a character class; no shell pattern matches an arbitrary number of digits. You can't make part of a pattern optional; the closest you get to optional components is the asterisk.

Patterns as a whole generally match as much as they can; this is called being *greedy*. However, if matching too many things with an asterisk prevents a match, the asterisk gives up the extra characters and lets other pattern components match them. If you match the pattern b* to the string banana, the * matches the text anana. However, if you use the pattern b*na, the * matches only the text ana. The rule is that the * grabs the largest number of characters it can without preventing a match. Other pattern components, such as character classes, literal characters, or question marks, get first priority on consuming characters, and the asterisk gets what's left.

Some of the limitations of shell patterns can be overcome by creative usage. One way to store lists of items in the shell is to have multiple items joined with a delimiter; for instance, you might store the value a,b,c to represent a list of three items. The following example code illustrates how such a list might be used. (The case statement, used here, executes code when a pattern matches a given string; it is explained in more detail in Chapter 3.)

```
list=orange,apple,banana
case $list in
*apple*)        echo "How do you like them apples?";;
esac
```

```
How do you like them apples?
```

This script has a subtle bug, however. It does not check for exact matches. If you try to check against a slightly different list, the problem becomes obvious:

```
list=orange,crabapple,banana
case $list in
*apple*)        echo "How do you like them apples?";;
esac
```

```
How do you like them apples?
```

The problem is that the asterisks can match anything, even the commas used as delimiters. However, if you add the delimiters to the pattern, you can no longer match the ends of the list:

```
list=orange,apple,banana
case $list in
*,orange,*)          echo "The only fruit for which there is no Cockney slang.";;
esac
```

[no output]

To resolve this, wrap the list in an extra set of delimiters when expanding it:

```
list=orange,apple,banana
case ,$list, in
*,orange,*)          echo "The only fruit for which there is no Cockney slang.";;
esac
```

```
The only fruit for which there is no Cockney slang.
```

The expansion of $list now has a comma appended to each end, ensuring that every member of the list has a comma on both sides of it.

Sometimes, you may find that shell patterns do not have the flexibility to represent what you want. When that happens, you may need to go to regular expressions; see the "Regular Expressions" section at the end of this chapter for more information.

Pathname Expansion

Pathname expansion (the POSIX term), or globbing (what everyone actually calls it), is one of the shell features most users are likely to be at least partially familiar with. The shell has a built-in facility for generating or matching file names. When an unquoted word contains any of the pattern-matching wildcards, it is subject to globbing. In globbing, the shell compares the pattern to files in the file system (using essentially the same pattern matching rules described previously) and expands the word into any matching file names. If there are no matches, the shell leaves the pattern alone. Instead of matching a single specified word against a pattern to produce a single true/false result, globbing matches multiple names and produces all the matches as results. There is, of course, an exception; the find utility uses globbing patterns to match file names but uses them for true/false matches.

Differences from Shell Patterns

Pathname expansion uses the same basic pattern-matching characters as regular shell patterns, but there are a couple of significant differences. When a pathname refers to a file not in the current directory, the full name used is called the *path* of the file. Each of the pieces of a path, separated by slashes (or possibly by other characters on non-UNIX systems), is called a *component*. In globbing, each section of a pattern (as divided by path separators) is matched against single components. So, if you wish to match the file bin/unsort, you can specify b*/ unsort, or b*/u*, or bin/*sort, but you cannot just use *unsort. If there are no path separators in a pattern, it matches against files in the current directory; if you are in the bin directory, *sort could match unsort. (Note that there is no portable unsort utility, but writing one makes a great exercise.)

Another way to think about this is that the special characters can never match a path separator; only a literal path separator can match a path separator in a file path. For example, bin[/]unsort does not match bin/unsort. The character class can only match path components, never a path separator. To search in directories with a pattern, you must explicitly include any path separators you wish to match.

If a path starts with a path separator, the path is called an *absolute* path. Otherwise, it is called a *relative* path. A relative path name is always interpreted relative to your current directory. In fact, even a file name with no separators is technically a relative path; it is just a very short relative path.

The decision to match only within specified directories may seem surprising, but it makes good sense. Given that a typical UNIX system can easily have hundreds of thousands of files, it is quite simply impractical to try to match against all of them; the desktop system on which I ran most of my test scripts has a bit over three and a half million files on it. The requirement to match directories explicitly is probably a good idea. (The zsh shell, however, offers globbing extensions to let you do crazy things like this if you want. They are not generally portable, though.)

Pathname expansion, like pattern expansion, is aggressive about trying to find a match. Many UNIX systems sort some binaries into both /usr/bin and /usr/sbin. Sometimes it is not obvious which directory a program would be in. While the idiomatic solution is to use which file to find a copy of a file in your execution path, this doesn't help if you've forgotten the exact name of the utility. The glob pattern /usr/*bin/*stat matches any file in either /usr/bin or /usr/sbin with a name ending in stat. When expanding each component, the shell makes a list of possible matches, then compares all of these to the next component. If one of the components never ends up producing any matches, it is discarded completely. There is one subtle difference, having to do with components, between globbing and pattern matching. In a UNIX path, // is always equivalent to /; however, a shell pattern like a/*/b does not match a/b. You cannot match an empty component with a pattern because there is never actually an empty component.

Wildcards never match a component with a name starting with a period (.). These files, called *dot files*, are not matched by patterns and are usually not displayed to the user; they are often called *hidden* files. This is not the same way in which some other systems allow a file to be tagged as being invisible. You can see and manipulate these files in most programs; they just don't get displayed in lists by default or matched by globs. This applies to all the components in a path, not just file names. Note that a period has no special meaning except as the first character of a file name, and even then the meaning is purely one of convention. UNIX file names may have as many (or as few) periods in them as they want. Some programs assign special meaning to suffixes starting with a period, but most UNIX programs give no special interpretation to the name of a file. The pattern *.name does not match a file named .name; the period in the pattern is not at the beginning of the pattern, so it can't match a period at the beginning of a file name.

CASE SENSITIVITY IN PATHNAME EXPANSION

Systems differ in their handling of letters in different cases. On a traditional UNIX system, files named readme and README can exist in the same directory because the names of files are case-sensitive; that is to say, capital and lowercase letters are distinct. Other systems have used two other conventions. Some file systems (most notably, the traditional MS-DOS FAT16 file system) store all names without reference to case. This policy is often called *case-insensitive*. On these systems, not only are README and readme the same name, there is no way to know which of them was used to create a file.

Some systems, most notably the Macintosh and Amiga, introduced a new (well, it was new in the 80s, and UNIX doesn't change much) policy called *case-preserving*. On a case-preserving file system, the exact name used to create a file is preserved in the file system, but matches against file names are typically case-insensitive. Thus you can see that the file was named ReadMe when it was created, but if you try to open a file named rEADmE, you get the same file anyway. This behavior is also quite common on the more modern (well, relatively speaking) FAT32 file system used by Windows 95, and commonly used on flash drives or external hard drives. However, it is dependent on the "long name support" introduced in that era, and some devices (such as cameras) may fail spectacularly to recover gracefully if a file's name uses this feature.

For the most part, the UNIX shell is totally unaware of this, which can be a major source of surprises when using a case-preserving file system. The most common case-preserving file systems in use today are the native ones of Windows and Macintosh machines. Since OS X is a UNIX system these days, and many users expect shell scripts to run in the various UNIX-like emulation environments available under Windows, this may impact your scripts some day.

Some shells may offer extra options to provide for pathname expansion that ignores case. With shells that do not, you have to be aware of the potential issues. Even if the shell handles this well, though, utility programs may or may not do so reliably. Some programs may scan a directory looking for matching names before trying to open a file, end up failing to see the file, and possibly later overwriting it. This is unusual, but not unheard of. Your best allies in this are experienced users, who are typically familiar with the case handling of their system and reasonably careful about it.

A common pitfall for users coming from DOS environments is to think that the pattern *.* should match any file. However, this convention relies on the distinction between a file's name and the characters after the period, called the *extension*. UNIX has no such distinction, and a file whose name does not contain a literal period (.) does not match this pattern. This pattern also does not match dot files. It is not enough to match the period literally; the period must be the first character in the relevant path component to match against a dot file.

In some cases, pathname expansion will not detect files that can be accessed explicitly by name. There are three cases where this may apply. The first is case-sensitivity issues (see the previous sidebar). The second is that some network disk services provide directories only when they are explicitly requested; echo * lists only those directories that are in use, not the ones that could be in use if you asked for them.

Finally, globbing relies on the ability to read directories, while access to files relies only on the execute permission bit. This is a reasonably arcane distinction, which most people rarely encounter. Normally, directories give neither or both read and execute permission to any given user. However, it is possible to grant execute permission alone to a directory. This might be useful, for instance, in a public file server, allowing people to access files by name, but not to obtain a listing of files. Globbing requires the ability to read the directory to obtain the list of files against which a glob pattern is matched; without that, no file ever matches a glob.

Some shells offer an additional kind of pathname expansion called *brace expansion*. This is not portable to standard shells, but this does not mean you can safely ignore it; it means that, in some cases, file names with patterns like {a,b} will not behave as you expect them to. Brace expansion is discussed in Chapter 7. It does not affect file names expanded through pathname expansion, or the results of parameter expansion, so you do not need to worry about it when interacting with generated file names.

Using Globs

All of the previous discussion is pretty useful, but it can be a bit hard to get a feel for how to use globs without a few examples. This section introduces a few of the most common shell pattern idioms and explains how each of them works; it also gives some key advice about using globs effectively, both interactively and in scripts.

The pattern .??* matches any file beginning with a period and following it with at least two characters; this is used to match dot files in a given directory. This pattern is constructed to match files with names beginning with a period (.), but exclude the two special directory entries . and .. (which match the current and parent directory, respectively). You might think that, since the initial period has to be matched explicitly, you could use .?*, but the second period in .. is not special and can be matched by a question mark. This pattern does not catch files with names like .a or .b, which can be a problem.

To match any file with a name ending in .png or .gif, use a pattern like *.[pg][ni][gf]. In fact, this pattern also matches a number of other possible names, but luckily the number of clashes is low. (This problem gets worse if you try to match many more file suffixes.) Patterns like this are useful in cases where you can think of two or three likely file name suffixes that might be in use, but you are not sure all of them will be in use. If you have a directory containing a number of PNG files (using the common suffix) but no GIF files, and use the pair of patterns *.png and *.gif, the second pattern matches no files, and is left untouched. By contrast, the pattern *.[pg][ni][gf] matches all the PNG files and is replaced by their names, even though there are no GIF files.

A similar technique is often used for case-insensitive file name matching; for instance, you might use *.[Tt][Xx][Tt] to match files with a .txt suffix. By convention, when using sets of character classes like this, you should use the same position in each class for a given component. Thus [pg][ni][gf] suggests png and gif to the reader; if you wrote [gp][ni][gf], people would think you were aiming for gng and pif.

Files with really long names often lend themselves to abbreviation using a wildcard expected to match only one file's name. This is probably one of the most common sources of crazy or unplanned behavior in interactive usage; be careful when picking the patterns you use! It is very easy to get thrown off by an * unexpectedly matching a very long string, or an empty string, when you were looking at a particular part of a path name. This can be done across multiple directories, as well; a Mac user might spell /System/Library/LaunchDaemons as /S*/L*/L*ons. Anchoring the first and last characters of a file name often narrows down the field very quickly.

Wildcards can also be used to avoid shell metacharacters without quoting; for instance, a file named a;b can be referred to as a?b, as long as there are no other files matching the pattern. The use of ? as a fill-in for spaces or other special shell characters is idiomatic.

EXERCISE CAUTION

Be careful with wildcards. Typos can create horrible problems. One of the most common typos I've seen (and made, repeatedly), is to try to remove .o files (created by the C compiler) and end up typing rm *>o. This removes every file (except dot files) in the current directory and redirects its output (which is usually empty) into a file named o. This typo may seem unusual, but the * is a shifted key on most US keyboards and so is >. Just remember: *There is no undo button.* Whenever you're about to type an rm command, especially an rm -f, be sure to check the command line out to make sure you haven't made any crucial typos. Do not alias rm to rm -i; this is a horrible habit, which breaks a lot of useful scripted features. Worse, it will make you careless. A poor-quality safety net is worse than no safety net at all.

Regular Expressions

A comprehensive review of regular expressions is too much to fit into a single chapter. Whole books have been written on the topic. This section provides a basic grounding in regular expressions, covering the main features of the most common varieties. Regular expressions are primarily used by programs other than the shell, although many shells have a built-in version of some command (typically expr) that uses them. However, they are not used in portable shell syntax. (Some shells offer relevant exceptions, discussed in Chapter 7.) The term *regular expression* is often abbreviated to either regexp or regex. While regexp is clearer to read, regex is pronounceable; the plural is regexes (or regexps, which is still unpronounceable). I use the abbreviation here for brevity.

There are two primary varieties of regexes; basic regexes (often called BREs) and extended regexes (EREs). Each uses slightly different rules. The basic regex syntax is actually slightly more powerful than the extended syntax, but it is harder to write clearly and concisely. Many implementations offer additional features bolted on to either of these, making it hard to be sure exactly which features are portable. What's worse, not everyone implements the official POSIX standard for regexes, so you cannot necessarily rely on the standard. The default in most tools is to provide basic regexes with at least a few extensions, which may be documented.

In addition to the traditional forms of regexes, there are other variants. The Perl programming language introduced a number of additional features, which have become popular and widely used. Many programs other than Perl now provide "Perl-compatible regular expressions," thanks to the efforts of the kind people at www.pcre.org. There are other pattern matching languages available, such as Lua's patterns, some of which are much simpler than regexes.

In any discussion of regexes, credit must be given to Henry Spencer's regular expression library, released long enough ago that free software was a relatively new concept. Before POSIX even existed, Henry Spencer wrote an essentially compatible clone (not derived from AT&T source) of the V8 UNIX regexp() family of library functions. While most systems now provide standard library functions to make regexes available to most programs, this was not the case back then, and many programs offer regex support in the first place only because the Henry Spencer regex library made it possible. It offered what were essentially extended regexes (and still does in a few programs, I'm sure). This code was written in 1986 and is still found in a few modern systems in compatibility libraries.

Basic Regular Expressions

Regexes are most famously used by the grep utility; its name is derived from the ed editor's usage g/regular-expression/p, meaning "global search for *regular-expression* and print." In fact, there are often several varieties of the grep utility on a system, and it may support more than one variety of regex; this can be a portability problem if you depend on one of the extensions. Toward the end of the chapter, Table 2-8 shows the common variants you are likely to encounter and where they are likely to be found. As with most tools, check the documentation and any available standards, don't just test behavior on a given system. This section begins with a discussion of basic regexes, then goes on to cover extended regexes. Some newer software now uses extended regexes by default, and behavior can vary surprisingly. However, the most common utilities (grep, expr, sed) default to basic regexes. Because of this, I start with basic regexes, then go on to a description of the differences between extended and basic regexes; it mostly boils down to putting a backslash in front of anything cool in a basic regex. This reverses the usual sense of backslash as suppressing special meanings.

Unlike shell patterns, regexes are considered to have matched if there exists a matching string anywhere in the string being matched, even if it does not fill the whole line; this is similar to the behavior of a shell pattern with a * on each end. You can override this by *anchoring* the regex, tying it to the beginning of the line with a leading ^ or to the end of the line with a trailing $. The shell pattern hello is equivalent to the regex ^hello$. In some cases, a regex is implicitly anchored; for instance, the expr utility's colon (:) operator matches a regex against the beginning of a string.

In regexes, the character that matches anything is period (.), not question mark (?). So, if you want to match multiple greetings, you'd use h.llo as a regex, not h?llo. Character classes are essentially the same, except that regexes use ^, not !, to negate a character class. (Some shells support this syntax in character classes as well, as an extension.) Support for the POSIX [[:class:]] feature (and the related =name= and .name. features) is slightly more common in regex implementations than it is in shells, but it is still not portable enough to rely on.

You may have noticed that ^ has two different meanings in regexes. The regex ^[0-9] matches a digit at the beginning of a string; the regex [^0-9] matches any character but a digit anywhere in a string. Many seemingly intractable regex problems have turned out to be typos closely related to this.

Where regexes really begin to differ from shell patterns is in the handling of *. In shell patterns, the asterisk itself is capable of matching parts of a string. In a regex, it modifies the previous character. The regex apples* matches either apple or apples (or applesssss, for that matter). Instead of matching something in addition to the preceding s, the * modifies the s. The * is called a *repetition operator*; it repeats something else, rather than matching anything itself. If you want the behavior of a shell pattern *, it is spelled .* in regexes; that matches any number of any character. Note that the repetition operator repeats the previous matching construct; .* can match any number of different characters, not just the same character over and over.

In fact, the * operator doesn't really operate on characters. It operates on indivisible chunks of regex, called *atoms*. A character is always an atom because there is no way to match just part of it. Another way to create an atom is to group things manually, using parentheses. Material between \(and \) is called a *subexpression*, and is matched as a single unit. For instance, the expression ba\(na\)* can match ba, bana, banana, or bananana, but it cannot match banan. The n and a have been grouped into an atom. Character classes and the period are also atoms. When an atom is repeated, it is possible for it to match a different thing each time. The regex [aeiou]* can match any string of vowels; each repetition of the atom is checked separately.

The same rules that allow a subexpression to join multiple characters into an atom allow multiple subexpressions to be joined; subexpressions can be nested. Good examples of nested subexpressions are rare in basic regexes; the best uses for them rely on additional operators not provided in historic implementations of basic regexes.

The more general repetition operator is \{x,y\}, indicating a repetition of between *x* and *y* copies of the preceding character; if *y* is omitted leaving only \{x,\}, any number of copies greater than or equal to *x* are matched. If the comma is also omitted, exactly x copies are · matched. Thus \{x\} is precisely equivalent to \{x,x\}.

The majority of what you need to know to write basic regexes can be summed up with a list of atoms and a list of repetition operators, as shown in Tables 2-3 and 2-4.

Table 2-3. *Basic Regular Expression Atoms*

Atom	Description
.	Match any character
[...]	Character class
\(...\)	Subexpression
Anything else	Individual characters are atoms

So, for instance, in the regex ab*, there are two atoms (a and b), and the repetition operator * modifies the second atom. In \(ab*\)c, there is a subexpression consisting of two atoms and a repetition operator, and the whole subexpression is itself an atom. Repetition operators are not atoms; they operate on atoms. An atom followed by a repetition operator is not an atom anymore. If you want to make an atom containing a repetition operator, you must wrap it in parentheses to create a subexpression.

Table 2-4. *Repetition Operators in Basic Regular Expressions*

Operator	Meaning
*	Zero or more
\{x\}	Exactly *x*
\{x,\}	At least *x*
\{x,y\}	Between x and y, inclusive

Backreferences

There is one other thing, which is neither an atom nor a repetition operator. In a basic regex, a backslash followed by a single digit is a special construct called a *backreference*. As the name suggests, a backreference is a reference to something earlier in the regex. When a group is parenthesized, it becomes a subexpression. The backreference \1 refers to the first subexpression. Unlike a repetition operator, a backreference refers to the matching string rather than the matching expression. So .\{2\} matches any two characters, but \(.\)\1 matches only two of the same character. Backreferences are extremely powerful, and some edge conditions exist.

Backreferences are counted by open parentheses, not closed parentheses; given the expression \(\(ab\)*c\)*, \1 refers to the outer subexpression and \2 to the inner subexpression. It is not at all clear what should happen if you write \(\(b\)*\2\), and use of nested subexpressions and backreferences within subexpressions is probably not safe or portable.

Using backreferences is a bit tricky. Very few regexes really need backreferences; in fact, they are omitted in extended regexes (though some implementations offer them as an extension). Even worse, their performance can be incredibly bad; a carefully crafted regex with many subexpressions and backreferences can take seconds or even minutes to match against a string, even on ludicrously fast modern hardware.

Extended Regular Expressions

Extended regexes (often called EREs) are much more powerful than basic regexes in some ways, but weaker in others. They are most prominently associated with the egrep utility. One of the most obvious differences is the simplification of syntax; parentheses used for grouping, and braces used for repetition, do not need backslashes in extended regexes. There are several possible ways to get a literal open brace, but the only portable one is [{]. (More on this in the "Common Extensions" section.)

Extended regexes offer two additional repetition operators, ? and +. The ? operator is equivalent to {0,1}, and the + operator is equivalent to {1,}. Both offer greatly improved readability, even though they do not offer new functionality.

One of the most significant enhancements of extended regexes is the alternation operator (|). This is usually pronounced "or," not "pipe," because it is the symbol used for logical or bitwise or operations in some languages. In an extended regex, a|b matches either a or b. This operator has a low precedence (lower than the joining of adjacent atoms), so hello|goodbye matches either hello or goodbye, not hellooodbye or hellgoodbye. Furthermore, it applies to atoms including subexpressions, which combines with nested subexpressions to make for a number of interesting patterns. The extended regex ((0[1-9])|(1[12]))? matches any number from 01 to 12, or an empty string. Patterns like this can be used to check for somewhat more structured data than can easily be checked for with basic regexes.

Extended regexes do not have backreferences (although many implementations offer them as an extension). They do have subexpressions, though. See Table 2-5 for the list of ERE atoms.

Table 2-5. *Extended Regular Expression Atoms*

Atom	Description
.	Match any character
[...]	Character class
(...)	Subexpression
Anything else	Individual characters are atoms

The repetition operators are similar, although there are more of them, as shown in Table 2-6.

Table 2-6. *Repetition Operators in Basic Regular Expressions*

Operator	Meaning
*	Zero or more
?	Zero or one
+	One or more
{x}	Exactly x
{x,}	At least x
{x,y}	Between x and y, inclusive

The interaction between the alternation operator and other components can be a bit confusing; even experienced programmers sometimes forget how it works. Table 2-7 illustrates how to use it.

Table 2-7. *Alternation and Atoms*

Expression	Meaning
a|b	a or b
good|bad	good or bad
c|hat	c or hat
(c|h)at	cat or hat
a|b{2}	a or bb
(a|b)c	ac or bc
(a)|(b)c	a or bc
(a|b){2}	aa, ab, ba, or bb

The case in which I have most often gotten confused with alternation is the difference between (expr1)|(expr2) and (expr1|expr2). These are, in fact, completely interchangeable, as long as you are not going to refer back to the subexpression later and as long as you don't have any other text in your pattern. If there is other text, though, they are different. Consider the following example:

```
(h[eu]llo)|(good(bye| night)) (world|moon)
```

It is pretty obvious what this is doing; it's matching any of four statements ("hello" or "hullo" or "goodbye" or "good night"), followed by either "world" or "moon." Unfortunately, while this is obvious, it is also wrong. In fact, it can match either "hello" or "hullo" with nothing following them. The | between the hello and goodbye subexpressions is dividing the whole expression; the space before (world|moon) is not special in any way in a regex, so it just continues extending the subpattern on the right side of the |. In terms of Table 2-7, this is actually (a)|(b)c, not (a|b)c.

Common Extensions

A number of extensions to both basic and extended regexes are quite common. Many implementations of basic regexes allow \? and \+ as synonyms for the extended regex ? and + repetition operators. Some also allow alternation using \|. Similarly, some implementations of extended regexes support backreferences. Another very popular extension is the special pseudo-anchors \< and \>, which match the beginning and end of a word; these may be found in both basic and extended regex implementations. Some systems spell these instead as [[:<:]] and [[:>:]]. Historical egrep did not support \{ as a literal open brace, but many modern implementations do. The POSIX standard specifies that a { not followed by a digit is also literal, but do not rely on this; even if computers always understood it, programmers would not.

Most modern systems tend to offer a sort of hybrid mode in which extended regexes support backreferences, and basic regexes support at least a few of the extended regex operators. On some systems, a plain ? may work even in an alleged basic regex. Text editors that support regexes are particularly likely to offer strange hybrid feature sets.

In terms of portability, nearly every system has some programs that support extended regexes, but many programs provide BREs by default, or exclusively, for compatibility reasons. Table 2-8 lists a few of the most common programs that support regexes of one variety or another.

Table 2-8. *Regular Expression Support*

Program	Regex Type	Notes
awk	Extended	Also true of awk variants, such as gawk or mawk.
emacs	Basic	Also supports ? and + (without backslashes) and | as a synonym for ERE |.
expr	Basic	Some versions may offer ?.
sed	Basic	Very few versions support ?.
grep	Basic	See also egrep.
egrep	Extended	Most commonly known variant; also known as grep -E on some systems.
fgrep	N/A	Does not actually use regexes; matches fixed strings only.
vi	Basic	nvi has an option to switch to extended REs; vim supports \? and \+.

Replacements

As has been previously pointed out, patterns are usually implicitly anchored to the ends of a string; to match a pattern anywhere in a string, you must write *pattern*. Regexes, by contrast, are not usually anchored. There is a particularly important reason for this; it is often desirable to be able to replace the matching text with something else. The most common place this is encountered in scripting is in sed's s/*pattern*/*replacement*/ operator. This finds any chunk of a string matching *pattern* and replaces it with *replacement*. If the pattern were implicitly anchored and had to start and end with .* to match text in the middle of a string, replacements would always replace the whole string. This is not usually what you want.

In general, replacement text allows some reference back to the matched string. In general, there are two ways to do this; one is by using \N to refer to subexpressions, much like a back-reference. The other is to use & (or \& in a few programs) to refer to the entire matched string. The sed substitution operator allows repeated matches, each starting from immediately past the previous match, with the g suffix; s/./&-/g replaces word with w-o-r-d-.

Elaborate replacement strings using subexpressions are one of the places where the simpler syntax of extended regexes is the most rewarding. It is fairly tedious to type a pattern with multiple subexpressions. Consider this simple pattern for replacing Random, John Q. with John Q. Random:

```
s/\([^ ]\{1,\}\), \([^ ]\{1,\}\) \([^ ]\{1,\}\)/\2 \3 \1/
s/([^ ]+), ([^ ]+) ([^ ]+)/\2 \3 \1/
```

The extended regex is quite a bit shorter and easier to read. Note that while extended regexes may not support backreferences, replacements using extended regexes typically support references to subexpressions.

Using Regular Expressions

Regular expressions are mostly found in external utilities (although some shells may implement expr as a builtin for performance reasons). Because of this, in cases where you can use a shell pattern instead of a regex, it may be more efficient to use the shell's built-in pattern matching, such as the case statement, instead of using an external utility. When using POSIX shells, the pattern-matching parameter substitutions (discussed in Chapter 7) make it even easier to get a lot done without needing regexes.

The expr utility offers a fairly flexible regex feature; expr string : pattern performs a regex match of string against pattern. In this case, the regex is implicitly anchored to the beginning of the string, as though it had a leading ^; to bypass this, start your pattern with .*. The value produced by expr depends on whether pattern has subexpressions. If there is at least one parenthesized subexpression, expr prints the contents of \1, or an empty string if there is no match. Otherwise, expr prints the length of the match, or 0 if there is no match:

```
$ expr foobar : foo
3
$ expr foobar : '\(foo\)'
foo
```

Unlike grep, expr does not consider a zero-length match to be a success; to grep (and most editors), the pattern b* matches the word hello because the word hello contains zero or more repetitions of the letter b. To expr, only a match of at least one character is a real match.

One use of the expr utility is extracting parts of file names. A pair of common utilities, basename and dirname, allow you to extract part of the name of a file from its path. These utilities are not completely portable, but you can do the same thing with expr:

```
$ expr /path/to/file : '\(.*\)/[^/]*'
/path/to
$ expr /path/to/file : '.*/\([^/]*\)'
file
```

Each of these expressions matches the same string; an arbitrarily long string of any characters whatsoever, followed by a slash and then any string of characters other than slashes. The difference is in which part of this pattern is marked as a subexpression; in the first pattern, it is the material before the slash, and in the second, it is the material after the slash. One weakness of expr is that you can only use it to extract the first subexpression of a regex. If you need to use a subexpression for grouping before the material you want, you will have to do something more elaborate to extract the desired text. However, in the most common cases, you can get what you want.

The preceding example assumes there is always a slash in the expression. What if there isn't?

```
$ expr filename : '\(.*\)/[^/]*'

$ expr filename : '.*/\([^/]*\)'
```

The expression doesn't match because there's no slash. So, of course, the thing to do is make the slash optional:

```
$ expr filename : '\(.*\)/\{0,1\}[^/]*'
filename
$ expr filename : '.*/\{0,1\}\([^/]*\)'
```

This doesn't work either. The second result might surprise you, but with the slash made optional, the .* on the left end of the expression can match the whole string; there is nothing to force it to leave any characters for the subexpression on the right to consume. In practice, you have to use another layer of testing to determine whether there is a slash before trying to split the string around it. (More advanced pattern-matching tools, such as the pcre library, could do this in one pass.)

Regexes are one of the most powerful tools of the UNIX system. With experience and practice, they become second nature; nothing is so maddening as a program where searching does not support regular expressions. The biggest problem users tend to have early on is confusing regexes with patterns; there seems to be no cure for this but practice and habit. In general, patterns are used only in the shell and in file name matching; everything else uses regexes. The equivalences are simple enough, and anything complicated in a regex generally cannot be done with a shell pattern to begin with. The hard part is getting the habit for which one to use when.

Something that might help you develop a feel for the differences between patterns and regexes is to run some tests and experiment. The following script shows how different strings do, or do not, match against patterns and regexes. (An explanation of how this script works will have to wait for a couple of chapters.)

```
#!/bin/sh
pattern="$1"
shift
for string
```

```
do
  if expr "$string" : ".*$pattern" >/dev/null 2>&1; then
    echo "regex: $string matched $pattern."
  else
    echo "regex: $string didn't match $pattern."
  fi
  case $string in
  $pattern) echo "shell: $string matched $pattern.";;
  *) echo "shell: $string didn't match $pattern.";;
  esac
done
```

To use this script, save it in a file and mark it as executable (chmod +x *filename*). Run it with at least two arguments; the first is a pattern you wish to test, and the second and later arguments are strings you wish to see matched against the pattern. Here's a sample:

$ ./patcheck '*' aardvark
```
regex: aardvark didn't match *.
shell: aardvark matched *.
```

Be aware that this script does not try to anchor regexes for you, and it even suppresses the default anchoring on the left provided by expr. If you want to compare only against anchored regexes, change the expr line to read as follows:

```
  if expr "$string" : "$pattern$" >/dev/null 2>&1; then
```

Regexes offer a number of improvements over shell patterns. The repetition operators allow for much more specific tests for common patterns, such as a string of unknown length containing only digits; the regex [0-9]* simply can't be expressed correctly in shell patterns. You can, however, use the pattern *[!0-9]* to detect any string that does not contain only digits.

Many utilities default to basic regexes, but optionally accept extended regexes. For the most part, if you haven't got a specific reason to think otherwise, any given program probably uses basic regexes as a default, usually with some extensions. More tips on managing the diversity of utility behaviors may be found in Chapter 8.

Replacing Patterns with Regular Expressions

Mechanically, it's quite easy to replace a pattern with a comparable regular expression. What is not so easy is getting the shell to use regexes in these places. The following discussion assumes some familiarity with statements and control structures, which are explained in the following chapters; you can come back to it later if too much of it is unfamiliar.

The two primary uses of shell patterns are file name matching and case statements. Replacing globs with regexes is not always easy. In the simplest case, you can use ls and grep together to generate a list. If you want a list of all files whose names have only digits in them before a particular suffix, such as .txt, you can express this as follows:

```
$(ls | grep '^[0-9]*.txt$')
```

The ls command, when running in a pipeline, lists each file name on a separate line by default; the grep command then shows only the lines matching the given regex. The $() construct (explained in Chapter 5; not portable to a few older shells) substitutes the output of this command, split into words. For files not necessarily in the current directory, this can be harder, and you may need to use the find command.

The case statement is hard to replace idiomatically. My advice is to replace it with a series of if and elif statements. Because only one branch of a case statement can match, these statements should be nested:

```
if expr "$1" : "$2" >/dev/null 2>&1; then
  echo "$2"
elif expr "$1" : "$3" >/dev/null 2>&1; then
  echo "$3"
elif expr "$1" : "$4" >/dev/null 2>&1; then
  echo "$4"
elif expr "$1" : "$5" >/dev/null 2>&1; then
  echo "$5"
else
  echo "no match"
fi
```

Another option, which may be more expressive in some cases, is to use regexes (and substitution) to generate a new string that is more amenable to pattern matching. Imagine that you wished to check for each of four flags, as in the previous example:

```
matches=""
expr "$1" : "$2" > /dev/null 2>&1 && matches="2$matches"
expr "$1" : "$3" > /dev/null 2>&1 && matches="3$matches"
expr "$1" : "$4" > /dev/null 2>&1 && matches="4$matches"
expr "$1" : "$5" > /dev/null 2>&1 && matches="5$matches"

case $matches in
*2*) echo "$2";;
*3*) echo "$3";;
*4*) echo "$4";;
*5*) echo "$5";;
*) echo "no match";;
esac
```

While this structure separates the matching operation into two passes, it preserves the semantics of the case statement precisely. On the down side, it does require processing all four tests before evaluating any of them.

Common Pitfalls of Regular Expressions

The two most common problems with regexes are matching too much and matching too little. In particular, it is extremely easy to be surprised when a .* matches nothing, and you expected it to match something, or to be surprised when it matches everything.

Some time ago, I wrote a script in which I intended to reverse the first two words of a line:

```
sed -e 's/\([^ ]*\) \([^ ]*\)/\2 \1/'
```

This did exactly what I expected; it selected everything up to the first space, and the next block of spaces, and reversed them. But then I wanted it to keep doing this to additional pairs, so I modified it:

```
sed -e 's/\([^ ]*\) \([^ ]*\)/\2 \1/g'
```

This seemed to work, but then I tried it on another system, and it didn't seem to work at all. While a b became b a, a b c d became b ac d. (In fact, there was a trailing space after this, which I did not initially notice.) In fact, "buggy" system was correct. The first iteration matches a b. The second matches an empty string of nonspaces, a space, and the letter c, and reverses them. Because I "knew" that my intent in writing [^]* was to match the largest available series of non-words, I forgot that the regex takes the first match it can find, matching as much as it can, not the longest match it can find no matter where it has to start to make that match. Interestingly, several systems had a bug, which caused them to skip that first character in this circumstance and "correctly" do what I wanted. (The bug seems to have been an unusual edge condition.)

Forgetting anchors or including extra anchors are both common mistakes made when trying to match something specific. Just during the time I've been working on this book, I've been bitten several times by the fact that expr anchors regexes implicitly to the beginning of the string.

When you have an expression that could be seen as matching a string in more than one way, the general rule is that the leftmost expressions are greedy first. So, if part of a string could go in either of two subexpressions, it will be in the leftmost one.

The distinctions between basic and extended regexes are another common source of confusion. If you have been using one heavily, and you switch to the other, all sorts of things go wrong. Subexpressions become literal parentheses, and vice versa; both are confusing. There is no such thing as a nontrivial regex that can be used both as a basic and an extended regex. If you have two editors, one that uses each syntax, expect to spend a lot of time puzzling over warnings about invalid repetition operators and unmatched parentheses, or wondering why a search didn't turn something up that is right there in the page.

What's Next?

The ability to decide which of several pieces of code to execute, or to execute code repeatedly, is essential to programming. Chapter 3 introduces the basic control structures that make the shell into a programming language rather than a mere macro language, as well as some of the tools the shell provides for the creation and manipulation of data files.

Basic Shell Scripting

This chapter introduces the basics of control flow in the shell. The shell's functionality is moderately baroque, and many shell features have elaborate interactions. This chapter glosses over the full (and rather gory) details of the shell's quoting and variable expansion features, leaving them for Chapter 4. Instead, this chapter introduces the basic programming features of the shell, showing how to control the execution of shell scripts, join programs together, and interact with files. This framework makes it much easier to provide meaningful examples while exploring the rather more complicated territory of the shell's expansion and quoting mechanisms.

Scripts presented without command prompts may be run directly on the command line or saved in a file and run as scripts.

Introducing Control Structures

By default, the shell executes commands in the order it encounters them, whether on the command line or on the keyboard. Certain inputs, however, instead of having direct effects of their own, cause the shell to change which commands it executes and in what order; these are called *control structures*. Control structures are what make the shell a programming language, rather than a very simple macro expansion language.

There are several kinds of control structures. Conditional execution causes the shell to execute some code, while skipping other code. This allows a script to adapt to different circumstances; for instance, a script might wish to ask a user for confirmation before taking a risky action. Iteration allows a script to run a given block of code more or fewer times. A typical example would be a program that performs the same operations on every file in a directory or on each line of input.

Control structures are sometimes used even when their function could be obtained without them; for instance, you might write a loop to perform a given task five times, rather than simply duplicating the code for that task five times. This makes it easier to generalize later (if the number of times you want to repeat the task varies, for instance) and also makes it easier to maintain code. This can also be done using shell functions, a feature introduced in Chapter 5.

In both cases, shell control structures depend on testing conditions. To make a decision about what to do, the shell has to be able to express the concept of a yes or no question; the shell has to have a concept of truth and falsehood, whether the question is "did the user say yes?" or "are there any more files?"

> ### A WORD ON STYLE
>
> The scripts used in this book employ a consistent indentation style. It is not necessary that you indent your scripts exactly the same way. The shell is, with rare exceptions, unaffected by your indentation choices. However, future readers will usually care quite a bit. A good indentation style ought to make it easy for the reader to see what is going on. Unfortunately, programmers rarely agree on what constitutes "easy to read." This book uses an indentation style familiar to readers of GNU shell scripts, with two spaces of indentation.
>
> One other important note: When modifying existing code, never change the indentation policy if there is one. It is more important that a given module be consistent than that you like the way your additions read. Users can learn nearly any indentation style fairly quickly, but they cannot hope to easily read code with inconsistent indentation.

What Is Truth?

In nearly every programming language, most control structures come down to tests and the concept of whether a condition "is true." In the shell, control structures are based on the exit status of commands. Every program that is run on a UNIX-like system has a numeric exit status (or return code), which indicates something about the final state of its execution. Two programs provided on all UNIX systems, true and false, are guaranteed to always yield a true or false exit status, respectively. The : built-in command always produces a true exit status. Under the hood, the return code is zero for a successful command execution, and non-zero for a command that is reporting any kind of failure or abnormality. This conflicts with the common convention in C-like languages of executing code inside if (1) and not executing code inside if (0). Many shell programmers use the : command, which is a synonym for true. I like the natural language form, but the use of : is quite common, too. It has advantages. While only some shells provide true as a built-in, : is a built-in command in every shell, making it more efficient. It is also shorter to type and to read. (And for those of you targeting minimal embedded systems, : works when /bin/true is missing. This is less important with /bin/false; if it is missing, the execution fails, so the false command always fails.) The examples in this book are written more for clarity than for performance, in this respect.

While people often think of control structures as applying only within script files, the shell happily accepts control structures typed directly on the command line. For instance, you can verify the behavior of true and false on the command line:

```
$ if true
> then echo "True!"
> fi
True!
$ if false
> then echo "False!"
> fi
$
```

The exit status is not the output of the program; it is a separate piece of data made available to the calling program, such as the shell. The true command doesn't print the zero value, it simply makes that value available to the program calling it.

For now, I ignore the question of whether commands are built in or external. It turns out not to matter; built-in commands produce a return code, just as external commands do, and use the same conventions. If you are curious about the return code of a command, you can echo the built-in shell parameter $? immediately after running it. After a successful command, this value will be 0. After an unsuccessful command, it will typically be non-zero. Standard POSIX shells have a feature where any command can be prefixed with !, reversing the return code of that command. For instance, the echo command usually succeeds, but ! echo hello performs the echo successfully, then yields a return code indicating failure. Unfortunately, a few shells omit this feature; in code that has to run on /bin/sh on every common system, it is best to avoid it. Here is an example of how to test for the function of the ! command prefix:

```
if eval "! false" > /dev/null 2>&1; then
  echo "This shell supports !"
else
  echo "This shell does not support !"
fi
```

```
This shell supports !
```

There are only a couple of shells (most notably /bin/sh on Solaris) that will run into this. You can replace !*command* with a construct like this:

```
if command; then false; else true; fi
```

One command is particularly important—the test command, which can perform a variety of logical tests, such as comparing numbers or strings, or testing attributes of files (such as whether they exist, have contents, or are accessible). Unlike many commands, the test command generally produces no output at all; rather, it indicates success or failure only through its return code. For historical reasons, and also because it looks pretty, the test command has an alias of [, which expects a trailing] after its arguments. If you have ever wondered why there is a file /bin/[, now you know. However, this variant can not be safely used in shell code being used with m4sh or autoconf, so it is a good habit to use the plain test form.

WHY IS TEST EXTERNAL?

This is sort of a trick question; in fact, in many shells, the test command (and [) are actually implemented internally by the shell for efficiency. The real question is why test is conceived of as a command rather than as some kind of syntactic feature of the shell. The answer is that the shell's syntax is more generic this way; you can write new programs, and they can immediately become part of the shell's extremely flexible control structure. The various tests (and there are many) performed by the test program are only a small subset of the sorts of things you might want to check for within a script. In general, in terms of portability, it does not matter whether a command is a built-in or external command, as long as its behavior is predictable.

When expanding variables as arguments to the test command, be careful about what could happen with variables whose expansions look like parts of the test command's argument grammar. While most of the time the test command figures out what was intended, it can be easier for everyone to ensure that arguments are unambiguous. A common idiom for this is to precede arguments with X where possible, as in the following example:

```
if test X"$answer" = X"42"; then
  echo "Forty-two!"
fi
```

There are three key points to this idiom. First, putting a letter in front of the variable ensures that, even if a user enters something like = or -f, test treats the argument as a plain string, not an operator. Putting quotes around the variable ensures that it will not be split into multiple words. Finally, putting the X outside the quotes on both sides makes the intent clearer. The user can easily see that the X is the same on both sides. Another common idiom is to reverse the positions of the values. This eliminates possible ambiguities, presenting test with an expression that can only be understood as intended:

```
if test 42 = "$answer"; then
  echo "Forty-two!"
fi
```

Of these two, I prefer the X form, simply because I find it easier to read "answer equals 42" than "42 equals answer." This is purely a style question; either is portable.

The test program performs string comparisons by default; the expression test 1 = 1.0 is considered false because the strings differ. However, it also supports numeric comparisons, which are spelled as hyphenated operators, like -eq; test 1 -eq 1.0 is true. Numeric comparisons are needed because string comparisons pay no attention to magnitude; test 100 < 2 succeeds because the digit 1 is before the digit 2 in standard character sets. Table 3-1 shows the relational operators supported in test.

Table 3-1. *Relational Operators in test*

String Operator	Numeric Operator	Meaning
a = b	a -eq b	a and b are equal
a != b	a -ne b	a and b are not equal
a > b	a -gt b	a is greater than b
a < b	a -lt b	a is less than b
a >= b	a -ge b	a is greater than or equal to b
a <= b	a -le b	a is less than or equal to b

Developers from other languages should note two distinctions. The first is that the == equality operator is not portable, although some variants support it as an extension. The second is that Perl precisely reverses the sense of these operators; in Perl, == is the numeric equality test, and eq is the stringwise one.

The test command supports a number of logical operations allowing you to combine or invert tests. First, any test can be preceded by ! to reverse the sense of the test. This is portable among shells and implementations of test, even in shells that do not allow commands to be preceded by !.

Some versions of test allow combinations of multiple tests, conjoined with -a (and) or -o (or) operators. This is not fully portable; instead, use the shell's && and || operators (which are explained in Chapter 4).

Introducing Conditional Execution

There are two primary mechanisms for conditional execution in the shell. The first is the if statement, which executes code if a specified condition is true. The second is the case statement, which can select among multiple sections of code based on the contents of an expression. In both cases, only one section of code is actually executed, and others are completely bypassed.

Introducing the if-then-else Statement

The if statement executes code if a specified command succeeds. The syntax of the if statement follows this basic pattern:

```
if command; then
  actions
fi
```

The use of fi, rather than something generic like end, reflects the original shell developer's fondness for ALGOL. The then part of the statement does not need to be on the same line as the if; in fact, it must be separated by a command separator (the semicolon in the previous example). Some users prefer to write if statements as follows:

```
if command
then actions
fi
```

In this book, I use the first structure, but they are equivalent. A simple program to check whether the reader can perform simple arithmetic could be implemented as follows:

```
printf "What do you get if you multiply 6 by 9? "
read answer
if test X"$answer" = X"42"; then
  echo "You read too much science fiction."
fi
```

If the user enters 42, the shell counters with a reference to a popular novel. But if the user enters anything else, the shell just says nothing. You could resolve this by checking for other values:

```
printf "What do you get if you multiply 6 by 9? "
read answer
if test X"$answer" = X"42"; then
  echo "You read too much science fiction."
fi

if test X"$answer" != X"42"; then
  echo "You do not read enough science fiction."
fi
```

As you can see, this has the potential to become large and unwieldy rather quickly. Furthermore, if some clever sort comes along and "corrects" the value used, it's quite possible that one of the statements will be changed, and the other will not, leading to inconsistent or unwanted behavior. Luckily, the shell has another keyword that may be used in if statements: else. The else clause of an if statement, if present, is executed if the specified command indicated failure. A more idiomatic implementation of the previous script would be as follows:

```
printf "What do you get if you multiply 6 by 9? "
read answer
if  test X"$answer" = X"42"; then
  echo "You read too much science fiction."
else
  echo "You do not read enough science fiction."
fi
```

As with then, else may be placed on the same line as the following actions; however, this is often harder for the reader to understand. Conditional statements may be nested arbitrarily, as well:

```
printf "What do you get if you multiply 6 by 9? "
read answer
if test X"$answer" = X"42"; then
  echo "You read too much science fiction."
else
  if test X"$answer" = X"54"; then
    echo "Boring, but arguably correct."
  else
    echo "You do not read enough science fiction."
  fi
fi
```

This works well as long as there are not too many alternatives, but imagine for a moment a test to determine whether the user has entered a valid state or province name using this pattern. Clearly, something more flexible is needed. One method is to use the optional elif test:

```
printf "What do you get if you multiply 6 by 9? "
read answer
if test X"$answer" = X"42"; then
  echo "You read too much science fiction."
elif test X"$answer" = X"54"; then
  echo "Boring, but arguably correct."
else
  echo "You do not read enough science fiction."
fi
```

Any command may be used as the controlling expression for an if or elif statement. Since most UNIX commands indicate their status in their return code, this can also be used for error detection during a script's execution. Most programs print their own error messages, but sometimes the output from a program would not be informative to the user.

```
if grep $user /etc/passwd; then
  echo "$user is already in /etc/passwd."
fi
```

```
seebs:x:1000:1000:Peter Seebach,,,:/home/seebs:/bin/bash
seebs is already in /etc/passwd.
```

The first line of output is the output from the grep command, not the intended error message. There are two ways to resolve this. One is to use the -q (or -s) command-line flag to grep; this suppresses output, causing grep to indicate success or failure only through its exit status. Unfortunately, these flags, while widespread, are not universal; some implementations support one, some the other, and some neither. The portable solution is to redirect the output of the command:

```
if grep $user /etc/passwd >/dev/null; then
  echo "$user is already in /etc/passwd."
fi
```

The output is redirected to /dev/null, preventing the user from seeing it. (Redirection is explained in the "Introducing Redirection" section later in this chapter.)

When you need to store a user preference or other decision, the simplest idiom is to store either true or false in a variable, then use the variable as a condition:

```
do_this=true
do_that=false
if $do_this; then
  echo "Do this."
fi
if $do_that; then
  echo "Do not do that."
fi
```

```
Do this.
```

This idiom is easy to read and runs efficiently. You can also store values such as Y or N in a variable and test for them using the `test` command, but using `true` and `false` is simpler and cleaner. Implemented with string values and the `test` command, the previous example becomes:

```
do_this=Y
do_that=N
if test "$do_this" = "Y"; then
  echo "Do this."
fi
if test "$do_that" = "Y"; then
  echo "Do not do that."
fi
```

```
Do this.
```

The behavior is the same, but the code is harder to read. Experienced programmers may prefer to use `:` and `false` for brevity or performance reasons.

You can test for patterns as well. While there is no portable way to match patterns or regular expressions using `test` (the regular expression operator is not universal), the `expr` command can be used to compare strings to regular expressions:

```
if expr "$do_this" : "[Yy].*"; then
  echo "Do this."
fi
```

In some cases, you will find that the `if` and `elif` constructs are not as expressive as you would like for a given problem, and what you really want to do is compare a string against a series of possible patterns, not just against an individual pattern. There is a way to do just that.

Introducing the case Statement

The `case` statement compares a string to a series of patterns. One of the advantages of this is that you can have multiple different tests without an ever-increasing indentation spiral of doom. One of the disadvantages is that, while `expr` tests regular expressions, `case` tests only shell patterns. However, shell patterns with alternation are flexible enough to serve well. The basic layout of a `case` command looks like this:

```
case word in
  pat1) actions;;
  pat2) actions;;
esac
```

As with `if`, the `case` command is ended by its own name, spelled backward. There may not be spaces between the two semicolons that terminate each list of actions. The value of *word* is expanded but is not subject to field splitting after expansion. So if *word* is just a single variable, you never need quotes around it. (The only time you could need spaces would be if *word* contains spaces prior to expansion; the value "$a $b" needs to be quoted, as the shell takes only a single word before the in keyword.) The value is checked against each pattern in turn, and the actions from the first matching pattern are executed. Some systems also provide pattern matching in test, but this is nonportable. Use case instead.

Pattern matching is explained in more detail in Chapter 2. This section assumes some familiarity with pattern matching but uses simple patterns to illustrate how the case statement works. For instance, the following test implements a draconian user interface policy:

```
printf "Would you like to play a game? (please enter yes or no): "
read input
case $input in
  yes) echo "I would like to play a game too, but I am only a sample script.";;
  no) echo "I am very disappointed.";;
  *) echo "I said to please enter yes or no. Now formatting your disk...";;
esac
```

User input that contains "yes" or "no" plus other contents will not pass muster in this example. For instance, if the user entered "yes, please," the script would not consider this valid input. A more forgiving writer might use something similar to the following:

```
printf "Would you like to play a game? (please enter yes or no): "
read input
case $input in
  [Yy]*) echo "I would like to play a game too, but I am only a sample script.";;
  [Nn]*) echo "I am very disappointed.";;
  *) echo "I said to please enter yes or no. Now formatting your disk...";;
esac
```

Additionally, it is permissible to provide multiple patterns for a single case, separating them with pipe characters (|). For instance, the following script accepts a number of variants but is not quite as general as the preceding example:

```
printf "Would you like to play a game? (please enter yes or no): "
read input
case $input in
[Yy]|[Yy][Ee][Ss]) echo "Me too, but I am only a sample script.";;
[Nn]|[Nn][Oo]) echo "I am very disappointed.";;
*) echo "I said to please enter yes or no. Now formatting your disk...";;
esac
```

This accepts y or yes in any combination of capitals, or n or no in any combination of capitals, but it will not recognize other inputs. If there is no way to manage what you want using shell patterns, you may have to fall back on if statements and expr or grep. See Chapter 2 for more information about patterns and regular expressions.

Between if and case, you can control the behavior of a great number of programs; but if you stop there, you will shortly notice that programs that need to repeat actions become very tedious to write and maintain, even with a modern text editor to handle your cut and paste needs. What you need is a way to do the same thing over and over, without getting bored; this brings us to *iteration*.

Introducing Iteration

The real strength of the shell (or of anything computers do) is not in doing a single thing, but in doing similar things over and over. The shell provides two primary mechanisms for iteration. The while loop (and its relative, the until loop) repeat as long as a condition is true (or false). The for loop iterates over a fixed list of items, processing each item once.

The while Loop

The simplest loop in the shell is the while loop, which performs a series of actions as long as a condition remains true. The basic syntax is this:

```
while command; do
  actions
done
```

As with the if statement, *command* can be any shell command. The actions can be a shell command or a sequence of shell commands. If *command* indicates failure, the shell leaves the loop. For instance, if *command* fails the first time the shell executes it, the actions are not performed even once. Otherwise, after each time performing actions, the shell runs *command* again. For instance, Listing 3-1 might induce a positive frame of mind.

Listing 3-1. *Positive Thinking Made Easy*

```
while test X"$answer" != X"yes"; do
  printf "Say yes: "
  read answer
done
```

This loop runs until the variable $answer contains the string yes. The variable is not initialized prior to the loop; assuming it wasn't already set somewhere else in the script, it simply expands to an empty string until the user supplies a response to the read command. It is not an error to use an uninitialized variable in the shell (but you can check for a value; see the discussion of variables in Chapter 4).

You can make the code inside the loop as complicated as you want, including using other features such as conditional execution, as in the following example:

```
while test X"$answer" != X"YES"; do
  printf "Are you ready? "
  read answer
  if X"$answer" = X"yes"; then
    echo "I can't HEAR you!"
  elif test X"$answer" != X"YES"; then
    echo "When I ask you a question, you say YES!"
  fi
done
```

For convenience, the shell also offers an until loop, which is precisely like a while loop, except the sense of the condition test is reversed. For instance, Listing 3-1 would be written as follows using until:

```
until test X"$answer" = X"yes"; do
  printf "Say yes: "
  read answer
done
```

Some writers feel that the until loop adds substantial clarity, but others dislike it. I recommend that you use it when it seems clearer. If a natural language description of the process would start with "do X until . . . ," then use until.

Introducing break and continue

Sometimes, you may find out early in a loop iteration that you cannot usefully continue. The shell only checks *command* at the top of the loop, though; the shell will not stop the sequence of commands halfway through just because *command* would indicate failure if run again. To escape the loop immediately, use the break command. In some cases, this is especially useful when combined with the true program, which always succeeds. For instance, you may want to ensure that a loop is run at least once (C programmers may be familiar with this as the do {} while () idiom). There is no explicit syntax for this. Idiomatically, you run an eternal loop, and break when the loop condition is no longer true.

```
while true; do
  printf "Say yes: "
  read answer
  if test X"$answer" != X"yes" ; then
    echo "Oh, come on now. You can do it!"
  else
    echo "You did it! Way to go!"
    break
  fi
done
```

Another possibility is that, while this particular iteration of the loop has lost interest for you, you wish to continue iterating. For this, you use the continue statement, which jumps back to the top of the loop. The continue statement jumps to the iteration test; if that test now fails, the loop exits.

Note that break and continue only have meaning within loops, such as while or for, not in terms of if or case statements. The break statement in this example skips out of the while loop. If you want to break out of more than one loop, the break and continue statements take an optional argument indicating how many nested loops to break out of.

```
while true; do
  printf "Are you bored yet?"
  answer=""
```

```
while test X"$answer" != X"yes" && test X"$answer" != X"no"; do
  read answer
  case $answer in
    no) ;;
    yes) echo "I never liked you either."
      break 2;;
    *) echo "I am but a humble script, and only understand yes and no.";;
  esac
done
done
```

The preceding example uses break 2 to leave both the inner loop (waiting for an answer it understands) and the outer loop. If the inner loop used only a plain break statement, it would jump to the end of the inner loop, but the outer loop would continue to iterate.

Introducing for loops

In the shell, the for loop does only one thing: iterate over a provided set of arguments. This is not analogous at all to the C for loop, which can iterate over essentially any circumstance. Perl users may be familiar with it as foreach. The basic form of the for loop is this:

```
for var in list; do
  actions
done
```

The value provided for *list* is subject to parameter substitution followed by globbing, and then subject to field splitting (unless it is quoted). The for loop runs once for each member of *list*, assigning that value to *var*. For instance, the following script looks almost like a very simple mail-merge program:

```
for name in "Occupant" "Our Friends" "Current Resident" "Postal Customer"; do
  echo "Hello, $name"
  echo "Look! A personalized letter! Buy our stuff!"
done
```

Because the most common usage of the for loop is to iterate over the arguments given to a script, there is a special syntax to do this. If the in *list* is omitted, the shell iterates over the arguments given to the script. (Actually, it iterates over the positional parameters, which are usually but not always the arguments given to the script; the positional parameters are discussed at length in Chapter 6.) However, this produces a rare portability issue; some older versions of bash do not cope well with a semicolon after the variable name. When using for without in, put a new line before the do keyword. For instance, the following script identifies the first file in its arguments that contains a given string:

```
string="test"
for i
do
  if grep "$string" "$i"; then
    echo "$i"
    break
  fi
done
```

As you can see, break works the same way in for loops that it does in while loops. This script has a number of flaws, but it can be used. The most obvious flaw is the display of the unneeded output from grep. Another flaw is that, if $string expands to something that looks like a grep option, the script misbehaves; similarly, some versions of echo may behave surprisingly with file names that have hyphens or backslashes in them. The following script is a little cleaner:

```
string="test"
for i
do
  if grep -e "$string" "$i" >/dev/null; then
    printf "%s\n" "$i"
    break
  fi
done
```

The -e option to grep specifies that the following argument is the expression to match, even if it might otherwise be interpreted as an option. The printf command displays the file name no matter what it is, suppressing the strange and unportable behavior of echo.

Thinking About Control Structures

The preceding introduction to control structures is not a substitute for using them frequently to get comfortable with them, but it should be complete enough to let you understand the sample programs used to illustrate other features. It takes some experience to know when to use the different control structures, and the best way to develop a good sense for this is probably to look at, and write, lots of examples. If you are new to programming, this is usually one of the hardest parts to get used to.

The shell control structures have names that describe their behaviors. You can usually decide which one to use by trying out verbal descriptions such as "for each file" (a for loop), "while there is more data" (a while loop), or "if the file exists" (an if statement). The case statement is the hardest to map to idiomatic English, but if a description of what you are doing can be phrased starting with "in the first case," it is probably going to map well onto case.

Some of the most powerful uses of these constructs depend on the use of additional tools. One of the most crucial of these is the ability to change the sources of input, and the destinations of output, of shell programs.

Introducing Redirection

In most cases, when you are using a shell interactively, commands accept input from your keyboard and direct output to your screen. When you run a script from an interactive session, it works the same way. UNIX systems treat files, keyboards, and other data sources in essentially the same way, calling them all *streams*. A stream is simply a source of data, or a place data can be written to. Some streams can be both read from and written to. Changing the source of a program's input, or the destination of its output, is called *redirection*. This section provides an introduction to redirection, although there are additional features to be explored later.

The examples in this section are often presented as interactive sessions, with user input in bold and shell prompts and output in plain text.

Here's an example of redirection in action:

```
$ echo "hello, world" > hello
$ cat hello
hello, world
```

This differs from the direct echo in that a new file, named hello, has been created. The output of echo is redirected into the file. When redirecting to a file, the shell empties the file first. If you want to add on to the existing contents, use >>, as in the following example:

```
$ echo "goodbye, now" >> hello
$ cat hello
hello, world
goodbye, now
```

A particularly common redirection target is the special file /dev/null. This special file is not a regular file storing data, but a special file that simply discards anything and everything written to it. For instance, the for loop example emitted unwanted output, until it was eliminated by the use of redirection to /dev/null; here it is again:

```
for i
do
  if grep -e "$string" "$i" >/dev/null; then
    printf "%s\n" "$i"
    break
  fi
done
```

Without the redirection, the user sees all of the matching lines in each file, followed by its name. This is annoying, but there is no portable way to tell grep not to produce any output. What you can do portably is redirect that output, discarding it; then, the script produces only the file names, rather than the grep output and the file names.

Similarly, commands can be run using a file as input instead of the keyboard, using a < for redirection. For instance, you might want to run one command on the output of another, like this:

```
$ ls > list
$ grep hello < list
hello
```

In this example, a complete list of files in the current directory is stored in a new file named list. Then, the grep command is used to display lines in that file containing the string hello. This is inefficient, though; you have to remember to clean up the intermediate file, and if the output is large, it takes up a lot of space. UNIX solves this with *pipes*. A pipe is a single stream that provides output from one program as input to another. For instance, the following command displays every file in the current directory with hello in its name:

```
$ ls | grep hello
```

On some (non-UNIX) systems, a similar syntax is available, but the shell implements it by writing the output to a temporary file, running the second program on that file, and then deleting the file. On UNIX, both commands can run simultaneously.

A series of commands joined by pipes is called a *pipeline*, and in general, a pipeline can be used in any case where a single command could be used. A pipeline can have more than two commands. This command displays a count of files in the current directory with hello in their names:

```
ls | grep hello | wc -l
```

The exit status of a pipeline is the exit status of the last command in it. So the first example can be used, combined with redirection, to create a simple test:

```
if ls | grep hello > /dev/null; then
  echo "you have a file with hello in its name."
fi
```

The output from the ls command is fed into grep as input. The grep command then prints any matching lines, but its output has been redirected to /dev/null. However, the grep command's exit status is success when it finds at least one match. So, without actually looking at the output, the shell can still tell whether grep would have printed anything, and thus whether there were any matching lines. Note that it does not matter at all what exit status the ls command yields; only the exit status of grep is being used by the shell. Thus this script won't work:

```
if  ls | grep hello | wc -l > /dev/null; then
  echo "you have a file with hello in its name."
fi
```

Whether grep produces any output or not, the wc (word count) command is unlikely to fail. This highlights the difference between the output of the command and its return code. If there are no matching files, wc -l prints 0 to standard output; if there are matching files, it prints the number of lines it received as input. However, its return code will be zero as long as no errors occurred. Because wc is the last program in the pipeline, it determines the return code of the whole pipeline.

Understanding File Descriptors

The discussion so far has talked about input and output streams, but it has not mentioned any other streams. UNIX programs usually start with three streams: standard input, standard output, and standard error. Standard input reflects the input to the program, whether that is a terminal, another program, or a file. Standard output is where the program's output goes, while standard error is a separate stream used for error messages. When standard output is redirected to a file or to another program, standard error is unchanged:

```
$ grep string nonexistent-file > /dev/null
grep: nonexistent-file: No such file or directory
```

If you are running in an interactive session, standard error is usually your terminal. As another example, when a CGI script is being run by a web server, it is common for standard output to be the eventual web page to be presented to the client and standard error to go into the web server's log files.

Streams have associated numbers, called *descriptors*. Standard input is always descriptor 0, standard output is descriptor 1, and standard error is descriptor 2. By default, output redirection redirects descriptor 1, and input redirection redirects descriptor 0. So, in this example, standard output is redirected, but standard error is not:

```
$ ls nonexistent-file > output
ls: nonexistent-file: No such file or directory
```

The file named output is created, but empty, because the ls command did not send any messages to standard output. You can specify the descriptor to redirect explicitly:

```
$ ls nonexistent-file 2> error
$ cat error
ls: nonexistent-file: No such file or directory
```

The ls command produces no messages to standard output, and its error messages are directed into the file named error. However, if the file did exist, the error file would be empty and the file name would be displayed; standard output has not been redirected. This kind of technique can be used to defer the display of an error message, or prefix it with some kind of explanation. Consider the preceding example with a loop calling grep. You might want to defer those messages or suppress them entirely:

```
string="test"
found=0
show_errs=true
for i
do
  if grep "$string" "$i" >/dev/null 2>error
    printf "%s\n" "$i"
    show_errs=false
    break
  fi
done
```

This writes any errors it encounters into a file named error; a more robust script would use a temporary file with a name that is not likely to clash with a user-created file. However, you need a way to report these errors. If there were errors encountered before a matching file showed up, it is undesirable to follow the file with errors. Thus the show_errs variable is created to indicate whether to display errors. It is used as follows:

```
if $show_errs; then
  echo "Couldn't find '$string' in any files."
  if test -s error; then
    echo "Errors were encountered:"
    cat error
  fi
fi
```

If the show_errs value still contains true, no matches were found, and it is useful to display an error message to the user. The if statement becomes if true; then, which executes the conditional code. On the other hand, if matches were found, show_errs has been set to false, and the conditional code is not executed; there is no reason to warn the user about possible errors reading other files when the file the user cared about was read successfully.

In the case where no matches were found, any error messages from the grep commands might be relevant, so they should be displayed. This is conditional on the test -s command, which checks that a file exists and has contents. Unfortunately, there is a subtle bug; since each call to grep is redirected separately, the file contains only any errors produced by the last file. Each run through the loop empties the error file before running grep. One solution would be to use >> redirection, but there is a simpler way. Redirection can be applied to any shell command, not just individual statements. Redirecting the whole loop truncates the file only once, at the start of the loop, and accumulates all of the errors. Another is to use a more robust name for the temporary file. That gives you the following improved script:

```
string="test"
found=0
show_errs=true
error=${TMPDIR:-/tmp}/err.$$
for i
do
  if grep "$string" "$i" >/dev/null; then
    printf "%s\n" "$i"
    show_errs=false
    break
  fi
done 2>"$error"
if $show_errs; then
  echo "Couldn't find '$string' in any files."
  if test -s "$error"; then
    echo "Errors were encountered:"
    cat "$error"
  fi
fi
```

Just as the shell restores the previous streams after redirecting a single command, it restores the previous streams after redirecting a compound command. The TMPDIR environment variable, when set, is used to hint at a location other than /tmp in which to store temporary files. By convention, temporary files usually embed the shell's PID in their names to avoid clashes. Each use of the file name error has been changed to "$error". The quotes protect the script in the event that someone has set TMPDIR to a name including spaces or new lines, which could otherwise cause the shell's field splitting to render the script syntactically invalid.

However, this script now has a serious bug. Its output is only sometimes the name of the first file containing the string. If there were no such files, its output is an error message. This requires any program using the output from this program to be more careful. What you want is some way to distinguish between the output of a script and diagnostic messages about it. And, as it turns out, that is exactly what standard error is for. Thus the following cleaned up version does the right thing:

```
string="test"
found=0
show_errs=true
error=${TMPDIR:-/tmp}/err.$$
for i
do
  if grep "$string" "$i" >/dev/null; then
    printf "%s\n" "$i"
    show_errs=false
    break
  fi
done 2>"$error"
if $show_errs; then
  echo "Couldn't find '$string' in any files."
  if test -s "$error"; then
    echo "Errors were encountered:"
    cat "$error"
  fi
fi >&2
```

As with the redirection of the for loop, the entire trailing if statement can be redirected. The redirection >&2 redirects the output of the if statement to standard error; this technique is explained further in a few paragraphs. If this command is used in a pipeline with another command which expects to receive the name of a file, the second command will get either a file name or nothing; this prevents the second program from trying to find a file named Couldn't find 'test' in any files.

In most cases, this is a useful feature. However, separating output and errors is not always desirable. In some cases, such as running large software builds, it is common to want to put standard output and standard error together in a single file. For instance, if you wanted both the output of a build and any error messages stored in a log file, you might try this:

```
make >log 2>log
```

This does not work as intended. The first redirection creates a file named log, truncates it, and starts writing output to it. The second opens the same file and starts writing to it. Unfortunately for you, this means that the output and error streams can overwrite each other because they are each writing separately to the same file. Each redirection has created a separate stream going into the same file, and each stream has its own notion of where in the file it will write next. What you want, however, is to have a single stream that both standard output and standard error appear in. The shell has a special syntax for this, allowing any file descriptor to be copied (also called being *cloned* or *duped*) from any other file descriptor:

```
make >log 2>&1
```

The ampersand (&), in this context, indicates cloning of an existing descriptor rather than opening of a file by name. Thus standard output is redirected into a file named log, and then standard error is redirected to wherever standard output goes—in this case, the file named log. The two descriptors are now both attached to the same stream for the duration of the redirection. Note that, although only a single > is used, duplication of a file descriptor does not truncate anything; it is not opening the file, but copying the already open stream to a new descriptor. As with any other redirection, this is temporary, and after the command exits, the descriptors go back to their original, separate streams. There are a number of other cases where this technique can be used, but joining standard error to standard output is by far the most common. The same technique can be used for input streams using <&.

Throughout this section, redirections have always been shown at the end of a command line. In fact, redirections can occur anywhere in a command line. Redirections are processed separately from arguments and are not visible to the command being run. In general, redirections are processed from left to right. However, in the case where a command is in a pipeline, redirecting standard error to standard output has the effect you probably want—standard error is merged into the pipeline.

Redirection Using exec

One other use of redirection is common enough to be worth mentioning. It is incredibly tedious to run a large number of commands all with the same redirection appending their output to a file. The shell allows you to redirect the shell's file descriptors, rather than just the file descriptors of a particular command, using the exec shell built in. If you call exec with some redirections, but no other arguments, it redirects those streams within the shell itself. Be very careful to do this only within scripts; if you do it on the command line, you can quite thoroughly hose your shell session. (This is a technical term.) Redirecting the shell's descriptors means that all future commands run by the shell will be affected by these redirections. For instance, the following line in a shell script stores all errors generated by future commands within that script in the file log:

```
exec 2>log
```

The exec command can be used to open and close streams. UNIX systems do not use a special character to indicate end of file. In a pipeline, the program receiving data needs to know whether there is more data coming. To distinguish between no data available yet, and no more data coming, UNIX uses a special condition called "end of file", which is not sent as a character on the stream. This means that streams can contain completely arbitrary data; there is no chance of accidentally terminating a stream. To indicate end of file on a pipe, the writer closes the pipe.

Closing files can matter under a number of circumstances, so a discussion of redirection needs to talk about it. The first case where closing occurs is when a program terminates; all of its file descriptors close. So, for instance, in a simple pipeline like ls | grep hello, when the ls command terminates, its output stream is closed. When the grep command finishes reading the data written into the pipe, it detects the end of file on the pipe. If a command is generating data slowly but has not terminated, there is no end of file; UNIX distinguishes between "end of file" and "no data available right now." The following example shows that, even if no data are ever written to a pipeline, it remains open for the duration of a command:

```
$ sh -c 'sleep 3' | ( date; cat; date )
Sun Jun 15 14:53:17 CDT 2008
Sun Jun 15 14:53:20 CDT 2008
```

The two date commands show how long it takes for cat to execute, so you don't even need a stopwatch to see how this works.

Secondly, when a descriptor is redirected, the previous descriptor is closed, even if the program is still running. When a redirection is temporary, as with a redirection on a particular command, the original descriptor is saved and is not closed. However, when you use exec to redirect a descriptor permanently, the original descriptor can be closed. Two variants on the previous fragment illustrate the difference:

```
$ sh -c 'sleep 3; exec >/dev/null' | ( date; cat; date )
Sun Jun 15 14:56:01 CDT 2008
Sun Jun 15 14:56:04 CDT 2008
$ sh -c 'exec >/dev/null; sleep 3' | ( date; cat; date )
Sun Jun 15 14:56:13 CDT 2008
Sun Jun 15 14:56:13 CDT 2008
```

When the sleep command executes before the redirection, the output pipe does not close until after the sleep command completes. When the output stream is redirected first, the output pipe closes immediately (and there is a three second delay before the shell prints a new prompt).

Between these two rules, you very rarely need to explicitly close a descriptor in shell programming. However, both input and output streams can be closed explicitly using the cloning syntax, giving - as the name of the descriptor to clone. For instance, the redirection 2>&- closes standard error for the command being redirected, and the command exec 2>&- closes standard error for the whole script. The preceding fragments could use >&- just as well as >/dev/null because the script actually produces no output. However, many programs will malfunction if they are run with standard output closed rather than merely directed to /dev/null.

Redirections of individual commands or shell structures are carefully isolated; the shell restores the previous state of its descriptors after running them. However, when you use exec to redirect streams, these changes can have permanent effects. For instance, after the previous command, it may not be possible to restore the previous value of standard error; if standard error was attached to a pipe, there is no way to reopen the pipe.

More complicated shell programs may use a surprising number of redirections to achieve particular goals. For instance, what do you do if you want to run a number of commands, with standard error redirected, then recover the old state of standard error? If you use exec to redirect standard error to a file, the old standard error stream is closed. One solution is to run such redirections in subshells (or functions).

However, there is another way to preserve a stream. If you have more than one descriptor attached to the same stream, the stream is not closed until the last descriptor attached to it is closed. The following fragment illustrates this:

```
$ sh -c 'exec 5>&1; exec >/dev/null; sleep 3' | ( date; cat; date )
Sun Jun 15 15:10:13 CDT 2008
Sun Jun 15 15:10:16 CDT 2008
```

The first redirection redirects descriptor number 5 to a duplicate of standard output, after which standard output is closed. You may notice that I have not previously described descriptor number 5. Descriptors numbered 3 and higher are not initially defined or opened, but you can redirect them wherever you want, using the same syntax used for the first three.

This is often useful if you want to temporarily alter your shell environment, preserving the ability to restore it. Much of this can be done by running commands in subshells, but sometimes explicit control is more expressive.

The following script illustrates the use of extra descriptors to control the display of both errors and output:

```
exec 3>&1                        # stash standard output in descriptor 3
exec 4>&2                        # stash standard error in descriptor 4
exec 1>output.tmp                # send output to output.tmp
exec 2>error.tmp                 # send errors to error.tmp
printf "Filename? " >&3          # display message on descriptor 3 (old stdout)
read file
printf "String? "   >&3
read string
grep -e "$string" "$file"        # output to output.tmp, errors to error.tmp
status=$?
exec >&3                         # restore standard output
exec 2>&4                        # restore standard error
if test $status = 0; then
  echo "'$file' contained '$string'."
else
  if test -s error.tmp; then
    cat error.tmp >&2
  else
    echo "'$file' did not contain '$string'."
  fi
fi
```

The control structures at the bottom of the script operate in the original environment, with descriptors 1 and 2 directed wherever they were at the start of the script. While it would generally be ridiculous to do something this elaborate in such a simple case (it would have been much simpler to redirect the output and error streams of the grep command), the principles apply well to larger and more complicated scripts.

There is no real standard for how to use descriptors 3 and higher. Unfortunately, this exposes a weakness of the shell; there is no convenient way to keep track of descriptors. You can mitigate this somewhat by using variables to store the values used for a given function, as in the following example:

```
exec 3>/tmp/log.txt
logfd=3
log() { echo "$@" >&$logfd; }
log "Hello, world!"
log "All done."
```

This script emits two lines to /tmp/log.txt. However, this technique is still imperfect. For one thing, it still offers no assurance that some other piece of shell code will not redirect descriptor 3. Secondly, you simply have to be sure to use the same descriptor number in both lines. You might think to try setting the variable first:

```
logfd=3
exec $logfd>/tmp/log.txt
```

This fails because redirection is shell syntax, and a redirection operator (such as 3>) cannot result from parameter expansion. You can work around this using eval, though:

```
eval "exec $logfd>/tmp/log.txt"
```

If this seems a bit much to keep track of, the m4sh utility (part of GNU autoconf) provides a somewhat automated way to keep track of descriptors and avoid clashes.

COMMON CONVENTION: USING - AS A FILE

A great number of UNIX programs, but not all, will treat the file name - as referring to standard input or standard output, whichever is appropriate. This is a very useful idiom, even in utilities that process standard input by default, as it allows standard input to be specified along with other files. For instance, the following trivial command displays its standard input between a pair of files named header and footer:

```
cat header - footer
```

Inconveniently, not every utility recognizes this convention. If you actually create a file named - and want to pass it to a utility that uses this convention, use the name ./-.

This is not related to the use of redirection to &- to close a descriptor.

Introducing Here Documents

Often, a program needs input that could be read from a file, but creating (and then removing) a small temporary file is awkward or inconvenient. The shell has a special syntax for this, which looks much like the syntax for redirection. A piece of text introduced using a << rather than a < for redirection is called a *here document*. The here document consists of every following line of input until a special string, which is called a *sentinel*. It is generally equivalent to creating a temporary file holding those input lines and redirecting input from that file. For instance, the mail merge program might well use a here document:

```
for name in "Occupant" "Our Friends" "Current Resident" "Postal Customer"
do
  cat <<EOF
Hello, $name
Look! A personalized letter! Buy our stuff! Really!

We are even expanding variables for you, $name!
EOF
done
```

In this, the `<<EOF` starts a here document, which continues until a line consisting only of the word `EOF`. Parameter substitution applies normally within the here document, although globbing and tilde expansion do not. You can embed a dollar sign literally by prefixing it with a backslash. A here document is subject to the same quoting rules as double-quoted text.

There are two special modifications available when using a here document. The first is that a hyphen after the `<<` tells the shell to strip leading tabs (but not leading spaces) from the text:

```
cat <<-EOF
        Not indented!
EOF
```

```
Not indented!
```

The second is that, if the sentinel is quoted, no substitutions are performed on the text; it is treated as pure literal data, like a string in single quotes. This can be useful if you want to produce text that uses dollar signs. For more details on how quoting works in general, see the discussion of quoting and expansion in Chapter 4.

It is possible to provide multiple here documents in a single command line. They are processed in the order they are specified. For instance, the following script fragment concatenates two here documents:

```
( cat <&3; cat <&4 ) 4<<EOF 3<<EOF
world!
EOF
Hello,
EOF
```

```
Hello,
world!
```

Note that, because descriptor 4 is redirected first on the command line, the first here document is used as descriptor 4, which is displayed by the second cat command.

However, if there are multiple here documents for the same descriptor (including the default descriptor 0) of the same command, only the last document's contents are presented.

```
( cat; cat ) <<EOF <<EOF
world!
EOF
Hello,
EOF
```

```
Hello,
```

In this case, the second redirection replaces the first, so only the second document is available on standard input. As always, redirecting a file closes the old one.

Redirection and Loops

Loops, such as a while loop, are themselves shell commands, and any shell command can have its input and output redirected. For instance, on an embedded system that lacks the grep binary, you can always cheat. (This script may also be faster in some cases than using an external command.) The following script is similar to a simple case of grep. Invoked as shellgrep *pattern files*, it shows all lines from *files* matching *pattern*, although it matches shell patterns, not regular expressions:

```
pattern="$1"
shift 1
cat "$@" | while read line ; do
  case $line in
    *$pattern*) printf "%s\n" "$line";;
  esac
done
```

(The "$@" construct is explained in more detail in Chapter 4, and you may also need to know about some special cases discussed in Chapter 7.) If you want to know which file each line came from, you have to make it a bit more complicated:

```
pattern="$1"
shift 1
for file
do
  while read line; do
    case $line in
      *$pattern*) printf "%s: %s\n" "$file" "$line";;
    esac
  done < $file
done
```

This script checks each file separately; if it finds a matching line, it echoes the name of the file before the line. If all you want is the names of matching files, you can do that, too:

```
pattern="$1"
shift 1
for file
do
  while read line; do
    case $line in
      *$pattern*) printf "%s\n" "$file"; break;;
    esac
  done < $file
done
```

This version jumps ahead immediately upon finding a matching line; the break in the inner loop prevents the script from repeating the names of files with multiple matches. Note the similarity to the previous examples using the external grep program to look at each file, or to the -1 flag provided by many versions of grep. Note that tricks like this are not only useful on tiny little embedded systems. Because commands like grep are external to the shell, and the case command structure is built in, performance may be better using an idiom like this. On systems with particularly expensive command spawning, such as Windows, the performance difference may be quite surprising.

One limitation of for loops in the shell is that they always perform field splitting; if you want lines split instead of words, you can use a redirected while loop. For instance, consider this example from earlier in the chapter:

```
for name in "Occupant" "Our Friends" "Current Resident" "Postal Customer"; do
  echo "Hello, $name"
  echo "Look! A personalized letter! Buy our stuff!"
done
```

If you have a file containing the names of your close personal friends, you might try to use command substitution to adapt this:

```
$ cat friendslist
Occupant
Our Friends
Current Resident
Postal Customer
$ for name in $(cat friendslist); do
>   echo "Hello, $name!"
> done
Hello, Occupant!
Hello, Our!
Hello, Friends!
Hello, Current!
Hello, Resident!
Hello, Postal!
Hello, Customer!
```

Well, that didn't go as planned, and now you know where that really weird junk mail comes from. What you need is a way to distinguish between word breaks and line breaks. A simple way to do this is to use a `while` loop, with its input redirected from the friends list. The read command exits successfully every time it reads a line and fails when it has no input:

```
$ while read name; do
>    echo "Hello, $name!"
> done < friendslist
Hello, Occupant!
Hello, Our Friends!
Hello, Current Resident!
Hello, Postal Customer!
```

This idiom is extremely useful and is often used in conjunction with programs such as `find`, which generate lists of file names. Just be careful; UNIX allows newlines in file names, which can produce surprising results. If you do not have control over the inputs to a loop like this, be very careful about relying on the inputs and sanitize them carefully.

What's Next?

Chapter 4 explains the core methods by which the shell interprets its input: parsing, quoting, and substitution. I introduce tokens and explain how the shell determines what parts of a shell script are commands, what parts are control structures, and what parts are arguments to commands. I then explain the basics of quoting, the mechanism by which you control how the shell interprets words and when it performs substitutions. Finally, I'll go over the basic ways in which the shell substitutes new text, such as replacing variable names with the values of those variables.

CHAPTER 4

■ ■ ■

Core Shell Features Explained

This chapter gives a more detailed explanation of the structure of shell programs and the interactions between some of the basic features introduced in Chapter 1. This chapter also introduces the basic grammatical structure of shell programs, then explores the interactions of the quoting, substitution, and globbing mechanisms.

There are a number of exceptions and special cases, which are explained throughout the chapter, but an overview makes it easier to follow what happens. The first thing the shell does is split input into words and special punctuation items, called *tokens*. After this, substitutions and expansions are performed, replacing variable references with the contents of variables, shell glob characters with file names, and so on. The order of operations is as follows:

1. Tokenizing. The shell splits inputs into tokens. Keywords and special shell syntax characters are identified at this point, before any substitutions or expansions have occurred.

2. Parameter and command substitution. Parameter and command substitutions are performed. Quoting may cause some strings that look like parameter or command substitutions to be ignored. (Command substitution is explained in Chapter 5.)

3. The results of substitution are subject to field splitting.

4. Globbing is performed on any words that have unquoted glob characters.

5. Commands and control structures are executed.

There are some complications (for instance, some shells might perform tilde expansion prior to parameter substitution), but this basic order of operations covers what the shell really does. Most of the time, confusion about what a script will do can be resolved by thinking through these steps. Why doesn't this script work?

```
IF=if
$IF true; then echo hello; fi
```

It doesn't work because tokenizing happens before parameter substitution. The shell identifies $IF as a word, not a keyword. When it is later replaced with text, it is too late for it to try to become a keyword.

Similarly, the expansion of a glob pattern into file names occurs after parameter expansion. Thus, even if there were a file named $PATH, echo * would not produce the same output as echo $PATH.

The `case` statement provides exceptions to rules about what happens after substitution; there is neither field splitting nor globbing after substitution in the control string or the patterns of a `case` statement. In fact, in the patterns, quoting suppresses pattern matching rather than preventing globbing.

Parsing

When reading input, the shell begins by breaking input into a collection of symbols, called tokens. For instance, in a simple shell command such as `echo hello, world!`, there are four tokens. The first three are the command name and its arguments, and the fourth is a new line (see Table 4-1).

Table 4-1. *What the Shell Sees*

Token	Description
`echo`	Word
`hello,`	Word
`world!`	Word
`<newline>`	Command separator

The spaces separating the arguments are not tokens; they just separate tokens. The meanings of tokens, and even which tokens a given string contains, are sometimes affected by context; something might have special meaning on one line of a shell script and be an ordinary word on another.

Tokens

There are several different kinds of tokens. The most common are plain words, such as command names and arguments. Some words that have special meaning to the shell, such as `if` or `for`, may be special tokens called *keywords*. Finally, special shell punctuation, such as redirection operators or semicolons used to separate commands, are also tokens.

The special characters are as follows:

```
|   &   ;   <   >       (        )                $
`   \   "   '   <space>   <tab>    <newline>        *
?   [   #   ~   =         %
```

Not all of these characters are always special; some may be special only in specific contexts. (In some traditional shells, ^ is also special and a synonym for |.)

Anything that is quoted, or which results from substitution, is always a plain word even if it looks like something else. For instance, a new line is normally a token that can end a command. However, a new line in quotes is no longer a special token. Instead, it is just another character that is part of a normal shell word. In this example, there are three tokens:

```
echo "hello,
world"
```

The first token is echo. The second is the quoted string hello,<newline>world, with a new line between the comma and the w. The third is the new line after the quoted string. Because it is outside a quoted string, that new line is a token. Similarly, any quoted characters at all in a word ensure that it is treated as a plain word, never as a shell keyword. The text \if is simply a plain word if, not the beginning of a control structure.

When forming tokens, the shell sometimes discards things; for instance, unquoted whitespace (such as spaces or tabs) separates tokens, but does not itself become a token. The process of splitting input into words around space is called *word splitting*. If the shell encounters a sharp (#, also called pound, hash, or octothorpe) while looking for tokens, it reads from that character to the end of the current line and discards the results as a comment. As a matter of style, many programmers prefer to only start comments at the beginning of a line, but it is often easier to read a script with short comments after individual lines.

The underlying principle of the shell's token parsing, common to shell and to many other languages, is that a token is always the longest possible series of characters. This is often called the *maximal munch* rule. While a # may start a comment, it can also be part of a word. Here's an example of how this works:

```
echo a #b
echo c# d
```

```
a
c# d
```

In the first line, the first argument ends at the space. The # is encountered in a place where it would have to start a new token, so it starts a comment; the #b is discarded. In the second line, the # occurs as part of a word. Since # can be part of a word, it simply is, and it does not start a comment is. Thus, if there is ambiguity about whether a character is part of the current token or starts a new token, it is always part of the current token.

Similarly, these two lines are very different:

```
ls hello 2>error
ls hello2>error
```

The first line tries to list the file hello, sending any error messages to the file error. The second line, however, tries to list the file hello2, sending any output to the file error. The 2 can be part of the word, so it is treated that way. This is a quirk of redirection parsing. You do not need space before a redirection if it is of standard input or standard output, but if you are modifying one of the other descriptors, you generally need a space in front of the redirection so the shell doesn't interpret the descriptor number as part of the previous word.

The redirection operators highlight this because the whole redirection operator is a single token. Thus a number followed by a greater-than or less-than sign is a redirection, but a number separated from a greater-than or less-than sign is not. However, that works only if the number is itself looking like a token; if it is the last part of the previous word, it can't start a new token. This also shows why you cannot use a variable to create a new file descriptor:

```
logfd=3
exec $logfd>/tmp/log.txt
```

As described previously, this ends up trying to execute the command 3. You cannot expand variables into special tokens, only into plain words.

On the other hand, the target of a redirection can be quoted, can result from substitution or globbing, or even both.

```
exec 3>"$logfile"
```

This does exactly what you would expect: it expands the variable $logfile and redirects descriptor 3 to it. The redirection (3>) is a token; the thing redirected to is a separate token, which can be any word.

Words and Keywords

A token such as if or while is called a *keyword*, and can only be recognized in certain contexts. Tokens with no special meaning to the shell are called *words*. A word may have the same spelling as a keyword but is not treated specially by the shell. For instance, in the following script fragment, if is just a word, not a keyword:

```
echo if
```

The results of substitution, globbing, or quoting are always words. As an example, consider the following script fragment:

```
X="Y=3"
$X
```

```
Y=3: not found
```

While the sequence Y=3 would normally be a variable assignment, it resulted from substitution, so it became a plain word. The right-hand side of an assignment can be any word and can result from substitution or globbing. However, the variable name and equals sign must be literals. Likewise, a redirection operator must be a literal, but the name of the file to redirect to can be any word, including one resulting from substitution or globbing. (You can get around this; see the "The eval Command" section in Chapter 5.)

Context often determines the meaning of something to the shell. Context determines whether a new line terminates a command or is simply more whitespace. As with some other languages, the shell interprets a new line as ending a command when the command line so far is grammatically valid and otherwise expects additional input. Similarly, the same characters that would be a variable assignment at the beginning of a line are just another word later in a line:

```
echo A=B
```

```
A=B
```

The shell usually looks for keywords only in particular places, such as the beginning of a line. Otherwise, words are simply accepted as tokens producing a series of plain words with no special significance to the shell. In the standard shell, the keywords are as follows:

```
!     {     }     case    do    done
elif  else  esac  fi      for
if    in    then  until   while
```

Command Lists

In the examples so far, simple commands and pipelines have been used as the controlling expressions for if and while statements. In fact, the controlling expressions for these have the same grammar as their bodies and are sequences of commands called *lists*. A list is a series of commands or pipelines, usually joined by some combination of semicolons (;), new lines, and ampersands (&), and terminated by one of these. In nearly every case, you can replace a new line with a semicolon. The shell does not distinguish between these two forms of the same command:

```
if test -f "$file"; then
  echo "$file exists."
fi
if test -f "$file"; then echo "$file exists." ; fi
```

A series of commands entered on the command line are a list, grammatically. The shell determines the end of a list to have occurred when a special keyword or token shows up that ends the list. For instance, the grammar of a simple if-then-fi statement is as follows:

```
if list
then list
fi
```

Starting from an if, the shell reads commands until it encounters a then. The set of commands read is a list. The exit status of a list is the exit status of the last pipeline within the list, just as the exit status of a pipeline is the exit status of the last command within that pipeline. The exit status of the various flow control statements is usually zero if no code was executed, or the exit status of the last code executed. The following contrived example illustrates this:

```
while if true; then false; fi do
  false
done
```

The if statement used as a conditional for the while loop always executes its body, which consists of a single false command. The overall exit status of the if statement is the exit status of the last statement executed, the false command, so the while loop terminates immediately, and the exit status of the whole chunk of code is zero (indicating success). The false command inside the while loop is never executed.

FLEXIBLE GRAMMAR

You may have been surprised to see no semicolon after the `fi` ending the `if` statement. The semicolon after `true` is needed because the shell has no other way to recognize that `then` is intended as a keyword rather than an argument to the `true` command. Similarly, the semicolon after `false` is necessary. However, after the shell has detected the `fi` token, it knows that it has finished parsing the `if` statement; it does not need a special separator or terminator to tell it to start looking for either a keyword or another statement.

While tricks like this can make scripts several characters shorter, you should generally avoid them. Write for clarity first. In general, expand constructs onto multiple lines. The shell will not be any slower, but future readers of your code will find it more comprehensible.

Similarly, the `if` statement's controlling expression can be any list, not just a single command. This list can contain a series of commands, including other conditional statements. For instance, the following example asks the user how picky it should be before asking another question:

```
echo "Would you like me to be picky?"
read picky
echo "So, do you have any grapes?"
read answer
if case $picky in
    [Yy]*) test X"$answer" = X"yes";;
    *) case $answer in [Yy]*) true;; *) false;; esac ;;
    esac
then
  echo "You said yes!"
else
  echo "I don't think you said yes."
fi
```

The condition for the `if` statement is a pair of nested `case` statements. If the user's answer to the first question begins with either a capital or lowercase Y, the program will accept only the exact text "yes" as an answer. Otherwise, the program will accept any string starting with a capital or lowercase Y as being close enough to a "yes." In each case, the exit status is simply the status of the last exiting command: either the `test` command, used to check for the answer, or the `true` or `false` commands used to yield a status from the second `case` statement.

New lines and semicolons are mostly interchangeable as command separators, with the exception that the shell will politely ignore a series of blank lines but will object to a series of semicolons. Each semicolon must follow a command. Regardless, whether you use semicolons or new lines, each command is executed sequentially, and each command completes before the following command starts.

While ampersands are syntactically command separators, their semantics are different. When a command is followed by an ampersand, the command is run asynchronously; the shell continues immediately, while the command continues running at the same time. This is called running the command in the *background*. While the most common usage of this on the command line is to run a single command in the background, the ampersand is simply a generic command separator; you can also write multiple commands on a line, separated by ampersands. Each command that is followed by an ampersand is run in the background.

Short Circuits

There are two other command separators, which perform logical tests. They are the "and" operator (&&) and the "or" operator (||). The exit status of a pair of commands joined by && is true if both commands had a true exit status, and false otherwise. Similarly, the exit status of a pair of commands joined by || is true if either command had a true exit status, and false otherwise. As in many programming languages, the shell only executes the second command if the exit status of the pair has not already been determined; this is called *short-circuiting*. This can be used to express the same functions as an if statement, but is shorter; for simple code, it is often idiomatically better to put the operations together like this. For instance, the following idiom emits a logging message if the variable verbose has been set to true:

```
$verbose && echo >&2 "Processing $i..."
```

When the first command supplied to one of the short-circuit operators is an imperative, the meaning is reasonably easy to keep in mind. For instance, the following code fragment might be described as "remove the file or emit an error message":

```
rm $file || echo >&2 "Could not remove $file."
```

When a command line contains only the previously discussed command separators, such as semicolons, commands are simply treated in order. The logical short-circuit operators, however, are special; commands joined with these operators are treated more like a single command. For instance, the following fragment has an exit status of success:

```
false && false; true
```

The second false is not executed, but the semicolon separates the whole && operation from the true command. The way in which commands group more closely around the logical operators than around the other command separators is often described as the logical operators having higher *precedence*. It is, however, possible to force the shell to group the second two commands together. To do this, you must tell the shell where you want the lists to be formed.

Explicit Lists

You can join a series of commands together into a single list, which can then be joined with other lists using pipes, used as one side of a short-circuit operator, or otherwise treated as a single unit. There are two ways to do this. The first is to put a list of commands inside braces ({}); such a list is often called a *compound statement*. In this case, the list of commands must be terminated by a statement terminator, such as a semicolon or new line; otherwise, there is no way for the shell to recognize that the terminating brace was not simply a parameter to a command. In fact, some shells (bash and zsh) recognize the trailing brace without an explicit terminator. Do not rely on this, but do not rely on being able to use an unquoted } as an argument part way through a list either.

Grouping makes a group of commands act like a single command. For instance, the previous example can be converted using braces to separate commands:

```
false && { false; true; }
```

This now has an exit status of false; the initial `false` command generates a false return code, so the compound command in braces is not executed.

The other way to group commands is to put the series of commands inside parentheses [()]. Parentheses have an additional effect beyond forcing commands into a single list; they create a new shell process, called a subshell. Subshells are explained in more detail in Chapter 5. In general, commands within a regular list can affect the environment of the shell, but commands within a subshell have no effect on the environment of the rest of the shell program. On many platforms, subshells are substantially more computationally expensive than compound statements. Avoid using them when you don't need to.

DEBUGGING SUBSTITUTION AND QUOTING

Throughout this chapter, you may find yourself unsure about the interactions of different kinds of quoting and substitution (or globbing). The following simple script shows you exactly what arguments it ultimately received:

```
#!/bin/sh
echo "$# argument(s):"
for arg
do
        echo "'$arg'"
done
```

Save this script to a file named `printargs` somewhere in your path, and make sure it is executable (chmod u+x). The special variable $# holds the number of arguments given to the script. To run the script, invoke the shell on the test file with whatever additional arguments you want:

```
printargs foo bar
```

```
2 argument(s):
'foo'
'bar'
```

A bit of explanation may be in order. The initial echo command uses quotes because (and) are special characters to the shell. Note the unusual quoting around $arg. That is a double quote, a single quote, $arg, a single quote, and a double quote. The double quotes ensure that the shell displays the argument exactly as it was passed in, and the single quotes around it make it easier to see whether the argument begins or ends with any spaces or tabs. Because the single quotes occur inside double quotes, they have no special effect; they are just plain characters that are then echoed. If you still have questions, keep reading, the rest of this chapter explains this in more detail.

The new line before do is there for compatibility with a few old shells that did not handle the shorter for arg; do syntax for a for loop without an in clause.

Shell Quoting

Quoting is the process of suppressing the special meaning of a character. Three different kinds of quoting are provided by the shell. Backslashes, often called escapes, suppress the special meaning of a single character and work in almost every context. Single quotes are used for purely literal text, while double quotes allow some of the shell's substitution behaviors.

Experienced UNIX users looking for a prank often start by creating files in a novice's home directory, which are hard to remove. The simplest way, addressed briefly in the introduction, is to put spaces in the name of a file. Each of the quoting mechanisms can overcome this.

Escaping Characters with a Backslash

The backslash is the most complex quoting mechanism because its behavior is almost, but not quite, perfectly consistent. Normally, a backslash followed by any other character is treated by the shell as that other character, deprived of any special meaning; this is called an "escaped" character. A backslash followed by a space is a space character that does not separate words. A backslash followed by a double quote is a double quote character that does not begin a quoted string. A backslash followed by a backslash is just a plain old backslash.

The first major exception is that a backslash at the end of a line does not create an escaped new line character. Instead, the backslash and the new line are both removed. Of course, it would be too simple if this were always true. If the backslash is inside a comment, it is completely ignored, but the new line has its normal effect. This is the backslash equivalent of the 400-year rule for leap years, and it comes up about as often.

The second is that, inside double quotes, backslashes are not mostly suppressed by the shell; they escape only dollar signs, new lines, backticks (grave accents), double quotes, and backslashes. A backslash followed by anything else is just a backslash in this context.

The third exception is that backslashes are in no way special inside single quotes. No matter how many or how few backslashes you put between single quotes, or what comes after them, they are just backslashes.

There is one other major source of confusion: Many programs do special things with backslashes. For instance, consider what happens if you use echo to test the behavior of backslashes in a single-quoted string:

```
$ echo '\\'
```

You would expect this to produce \\ as output. In most shells, it will. However, if you try this in zsh, you get only a single \. The problem is that, while the shell has not done anything special with the backslash, the built-in echo in zsh does, in fact, use backslashes specially. You can try to outsmart the shell by calling /bin/echo explicitly, but there is an astounding variety of ways in which the echo command can differ from one system to another. Utility portability is discussed in more detail in Chapter 7. In the meantime, be aware that people have been complaining about the complete nonportability of any but the simplest uses of echo for well over 20 years.

SLASH AND BACKSLASH

Many users find it difficult to distinguish between forward slashes and backslashes. On a US keyboard, the forward slash is the one under the question mark; it is the one that is leaning "forward"—that is to say, the top is farther to the right than the bottom. This confusion is amplified by the tendency of Windows users to think of backwards slashes as path separators, while UNIX users tend to use forward slashes. (In fact, under the hood, Windows uses forward slashes, too; the command interpreter translates backslashes into forward slashes.)

My first thought was to say, "Slash is the one that is used in URLs," but I have seen hundreds of advertisements, business cards, and other things that use backslashes. The problem seems to be not only that people are not sure which one they want, but that many people have the words themselves confused, and thus carefully verify the word "backslash" only to actually mean the thing that everyone else calls a forward slash.

To save you trouble, here's the complete list:

* Forward slash: /

* Backward slash: \

* In general, unqualified slash means forward slash.

Escaping Characters with Single Quotes

Single quotes are very simple. Absolutely everything from a single quote to the next single quote is literal. New lines, backslashes, dollar signs, it doesn't matter. Everything is literal. This means that there is no way to include a single quote inside a single quoted string. You will occasionally see this idiom:

```
echo 'Peter'\''s favorite language'
```

```
Peter's favorite language
```

The first single quote starts a string, and the second ends it. This is followed by an unquoted backslash, which escapes the next character, which is a single quote. This results in a quoted single quote; because it is quoted, it does not start a new string. The next character after that is another single quote, starting a new single-quoted string that runs to the end of the line. Because the character between the two strings was not an unquoted word separator, the two strings, and the character between them, are joined into a single string.

Escaping Characters with Double Quotes

Double quotes suppress the meaning of many special characters, but parameter substitution (see the "Understanding Parameter Substitution" section later in this chapter) occurs normally within them. Double quotes are probably the most commonly used form of quoting, as they give the useful combination of allowing for parameter substitution while preventing field splitting. Knowing this, you now know what one of the lines in the argument printing script does:

```
echo "'$arg'"
```

The double quotes eliminate the special meaning of the single quotes, allowing the contents of the variable $arg to be expanded. However, the double quotes perform an additional function, which is to prevent globbing or field splitting from being performed on the contents of the variable $arg. Thus if the user passed a string with multiple spaces in as an argument, the string echoed back by the shell will preserve those spaces.

Quoting Examples

The interactions of the different quoting mechanisms can be fairly confusing at first. In general, use single quotes for maximal predictability, double quotes for material that needs parameter substitution, and backslashes to suppress the value of a single special character, such as $.

There are many things you may wish to write that cannot be done within a quoted string of any sort or are excessively awkward in one kind of string but easy in another. In many cases, the simplest thing to do is to use a double-quoted string and use backslashes to suppress additional special meanings. However, if you have a string that uses a great number of backslashes and special characters, you may find single quotes preferable. If you find single quotes useful, but you want to interpolate a single variable, the following idiom may prove useful:

```
'some text'"$VAR"'more text'
```

This concatenates the value of $VAR with the surrounding text, while protecting that text from all varieties of shell substitution.

Substitution and Expansion

When processing input, the shell replaces parameters with their values. This replacement is called *parameter substitution, parameter expansion,* or (rarely) *variable interpolation.* I use the term substitution because the term expansion might be taken as suggesting that the resulting text is always larger. The POSIX spec uses the term expansion. After parameter substitution, the shell expands certain patterns into file names; this is called *pathname expansion,* or globbing. This section reviews the basics of parameter substitution and globbing. Chapter 5 discusses command substitution, which is similar in many ways to parameter substitution. Some shells offer additional parameter substitution options that are not portable; these are discussed in Chapter 6.

PARAMETERS OR VARIABLES

What is the difference between a variable and a parameter? The answer depends on which book or manual you are reading. The POSIX spec uses the term *parameter* for the general case; *variables* are parameters whose names are identifiers (alphanumeric characters and underscores, with the first character being a letter or an underscore). The special parameters which refer to the arguments of a script program or the shell are called *positional parameters.*

Many users are more familiar with the term parameter being used to mean arguments; these are what the POSIX spec calls the positional parameters. Someone who refers to $* as a variable rather than a parameter will probably call $1 a parameter rather than a positional parameter.

Substitution and Field Splitting

Often, when parameters are substituted, the output is described as being subject to *word splitting.* In fact, what really happens to them is something different, called *field splitting.* The original splitting of input into tokens always uses the same rules; words are split around whitespace (spaces, tabs, and new lines). When a substitution is split, however, different rules may be used.

The shell defines a special variable, $IFS, which defines the field splitting rules. If $IFS is not set, the shell behaves as though it contained space, tab, and new line characters (in that order). If $IFS is set to an empty string, fields are not split at all. Finally, if $IFS is set to a string, then the characters in that string are used to split fields, just as whitespace splits words. The following example illustrates the difference:

```
$ IFS=:
$ a="hello:world"
$ echo hello:world
hello:world
$ echo $a
hello world
```

When expanding $*, the shell joins the positional parameters with the first character of $IFS; if $IFS is an empty string, the parameters are concatenated.

Setting $IFS allows you to parse more complicated input. You can check the components of $PATH using $IFS and a for loop:

```
IFS=:
for dir in $PATH; do
  echo $dir
done
```

A similar idiom, using the set command to reset the positional parameters (discussed in detail in Chapter 6), is as follows:

```
IFS=:
set -- $PATH
for dir
do
  echo $dir
done
```

As a side note, you cannot put the assignment to $IFS on the same line as the command. The command is parsed before the assignment takes effect, even though the command is run after the assignment takes effect.

Although the name $IFS is capitalized, $IFS is not usually exported. The behavior of child shells to which $IFS has been exported is not portable. Don't do that.

Understanding Parameter Substitution

Parameter substitution occurs only in double-quoted strings or outside of any quoting and is introduced by a dollar sign. A dollar sign that has been escaped, or that occurs in a single-quoted string, has no special meaning. If the first character after the dollar sign is a punctuation mark that denotes a built-in shell parameter or a digit, it is taken as the name of a built-in shell parameter to substitute. There are a number of built-in parameters, and many shells define additional such parameters. For now, the short list in Table 4-2 of common parameters will suffice.

Table 4-2. *Common Shell Parameters*

Parameter	Description
$0	Name of current program; usually the name of a script file, or just the shell's name.
$1	First parameter of current script or function.
$2	Second parameter of current script or function. (This pattern continues, but parameters 10 and higher require special treatment.)
$*	All parameters of current script or function, separated by spaces.
$@	All parameters of current script or function. Outside of quotes, identical to $*. Inside double quotes, expands to each parameter inside separate double quotes.
$$	The process ID of the shell.
$#	The number of positional parameters.

If the first character after the dollar sign is a letter or underscore, the shell takes that character, plus any following letters, numbers, or underscores, to be the name of a variable to expand. This creates an interesting problem: What do you do if you want to append some characters after the substitution of a variable? For instance, the following script might have been intended to produce "hello, world," but it actually produces only an empty line:

```
$ hello="hello, "
$ echo $helloworld
```

The output is an empty line because the shell is expanding the unset variable helloworld, not the recently set variable hello followed by the text "world." There are a number of clever or sneaky tricks to get around this, but the best solution is to use braces to delimit the variable:

```
$ echo ${hello}world
hello, world
```

When the shell sees a curly brace after the dollar sign, it searches for the next matching brace to determine which parameter to substitute. Braces are also needed to refer to positional parameters ${10} and higher. The shell replaces $10 with a literal "0" appended to the value of $1; this is the reverse of the behavior that mandates the use of parentheses when working with identifiers. Older shells do not recognize ${10}; in these shells, you must use shift to access positional parameters past $9. (See Chapter 6 for more discussion on positional parameters.)

Sometimes, you may be unsure of whether a variable will have been set or not before a given piece of code executes. The shell has a variety of features to allow for alternative substitutions in place of variables that are not set (or set to an empty string, also called a *null string*). The most commonly used variant is the ${*parameter*:-*word*} construct, which is equivalent to ${*parameter*} if it has a value, or *word* otherwise. In the case where the construct is substituted with *word*, that is subject to substitution as well. The following fragment greets the user in an even less-efficient way than usual:

```
foo=""
bar="world"
echo hello, ${foo-$bar}
```

```
hello, world
```

The substitution rules in Table 4-3 are a common and well-supported subset of those available in standard shells (and even a number of prestandard shells).

Table 4-3. *A Subset of Special Parameter Substitutions*

Pattern	Description
${*parameter*:-word}	If *parameter* is null or unset, substitute *word*; otherwise, substitute *parameter*.
${*parameter*:=word}	If *parameter* is null or unset, assign *word* to parameter. Then substitute *parameter*.
${*parameter*:+word}	If *parameter* is null or unset, substitute null; otherwise, substitute *word*.
${*parameter*:?word}	If *parameter* is null or unset, print *word* (or a default message if *word* is null) to standard error and exit the shell.

In each of these substitutions, the colon may be omitted; in this case, the shell tests only for a parameter that is unset, not an empty string (also called a null value). With the colon, an empty string is treated the same as an unset parameter. Each of these forms is useful under different circumstances.

The hyphen form of substitution is primarily used to provide a default value, while allowing a user to override it. This is especially likely to be useful with environment variables, allowing the user to override the default behavior of a script. A typical example from a compilation script would be to provide a default value for the CFLAGS environment variable, which is used by convention to hold compiler options:

```
cc ${CFLAGS-"-O2"} -o hello hello.c
```

If the CFLAGS environment variable is set, it is passed to the compiler. Otherwise, the value -O2 is passed in as a default. The quotes around the flag are not needed but are allowed; in this case, I used them because it helps visually distinguish between the hyphen in the shell syntax and the intended replacement text. Also, it is useful to get in the habit of providing quotes in cases where they might or might not be necessary because the alternative is usually to omit them when they were necessary. Program defensively.

Of course, in a longer script, it is quite possible to imagine a lack of interest in typing that same construct over and over. One improvement is to use the equals sign substitution rule the first time and thereafter use the variable's value:

```
cc ${CFLAGS="-O2"} -o hello hello.c
cc $CFLAGS -o goodbye goodbye.c
```

When the shell expands ${CFLAGS="-O2"}, one of two things happens. If the CFLAGS variable was already set, it expands, and its value is unchanged. If the variable was not set, or was empty, it is replaced by the assigned value (-O2, in this case), and then expanded. Thus, whether or not the variable was set before the first line was executed, it will definitely be set after that line is executed.

This is functional but a little clumsy. It creates an unfortunate ordering dependency on the lines in the script; if you later discover that your new boss lives backward in time and requires that goodbye.c be compiled before hello.c, you cannot simply reverse the lines in the script; you have to edit both of them. (While the particular circumstance may seem unusual, being obliged to reorder operations in a script is quite common.) You have two workable options. One is to switch to a more elaborate construct, possibly using test to check the existing value of the variable before assigning it. You should not simply place the variable substitution on a line by itself; the substitution would then be executed as a command. However, you can use it as an argument to a command that does nothing:

```
: ${CFLAGS:="-O2"}
cc $CFLAGS -o hello hello.c
cc $CFLAGS -o goodbye goodbye.c
```

This is a very expressive idiom. In this case, true and : are not equivalent; some implementations of true inexplicably react to some possible combinations of parameters by doing something:

$ /bin/true --version
```
true (GNU coreutils) 6.10
Copyright (C) 2008 Free Software Foundation, Inc.
License GPLv3+: GNU GPL version 3 or later <http://gnu.org/licenses/gpl.html>
This is free software: you are free to change and redistribute it.
There is NO WARRANTY, to the extent permitted by law.

Written by Jim Meyering.
```

This kind of thing can be fairly disruptive of the output of a script. Stick with : for such usage.

The plus sign substitution rule has an interesting history. One of its most powerful uses is nearly entirely obsolete now, and it involves the special shell parameter $@. In some very early shells, if there were no parameters at all, "$@" substituted a quoted empty string rather than to nothing. (The more convenient behavior is specified by POSIX and is reasonably close to universal in modern shells. For details, see the discussion of shell versions in Chapter 7.) One idiom for working around this is ${1+"$@"}. This expands to "$@" if $1 is set; otherwise, it's set to null. In this case, using the colon would undermine the entire point of the exercise; it would result in an incorrect substitution for the arguments of a script whenever the first argument was an empty string. It is useful in this and other cases where you wish to avoid substituting something unless there is something to substitute.

The +: form is a little harder to find really good uses for, but it has its place, too. As an example, consider appending a series of words together. You want spaces between words, but you do not want extra spaces. You can write an elaborate hunk of code to append spaces suitably, keeping everything quoted, or you can use ${var+:" $var"}. This expands to a space followed by $var, if var has a nonempty value, or to nothing at all, if var was empty or unset.

The question mark substitution rule is of limited utility. In most cases, you will want to write your own, more robust, error handling. On the other hand, if you really do not feel there is any sensible default, you can always use this to force people to pick one:

```
cc ${CFLAGS?:Cannot compile without compiler flags.} -o hello hello.c
```

```
build.sh:1: CFLAGS: :Cannot compile without compiler flags.
```

The exact format of this error message may vary between shells.

When a parameter substitution occurs outside of double quotes, the results of the substitution are usually subjected to field splitting and globbing, but never to parameter substitution again; if a variable expands to $FOO, it does not get expanded again. Inside double quotes, nothing happens after parameter substitution. (Parameter substitution cannot occur within single quotes, making the question of what would happen if it did moot.) As a rather unusual special case, the word used as the controller for a case statement is subject to tilde expansion, and then parameter substitution, but the results of the parameter substitution are not subject to any further modifications, not even field splitting. The common habit of quoting a single variable used to control a case statement is unnecessary, although some people prefer it as a matter of style.

Tilde Expansion

Tilde expansion is a special expansion that replaces certain strings starting with tildes (~) with the home directories of named users, or the current user if no user is named. An unquoted tilde at the beginning of a word may be subject to tilde expansion. If a user name is provided (consisting of everything from the tilde to the first unquoted slash, or simply the whole word), that user's home directory replaces the tilde and user name. If no user name is provided, the tilde is replaced by the current user's home directory. For instance, ~bob is replaced with the home directory of the user bob. If there is more text, it is appended to the results of the expansion. For instance, ~/bin refers to the bin subdirectory of $HOME. Tilde expansion does not check its results against the file system; it expands only based on user account information or the $HOME environment variable. The behavior if a nonexistent user is named is nonportable, although many shells simply omit any substitution. Tilde expansion can occur after colons in a variable assignment. For instance, the shell expands tildes in the following:

```
PATH=/bin:/usr/bin:~bob/bin:~amy/bin
```

Standard shells expand both ~bob and ~amy in the preceding example (assuming both users exist). Tilde expansion is universal among POSIX shells, but some older shells do not provide it.

Globbing

The basic globbing rules were described in Chapter 2, along with shell patterns (which they somewhat resemble). Although multiple matching path names expand into multiple words, the individual file names are not subject to field splitting.

Globbing never occurs within quotes, because glob characters have no special meaning within quotes. Glob characters next to quoted text are expanded with the quoted text as part of the pattern. Quoting is often useful when you wish to match a path that includes a variable substitution. For instance, the following shell command has a hidden bug:

```
rm -rf build/$version/*.log
```

As long as $version is something simple, like 4.2 or 3.1415, this command behaves as expected. However, imagine your chagrin should you ever attempt this on a version with spaces in it, such as 1.2 / prerelease. The result would be the following:

```
rm -rf build/1.2 / prerelease/*.log
```

This may be one of the few cases where one might, for a brief moment, wish for the csh feature of responding "No match" when a glob fails. The shell simply performs no globbing, leaving you with a command that, if you are very smart and were not running as root, probably eventually tries to remove prerelease/*.log and fails. Worse yet, the -f flag means you do not even get a warning message. You might try to resolve this by quoting as follows:

```
rm -rf "build/$version/*.log"
```

However, glob characters have no effect inside quotes, so rm simply tries to find a file with the literal name build/1.2 / prerelease/*.log, and it probably fails. The solution is to combine quoted and unquoted text:

```
rm -rf build/"$version"/*.log
```

This causes the shell to try to find every file in build/1.2 / prerelease with a name matching the pattern *.log, and then pass their names as arguments to rm. This still may not do what you want, as it denotes a directory named " prerelease" inside a directory named "1.2 ," but at least it won't turn into a 16-hour night with the backups. You did make backups, right?

UNUSUAL FILE NAMES

The greatest weaknesses of the shell are two simple characters: space and new line. The classic UNIX file system allows all but two characters in file names; one is the slash, used as a directory separator, and the other is the ASCII NUL byte (with the integer value 0, which is not the same as a literal 0 digit). Unfortunately, many shell programs and scripts do not cope gracefully with file names containing spaces. Many, many more can do horrible things given a file name containing a new line.

You can mostly work around the space character with experience and practice. For the new line, there is often nothing you can do. The utility features needed to let you work reasonably safely with names containing new lines are not portable enough.

Spaces, while they can be dealt with given sufficient care, are simply too hard to get right for it to be safe to assume that arbitrary script programs will deal with them gracefully. Do not use spaces in file names.

With the widespread adoption of Mac OS X, many more UNIX developers are becoming familiar with environments in which spaces in file names are more common. Still, don't take chances when you don't have to.

If a glob pattern is assigned to a variable, nothing special happens; the text of the pattern is stored in the variable. However, when the variable is substituted, it will generally be subject to globbing.

What's Next?

Now that you understand the quoting and substitution rules, you can write a broad variety of very powerful shell scripts. However, there are a few things that can't be done without more powerful tools. The next chapter introduces ways to organize and reuse code, as well as how to run pieces of code as if they were separate scripts, giving you a lot of additional flexibility.

■ ■ ■

## CHAPTER 5

Shells Within Shells

This chapter discusses the relationship between the shell and the programs it calls, with a particular focus on *subshells*—additional shells run by a shell script in a new process. This chapter also discusses shell context and the distinction between shell variables and environment variables.

Understanding Processes

This chapter relies more heavily than previous chapters on a firm understanding of the UNIX process model. (While Windows does not use this model, UNIX-like shell environments running on Windows tend to emulate it at least some.) UNIX systems can run multiple programs at once. In fact, not only can multiple programs be running at once, but multiple instances of a single program also can be running at once. Each instance of a running program is called a *process* and has a unique numeric process identifier, or *pid*. The pid of the shell is expanded in the shell parameter $$. While a pid may be reused after a process has exited, a process keeps its assigned pid for its entire lifetime, and there can never be another process with the same pid during that lifetime. Each process has its own separate memory space, although in some cases processes may arrange to share memory. The ps command gives a list of processes currently running. UNIX does not distinguish as some systems do between "applications" and other kinds of processes; all programs run the same way. Note that the output of the ps command is nonportable; you cannot use it safely in a portable shell script, as the formatting of the display varies from one system to another, as do the options used to specify what to display. There is no useful portable subset. It is generally easy for humans to read, but not very useful to shell programmers.

The fundamental tool of UNIX process creation is the *fork*, in which a single process becomes two identical processes. In a lower-level language, such as C, this is done by using the UNIX system call fork(). When a process invokes this fork() successfully, the process is duplicated, and both processes then return from fork(), differing only in the return status of the fork() system call. In the original process (called the parent), the fork() system call returns the pid of the child; in the child, the fork() system call returns 0. Apart from that, each process has the exact same environment; the same objects are stored at the same addresses in memory, for instance. However, the child process has a distinct copy of these objects; modifications in the child have no effect on the parent. (The fact that two processes can have the same memory locations holding different values can be a bit of a surprise; each process has its own distinct mapping from memory addresses to physical memory.)

There is no UNIX system call to launch a new program as a subprocess. The fork() system call does not launch a new program, but rather duplicates an already-running one. The exec() system call (actually a family of related system calls) allows the replacement of the current process with a named program. Thus to spawn a new process, you first use fork(), then in the child process use exec() to launch the new command. The C library includes a wrapper function, system(), to run a command as a subprocess; on UNIX systems, this function works by passing the provided command to the shell. There is no way to explicitly fork in a shell script; instead, you run commands, create pipelines, or run subshells. The shell offers common tasks built in terms of fork() and exec(), rather than giving direct access to the system calls.

In some cases, a process may have multiple simultaneous paths of execution, called *threads*. I mention these only to stress that the UNIX shell does not use threading; each process started by the shell is a fully separate process. Within a portable shell script, you generally do not need to even be aware of threading. If you do find yourself using the output of ps, though, be aware that one of the least portable things is whether or not threads might show up in the output of ps, possibly giving several lines of output for a single pid. Be cautious.

Threading is newer than the shell and is not all that heavily used in the basic UNIX environment. On UNIX systems, the cost of launching a new process is fairly low, so there is little incentive to avoid spawning new processes. One of the greatest challenges of shell programs that need to run on Windows systems in emulated UNIX-like environments is that process creation costs are extremely high on Windows. If you anticipate a need to run your code on Windows, you may want to pay extra attention to the cost of new processes; avoid anything that would imply a fork() on UNIX, such as subshells or external commands, whenever you can.

All of this may seem rather complicated and even irrelevant, but the shell's behavior is closely tied to this underlying model. Whenever the shell runs any external command, it does so by this fork()/exec() pair. The one exception is the use of the exec built-in command to replace the currently running shell with another program; in this case, the shell uses only the exec() system call.

Variables and the Environment

So far, the discussion of variables in this book has looked at how they are used within a shell script. Some variables are available not only to the shell, but also to any child process it starts. These variables are called *environment variables*, and the set of environment variables in a given process is called the *environment* of that process. Environment variables are available to any program, not just the current script. Any programming language used on UNIX-like systems will typically offer some way to access (and possibly modify) environment variables. Processes have additional state beyond their environment variables, such as the collection of open file descriptors or current working directory. I refer generally to the set of environment variables and other per-process state as the *context* of a process.

The set built-in command, called without arguments, prints all shell variables, whether or not they are in the environment. The env utility, called without arguments, prints its environment.

A common convention among shell programmers is to use capital letters exclusively in the names of environment variables (e.g., $PATH) and use all lowercase names for unexported shell variables (e.g., $answer). This is an excellent convention, and this book uses it. Many developers put all shell variables in all caps. However, because there is no reasonable portable way to determine whether a variable has been exported, it is generally better to use the former convention. Shell variable names should use underscores (_) to separate words, not mixed capitals and lowercase letters. (The shell doesn't care, but future readers do.)

Manipulating the Environment

There are three primary changes you can make to the environment: You can add variables to it, remove variables from it, or modify variables in it.

Adding variables to the environment is sometimes called *exporting* them, probably because it is done using the export command. The export command adds its named arguments to the environment. As with assignment, you do not use a dollar sign ($) to mark the names of the variables. For instance, the command export FOO adds the variable FOO to the environment. A common idiom is to assign a variable, and then immediately export it:

```
NAME=John
export NAME
```

Many recent shells allow variable assignments to be used on the export command line, providing an equivalent, but not fully portable, shorthand:

```
export NAME=John
```

If you are comfortable relying on POSIX shell features, you can use this, but it offers little advantage. There is no portable way to remove a variable from the environment. The unset command removes a variable from both the environment and the current shell, but is not universally portable. For purposes of a shell script, it is typically enough to set a variable to an empty value, then make sure to use the colon (:) variants of the shell's substitution rules, for instance, using ${foo:-bar} instead of ${foo-bar}. However, this still leaves an empty string in the environment. If you really need to remove environment variables, you will need to rely on POSIX shell features; consider using an execution preamble (see Chapter 7) and the unset command. An unset variable that is later assigned a value does not become part of the environment without being exported again.

Environment variables are modified like any other variables, using the shell's assignment operator. You cannot portably check whether a variable has been exported; this is one of the reasons a naming convention is so useful.

The environment is passed to child processes, but there is no way for children to modify the environment of the parent process. For instance, the following script does not do what its author perhaps intended:

```
$ cat path.sh
#!/bin/sh
PATH=$PATH:/usr/local/bin
$ echo $PATH
/bin:/usr/bin
$ ./path.sh
$ echo $PATH
/bin:/usr/bin
```

The user probably expected the shell assignment in path.sh to alter the PATH variable. In fact, it did alter the PATH variable in the new shell that ran the script; however, this had no effect on the shell that invoked the script. Ways to modify the shell's environment are discussed in the section, "Modifying the State of the Shell," later in this chapter.

Issues like this are extremely widespread. Many UNIX systems use startup scripts with names like /etc/rc or /etc/rc.local. While researching shell features, I stumbled across a fascinating discussion among users trying to get an environment variable set on their system at boot time so that all users would share it. Their discussion revolved around adding the variable setting to /etc/rc.local, a file for local system administrator additions to the system's startup scripts. Here's how that system runs its rc.local script, if it exists:

```
if [ -f /etc/rc.local ]; then
  sh /etc/rc.local
fi
```

Since the rc.local script was being run by a separate shell, the variables would not have propagated anyway. Of course, sometimes you do not want a chunk of code to be able to modify your environment; I suspect the preceding code was written with the conscious intent to prevent the local script from making changes to the environment of the parent script, which could have affected the rest of the boot process.

Temporary Changes

Many UNIX utilities rely on environment variables, so it is common to set variables to influence their behavior. This can lead to a cluttered environment in which future script code behaves unexpectedly because of values left in the environment. There are several ways to resolve this. Some scripts simply set an environment variable, run code depending on that setting, then unset it. This technique has a couple of flaws. One is that, if the variable had a previous value, it is lost. Another is that some scripts need to be portable to systems without unset. What is needed is a way to restore the previous value. There are three options.

The first is to stash the value in a temporary variable. Save the old value, set the new one, then restore the previous value. As an example, running make with a modified path might be implemented as follows:

```
save_PATH="$PATH"
PATH="/usr/local/bin:$PATH"
make
PATH="$save_PATH"
```

In this example, the make command is run with the /usr/local/bin directory in $PATH, but the previous value of $PATH is restored afterward. This works, and it may even be useful in the case where you want to run a number of commands with a temporary variable assignment. Saving previous values becomes more useful in cases where you need to change a value back and forth.

A particularly common case of this is using a similar idiom to change the $IFS shell variable. You can iterate through $PATH by setting $IFS to : and using a command like for dir in $PATH. However, you might want to restore the old value again occasionally during the loop:

```
save_IFS=$IFS
IFS=:
for dir in $PATH; do
  IFS=$save_IFS
  # now you can run commands with the normal value of $IFS restored
  echo "$dir"
done
IFS=$save_IFS
```

The second way to get a temporary change to the environment is to use the external env command. The env command can modify its environment and then run another program. For instance, the following script has the same behavior as the previous example:

```
env PATH="/usr/local/bin:$PATH" make
```

This has two limitations; the first is that it can run only a single command and the second is that the command it runs must be an external program, not a shell builtin (see the "Shell Builtins" section later in the chapter for more information about builtins). One likely pitfall of this technique is that parameter substitution occurs in the calling shell, which means that it uses the existing value, not the value passed in:

```
X=yes
export X
env X=no echo $X
```

```
yes
```

Although the echo command is run with the environment variable $X set to no, the argument passed to it is the already-substituted value from the parent shell. The command executed is echo yes, and it does not matter what $X is when this is executed. You can force the substitution to occur in the called program by using a shell with a quoted string argument:

```
X=yes
export X
env X=no sh -c 'echo $X'
```

```
no
```

The third technique for temporary variable assignments is to prefix a command with one or more variable assignments. This special syntax tells the shell to make an exported assignment only for the duration of a single command. A previous example is simplified a little further this way:

```
PATH="/usr/local/bin:$PATH" make
```

This syntax creates a temporary environment variable. The existing value (if any) of the variable assigned is not changed. If the variable assigned was not an environment variable before, it is not exported after the command runs, but only while the command is running. As with the env technique, this works only for a single shell operation. The command must be a simple command or pipeline; you cannot use braces or parentheses to group commands used this way. As with the env technique, the command is substituted, globbed, and subjected to field splitting before the variable assignments take effect. So, for instance, you cannot use the following to change $IFS:

```
IFS=: echo $PATH
```

This echo command shows you $PATH subject to field splitting using the previous value of $IFS. The shell first substitutes and splits the arguments, then creates the environment (assigning the new value to $IFS) and runs the echo command. This technique has a portability limitation; it is not safe to use this with built-in commands, such as read or cd. In general, it is probable that a shell will keep any variable assignment made in that context. Modern (POSIX) shells will restore previous values if the built-in command is eval or set, but older shells may not. This topic is explored further in the section "The eval Command" later in this chapter.

Exploring Subshells

The term *subshell* refers to a second instance of the shell program run under the control of an existing shell. A subshell is simply a shell context created by calling fork(). The subshell does not need to load the shell's executable from disk, perform any kind of initialization, or otherwise do anything at all except execute a command or list of commands; typically, the commands have already been parsed for it by the calling shell. What this means is that, even though a subshell is another process, the performance penalty of launching one is much smaller than people typically expect for a new process (except on Windows, where it is still quite high). Subshells may be created explicitly or implicitly. When () is used to separate out a list, this creates a subshell. Commands in a pipeline typically run in subshells.

A subshell is a separate shell context, and like any child process, it cannot modify the state of the parent shell. Directory changes, variable assignments, and redirections within subshells do not affect the parent shell. This is often useful, and subshells are used to make temporary changes to the shell's environment or state. Note that although command-line variable assignments are temporary and do not affect the shell's environment permanently, they do not create an implicit subshell.

Subshells and External Shells

A subshell is not the same as running a new shell to execute a command. You can issue a command to the shell using the -c command-line option or feed commands to another shell either through a script file or using a pipe to the shell's input. There are several major differences between an external shell and a subshell. A separate shell invocation parses the command (or commands) provided, performs word splitting, substitution, globbing, and so on. A subshell starts with material that has already been split into words but still performs substitution, globbing, and field splitting; it mostly executes the already-parsed material in a new process context. A separate invocation of the shell inherits environment variables but not unexported shell variables. By contrast, a subshell has all of the parent shell's variables accessible to it. As a special case of this, the subshell keeps the parent shell's value of the special shell parameter

$$. Finally, a separately invoked shell may (depending on the shell) run some standard initial-ization or startup scripts, which may cost substantial time or produce surprising behavior. For more information on shell startup, see the discussion of shell invocation in Chapter 6.

Command Substitution

Subshells are used in a kind of substitution that I glossed over in the previous section on substitution: *command substitution* (also often called *command expansion*). In command sub-stitution, the shell replaces a string of text with the output from running that string of text as a command. The command is run in a subshell, and any substitution or globbing occurs in the subshell, not in the parent shell.

The output of the subshell is treated the same way as the results of parameter substitu-tion. For instance, the output is subject to field splitting and globbing (unless it is in a context, such as the control word for a case statement, where these are not performed), and the sub-stitution can be put in double quotes to prevent this. Standard error from the command is not included as part of this output; it goes to the shell's regular standard error unless explicitly redirected.

Just as pipes allow you to use the output of a program as input to another program, command substitution allows you to use the output of a program as arguments to another program. There are two crucial differences beyond the difference in how these are used. The first is that argument lists may have limited length, while pipes can consistently handle giga-bytes of data. The second, closely related, is that commands in a pipeline run simultaneously, but when you use command substitution, the command being substituted must run com-pletely before its output can be used.

The shell's original syntax for command substitution, which is still universally available, uses backticks (`, also called backquotes) to delimit command substitutions, as in `command`. The text of *command* is executed in a subshell (which performs any substitutions or globbing), and the backticks and their contents are replaced with the output of *command*. As an example of usage, you can extract the name of a file using expr and store that name using command substitution:

```
filename=`expr "$file" : '.*/\([^/]*\)$')`
```

In most modern shells, another syntax for command substitution is $(*command*). Unfortu-nately, there are a few shells left where this is not portable; most notably, the Solaris and Irix / bin/sh. For some scripts, you may prefer to use the older form, but you may also prefer to use a preamble to get your script into a more recent shell (see Chapter 7). In newer shells, the pre-vious example could be rewritten as:

```
filename=$(expr "$file" : '.*/\([^/]*\)$')
```

This sets the variable filename to the file name component of a longer path. The $() syn-tax may be nested:

```
all_files=$(find $HOME -name $(expr "$file" : '.*/\([^/]*\)$'))
```

There is no easy way to nest command substitution using the backtick syntax. The reason is that backticks do not have distinct left and right forms, so the shell simply treats text up to the first backtick it encounters as being a single subshelled command. For instance, imagine that you were to try to perform the preceding find assignment using backticks:

```
all_files=`find $HOME -name `expr "$file" : '.*/\([^/]*\)$'``
```

The shell sees an opening backtick, then reads until it finds another backtick. So the first command is find $HOME -name . The expr command (and its arguments) show up outside of backticks, and the two backticks at the end look like substitution of an empty command. So this is treated by the shell as though you had written the following (using the other syntax):

```
all_files=$(find $HOME -name )expr "$file" : '.*/\([^/]*\)$'$()
```

The results of the empty $() construct are simply empty strings, and $(find $HOME -name) also produces no output. (The error message about a missing argument to -name goes to standard error). So after substitution of the commands, this becomes the following:

```
all_files=expr "$file" : '.*/\([^/]*\)$'
```

The net result is that the shell sets $all_files to the string expr and tries to execute $file as a command with the remaining arguments you had meant for expr as its arguments. On some shells, you can obtain the expected results by escaping the inner backticks:

```
all_files=`find $HOME -name \`basename $file\``
```

Now the parent shell sees escaped backticks, which do not end the command it is constructing, and it passes them into the child shell, which executes the subcommand as expected. This is hard to read, gets harder to read if you add more nesting, and is not completely portable. Do not do it. There is a much simpler solution:

```
file_name=`basename $file`
all_files=`find $HOME -name "$file_name"`
```

In this case, the output of the first command is used as an argument to the second. The complete list of files generated is assigned to the all_files variable. The behavior of backslashes in backticks may not be consistent between shells; avoid it. Backslashes in $() command substitution seem to be consistently passed unaltered to the subshell.

```
file_name=`expr "$file" : '.*/\([^/]*\)$'`
for path in `find $HOME -name "$filename"`; do
  echo `expr "$path" : '\(.*\)/\([^/]*\)$'`
done
```

The command substitution's results are subject to field splitting, providing a list of files in $HOME with the specified name. Note that this does not behave well if some of the file names have spaces in them. If you want to prevent field splitting, you can use backticks (or the $() syntax) inside double quotes. If you do this, you have to escape any nested quotes.

The choice of which command substitution syntax to use is more complicated than some shell portability decisions. The $() syntax is substantially better, except for the surprise of running into a system that doesn't support it. These issues are discussed more in Chapter 7's discussion of shell language portability. If you have other reasons to require a POSIX shell,

I would recommend the $() syntax, but it is probably not in and of itself enough justification to make the additional requirement.

In general, the best way to handle nested command substitution is not to use it; use temporary variables to hold intermediate results. Nesting of command substitution is a frequent source of confusion or bugs in shell scripts. Avoid it. By the way, while the $() syntax is more robust in the face of nesting, it has its own limitations; some shells behave surprisingly if you try to use command substitution of shell code that has mismatched parentheses, such as a case statement. (The workaround of using (pattern) in case statements is also nonportable.)

Implicit and Explicit Subshells

Subshells can be formed implicitly under several circumstances. The most important to know about for most scripts are pipelines and background tasks (background tasks are discussed in Chapter 6). In a pipeline, every command may be run in a subshell. There is no explicit () to indicate where the subshells go, but there will typically be one per command or possibly one for each command but the first or last. In a portable script, you must not assume that any command in a pipeline runs in the parent shell. A common idiom to allow you to use the output of a pipeline is to use a while loop as the last command in the pipeline; you can then access the output of the pipeline within the loop, but be aware that changes to shell variables may not affect the parent shell. (Worse yet, they may affect the parent shell, so you should not casually assume you can overwrite variables the parent shell is using.)

Here's a script I wrote once with the intent that it would list the contents of all subdirectories of the current directory:

```
#!/bin/sh
ls | while read file
do
  cd "$file"
  ls
done
```

This script has a surprisingly high density of bugs for such a tiny program. In fact, the only time it will work is when it is in a completely empty directory. If $file is not a directory, the cd command prints an error message, and the script runs ls in the current directory; this is probably not what I want. If $file is a directory, the shell changes to that directory and lists its contents as expected. So what's the bug in that case? The shell never changes back to the parent directory, so the next cd command will probably not work as expected. Finally, it is possible (and even common) that the ls command is subject to aliases that could cause it to behave differently or to environment variables that set default options causing it to, for instance, emit output in color. You can avoid the aliases by specifying the path to ls. The environment variables are harder to address; for more information on the portability problems such features can create, and how to avoid them, see the discussion of utility portability in Chapter 8.

There are a number of ways to address these issues. The first thing to do is distinguish between directories and files. In the case where $file is a directory, I want to change to it, run ls, and change back out.

```
#!/bin/sh
/bin/ls | while read file
do
  if test -d "$file"; then
    cd "$file"
    ls
    cd ..
  fi
done
```

Now this will work in the most common cases. However, there is a new problem. If one of the directories in question has permissions such that cd "$file" fails (or if the script writer made the extremely common mistake of not quoting $file and one of the directories has spaces in its name), the cd .. moves the script back up into the shell's parent directory, leaving the script once again behaving unexpectedly. You can resolve this at least in part by using &&:

```
#!/bin/sh
/bin/ls | while read file
do
  if test -d "$file"; then
    cd "$file" &&
    ls &&
    cd ..
  fi
done
```

This now works in most cases. The only case where it will fail is where you can change your working directory to a given directory, but ls fails in it, and this is pretty uncommon. However, there's a much simpler way; you can use an explicit subshell:

```
#!/bin/sh
/bin/ls | while read file
do
  if test -d "$file"; then
    ( cd "$file" && ls )
  fi
done
```

Because the cd command is now in a subshell, the parent shell doesn't have to do anything; it just keeps on executing in the directory it came from, rather than trying to figure out how to get back to the right directory. Note that, unlike the {} command group, a subshell does not need a trailing semicolon. This is because the) character is a metacharacter, which the shell recognizes unless it has been quoted, while } is merely a very terse keyword.

Explicit subshells are often used simply to group commands; this may be inefficient on any system, but it is especially inefficient if you need to worry about portability to Windows. If all you need is to group a few commands together, use {}.

Modifying the State of the Shell

Sometimes, it is desirable to change the environment of the current shell. Subshells are used to prevent changes to the child shell's context, especially the environment or current directory, from affecting the parent shell. However, sometimes you want precisely the opposite effect; you want to force something to have an effect on the parent shell. Many shell builtins exist to change the shell's state. You could not implement cd as an external program in UNIX because it would only change its own directory. The shell offers three other ways to run chunks of shell code within the current shell's environment: shell functions, the eval command, and the dot (.) command.

Shell Builtins

There are two major reasons for some commands to be built into the shell. The first is simple performance; for instance, many modern shells implement test as a built-in command so conditional operations do not require a process to be spawned. When a program is a builtin for this reason, it mostly matches the behavior of an existing program that is found in the file system. For instance, the built-in test program can generally accept any standard arguments that /bin/test would work with. While the external utility programs and the shell builtins may both provide extensions, the standardized part of their behavior is usually the same. On the other hand, the nonstandard behaviors may vary widely. There is more discussion of utility (and built-in command) portability in Chapter 8. In general, whether something is a builtin or not, you should be careful about relying on extensions.

The second reason for a command to be a builtin is that it has to modify the shell's context. For instance, the cd command is a builtin because a program that changed its own working directory would be useless to the shell calling it. Commands that modify or view shell variables have to be builtins. The env command is not a builtin because it does not view unexported shell variables, and because it never changes the caller's environment. By contrast, the set command is a builtin. The set command can display unexported shell variables or control shell options; both of these functions require it to run as part of the shell process.

Shell Functions

Shell functions offer an interesting compromise between running within the shell's environment and creating a new environment. A *shell function* is a block of code that is assigned a name and can thereafter be used just like a builtin command. This section introduces the common and portable subset of what you can do with shell functions; there is a great deal of variance between shells. (Some rare shells lack functions entirely; use a preamble to get to a real shell on those systems.) Shell functions are defined with the following syntax:

```
name () block
```

By convention, `block` is nearly always a {}-delimited list. However, you can use a ()-delimited list, in which case the function's body runs in a subshell. The block should be one of these two lists; other options are not portable. For instance, you cannot use a plain pipeline or list as a function body using this syntax. Some shells offer other syntax for defining functions or even accept a plain pipeline as a function body. In many cases, shells that accept multiple ways to declare functions provide different semantics for different types of functions. The previous structure, whether with {} or () for the body, is the only portable option.

Functions operate a little like separate scripts. For instance, during the execution of a function, the positional parameters refer to the function's arguments, not the calling script's positional parameters. ($0 may or may not be changed; do not rely on either behavior.) However, calling exit within a function exits the whole script. If you wish to return early from a function, the special return built-in command exits the current function with a specified return code; in portable scripts, this still has to be a small integer value, the same as any other exit status. Once the function completes, the positional parameters are restored. The function runs in the shell's environment, so code within the function can modify the shell's state; for instance, it can change the working directory or modify variables in the calling shell.

The name of a function may clash with the name of a variable; because of this, it may be beneficial to use a consistent prefix, such as func_, on function names. Some shells distinguish between function names and variable names, but older shells may not.

If you want to return a more complicated value or a string, you can store the result in a shell variable or design your function to be used with command substitution. For a shell variable, I recommend the name $*function*_result, as in the following example:

```
func_display_dpi () {
  func_display_dpi_result=$(xdpyinfo | awk '/resolution:/ { print $2; exit }')
}
```

The typical result of this function (a string like 75x75) would not be a possible return value in some shells, but it can be stored in a variable. Of course, it could also be simplified if the function just displays its output, and you use command substitution when calling it:

```
func_display_dpi () {
  xdpyinfo | awk '/resolution:/ { print $2; exit }'
}
```

I tend to favor the command substitution path when defining functions with useful outputs. It is more terse and usually more idiomatic; on the other hand, each call to such a function has to be run in a subshell, which can impose performance costs. The uniquely named variable offers better performance in most cases. (Not in the preceding example, though, where there's a subshell anyway.)

In shells other than zsh, redirections at the end of a function's definition are performed every time the function is called, but only for the duration of the function. For instance, the following script logs multiple lines to the /tmp/log file:

```
func_log () {
        echo $*
} >> /tmp/log
func_log hello
func_log goodbye
cat /tmp/log
```

```
hello
goodbye
```

Each invocation of the `func_log` function results in output to /tmp/log; note that >> must be used, or each invocation of the function would truncate the file. Because the redirection affects the entire function body, individual statements within it do not need separate redirection. However, the shell's standard output is not redirected, so the cat at the end displays the log file normally. This offers an interesting compromise between individual redirections and using exec to redirect the whole shell. This technique may be better avoided if you may need to target a system where zsh is otherwise the best POSIX-like shell available; it is also quirky enough that it may be better avoided if other people need to read your code—which they do.

While every modern shell provides some way to provide local variables within shell functions, there are differences between the shells, and no one method for doing this is portable. This is actually more frustrating than it would be if there were simply no way to do it at all in some shells. You can sometimes obtain results similar to local variables by using a couple of tricks.

One solution is to run a chunk of code that needs local variables in a subshell. Getting data out of such a function is hard; if you need results from it, you must use command substitution to obtain them. If your function uses a subshell, and then you always call it in another subshell for command substitution, Windows users will hate you.

Another option is to use shell variables with names that are unlikely to clash. For instance, you could extend the *function*_result idiom to other values you need during the execution of a function.

If you really need local variables, though, you can use a subshell for them. You can simply declare the function using a subshell as the function body; the subshell code can create or modify variables freely without worrying about affecting the parent shell environment. For instance, this script uses a subshell to avoid stomping on the parent shell's variable value:

```
func_add () (
  value=0
  for i
  do
    value=$(expr $value + $i)
  done
  echo $value
)
value="Save me!"
func_add 3 4 5
echo "Value: $value"
```

```
12
Value: Save me!
```

The func_add function stomps on the variable value, but only in its subshell. The code outside the subshell does not stomp on any variables, so it can be called safely. If you need to modify the parent shell's environment, you can use braces for the function body, then use a subshell within the function's body. You can use command substitution to get information out of the subshell, as in this nearly equivalent example:

```
func_add() {
  add_result=$(
    value=0
    for i
    do
      value=$(expr $value + $i)
    done
    echo $value
  )
}
value="Save me!"
add_result="Overwrite me!"
func_add 3 4 5
echo $add_result
echo "Value: $value"
```

```
12
Value: Save me!
```

The variable value is preserved, as it is modified only in the subshell. However, the add_result variable is given a new value. You could execute other shell code from the subshell, too; it is not limited to variable assignments. This technique allows you to distinguish between "local" variables in a function and shell globals. However, it has two key limitations. The first is that it really requires nested command substitution (at least in the case where the function's core behavior involves the output of external commands). This restricts portability to relatively modern shells. The other is closely related; this technique uses a couple of subshells, and as such, may perform poorly on Windows machines.

The behavior of temporary assignments made on the command line is not quite portable when the command is a function; in pdksh, such assignments are not reversed after function execution unless the function was declared using an alternative syntax (discussed in Chapter 7). To pass data to a function without altering the caller's environment or context, pass the data in as arguments and access them using the positional parameters ($1, $2, etc.) in the function. (Do not assume that $0 refers either to the function's name or the script's previous value for $0; it might be either.)

Although they have their limitations, shell functions are exceptionally useful in developing larger shell programs. Functions offer a quick way to bundle up frequently used code and reuse it, generally without the expense of spawning subshells. Many users are unaware of the availability of shell functions or assume they are an extension. While many function features are extensions (and no two shells offer quite the same set of features), functions themselves are essentially universal.

The eval Command

The eval command executes its arguments as shell code. It may seem odd to need a special command for this; if you have code you wish to execute, why not just write it? There are two factors that make eval necessary. The first is code that is being generated in some way, usually through parameter substitution or command substitution. Because the results of substitution can never be keywords or other shell syntax features, such as variable assignments, anything that generates code needs to be parsed again by the shell. However, that could easily be handled by feeding the resulting code to another shell. The second factor is the desire to execute that code within the current shell. This is most obvious with variable assignments, although in some cases it is simply a matter of efficiency.

The eval command takes its arguments and concatenates them (separated by spaces) into a string that is then parsed and executed. Because the arguments to eval often include bits of shell syntax or metacharacters, many programmers habitually pass a single-quoted string as an argument. The quotes are not always necessary, but it can be a good habit to include them when the arguments are complicated or contain metacharacters so that you can be sure whether it is the calling environment or the eval command performing any splitting, substitutions, or globbing.

One usage of eval is to create a shell syntax item, such as a variable assignment, by assembling it from other components (such as an escaped dollar sign and a name). Since there are no arrays in standard shells, programmers sometimes use sequences of variable names to similar effect. For instance, instead of using an array named a, you might use a series of variables named a_0, a_1, and so forth. If the variable count holds the value of an item of the array, you can assign a value to that member like this:

```
eval "a_${count}=$value"
```

This does not work if $value contains spaces or other special shell characters. The first step in correcting this is to use quotes:

```
eval "a_${count}=\"$value\""
```

This works unless $value contains double quotes or dollar signs. The trick is to prevent the shell from expanding $value until it is inside the eval so that it only gets expanded once. To solve this, escape the dollar sign so the shell passes the dollar sign and variable name to eval rather than the substituted string:

```
eval "a_${count}=\"\$value\""
```

Now, no matter what string $value contains, the eval command executes the following code (assuming $count was 0):

```
a_0="$value"
```

Nothing generated by parameter substitution is a special syntax character; no matter what $value contains, the result of the substitution is a plain string inside double quotes, and the contents of the string are reliably stored in $a_0. In fact, you can go a little further. The shell does not perform field splitting on the right-hand side of an assignment, so you can omit the inner quotes now that the dollar sign is escaped:

```
eval "a_${count}=\$value"
```

Even the outer quotes are actually unneeded. There is only one argument, and it contains no spaces or special characters that require additional protection:

```
eval a_${count}=\$value
```

The following fragment stores a collection of file names in a series of named variables, which can later be used somewhat like an array:

```
count=0
for file in *; do
  eval a_${count}=\$file
  count=`expr $count + 1`
done
```

On the first iteration, the shell assigns the name of the first file to a_0. This can only be done using eval. If you used a second shell, it would not affect variables in the parent shell, and if you didn't use eval, the shell would fail because there is no command named a_0=file. On the second iteration (assuming there are multiple files), $count is 1, so the second file is assigned to the variable a_1. This allows you to store the results of a glob separately and access them individually later. This gives you a safe way to treat a list of results as an array.

Most shell programs use a simpler idiom, simply accumulating values within a single variable:

```
for file in *; do
  a="$a $file"
done
```

While this is common and idiomatic, it is not quite as reliable. There is no way after this has run to distinguish between a file name containing spaces and two separate file names. You could use a different idiom, using other characters (such as colons) as separators, but any character can exist in a path name. In the special case where you are looking only at file names guaranteed not to have directory components in them, you could use path separators safely.

The eval command is also needed to extract these variables. The shell cannot handle nested substitutions like ${a_${count}}. Some languages, like Perl, can. For the shell, you must use eval. You can use the same kind of expression used to create dynamically named variables to access them later:

```
eval value=\$a_${count}
```

The shell generates the string value=$a_0, then evaluates it. The contents of $a_0 are substituted and stored in $value. Again, the right-hand side of the assignment is not subject to field splitting, so there is no need for quotes.

The following function provides a moderately complete implementation of arrays using a shell function interface:

```
func_array () {
  func_array_a=$1
  func_array_i=$2
  case $# in
```

```
  2)
    eval func_array_v=\$func_array_${func_array_a}_${func_array_i}
    return 0
    ;;
  3)
    func_array_v=$3
    eval func_array_${func_array_a}_${func_array_i}=\$func_array_v
    return 0
    ;;
  *)
    echo >&2 "Usage: func_array name index [value]"
    func_array_v=''
    return 1
    ;;
  esac
}
```

This function can be called to either set a named variable or extract its value. The values are all stored in variables using the prefix func_array_ to avoid name clashes. If you call func_array a 1 hello, this function stores the string hello in a variable named func_array_a_1. If you call this as func_array a 1, it then stores the current value of $func_array_a_1 in $func_array_v. You could easily change this to generate an error message for access to an unset array member; as is, it honors the shell's normal convention of substituting an empty string for an unset variable. Note that the index need not be numeric; it can be any string consisting only of underscores, letters, and numbers. This function could do with more error checking for valid indexes, but it illustrates the flexibility of eval.

Another use of eval would be displaying commands before running them for debugging or feedback purposes. The following function runs its arguments using eval, after optionally displaying them:

```
func_do () {
  cmd=$*
  if $verbose; then
    printf 'running %s\n' "$cmd"
  fi
  eval "$cmd"
}
```

The printf command displays the command prior to any substitutions or globbing, which is usually the most informative choice. Printing out the results after substitutions is quite a bit harder; there is a working example of how to do this embedded in libtool. In essence, you do it by using other tools (such as sed) to generate multiple versions of the text to be used in different contexts (for instance, inside and outside of double quotes). If you need to do this, pick up the existing code rather than trying to reinvent it, as there are a number of special cases to deal with.

In the section "Introducing Redirection" in Chapter 3, I pointed out that you cannot write code that tries to pick streams to redirect out of a variable. For instance, this code doesn't work:

```
logfd=3
exec $logfd>/tmp/log.txt
```

This fails, because the 3 which replaces $logfd is not seen as part of a redirection; instead, the shell looks for a command named 3, which it can execute with standard ouptut directed into /tmp/log.txt. The eval command makes this possible, however:

```
logfd=3
eval "exec $logfd>/tmp/log.txt"
echo "hello" >&$logfd
```

This example echoes hello into /tmp/log.txt. The shell substitutes $logfd, producing the string exec 3>/tmp/log.txt, then eval executes that string in the current shell environment.

The string passed to eval must be syntactically correct, or the shell reports a syntax error. The following fragment is just an elaborate syntax error:

```
eval "if $condition; then $action; "
fi
```

The eval statement fails because the if statement is incomplete; the following fi is a syntax error because it does not occur at the end of an if statement. You can use control structures within eval, but the entire control structure has to be within the code evaluated. By contrast, break and continue statements can be executed from within eval; the break statement is not a part of the syntax of the enclosing loop, but a command that affects the shell's flow control.

If the code passed to eval is syntactically valid, the return status of eval is the return status of the evaluated code. Otherwise, eval indicates failure (and displays an error message on standard error).

In modern shells, the eval command can be used to make a temporary assignment to $IFS:

```
IFS=: eval echo \$PATH
```

The eval command is run with $IFS changed, so when it substitutes $PATH, the shell uses the temporary value (a colon) for field splitting. Temporary variable assignments preceding built-in commands are not reverted with most built-in commands, but POSIX shells do this for eval or set. Unfortunately, some older shells do not handle this as expected.

Another common usage for eval is to run shell code (nearly always assignments) generated by other programs. Programs that want to generate modifications to the shell environment, such as the tset utility (which manipulates terminal settings), often have a mode in which they emit a series of shell commands. These commands are designed to be incorporated into the shell environment using command substitution and eval. For instance, the tset utility can produce shell assignments as output, intended to be evaluated by the calling shell:

```
eval `tset -s`
```

This displays basic terminal setup commands to ensure that other settings (such as those controlled by stty) are synchronized with the terminal type. (Many users also use the -Q option to prevent tset from overriding the choice of character used to erase the previous character typed, as this is typically idiosyncratic.) The tset utility also makes an interesting use of standard error; in its normal usage, it sends terminal reset instructions to standard error once it has identified a terminal type. If you have inadvertently displayed binary data to a terminal, and the terminal is displaying characters incorrectly, running tset will often correct this. The standard error stream is used so that, even when standard output is being directed to the shell (for command substitution), the special reset sequences go to the terminal anyway.

Another good example of a command with shell command output is the widely available ssh-agent command. The ssh-agent command provides a uniform way to handle secure shell authentication for a number of programs. When programs are run as children of ssh-agent, or children of another program (typically a shell) that ssh-agent started, they can get the information they need to use these authentication features from the environment. What about programs started elsewhere? To resolve this, the ssh-agent program can produce a series of environment variable assignments on standard output. Thus running eval `ssh-agent -s` gets variables into the current shell's environment for use by the shell and its children.

In most cases, the code generated by such programs is limited to variable assignments. In the case of ssh-agent, there is also an echo command to display additional information:

```
$ ssh-agent -s
SSH_AUTH_SOCK=/tmp/ssh-00024095aa/agent.24095; export SSH_AUTH_SOCK;
SSH_AGENT_PID=29018; export SSH_AGENT_PID;
echo Agent pid 29018;
```

Of course, displaying these values to standard output is useless (unless you're writing a book); the agent is now running, but no variables have been set in the calling shell. Programs expecting to be run in this manner tend to emit semicolons after every command to ensure that their output will be usable even if it has been combined into a single line by field splitting.

The purpose of this command is not just to allow programs that use an SSH agent to access it, but also to let you avoid rerunning the agent if you do not need to. For instance, this chunk of (nonportable, sadly) profile code would reuse an existing ssh-agent process if one existed:

```
if test -n "$SSH_AGENT_PID" &&
   ps x | grep ssh-agent | grep $SSH_AGENT_PID >/dev/null; then
   echo "Existing ssh agent: $SSH_AGENT_PID"
else
   eval `ssh-agent -s`
fi
```

The nonportability in the preceding code is the option specified to ps; there is no universally portable set of options that will display background processes. You could also use kill -0 $SSH_AGENT_PID to check for a process with the expected pid, but this would not prove that it was an ssh-agent process.

There are a number of security concerns with running eval on code generated by external utilities, as there is no way to constrain the code. When running eval in a production script, always specify the full paths to programs whose output you will be running. Of course, you may not be able to predict those paths; ssh-agent, for instance, might be in any /usr/bin, /usr/local/bin, /opt/gnu/bin, or any of a number of other common paths, depending on the system. You can search the common or reasonable places; beyond that, you have to make a security policy decision about how much to trust the user.

If you know a fair bit about the output you are expecting, you may be able to perform some sanity checks on it before executing it. In the fairly common case where you are substituting only a small portion of a piece of code, such as the name of a variable, you can check to make sure that the substitution is reasonable before executing it.

The dot (.) Command

The dot (.) command reads a named file in and executes it in the current shell. (The name "dot" is not the actual name of the command; you cannot invoke dot at a shell prompt, but people often refer to the command as "the dot command" for clarity in English, where a single period on its own is not a word.) This is often called *sourcing* the file, and bash accepts source as a synonym for ., although this is not portable to other shells (in fact, it's a csh feature). The named file is searched for in the current execution path; if you want to execute a program in the current directory, you must specify its path explicitly (unless you have the current directory in your path, in which case you should change that, as it is a very bad idea). Apart from the use of a search path, . file is generally equivalent to eval "$(cat file)".

DO NOT PUT . IN PATH

Do not put . in your $PATH. It is even worse if you put it at the front of your path, but even at the end, it is dangerous. In the real world, people make typos. An attacker who can arrange to have a file named sl in a directory where you run a command can cause you to execute that file; if it prints the error message you'd have expected from your shell, you might not even notice. This is most important when working on shared machines, but even for personal use systems, it is a good habit to use commands in . only by explicitly specifying a path of ./command.

There is an additional reason, other than security, to care about this. If you are used to . being in your path, you will make more mistakes. For instance, you may write a simple script that uses a helper script, only to discover that it works only when you are in a given directory. Better to specify paths and directories consistently.

Note that a path with a leading or trailing : also searches the current directory. Don't do that either.

The . command is mostly used for setup scripts that configure the shell's environment. For instance, the previous script intending to modify the user's path can be sourced by the shell, in which case it works:

```
$ cat path.sh
#!/bin/sh
PATH=$PATH:/usr/local/bin
$ echo $PATH
/bin:/usr/bin
$ . ./path.sh
$ echo $PATH
/bin:/usr/bin:/usr/local/bin
```

Sourcing can also be used in cases similar to those where you would use eval, but where it is convenient or desirable to create a file to store a series of commands you wish to run in the current shell.

Using Shells Within Shells

The various ways of spawning subshells have some overlapping functionality, but there are significant differences between them. The primary differentiations between ways of running subshells (or external shells) are whether the code can affect the parent shell's environment, whether the parent shell performs substitution on the code, and whether the child shell performs substitution (see Table 5-1).

Table 5-1. *Shells Calling Shells*

Shell Type	Affects Caller Context	Parent Substitutes	Child Substitutes
sh, sh -c	No	Yes	Yes
eval, .	Yes	Yes	Yes
()	No	No	Yes
fn ()	Yes	No	Yes
`` , $()	No	No	Yes

When arguments are passed to eval or to sh -c, they are plain strings to the parent shell and subject to normal shell substitution rules. However, when the parent shell creates a subshell, whether for command substitution or not, the code passed to the subshell is not subject to substitution in the parent. Similarly, the bodies of shell functions are subject to substitution and globbing each time the function is called, not when it is defined. If the body of a function consists of a subshell, it cannot modify the parent shell's context.

When to Use an External Shell

A full external shell should be used when you want to run code in a completely separate context and want the shell to parse that code. External shells have the highest cost of any of the shell execution mechanisms, but they give the cleanest behavior least affected by the current shell's context. External shells have a comparatively high cost, however. In most cases, wrapping an eval in a subshell is an acceptable substitute for launching a command with sh -c and may perform marginally better.

The external shell's arguments are potentially subject to parameter or command substitution before they are created, but the external shell will not have any local shell variables you have set. Similarly, it will not have any shell functions or other unusual local environment setup. Use an external shell instead of eval when you want to run a command that might affect the shell's environment or be affected by the shell's context. Similarly, use an external shell instead of . when you want to run an external shell script in a separate context.

External shells do have one very significant portability weakness: If the standard system shell lacks features, and you've used an execution preamble to get into a more modern shell, sh -c will probably call back to the old-fashioned shell. Pay attention to which shell you are calling when you use external shells.

Idiomatically, external shells are often used to express self-containment of a command; in many cases, the external shell command could have been run in a subshell quite easily. One other thing external shells can do is completely detach a child process from the parent shell. A job run in the background is still affiliated with the shell that started it. By contrast, a grandchild process can be completely disconnected. Processes designed to run as daemons often do this internally, but some lightweight programs expect the caller to do it. So one use of an external shell is to start a completely independent background task:

```
sh -c "background_task >/dev/null 2>&1 </dev/null &"
```

The external shell runs *background_task* disconnected from all the standard streams, then exits. After the external shell has exited, *background_task* is not connected to the parent shell in any way. Redirection of the standard streams is important; otherwise, *background_task* might still have the parent shell's input or output streams open, preventing those streams from closing when the shell exits.

Other typical uses of an external shell might look like this:

```
sh -c "tar cf - $dir | bizp2 | ssh user@remote "bzip2 -dc | tar xf -" &
```

This copies a directory tree to a remote host (and only works if ssh has been set up to allow passwordless access to that site).

```
bash installer $source $target > install.log 2>&1
```

This runs an external script explicitly. You would not want to use . to run the script; it might change the shell's context radically. The choice of a specific shell suggests that perhaps the installer script depends on bash extensions.

```
for shell in ksh ksh93 sh bash; do
  $shell test > test.$shell
done
ok=true
echo "---output---"
cat test.sh
echo "------------"
for shell in ksh ksh93 bash; do
  diff -u test.$shell test.sh || ok=false
done
$ok && echo "All shells matched!"
```

This scriptlet would provide a very minimal start on testing whether a test script's behavior is consistent across a small range of shells. In this case, the explicit choice of which shell to execute is very much intentional.

When to Use eval or dot (.)

The eval command is used when you want to assemble a chunk of shell code and evaluate it within the current shell context. You should use eval instead of an external shell primarily if you need to modify the current shell's context. In some cases, though, the performance advantage of not starting a new shell may be worth it as long as executing code in the current context does not cause problems. The eval command is useful when the generated code involves shell syntax or when you need to perform another pass of substitution on the results of a parameter or command substitution. If you need to interact with a variable, but which one must be determined dynamically, you need eval. Likewise, because substitution cannot create shell syntax features, such as control structures, you need eval to generate control structures.

The . command is used mostly for existing code rather than dynamically generated code. Larger projects written in shell may use . to incorporate a set of shared shell commands written as functions. The system startup scripts on several Linux systems, as well as many of the BSDs, use shell functions to provide consistent and reliable implementations of common tasks used in startup scripts. For instance, nearly every startup script on NetBSD starts with the following:

```
$_rc_subr_loaded . /etc/rc.subr
```

The rc.subr script provides a number of function definitions to simplify the development of startup scripts. At the end of the script, the $_rc_subr_loaded variable is set:

```
_rc_subr_loaded=:
```

If the support file has not already been loaded, the line expands to . /etc/rc.subr and loads the support file. If it has been loaded, the line expands to : . /etc/rc.subr, which does nothing.

Supporting files like this are useful for a number of reasons. Shell functions are generally faster than external commands. Furthermore, they can modify the environment of the script using them. This makes them essentially new built-in commands that can be written on the fly, allowing a great deal of convenience and flexibility in scripting.

When to Use Subshells

Subshells are often used because the parentheses offer a visually intuitive way to group commands. However, if you do not need any of the additional features of the subshell, using a command list (enclosed in braces and terminated by a semicolon or new line) is typically more efficient.

Any time you find yourself about to save, modify, and then restore part of your shell context or environment, a subshell is probably better. One of the most widely used examples of a subshell is this idiom for copying files:

```
tar cf - . | (cd target; tar xpf -)
```

Unlike the cp command, this preserves a broad variety of nonstandard files, such as device nodes. If run with root privileges, it also preserves ownership. Users on systems that provide it may prefer the pax utility, which can perform this operation with a single command. However, the pair of tar commands lends itself to another common idiom, which cannot be done using only a single command, doing the same thing to or from a remote machine:

```
ssh user@remote 'cd source; tar cf - .' | ( cd target; tar xpf - )
```

Whether local or remote, the unpacking operation could be done instead using plain shell compound commands, but then the current directory of the shell would be changed. Using a subshell is more idiomatic. If you are using a remote shell, remember that it cannot expand local shell variables; make sure any variable arguments sent to the remote shell have already been expanded on the local end.

When to Use Command Substitution

Command substitution is one of the central strengths of the shell, allowing arbitrary new functionality to be added to the shell on the fly. Common uses of command substitution include generation of data and performing operations that the shell does not provide natively. For instance, although some modern shells have built-in arithmetic evaluation, historically shell scripts have used the expr utility to perform arithmetic, and you should stick with it in code that you expect to ever need to port. For instance, when using getopts (see Chapter 6; of course, this isn't all that portable either) to parse options, the shell sets a variable $OPTIND to the index of the first nonoption parameter. To remove the options from the parameter list using shift, you need to shift one less than that many values off the parameter list:

```
shift `expr $OPTIND - 1`
```

There may still be shells that only let you shift one argument at a time (because their shift command takes no arguments), in which case you must use a loop to accomplish this, but I haven't been able to find one. Similarly, you may want to count files that match a given test:

```
total=0
for file in *
do
  test -d "$file" && total=$(expr $total + 1)
done
echo "$total file(s) are actually directories."
```

Another very common use of command substitution is modifying strings using the sed or tr utilities (with which there are many portability issues; see Chapter 8). For instance, a script that wishes to shout at the user might use tr to uppercase a message:

```
func_toupper () {
  func_toupper_result=`echo "$@" | tr a-z A-Z`
}
func_toupper "I can't hear you."
printf "%s" "$func_toupper_result"
```

```
I CAN'T HEAR YOU.
```

In this case, of course, it might make sense to remove the command substitution and simply display the output immediately. A common pitfall when using command substitution is to carefully store the output of a command, only to immediately display it. This habit probably reflects the idiom in many languages, where you use a special command to display things; thus if you want to display the result of an operation, you obtain the result and then display it. Be careful about falling into this habit. The example displays the output immediately because its only purpose is to display the output. In a real program, if you were always going to display the output immediately, it might make more sense to write the function to display output rather than returning a result:

```
func_toupper () {
  echo "$@" | tr a-z A-Z
}
```

Command substitution like this is often used when a given data manipulation exceeds the native capability of the shell to perform pattern operations. Some shells offer substantially more flexible variable manipulations, but the basic pattern remains, and there are always things that external utilities are better at.

It is important to note that the commands in a command substitution do not need to be external programs and do not need to be simple shell commands. You can expand the output of functions, lists, or shell control structures, such as while loops.

Combinations

One of the most common idioms with all of the previous is combining them. As you have probably noticed, many of the examples of how to use eval use it on the results of command substitution. The shell is fundamentally a glue language, and each of these mechanisms is used for a different kind of glue. The following example lumps everything together:

```
: ${MD5SUM="md5sum"}
find . | while read file; do
  test -f "$file" || continue
  md5=`"$MD5SUM" < "$file"`
  eval assoc=\$md5_$md5
  if test -z "$assoc"; then
    eval md5_$md5=\$file
  else
    printf 'duplicate: "%s" and "%s"\n' "$file" "$assoc"
  fi
done
```

A few words of explanation may be in order. This script attempts to identify duplicate files in the current directory, using the MD5 checksum algorithm. (This may not be available on all systems; on some systems, it may be named md5, or not be installed at all.) The essential loop, on the outside, looks like this:

```
find . | while read file; do
  # DO SOMETHING WITH $file
done
```

This loop uses the output of the find command (a list of file names, one to a line) as a list of file names to process. Now, what exactly is happening inside the loop?

```
test -f "$file" || continue
```

The first operation is a check that the file is a plain file, as opposed to a directory or a UNIX special file (such as the file system representation of a physical device). The short-circuit operator is a little terse, but expressive. This kind of usage is idiomatic in shell; while it might be dismissed as unwarranted "clever" programming if it were not a common idiom, familiarity makes up the difference. This idiom is very similar to the Perl idiom condition || next.

```
md5=`"$MD5SUM" < "$file"`
```

This line sets a variable, $md5, to the output of the selected checksum command. The md5 and md5sum programs I used are verbose when invoked on a named file, but nicely terse when invoked with only an input stream, producing nothing but a 32-character string. This string is a 128-bit number derived from the file contents, which is typically different for any two files that are different. Of course, there are many possible clashes, but in practice the chances of a clash are low (extremely close to one in 2^{128}, if you can believe that).

```
eval assoc=\$md5_$md5
if test -z "$assoc"; then
  eval md5_$md5=\$file
else
  printf 'duplicate: "%s" and "%s"\n' "$file" "$assoc"
fi
```

This is the actual guts of the script. If you store a list of files and their MD5 checksums, you must search the whole list for each potential clash. This is annoying. In a language that supports associative arrays (also often called *hashes*), you would probably store each file name as a value with its checksum as a key. In fact, you can do nearly the same thing in the shell using computed variable names. Computed variable names, of course, mean using eval. Let's have a closer look at the bolded code fragment:

```
eval assoc=\$md5_$md5
```

This is a useful idiom for obtaining the value of a variable whose name you must compute at runtime. If the MD5 checksum of a file were 12345678 (it wouldn't be; it'd be four times that long, but a short name is more readable), this would expand to the following:

```
assoc=$md5_12345678
```

This stores the value of the dynamically selected variable in a variable with a predictable and constant name.

If the MD5 variable had a value, it must have been stored from a previous match, and you have a duplicate; you have identified a match between the new file $file and the file name now stored in $assoc. If it has not, you want to stash the name of the current file in that variable:

```
eval md5_$md5=\$file
```

Because the calling shell does not substitute $file, you do not need to worry about special characters; the eval command does the substitution, and the results are guaranteed to be treated as a plain word, not as shell metacharacters, even if the file name contains quotes, new lines, spaces, or other unusual characters.

The use of assignment reduces the number of subshells and command substitutions you might otherwise need. A very common idiom is to use eval in a command substitution to extract the value of a variable:

```
assoc=`eval printf %s "\"\$md5_$md5\""`
```

Direct assignment is quite a bit simpler to use, but be aware of this idiom, as you may see it frequently. The combination of eval and command substitution merits attention because this combination is fairly common. In general, using eval and echo (or printf) to obtain the output of dynamically generated code is a useful idiom. The eval command lets you generate a variable name dynamically, printf lets you display its contents, and command substitution lets you embed those contents into another command or variable assignment. The weakness of this idiom is that command substitution implies field splitting and removal of trailing new lines, so it does not preserve all contents precisely. This may be unavoidable, when the dynamically generated code includes references to external commands.

What's Next?

Chapter 6 goes from fiddly little details of shell syntax into gory details of shell invocation and execution. I explain more about the positional parameters, the meaning and nature of shell options, and the grand unified theory of why the shell is not doing what you expected it to do, as well as some of the debugging tools and techniques that may become necessary if a script is misbehaving.

CHAPTER 6

■ ■ ■

Invocation and Execution

This chapter discusses the runtime of the shell. The shell must be started in some way; this is discussed in the next section, "Shell Invocation." Once the shell is running, it is important to understand what the shell actually does, the order in which substitutions occur, and the way the shell interacts with other processes. It may even be necessary on rare occasions to use additional tools to debug a script that behaves unexpectedly.

Shell Invocation

This section discusses the process of starting the shell (or a shell script) and telling it what to do; this is called *invocation*. The shell itself is a command, like any other, which takes command-line options and arguments; similarly, each shell script becomes a command that can be invoked, and most take options, arguments, or both.

The words following a command's name on the command line are generally called *parameters* or *arguments*. I use the term arguments to avoid confusion with shell parameters (which are sometimes called variables to avoid the same confusion). Many commands take special arguments, called *options*, which change the way the program behaves. The UNIX convention is that options are generally introduced with a hyphen and typically have single-letter names. Multiple options can be combined; foo -ab is usually the same as foo -a -b. Some options may take an additional word as an argument, such as the -e option to grep, which takes a regular expression as an argument.

The meaning of arguments that are not options may vary. Many UNIX utilities treat all of their arguments the same, typically as a list of file names. However, there are many exceptions; it is also common for the first nonoption argument to a command to be special. In grep, for instance, if no -e option is provided, the first argument is a regular expression, and following arguments are file names.

How UNIX Runs Scripts

When a UNIX-like system tries to execute a file, the kernel checks to see what kind of file it is. If it is a regular file with execute permission, the kernel tries to execute it. The kernel starts by examining the file to see if it is a known type of executable by looking for a distinctive header; for instance, on many modern systems, the kernel checks for an Executable and Linking Format (ELF) header denoting an executable in the ELF format.

On essentially every "real" UNIX-like system (all UNIX systems and all UNIX clones), there is a common standard executable script format—a file starting with the characters #! (called a *shebang*, short for *sharp-bang*). Strictly speaking, this behavior is not mandated by POSIX, and there are subtle variances between systems; in practice, it is universal as long as you are reasonably cautious. Such a file is taken to be a script file to be run by an interpreter. The rest of the first line of the file indicates what program the script is to be used with. For instance, the common shell header #!/bin/sh indicates that the script is to be used with /bin/sh. To execute the file, the kernel executes the command /bin/sh with the name of the script as its first argument. Spaces after the ! are permitted but ignored; you can ignore the occasional rumors that it is nonportable to omit the space.

The command name in a shebang line is nearly always an absolute path. The kernel does not search $PATH for a binary; it just tries to find a file of the given name. So a script starting out #!sh is treated as a script for the sh program in the current directory. The command cannot itself be another #! script.

Traditional shells treat a file marked as executable, but lacking a header, as a shell script. This behavior is required by POSIX, but you should never rely on it. In particular, it is harder to tell which shell will be used to run a script invoked in this way, especially if it is being invoked by a shell other than the standard shell. Some shell documentation describes a script run this way as a "subshell," but the shell context (functions, aliases, shell variables, and so on) is cleared out as though it were a new shell.

Interestingly, the POSIX definition of the shell explicitly does not specify what happens if a file starts with #!; this is because a hypothetical non-UNIX system could comply with POSIX but treat all scripts as shell scripts. In fact, many UNIX systems simply treat all executable files (which are not recognized by the kernel) as shell scripts, even if they are not text files! A typical result from trying to execute an executable from another machine is a cryptic error message:

```
$ ./somega
./somega: 1: Syntax error: "(" unexpected
```

This file was an old executable compiled on an older machine and copied around with the rest of my files. Because the executable was not compatible with the hardware I tried it on, the kernel failed to execute it. Since it was marked executable, the shell tried to execute it anyway. POSIX allows the shell to print a warning and fail to execute non-text files, but many shells don't bother.

Warning The shell does not necessarily check whether an executable file is actually a shell script!

There are two places where other arguments may be passed to the new script. If there is a space after the command's name, anything else on the line is also passed to the command, before the script's name; for example, #!/bin/sh -x runs a script in trace mode. The remainder of the line may or may not be split into multiple arguments; most systems pass it as a single argument, even if it contains spaces—but do not rely on this. If a script's header is #!/bin/sh -x -y, the options are usually passed as a single argument containing a space, not two separate arguments.

Secondly, if the script command originally had arguments, those arguments are passed after the script file's name. If a script starting with #!/bin/sh -x is invoked as ./script hello, the original arguments passed to the shell are /bin/sh, -x, ./script, and hello. The shell interprets -x as an option. It then uses ./script as a script file (setting $0 to ./script, and reading commands from that file instead of standard input) and passes hello as $1. This behavior is precisely the same as you would get by explicitly invoking the shell on the file.

#! NOTATION AND $PATH

An obvious problem with shebang notation is that the path to a program may not always be consistent or predictable. While this has no immediate effect on most shell scripts, it can crop up in some cases (such as where you are writing a script for a particular shell), so a brief discussion is in order.

If you want a script to run on two systems and both provide ksh, but one provides it in /bin and the other in /usr/local/bin, it is quite easy to end up with the script failing on one system or another just because the shebang line is wrong. One surprising solution is to use the env command; when it runs its nonassignment arguments as a command, it searches the $PATH environment variable for the command. If you know that you want to run ksh, and you are confident that it is in the user's path, a script starting with #!/usr/bin/env ksh executes ksh correctly. The env utility can be used to run another program, even if no variable assignments have been provided.

There are a couple of limitations to this trick. One is the existence of a few systems where env is in /bin, not in /usr/bin. Furthermore, most systems do not allow you to specify multiple program arguments on the shebang line; if you change the line to #!/usr/bin/env ksh -x, the env utility may try to find a program named ksh -x to run, rather than trying to run the ksh program with the -x argument. Execution preambles (see Chapter 7) may allow you to avoid some of these issues.

The POSIX spec recommends the use of the getconf utility to obtain the default system search path (getconf PATH) and iterate through it looking for the standard shell. Another option is to use the command utility; command -v sh should give you a path to the shell, for instance.

Shell Options

Options passed to the shell control various implementation choices or settings, some of which are visible within a script as flags. Some command-line options set flags that can be changed later using the set command. You can see the current status of shell flags in the special shell parameter $-, which represents them as a string:

```
$ echo $-
ilms
```

This means that the shell has the -i, -l, -m, and -s flags set. These options may not apply to all shells, and not all shell options are portable. If you want to check for a given option, check to see whether its letter is present. For instance, a script can determine whether or not it is in trace mode:

```
case $- in
*x*) ;;
*)   echo "+ $cmd" >&2;;
esac
```

This rather quirky bit of code displays $cmd on standard error if the trace flag is not set. The trace flag displays simple commands before executing them, but it does not display shell control constructs, such as case statements; if it is set, no simple commands are executed, so none of this code is displayed.

The most common flag to check for is the -i flag, which is set in an interactive shell session (discussed in more detail in the section "Shell Startup and Interactive Sessions").

Additional settings may be available using the special -o option; for instance, in ksh or bash, set -o vi enables vi-style command-line editing. These settings are generally not portable between shells. Furthermore, some shells may abort if asked to set an unknown option. Be aware of this, but avoid it in scripts.

Using Positional Parameters

Any additional words after the last shell option are arguments to the shell. If no commands are provided using the -c option, the shell treats its first argument as the name of a script to run, and following arguments as arguments to that script. Otherwise, all arguments are passed on to the script.

The arguments passed to the shell are stored in special shell parameters named $1, $2, and so on. These are called the *positional parameters*. The name of the shell itself is stored in $0 for an interactive session, but when the shell is running a script, $0 holds the name of the script. Although the shell in the previous example actually received four arguments (the first being the path of the shell executable), it sets $0 to ./script and $1 to hello. The name of the shell, and the command-line options to the shell, are consumed by the shell and not exposed to the script program. The number of positional parameters is stored in the special parameter $#. For historical reasons, the shell's parser treats $10 as the value of $1 with the string 0 appended to it. To use parameters past $9, use ${N} in a modern shell. Older shells, including the SVR4 shell, will not accept larger values under any circumstances; in these, you must extract earlier values and use shift to move other parameters into the first nine slots.

Although some shells offer extensions providing for array variables, the positional parameters are the only array conveniently available to a portable shell script. Because of this, they are used for much more than just argument processing. One common idiom is to extract all options and arguments from the positional parameters at startup to free them up for later use in argument parsing. (Trickery such as using many similarly named variables to substitute for arrays, while portable, is awkward and not always efficient.)

The set Command

Unlike variables, the positional parameters cannot be directly set using variable assignment; 1=2 is just an unknown command to the shell, not an assignment into $1. The set command can be used to set the positional parameters.

The set command takes a special option (--) to indicate that you are setting something other than shell options; any following arguments are assigned to the positional parameters, with the first argument going into $1. The general syntax for this usage is set -- *values*. Although set is a special shell builtin, the arguments are processed normally; parameter and command substitution, globbing, and field splitting all apply.

WHAT IS DUMMY AND WHY IS IT BEING SET?

A common idiom in older scripts is to use the word dummy instead of -- when setting the positional parameters. Very old shells did not recognize -- as the end of shell options and the beginning of the parameter list. As a result, you had to put something that was definitely not a shell option in front of the parameters. In a shell that didn't know about the -- convention, set -- makes the shell set $1 to the string --.

An idiomatic resolution is to use the word dummy, which does not start with a hyphen, then immediately shift it off the parameter list:

```
set dummy $array ; shift
```

This is moderately idiomatic (some people prefer shorter names like X, but I find dummy to be particularly self-documenting). However, it may not be necessary anymore; the shells I have access to, including the traditional SVR4 shell, all work using the modern syntax. (It was probably added in the System III shell in 1981.)

There is one other reason to use this. The SVR4 shell can set positional parameters with set -- *args*, but plain set -- does not clear them. To clear the positional parameters, use shift $#.

In some scripts, this is used as a simple way to get access to the results of variable expansion and word splitting applied to one or more variables, or to add values to the positional parameters before executing something. For instance, if you want to insert a value in front of the existing arguments, you can use $@ and the set command:

```
set -- new "$@"
```

Another common idiom is to use $IFS and the set command to split a value around something other than whitespace. For instance, a classic UNIX password file entry uses colons as separators. You can read it in the shell using the following idiom:

```
save_ifs=$IFS
IFS=:
set -- $passwd
IFS=$save_ifs
```

The set command is not particularly complicated in and of itself, but using it effectively can be complicated. Setting all of the arguments at once can be awkward when you want to build or modify argument lists. You can also append additional arguments:

```
set -- "$@" "$new"
```

This appends $new to the argument list at the end.

Removing Positional Parameters

It is sometimes desirable to remove parameters from the shell's parameter list. This is done using the shift command, which removes positional parameters. You can use shift with or without an argument. With an argument (shift *N*), it removes the first *N* positional parameters, renumbering the later parameters to the front of the list. Without an argument, it removes the first parameter. The standard `for` loop that iterates through the positional parameters is nearly equivalent to the following `while` loop:

```
while test $# -gt 0; do
  echo "$1"
  shift
done
```

The equivalent `for` loop is as follows:

```
for i
do
  echo $i
done
```

In fact, there is a significant difference between these loops. After the `for` loop completes, the positional parameters are unchanged, but after the `while` loop completes, there are no positional parameters remaining. This can be useful. A common idiom for parsing command-line options is to consume options, leaving arguments for further processing:

```
opt_a=false
opt_b=false
opt_c=""
while test $# -gt 0; do
  case $1 in
  -a)  opt_a=true ;;
  -b)  opt_b=true ;;
  -c)  opt_c="$2"; shift ;;
  --)  break ;;
  esac
  shift
done
for arg
do
  # process non-option argument $arg
done
```

The first loop consumes any arguments that look like known options. The special option `--` indicates the end of options, allowing the user to specify an argument that happens to start with a hyphen. This provides robustness in the face of programs whose arguments might otherwise look like arguments. This is one of the ways to deal with problems, such as needing to remove a file named `-rf`.

Manipulating Parameters for Fun and Profit

Individually, the tools the shell provides for argument manipulation may seem a little weak. There is no way to assign a single parameter or to insert a parameter later in the list. There are a number of shell idioms for argument list manipulation, but many of them are unreliable when confronted with arguments containing spaces. Consider the following simple loop, intended to extract options and separate them out from file arguments:

```
files=""
opts=""
for arg
do
  case $arg in
  -*) opts="$opts $arg";;
  *)  files="$files $arg";;
  esac
done
set -- $opts -- $files
```

This works pretty well, as long as none of the files, or options, contain spaces. (If you want this functionality, without those bugs, you should probably use getopt or getopts, discussed in the section "Handling Options and Arguments"; I picked the example because it is tricky to get it right and interesting to think about.) There are several ways to attempt to resolve this difficulty.

If you can think of a character that you are confident cannot occur in any of your options, this is actually easy to do. Unfortunately, techniques like this are pretty limited; they rely on coincidence in many cases. For instance, very few file names contain colons; so you might use colons to separate a list of files, but then a file with a colon in its name can wreck your whole day. Here is an example of how you could use a colon to separate words:

```
files=""
opts=""
for arg
do
  case $arg in
    -*) opts=${opts+$opts:}$arg ;;
    *)  files=${files+$files:}$arg ;;
  esac
done
save_IFS=$IFS
IFS=:
set -- $opts -- $files
IFS=$save_IFS
```

There are three major changes here. The first is the use of a different character (in this case, a colon) to separate words within the $opts and $files variables. The second is the use of a corresponding value of $IFS to split the variables again. The third, closely related to the second, is a more complicated inner assignment. Without this, the shell generates a spurious empty argument at the beginning of each list. For example, if the arguments were foo bar, $files would end up set to :foo:bar. Note the subtle difference between this behavior and what happens when $IFS is unset (or has its default value); normally, a variable with a leading space does not expand into an extra field.

You can use other values for $IFS. Some scripts use control characters for this, precisely because they are very unusual in file names. However, there may be quirks; for instance, at least one version of bash can't handle $IFS being set to control-A.

You can also use simulated arrays using eval (as explained in Chapter 5) to store arguments without worrying about separators:

```
filec=0
optc=0
for arg
do
  case $arg in
    -*) eval opt_$optc=\$arg
        optc=`expr $optc + 1`
        ;;
     *) eval file_$filec=\$arg
        filec=`expr $filec + 1`
        ;;
  esac
done
shift $#
while test $filec -gt 0; do
  filec=`expr $filec - 1`
  eval 'set -- "$file_'$filec'" "$@"'
done
set -- "--" "$@"
while test $optc -gt 0; do
  optc=`expr $optc - 1`
  eval 'set -- "$opt_'$optc'" "$@"'
done
```

The array code here is similar to what was done in Chapter 5. The script extracts the arguments, then clears the argument list and repopulates it using while loops.

Each while loop goes through pushing arguments to the front of the list. Single quotes are used to reduce escape characters. For the first file argument, the eval command string ends up as follows:

```
set -- "$file_0" "$@"
```

No matter what values the variables contain, this works—they are substituted in as plain words, not keywords or shell syntax. The "$@" expansion preserves the existing arguments as separate arguments, regardless of their contents. In fact, the same basic techniques allow you to do arbitrarily complicated things, such as replacing a specific parameter while leaving the rest alone.

The most obvious limitation is that it does not work if you try to bundle it into a shell function. As shell functions have their own local set of positional parameters, modifications to the positional parameters within a function have no effect on the calling script.

Handling Options and Arguments

Although it is certainly possible to manually process arguments, as in the previous example, the task is common enough to have been solved repeatedly. Unfortunately, the solutions are not entirely portable. The first is the getopt command, which parses a command line and produces a new command line conveniently ordered. The syntax is getopt *string parameters*, and the output of the command is the *parameters* reordered, with options separated out and identified, according to the list of options in *string*. (In fact, the previous loop does most of the work of implementing getopt.) The options string lists the letters of accepted options; options that take an argument are followed by a colon.

Because the getopt command is not a shell builtin, and does everything by producing output, you can experiment with it at the command line to see how it works:

```
$ getopt a hello, world
 -- hello, world
$ getopt a -a hello, world
 -a -- hello, world
$ getopt a -b hello, world
getopt: illegal option -- b
 -- hello, world
$ getopt ab -ab hello, world
 -a -b -- hello, world
$ getopt ab: -ab hello, world
 -a -b hello, -- world
$ getopt ab: -ba hello, world
 -b a -- hello, world
```

The output of the getopt utility is *options -- non-options*. As each parameter beginning with a hyphen is evaluated, it is converted into a series of options. If an option that takes an argument is encountered, its argument is either the rest of the word (if there is any left) or the next word, whatever that may be. Options in clusters are separated out; -ab becomes -a -b. As with many utilities, getopt treats -- as ending options and beginning the nonoption parameters. The output of the getopt utility is intended to be used to replace the positional parameters; the canonical usage is combined with the set command:

```
set -- `getopt options "$@"`
```

This usage is portable on recent systems. You can then iterate over the positional parameters, extracting options, without having to worry about exactly what characters are part of which options. Doing this by hand is exceedingly difficult in shell and not really worth the trouble. However, the getopt utility does have one crucial limitation—it cannot gracefully handle parameters containing whitespace.

Modern shells generally provide a getopts built-in command, which is able to set shell variables, and thus provide more reliable handling of parameters. As the phrase "modern shells" suggests, this is not completely portable yet. Surprisingly, the shell in older versions of Cygwin was compiled so that it included the code for getopts, but it did not actually recognize the command. This has been fixed in modern releases.

The getopts command is used more like the read command, returning true or false depending on whether or not there is a next option, and returning one option at a time. The syntax of the command is getopts *string variable parameters*; if *parameters* are omitted, getopts uses the positional parameters. Each time getopts is invoked, it looks for another option and stores the option character in $variable. If there are no more options, getopts returns false. If there is an error, getopts returns true and sets $variable to ?. A typical usage of getopts looks like this:

```
while getopts ab: o; do
  case $o in
  a)  echo "received flag a";;
  b)  echo "received option b: $OPTARG";;
  esac
done
shift `expr $OPTIND - 1`
```

The special shell variable $OPTARG holds the argument provided for an option that requires an argument. The special shell variable $OPTIND holds the number of the first nonoption positional parameter. For example, if there are no options, $OPTIND has the value 1 after getopts has run (and returned false). Because the positional parameters number from one, executing shift $OPTIND would remove the first nonoption parameter from the list. Like getopt, getopts recognizes -- as the end of options and uses the remainder of a word as an argument if an option expects an argument.

Because getopts can handle arbitrary arguments reliably, I prefer it. While traditional shells did not provide the getopts builtin, modern shells, including the SVR4 shell, do.

Older Shells: Now What?

While nearly all modern shells support getopts (and you could write it as a function fairly portably), it may occasionally become necessary to work with a very old shell that lacks this feature. The following boilerplate code handles a broad variety of arguments fairly well. (Many of the names are placeholders used to illustrate how to handle common tasks in shell code.)

```
opt_boolean=false
opt_accumulator=0
opt_argument=''
# opt_list=''  this is unset so that ${opt_list+item} will work

# sed scripts:
my_sed_single_opt='1s/^\(..\).*$/\1/;q'
my_sed_single_rest='1s/^..\(.*\)$/\1/;q'
my_sed_long_opt='1s/^\(--[^=]*\)=.*/\1/;q'
my_sed_long_arg='1s/^--[^=]*=//'

while test $# -gt 0; do
  opt=$1
  shift
  case $opt in
    # standard usage patterns:
    -a|--accumulator)   opt_accumulator=`expr 1 + $opt_accumulator` ;;
    -A|--argument)      opt_argument=$1
                        shift
                        ;;
    -b|--boolean)       opt_boolean=:
                        ;;
```

```
--composite)          set dummy --boolean --list element ${1+"$@"}
                      shift
                      ;;
--list)               opt_list=${opt_list+$opt_list:}$1
                      shift
                      ;;

# Add your own long and short option branches here, and then
# change the branch match expressions below to match the
# appropriate options for splitting and reparsing...

# Separate optargs to long options:
--argument=*|--list=*)
                      arg=`echo "$opt" | $SED "$my_sed_long_arg"`
                      opt=`echo "$opt" | $SED "$my_sed_long_opt"`
                      set dummy "$opt" "$arg" ${1+"$@"}
                      shift
                      ;;

# Separate optargs to short options:
-a*|-p*|-q*|-r*)
                      arg=`echo "$opt" |$SED "$my_sed_single_rest"`
                      opt=`echo "$opt" |$SED "$my_sed_single_opt"`
                      set dummy "$opt" "$arg" ${1+"$@"}
                      shift
                      ;;

# Separate non-argument short options:
-b*|-x*|-y*|-z*)
                      rest=`echo "$opt" |$SED "$my_sed_single_rest"`
                      opt=`echo "$opt" |$SED "$my_sed_single_opt"`
                      set dummy "$opt" "-$rest" ${1+"$@"}
                      shift
                      ;;

-\?|-h)               func_usage                                 ;;
--help)               func_help                                  ;;
--version)            func_version                               ;;
--)                   break                                      ;;
-*)                   func_fatal_help "unrecognized option \`$opt'"  ;;
*)                    set dummy "$opt" ${1+"$@"}; shift;  break   ;;
      esac
done
```

While this may seem like a lot of work to avoid getopts, it is worth noting that this supports a number of helpful idioms, such as long argument names. The functions used for the
last few options are left as an exercise for the reader; their behavior should be obvious from

the context. Of particular interest is the code used to separate out multiple options given as a single argument. If you call this code with -bx as an option, the first pass through the loop replaces this with -b -x. You would have to define the -b) case for this to be processed correctly, though. As long as the -b case occurs before the -b* case, the first one matches and the shell processes the argument appropriately.

For extra credit, modify the preceding example to detect and warn the user if no argument is provided for an option requiring one.

Shell Startup and Interactive Sessions

There are several different kinds of shell sessions. If the shell is expecting to read commands and respond with prompts, that is called an *interactive* session. When the shell reads commands from a file, it generally is not an interactive session. A shell taking input from a pipe is also not an interactive session; the distinction is whether the input device is considered to be a tty (a terminal device; the name is short for "teletype"). Some shell sessions are further considered to be login sessions; a login session is normally interactive.

During startup, the shell may read (and execute) one or more startup scripts. The exact rules for this are, sadly, nonportable between shells. If your home directory contains a file named .profile, an interactive login shell will probably execute it during startup. Unfortunately, this is merely probable, not certain; as an example, bash looks for files named .bash_profile or .bash_login first, and it does not execute .profile if it finds one of the others. The intended benefit, of course, is that you can have a startup specific to bash that need not be portable to other shell variants. However, if you have a standard .profile you bring from one machine to another, it can be surprising trying to debug why it isn't being used.

Shells other than login shells may also run startup scripts. This is even less predictable and may be subject to strange rules. For example, many POSIX shells will execute the file named by the environment variable $ENV at startup. Pre-POSIX shells do not, and bash executes $ENV only if it is being run in its POSIX mode or was invoked under the name sh; otherwise, it uses $BASH_ENV instead. Contrary to its behavior with .profile, bash does not execute $ENV just because $BASH_ENV is not set. In short, you can not rely on startup behavior in a portable script. What's worse is that you cannot rely on such files being run at startup; but also you cannot rely on them *not* being run at startup.

This brings us to one of the few genuinely intractable problems of portable shell scripting: A hostile user can misconfigure the shell so that it will not work by creating a startup file which prevents successful execution of your script, most commonly by creating aliases for common commands (the alias command is described in Chapter 7). You can override this somewhat by specifying full paths or quoted names for most commands, but it is very difficult to get right.

There is not very much you can do about the possibility that someone, somewhere, will end up feeding your script to a shell that is configured to alias various common commands on startup. However, you can avoid doing this to your own scripts. In any file that affects shell startup, be sure to execute aliases and similar code only when you are not in an interactive shell. The safest idiom to use for this is as follows:

```
case $- in
*i*) alias yes=no
     echo "Do you want me to hit you?"
     ;;
*)   ;;
esac
```

This causes the shell to execute its initialization commands only when the shell is not interactive. I have seen a different idiom for this:

```
case $- in
*i*) ;;
*)   return 0;;
esac
```

This is not safe. While there are shells in which the `return` command (used, in some shells, to exit from a function) can also end the execution of a file being executed by the shell using `.`, there are shells in which a `return` command outside of a shell function exits the entire shell. As it is not unheard of for a startup script to end up getting picked up by a different shell, this can cause a perfectly ordinary shell script to unexpectedly terminate without any diagnosis of errors.

When looking at startup scripts, there are three common cases. A login shell typically needs to perform additional setup to populate the environment; on many systems, this would also be the place to configure things like terminal types or start an `ssh-agent` process. After this has been done, other shells can simply inherit this environment. Among non-login shells, there is still a noticeable difference between interactive and noninteractive sessions. If you are working with a shell that can execute a startup script in a noninteractive session, be sure your startup scripts don't do anything time-consuming or interactive in a noninteractive session.

Execution

It is possible to program fairly effectively in shell without needing to know the exact details of how certain things are done. The shell reads and executes code. However, there is some possibility for confusion. When does the shell parse? What order do various substitutions occur in? Where is this error message coming from?

This section gives a more detailed view of the runtime behavior of the shell and introduces some of the debugging tools that may come up when the shell behaves unexpectedly.

More on Jobs and Tasks

Job control features, allowing a shell to control or manipulate multiple tasks, are mostly used on the command line, but there are cases in which you can take advantage of the shell's ability to manipulate multiple tasks to simplify some shell script design tasks. Some shells offer extensions (such as ksh's co-process feature) that make additional use of background tasks. For portable scripting, the primary thing you can do with background tasks is continue doing some other work while a long task processes. For instance, you could have a script that plays a game with the user while waiting for an archive to unpack—although most users would probably rather you didn't.

Signals and Interprocess Communication

It is often necessary to communicate between processes. UNIX provides several mechanisms for interprocess communication (IPC), of which three are available to the shell. Two of them have already been introduced: exit status and pipes. The exit status of a process is only sort of an IPC mechanism, but it allows for a child process to communicate to its parent whether or not it has succeeded. Pipes are an exceedingly flexible IPC mechanism, but the shell pipe syntax only allows one-way communication between a pair of programs.

The other IPC mechanism available to the shell is *signaling*. Signals are unusual in that the recipient of a signal may not have any opportunity to interact with it. Signals can simply terminate the receiving process. However, most signals may be intercepted by a program, which can define a piece of code to execute when it receives the signal. This piece of code is called a *signal handler*. The shell allows the user to define handlers for several of the common signals.

Signals are referred to by their names or by their numbers; there is a consistent mapping of names to numbers for the most common signals. The signals most likely to be used in shell programming are outlined in Table 6-1.

Table 6-1. *Signals by Number*

Number	Name	Trap	Description	Default Behavior
0	EXIT	Yes	Shell is exiting.	
1	HUP	Yes	Session ended.	
2	INT	Yes	Interrupt.	
9	KILL	No	Kill.	
13	PIPE	Yes	I/O error on pipe.	
14	ALRM	No	Timer expired.	
15	TERM	Yes	Default termination signal.	
17	STOP	No	Process stopped.	
18	TSTP	No	Process stop request from terminal.	
19	CONT	No	Continue stopped process.	
21	TTIN	No	Stopped waiting for input.	
22	TTOU	No	Stopped waiting for output.	
30	USR1	No	User-defined signal #1.	
31	USR2	No	User-defined signal #2.	

The default effect of a signal varies. For HUP, INT, TERM, ALRM, and KILL, the default behavior is for the process to terminate. If a process is killed by a signal, its exit status is generally reported as 128 plus the signal number. For instance, a program interrupted by an INT signal has an exit status of 130. The USR1 and USR2 signals are usually ignored. They exist to allow programs to define specific behaviors in response to those signals without changing handling of any of the standard signals that normally have an effect.

The STOP and TSTP signals, as well as TTIN and TTOU, cause a process to cease execution but not to exit; execution resumes on a CONT signal.

Some signals are generated automatically by the UNIX kernel. Any signal can also be generated artificially. You can send any signal to any program (running with the same user ID) using the kill command. The default signal (sent if no signal is specified) is TERM. Other signals can be specified using their name or number with a leading hyphen. For example, kill -9 *pid* sends a KILL signal to the process with process ID *pid*, as does kill -KILL *pid*. Numbers are more portable.

Signals can be caught by a shell program using the trap built-in command, although only some signals may be trapped portably. This command specifies an action to be taken in response to a signal. The syntax for the command is trap *action signals*. If *action* is omitted or an empty string, the shell ignores the given signal or signals. If *action* is a hyphen (-), the shell resets the signal to its default behavior. Otherwise, *action* is executed as though passed as an argument to eval when the signal is received; this replaces the usual behavior for the signal. Multiple signals may be specified in a single trap command, and signals may be specified by number (portably) or name (on modern systems). However, only one action may be specified; if you want to run multiple commands, you must quote them (and separate them with semicolons or new lines) or use a shell function.

Do not assume that $? is passed into a trap handler correctly; some shells do not do this. In general, avoid starting a trap handler with a shell function call.

When a signal is generated by the kernel, it may be sent to the shell and its child processes rather than only to the shell. For instance, if you hit Ctrl-C while running a script, the shell process and its associated children all receive the INT signal. The trap command only affects the signal received by the shell itself; child processes can still receive, and be affected by, signals.

The shell defines a special signal, signal number 0 (named EXIT), that is handled when the shell exits. For instance, the following shell script greets the user:

```
NAME=world
trap "echo Hello, $NAME!" 0
```

```
Hello, world!
```

The action specified in the trap command executes automatically at the end of the script. The handler for signal 0 is frequently used for cleanup of temporary files created during the execution of a script. Note, though, that the exit handler is not invoked if the shell is terminated by another signal. The special value 0 (but not the symbolic name EXIT) may be used as a signal for the kill command, too. In this case, kill sends no signal but yields a return code indicating whether or not the process exists. A successful return indicates that the process exists, and a failed return indicates that it does not. No signal is delivered by kill -0, so a handler for signal 0 does not execute except when the script exits.

Run with no arguments, trap prints a list of the current signal handlers, quoted such that evaluating this output restores the signal handlers:

```
$ trap 'echo "you cannot defeat me so easily!"' TERM
$ trap
trap -- 'echo "you cannot defeat me so easily!"' TERM
```

It is not portable to attempt to save only a single signal's output from this list by scanning the list for a particular value, as the existing handler might be more than one line of code. In this case, the shell command to recreate it would also be more than one line of code, and a simple check of matching lines would fail. However, if you have full control over a script, you can resolve this by ensuring that all signal handlers are a single line of code, allowing you to save individual values. The obvious solution is to pipe the output of trap into a while loop; this does not work because signal handlers are reset to their defaults within a subshell. To store trap values, store the output in a file, then read the file:

```
trap 'echo "you cannot defeat me so easily!"' TERM
trap 'echo "whoops, driving under a bridge."' HUP
trap > /tmp/trap.$$
while read sig
do
  set -- $sig
  eval "signum=\${$#}"
  eval "sig_$signum=\$sig"
done < /tmp/trap.$$
rm -f /tmp/trap.$$
set | grep ^sig_
```

```
sig_HUP='trap -- '\''echo "whoops, driving under a bridge."'\'' HUP'
sig_TERM='trap -- '\''echo "you cannot defeat me so easily!"'\'' TERM'
```

The output of this script may vary between shells. In bash, the signals are spelled out as SIGHUP and SIGTERM, while ksh93 uses an extension to simplify the quoting of the strings. This means you cannot reliably expect one shell to correctly read or execute the output of a trap command run in another shell. However, all the shells are internally consistent; the output of the trap command in a given shell can be evaluated by that shell. Once you have saved the current signals, you can modify them or restore them individually. After running the preceding script, you could temporarily remove the HUP handler, then restore it:

```
trap - HUP
echo "Doing something long and boring. Will accept SIGHUP."
sleep 5
eval $sig_HUP
```

There are a few conventions about the use of signals. Interactive utilities generally abort upon receiving a HUP signal. Long-running daemons, though, often use the HUP signal as a cue to refresh their configuration, possibly rereading configuration files. Some use USR1 or USR2 for related tasks, such as refreshing or reopening log files.

Understanding Background Tasks

Background tasks and subshells have unique pids. When a task is launched in the background, the parent shell gets the child's pid in the special shell parameter $!. However, if the job is running in a subshell, it does not know its own pid; it gets the parent's pid in the $$ parameter. By contrast, a job run with sh -c gets its own pid in the $$ parameter.

Shell background tasks may be distinguished by their pids. Background tasks (along with interactive control of multiple jobs, called *job control*) are primarily used interactively. However, it is possible to make some use of background tasks in shells.

Background jobs are always run in subshells, so they do not affect the parent shell's context. A background job cannot change the calling shell's directory, set variables, or otherwise modify the caller except by sending signals. If you wrote a loop to read values from a file and ran it in the background, it would not set variables in the calling shell. Similarly, you cannot change a directory in the background:

```
cd /tmp &
```

This creates a subshell that changes its working directory to /tmp, then exits. The parent shell is unaffected.

So what do background jobs do? Background jobs are often used when you want to run a longer command while you continue working; for instance, at the command line, it is quite common to run a long compile process or file operation in the background. In a script, you might still want to run a long task in the background. To do so, you need to be able to determine whether the task is still running, wait for it to complete, or even abort it if you change your mind. All of this can be done.

Shell scripts that wish to use background tasks can keep track of them using their pids. Immediately after launching a background task, you can obtain its pid from the $! shell parameter. This can be used to send signals to the background task (using the kill command) or to wait for it later. If you have a large file-manipulation task to run, which may take several minutes and requires no user interaction, it might make sense to start it in the background, perform other tasks, then wait for it after those tasks are finished.

The wait command waits for background tasks to complete. Without arguments, it waits for all background tasks to complete and returns a successful exit status. If you specify the pid of a specific background task, it waits for that task to complete and returns the return code of that task. If the task has already completed, or the pid in question is not the pid of a child process of this shell, the wait command returns immediately indicating failure. The following trivial script begins an operation, then waits for it to complete:

```
tar cf archive.tar files &
child=$!
echo "Waiting for archive..."
wait $child
```

While waiting for a child is easy, and killing it is also easy, it is a little harder to check whether it is still running. The command kill -0 *pid* might work; if it succeeds, you know that there is a process numbered *pid* and that you have permission to send signals to that process. However, you do not know for sure that it is the child process you started; that process could have ended, and the pid then recycled.

Making Effective Use of wait

The wait command exits immediately if you ask it to wait for a process that is not a child of the current shell. However, if the process is still a child, the wait command waits for it. There is no portable way to check reliably whether a given process is a child of the current shell. The wait command runs in the calling shell, so to interrupt it, you must send a signal to the parent shell. If the signal would normally interrupt the shell, the signal will terminate the shell unless the signal is trapped.

If you send a signal to the shell while it's waiting, and the signal is trapped, the resulting behavior is unportable. Possible outcomes include the wait command aborting immediately or continuing until the child dies. Typically, the trap executes after the wait completes, but in zsh the trap executes immediately and the wait command continues anyway. This varies not only between shell families but between systems; the ash in use on NetBSD and FreeBSD systems differs from dash on Linux.

So, once the wait is started, you can't reliably interrupt it without killing your shell. You can't run wait on a background task in a subshell because the subshell is not the parent of the background task.

In practice, you can usually get away with checking the pid with kill -0 and expect that this will give you a good guess as to whether the child process is still running. This is not perfectly reliable, but is usually pretty good.

If you only need to monitor a single background task, you can solve the problem by having the background task notify the parent shell when it is done, rather than the other way around. To do this, you can have the child process send the parent shell a USR1 signal, which you have cleverly trapped. The following script prints "Nope, still waiting. . ." three times, but it could perform any activities you wanted while waiting; the point of the example is that you can tell when the subshell has exited:

```
done=false
trap 'done=true' USR1
(sleep 3; kill -USR1 $$) &
while if $done; then false; else true; fi; do
  echo "Nope, still waiting..."
  sleep 1
done
```

The subshell keeps the parent shell's pid as $$, so the kill command sends a USR1 signal to the parent shell after the previous command completes. It is a bit harder to use this with more than one background task; you cannot tell which process sent you a particular signal.

A similar technique can be used to once again invert the sense of the problem. Imagine that you have a task you wish to run, but you do not want to run it forever because it might hang. If it has not completed within a given amount of time, you want to kill it. The following rather ugly one-liner does fairly well at this:

```
sh -c 'sh -c "sleep '$delay'; kill $$" >/dev/null 2>&1 & exec sh -c "'"$*"'"'
```

This shell fragment runs the provided arguments ($*) in a child shell, but it terminates that shell after $delay seconds if the child shell has not already exited. The exit status is the exit status of the child shell, which reflects the abnormal exit if the kill command fires. This example shows off a variety of expansion rules, subshells, and quoting behaviors. The first thing to note is that, at the top level, this command invokes a shell (using sh -c) that actually executes a command in which some variables have been expanded. Assuming that $delay contains the number 5, and the positional parameters contain the string *command*, the child shell then executes this:

```
sh -c "sleep 5; kill $$" >/dev/null 2>&1 & exec sh -c "command"
```

The command line is assembled from a single-quoted string (up through sleep and the space after it), the expansion of $delay, another single-quoted string (up to the last sh -c and the following double quote), a double-quoted expansion of $*, and finally a single-quoted double quote. This brings us to the question of what this elaborate list actually does.

The child shell executes two commands. The first is another child shell, which I'll call the grandchild for clarity, running the command sleep 5; kill $$. Because $$ occurs in double quotes, it is expanded by the child shell, not by the grandchild shell; this matters because the grandchild shell is not a subshell and does not inherit the child shell's $$.

The grandchild shell's output and error streams are directed to /dev/null. So, after 5 seconds, the grandchild shell attempts to kill the child shell. Meanwhile, because the shell command that started the grandchild ends with the & separator, the child shell goes on to execute the next command in its list. This command is another shell, which runs the external command. The command is passed to a new shell to allow it to be parsed, to contain arbitrary keywords, and so on. However, to ensure that this process can be stopped, the script must know the process ID it will run under. Conveniently, the exec command runs the new command in place of the caller; thus the new shell is run using the same process ID—the one that was passed to the grandchild shell to be killed in $delay seconds.

This has a couple of weaknesses. The first is that, if the grandchild process (containing the command you are actually interested in) exits quickly, the kill command fires anyway. This could result in a new process getting sent the signal, if the pid is reused. This is uncommon, but not impossible. Also, it is often better to send more than one signal (first a polite reminder, then an actual KILL signal) so commands that need a second or so for shutdown can do it cleanly. This actually increases the window for possible problems, but it improves the reliability of execution in the common case where the child process has important cleanup work to do before exiting. The following code is based on an elegant solution suggested by Alan Barrett, used by his kind permission:

```
func_timeout() (
  timeout=$1
  shift
  "$@" &
  childpid=$!
  (
    trap 'kill -TERM $sleeppid 2>/dev/null ; exit 0' TERM
    sleep "$timeout" &
    sleeppid=$!
    wait $sleeppid 2>/dev/null
    kill -TERM $childpid 2>/dev/null
    sleep 2
    kill -KILL $childpid 2>/dev/null
  ) &
  alarmpid=$!
```

```
wait $childpid 2>/dev/null
status=$?
kill -TERM $alarmpid 2>/dev/null

return $status
)
```

This is a rather elaborate shell function and deserves some careful explanation. The first four lines are straightforward:

```
timeout=$1
shift
"$@" &
childpid=$!
```

The first two lines extract the timeout value (passed as the first argument to the function) from the positional parameters of the function, then remove it from the positional parameters. The function then executes the remaining arguments as a command. Note that they are executed as a single command, with no shell syntax (such as semicolons); if you wanted to support additional shell syntax, you would have to pass them to a new shell, probably using `sh -c`. The shell then obtains the pid of the background task, storing it in the shell variable `$childpid`.

```
(
    trap 'kill -TERM $sleeppid 2>/dev/null ; exit 0' TERM
    sleep "$timeout" &
    sleeppid=$!
    wait $sleeppid 2>/dev/null
    kill -TERM $childpid 2>/dev/null
    sleep 2
    kill -KILL $childpid 2>/dev/null
) &
alarmpid=$!
```

This is where the magic happens. This runs a second background task in a subshell. The task starts by trapping the TERM signal. The handler kills `$sleeppid`, then exits. The handler is specified in single quotes, so `$sleeppid` isn't expanded yet, which is good, because it hasn't been set yet either. (If this subshell gets killed before it gets any farther, the handler executes the command `kill -TERM`, with no arguments; an error message is emitted to `/dev/null` and nothing happens.)

The subshell now launches a background `sleep` task, stores its pid in `$sleeppid`, and waits for the `sleep` to complete. If the `sleep` command completes normally, the subshell then tries to kill the original child, first with a TERM signal, then with a KILL signal. This whole subshell is run in the background, and its pid is stored in the variable `$alarmpid`.

```
wait $childpid 2>/dev/null
status=$?
kill -TERM $alarmpid 2>/dev/null

return $status
```

Now the parent shell waits for the child process. If the child process has not completed when the background subshell finishes sleeping, the background subshell kills it. Either way, when the child process terminates, the parent shell extracts its status, and then tries to kill the alarm process. There are two ways this can play out. The first is that the child process might not die from the TERM signal, in which case, the alarm process tries to kill it with a KILL signal and then exits. In this case, the parent shell's attempt to end the alarm process could theoretically hit another process, although the window is very narrow. The second (more likely) possibility is that the child process dies from the TERM signal, so the parent shell kills the alarm process, which then tries to kill its sleep process (which has just exited) and then exits. In any event, the function returns the status of the child process; if it was terminated by a signal, the status usually reflects this. (Some shells may strip the high bit, which indicates that a process was terminated by a signal.)

The variables set locally in the function, such as $childpid, do not show up in the calling shell because the whole function is run in a subshell. Of course, the nested subshells and background tasks impose a noticeable performance cost, especially on a Windows system, but on the other hand, this kind of code is likely only to be run with tasks that can run for some time. Even if spawning subshells takes a noticeable fraction of a second, a 10- or 20-second runtime will dwarf that cost completely.

Techniques like this can be very useful while trying to perform automated testing, but a caveat is in order: There is no safe estimate available for what $timeout should be. If you are using something like this to catch failures, be sure you have thought about the performance characteristics of the command you want to time out waiting for. For instance, retrieving a web page typically takes only a couple of seconds, so you might set a time limit of 10 seconds. However, if a DNS entry has gotten lost or misconfigured and a web server is trying to look up names, it is quite possible for a connection to a host to take over 30 seconds simply to start up. Aborting too early can give misleading results.

Understanding Runtime Behavior

Previous sections of this book have introduced a number of things the shell does to its input. Input is broken into tokens, parameters and commands are substituted, and globs are replaced. Nearly every time a shell script has really mystified me, it turned out that I had forgotten the order of operations or the special circumstances under which an operation did not occur. The first thing to know is the basic order of operations, as shown in Table 6-2.

Table 6-2. *Shell Operations in Order*

Order	Operation	Notes
1st	Tokenizing	Creates tokens. This is the only phase that can create keywords or special shell punctuation. Words are split on whitespace.
2nd	Brace expansion	Only in some shells; see Chapter 7.
3rd	Tilde expansion	Replaces tilde constructs with home directories. Not universal.
4th	Substitution	Variable and command substitution (also arithmetic substitution in some shells; see Chapter 7).
5th	Field splitting	Results of substitution split on $IFS.
6th	Globbing	Glob patterns expanded into file names, possibly producing multiple words.

Continued

Table 6-2. *Continued*

Order	Operation	Notes
7th	Redirection	Redirection operators processed, and removed from command line.
8th	Execution	Results executed.

Of course, nothing in shell is this simple. There are two contexts in which field splitting and globbing are not performed. These are the control expression of a case statement and the right-hand side of variable assignment. Quoting also changes many behaviors. In single quotes, no expansion, substituting, splitting, or globbing occurs. In double quotes, tilde expansion, field splitting, and globbing are suppressed; only substitution is performed.

In the case where the command executed is eval, the arguments are subject to all of these steps again and subject to the same rules (including quoting, if there are any quotes in the arguments to eval).

These steps are taken one command at a time. The shell does not parse a whole script before beginning execution; it parses individual lines. At the end of each line, if the shell needs more tokens to complete parsing a command structure or command, it reads another line. When the shell reaches the end of a line (or the end of the whole script file) and has one or more valid commands, it executes any valid commands it has found. The following script always executes the initial echo command, even though the line after it is a syntax error:

```
echo hello
case x do
```

```
hello
script: 2: Syntax error: expecting "in"
```

However, if the commands are joined by a semicolon, the shell tries to finish parsing the first line before running the command:

```
echo hello; case x do
```

```
script: 1: Syntax error: expecting "in"
```

Even if the command is long and complicated, such as a case statement containing nested if statements, the whole command must be parsed before anything is executed.

Behavior with subshells is more complicated. Some shells perform complete parsing (but no substitution) of code that will be executed in a subshell. Others may let the subshell do some of the parsing. Consider the following script fragment:

```
if false; then
  ( if then )
else
  echo hello
fi
```

Should this script work? We can tell by inspection that the subshell command (which is invalid) is never run. However, every shell I have tried rejects it for a syntax error. A more subtle variant may escape detection:

```
if false; then
  ( if then fi )
else
  echo hello
fi
```

This version passes muster with ash and zsh, but it is rejected by ksh93, pdksh, and bash. Replacing the subshell with command substitution makes it easier to get shells to accept such code, but even then ash rejects it if the fi is omitted.

In practice, the best strategy is the simplest—ensure that code passed to subshells is syntactically valid.

Command Substitution, Subshells, and Parameter Substitution

When commands are executed in subshells, they are not subject to any kind of expansion, substitution, field splitting, or globbing in the parent shell. This is true whether you are dealing with an explicit subshell or the implicit subshell used by command substitution.

This behavior is closely tied to the fact that nothing can ever expand to a keyword. The parent shell can always determine which tokens belong in a command to be passed to a subshell without performing any kind of substitution; it simply passes those tokens to the subshell, which performs any needed substitutions.

This is generally true even for implicit subshells used in a pipeline, although it is not true of zsh in some cases:

```
true | true ${foo=bar} | true
```

In zsh, if $foo was initially unset, it is set to bar. In other shells, it remains unset.

The previous example may seem a bit contrived. There are very few reasonable cases in which it matters at all whether it is the parent shell or a subshell performing substitutions; outside of the = form of variable assignment and special variables like $BASH_SUBSHELL, it simply never matters. However, understanding it can make it easier to see how the shell works.

Quoted and Unquoted Strings

It is easy to understand the behavior of both quoted and unquoted strings when each token is one or the other. The shell's behavior when quoted and unquoted strings are not separated by space is a bit more intricate, but you have to use it sometimes; very few interesting scripts can be written without combining quoted and unquoted text.

For the most part, quoting is predictable. Each quoted block is interpreted according to its own quoting rules, and the results are concatenated into a single string. Substitution occurs only within unquoted or double-quoted text, and field splitting occurs only outside of quotes.

The interaction of globbing and quoting, however, can be confusing. If you have quoted and unquoted glob characters in a single string, the quoted ones remain literal and the unquoted ones are available for pattern matching. Thus the pattern `'*'*` matches file names starting with an asterisk.

The interaction of tilde expansion with quoting is not portable; some shells will expand `~'user'` the same way as `~user` and others the same way as `'~user'`. Since tilde expansion itself is not completely portable, this has little effect on portable scripts.

Quoting in Parameter Substitution

A number of parameter substitution forms contain embedded strings. The quoting rules for these are not entirely portable. In general, omit quotes in these strings and rely on quoting around the substitution. If you need to escape a dollar sign or similar character in a literal, use a backslash. If you want to prevent globbing, quote the whole substitution, not just the right-hand side.

The examples in Table 6-3 assume two variables, $a and $e; $e is unset and $a holds an asterisk.

Table 6-3. *Trying to Predict Shell Expansion*

Expression	Output
`${e}`	Empty string
`${a}`	Expansion of glob *
`${e:-$a}`	Expansion of glob pattern *, except in zsh where it is literal
`"${e:-$a}"`	*, except in ash, which expands the glob
`"${e:-*}"`	* expression
`"${e:-"*"}"`	*, except in ksh93, which expands the glob
`"${e:-"$a"}"`	*, except in ksh93, which expands the glob
`"${e:-\$a}"`	$a
`${e:-'$a'}`	$a
`"${e:-'$a'}"`	'*', except in pdksh, which gives $a
`'${e:-'$a'}'`	${e:-*} as a glob pattern, except in zsh, where it is literal

To make a long story short, it is hard to predict the behavior of nested quotes in variable substitution. Avoid this as much as you can. However, be aware that you may need quotes to use assignment substitution. The following code does not work in some older shells:

```
$ : ${a=b c}
bad substitution
```

To work around this, you can quote either the right-hand side of the assignment or the whole operator. Quoting the word only is more idiomatic:

```
$ : ${a="b c"}
```

In the preceding example, if $a has a value, that value is expanded outside of quotes, but if it did not have a value, the assigned value is in quotes:

```
$ sh echoargs ${a="b c"}
b c
$ sh echoargs ${a="b c"}
b
c
```

Trying to predict this behavior is essentially futile; there are simply too many specialized bugs or special cases. In general, the interactions between assignment substitution and other quoting rules make it best to use this substitution form only as an argument to : commands, not in cases where you have any expectations about the substituted value.

The POSIX expansion forms using pattern matching (discussed in Chapter 7) treat the pattern as unquoted by default, so you must quote pattern characters in them. As you can see, this behavior may be hard to predict consistently. Backslashes are usually safe for escaping single characters.

A Few Brainteasers

While all of the shell's rules are individually comprehensible, it is easy to think so hard about one of the shell's quoting or substitution behaviors that you forget about another one. This section gives a handful of code fragments that have surprised me or other people I know, resulting in confusion about why a given shell fragment didn't work or even confusion about why it did.

```
$ echo $IFS
```

I am a little ashamed to admit that I've used this several times to try to debug problems with the shell's behavior. It seems perfectly sensible, and if you think $IFS is unset or contains only whitespace, it even does what you expect. The problem is that unquoted parameter substitution is subject to field splitting. This means that any characters in the value of $IFS that are found in the value of $IFS are taken as field separators. If a word expands to nothing but field separators, there is no word there; all this does is pass no arguments to echo, producing a blank line. You wouldn't think it surprising that the characters in $IFS are in $IFS, but the habit of using echo $var to display a value is pretty well set in many shell programmers.

```
$ a=*
$ echo $a
```

This fragment clearly shows that the shell performs globbing on variable assignment; after all, $a was set to a list of file names, right? In fact, it is quite the opposite; $a was set to *, but since the substitution isn't quoted, the results are globbed.

The next example shows a case that seems surprising if you don't know that field splitting does not occur in an assignment operation. Most shell users are familiar with the problem of trying to assign multiple words to a variable:

```
$ a=one two
sh: two: command not found
$ echo $a

$ a="one two"
$ b=$a
```

The second assignment does not need quotes; there is no field splitting in the assignment. However, you will see quotes used there quite often, mostly by people who have been burned by trying to assign a list of words to a variable without quotes. This is the big difference between word splitting (tokenizing) and field splitting. An assignment must be a single word, so if it is to contain spaces, they have to be quoted. However, once the assignment is identified, the right-hand side is substituted without any field splitting or globbing.

```
case $var in
"*")
  echo "*";;
*" "*)
  echo "* *";;
*)
  echo "anything else";;
esac
```

The case statement has two interesting special cases, if you'll pardon the term. The control expression is not subject to field splitting or globbing. The pattern expressions are stranger still. Shell pattern characters in the patterns are obviously treated as pattern expressions (rather than globs) when unquoted. To get literals, you must quote them. However, other shell characters may need to be quoted; the quotes in *" "*) are needed, or the script becomes a syntax error. This is understandable if you think of the abstract form of the syntax:

```
case expression in
word) commands ;;
esac
```

All you have to do is remember that each test expression has to be a single shell word at tokenizing time; it is not subject to field splitting or to globbing.

Debugging Tools

This section is, of course, not very important. Your scripts will work on the first try because you are paying very careful attention to all the wonderful advice on how to write good code. Perhaps you even have flow charts. However, on the off chance that you might sometimes find a script's behavior a little surprising, a discussion of debugging tools is called for.

The shell's trace mode (-x) is fairly close to a debugging tool, but it is, unfortunately, fairly limited. All it can show you is actual simple commands as they are executed; control structures are not shown. The verbose flag (-v) shows the shell's input as it is read, but this doesn't show you the flow of control.

It is sometimes useful to display commands before executing them, but the usual mechanisms work only for simple commands or pipelines. If you have a variable containing a command, you can display it easily enough with echo "$*command*". However, you cannot necessarily execute it and get the results you expect. If you simply use the variable as a command line, any shell syntax characters or keywords will be ignored; if you pass it to eval, however, a whole new pass of shell substitutions and quoting takes effect, possibly changing the effect of the command. Each of these conditions may prevent you from using this technique generically, but in the majority of cases, it can be used.

To debug shell scripts, you must use a variety of tools, depending on the problem you are having. You can generally start with trace mode to see at least where in the script things are acting up. Once you have isolated the approximate location, inspection is often enough to reveal the bug. When it isn't, you will need to use additional code to figure out what the shell is doing. For instance, if you have a case statement, trace mode will not show you what branch it takes, but seeing the code executed may tell you what you need to know. If not, start by displaying the value you used to control the case statement right before executing it.

Sometimes, especially with a larger script, reproducing a problem can take a long time per run. You can copy chunks of code out of your script to see what is happening; for example, if you have a misbehaving case statement, first modify the script to display the control value, then copy the case statement into a temporary file and change the contents of the branches to display which branch is taken. The temporary file can be run as a miniature script.

When you are debugging a script, be aware of enhancements or local features a given shell provides. While you should stick to portable code for the final version, sometimes an extension can be extremely useful for debugging. For instance, bash offers special traps like DEBUG, which lets you run a trap before every shell command. This can be very useful for tracking a shell variable that is getting changed unexpectedly. The DEBUG trap is also available in ksh, but not in pdksh; in ksh93, it also sets the parameter ${.sh.command} to the command that is about to be executed.

In general, debugging in the shell is not all that different from debugging in any programming language, although the tools available are generally more primitive. For a really difficult bug, you may wish to look into the bashdb debugger, which works only with bash but offers a variety of useful debugging tools for interactive debugging of scripts. A similar debugger exists for ksh and was introduced (with source code) in *Learning the Korn Shell (2nd Edition)* by Bill Rosenblatt and Arnold Robbins (O'Reilly, 2002).

Focus on developing a way to reproduce the bug reliably, isolating it by removing irrelevant components, and you should be able to track the bug down.

What's Next?

Chapter 7 explores the portability of shell language constructs and introduces a few common extensions that you may find useful in more recent shells. It also discusses ways to identify which shell a script is running in, and possibly find a better shell if the shell you've been given isn't good enough for you.

CHAPTER 7

■■■

Shell Language Portability

So far, this book has mostly discussed the portable subset of shell languages, with an occasional warning that a useful technique may not always be portable. This chapter discusses shell portability in much greater detail, starting with more discussion on what portability is and how bugs and features differ. The next sections discuss some of the most common additional features and extensions, with brief notes on where you might find them. This includes substitution rules, redirections, and even additional syntax structures found in some shells. There is also a discussion of which features may be omitted for a stripped-down shell.

Following the discussion of extensions is a list of common shell variants, including ways to identify them and ways to invoke them to get behavior closer to the POSIX standard. Following this is a discussion of ways in which a script can configure itself for more complete shell functionality, whether by defining additional features as shell functions or by searching for a more powerful shell to execute itself with.

More on Portability

A portable program is one that runs correctly on any standard system. But what about nonstandard systems? What about buggy systems?

There is no perfect answer. When writing portable code, give some thought to what you are likely to run into. The autoconf maintainers recommend avoiding any features introduced more recently than V7 UNIX (1977). Most modern systems have a shell at least a little newer, although some famously continue to ship with a "traditional" Bourne shell. This advice may sound very drastic, but it is almost certainly the right choice for autoconf scripts because the entire purpose of autoconf is to be able to figure out what is wrong on your system and work around it. In that case, having a script fail on an old system would be exceptionally frustrating. If you are writing the installer for a set of 3D video drivers for X11, by contrast, you can probably make few more assumptions about your target platform.

Err on the side of caution. The assumption that Linux systems would always use bash as the primary shell probably seemed reasonable once, but Debian and Ubuntu desktop systems have switched to dash. Furthermore, many Linux programs have been run in emulation on BSD systems, where their installers get run using the BSD /bin/sh, usually an ash derivative.

Think about your use cases. A script that is going to be run by end users probably needs to simply work out of the box on their systems. A script that is used by developers and is expected to be installed and ported to a new system can be a little more flexible; it's enough that it is easy to make it run. For something that is used internally, it may be fine to need a few minutes to migrate a script to a new box. Even then, attention to portability makes your life easier; a few minutes is a lot easier to manage than a few days.

In theory, you are usually best off avoiding extensions. However, extensions may not always avoid you; you may have to port existing code that relies on them, or you may find that an extension changes the behavior of a program that was written without it. Likewise, while it would be nice to simply avoid prestandard or broken shells, sometimes you have no choice.

Standardization

Standardization offers a useful way to think about the shell portability question, as it does for most other portability questions. If you are not quite sure what to do, targeting the POSIX shell is a good first step. This gives you a good baseline that nearly any system can meet with only a little work. This may not be enough for some programs; for instance, it is not enough for autoconf and may be a poor choice for something like an installer. Dependencies beyond the POSIX spec are almost always a poor choice. While ksh, bash, and pdksh are quite common, they are not universal. If you are finding that the additional features in these shells are particularly crucial to a script, it may be a warning sign that you have gotten into an area where another programming language may be a better choice. While the shell can certainly be used as a general-purpose scripting language, it is probably not as good of a general-purpose scripting language as Perl, Python, or Ruby. One of the shell's core strengths is its universality; if you start relying on specific features of bash version 3 or ksh93, you have lost that universality.

Most systems provide at least one shell that is reasonably close to a POSIX shell, but it is not always /bin/sh. In some cases, the best POSIX-compliant shell on a system may be an optional component, so some users won't install it. Depending on your target audience, it may be perfectly adequate to declare such a shell to be a system requirement, and tell people where to get it for their particular target system.

Standardization of a programming language describes two sets of requirements. One is implementation requirements—a shell must meet these requirements to be considered compliant with the standard. The other is requirements of programs in the language—a program must meet these requirements in order to run reliably on implementations. It is often helpful to view a standard as a contract; a vendor claiming POSIX compliance for a shell is promising to run your code correctly if you write your code correctly, allowing you to refer to the standard to determine whether something is a bug or not.

The POSIX standard distinguishes between behavior required for conformance, behavior permitted in a conforming shell, and optional extensions. Support for $() command substitution is required; a shell that lacks this is not conformant. When running commands in a pipeline, a shell may run any or all of them in subshells; the standard allows for one of the commands to be run in the parent shell (as the Korn shell does) but does not require it. A program that relies on a particular decision about which commands are run in subshells is not portable among POSIX shells, but any answer a shell gives to that question is compliant with the POSIX standard.

POSIX explicitly blesses some extensions, warning that they may exist and have special behavior; for instance, POSIX reserves the [[token as having possible special meaning to the shell, even though it does not specify anything at all about the syntax or semantics of such a token. This allows ksh and bash to be considered compliant (at least on this issue) even though they provide an extra feature (see the section "Built-In Tests" later in this chapter).

Brace expansion (also described in this chapter in the section "Portability Issues: Welcome to the Club") actually violates the POSIX standard; it causes at least some well-formed shell programs to behave contrary to the standard, but the standard doesn't make any allowances for this. Many extensions are arguably standard violations, and shells that provide them may allow you to disable them. However, in portable code, you have to be aware of these extensions and avoid tripping on them.

Bugs

Previously, I've mostly ignored the topic of bugs. Bugs are not the same thing as lack of a standard feature; they are special cases where a particular feature misbehaves. Bugs are usually more narrowly defined. A shell that lacks $() command substitution simply lacks it all the time; any test program will confirm its absence. A bug often manifests only under particular circumstances, making it much harder to figure out what went wrong. For instance, one early shell (long since patched) omitted the last trailing slash of any command-line argument containing two trailing slashes. The shell doesn't lack the ability to pass slashes in arguments, or even pairs of slashes, and it doesn't truncate characters otherwise; it's just a special case. Finding this out and identifying the problem could be a real pain.

Unfortunately for shell programmers, obscure bugs are plentiful. The worst are mostly in systems that have mostly left commercial use, but there are plenty left floating around. The good news is that you will rarely encounter them, but there are plenty of special cases. Most bugs are specific to a particular version of a shell; a bug might exist in zsh 4.x, but not in zsh 3.x. While features are usually added but not removed in newer shells, bugs can come and go. The documentation for autoconf has a particularly large list of shell bugs, including a few you can probably safely ignore:

www.gnu.org/software/autoconf/manual/html_node/Portable-Shell.html

Portability Issues: Welcome to the Club

These portability issues are not unique to shell programming; C programmers have been living with a similar problem for a very long time. The ANSI/ISO C89 standard, released in 1989 (and again in 1990, which is a long story), offered substantial improvements to the language; and code written in "C89" offers substantial improvements for developers, compared with code written for previous language versions. However, many vendors continued to ship compilers that did not implement this language at all for a long time. The net result is a complicated tangle of portability rules, habits people have developed, urban legends, and more. A huge number of the tests generally performed by configure scripts have been essentially guaranteed to produce particular answers on many modern systems; indeed, most of the systems where they wouldn't work as expected never got Y2K upgrades.

When the ANSI/ISO C99 standard came out, I decided that I had probably had about enough of worrying about portability to pre-ANSI compilers. While it is true that they still exist, and some vendors still ship them, there is not much point in trying to deal with them; instead, if I even find myself on such a system, I'll get gcc and move on. This is practical for C code because I already know I'm going to have to compile it on a new target system. It is not as practical for shell code because it imposes an additional step of shell development that might not otherwise apply.

Common Extensions and Omissions

This section introduces features common enough that you should be aware of them, even if you don't plan to use them. They matter anyway because they may change the behavior of programs that were otherwise valid. Furthermore, you may find them useful enough to justify imposing some requirements on shells your code will run on. Some, like the additional POSIX parameter expansion features, are found in nearly all modern shells. Others are found only in a few shells, such as ksh, zsh, or bash.

Other Kinds of Expansion and Substitution

The parameter substitution and globbing rules shown so far are a minimal subset widely available even on fairly old shells. However, there are a number of additional options you might run into. This section introduces brace expansion, additional forms of parameter substitution common to POSIX shells, arithmetic substitution, and some additional globbing features.

Brace Expansion

Brace expansion is a variety of expansion introduced by csh, and later adopted by ksh, bash, and zsh. While brace expansion is primarily used with file names, it is not a form of file globbing. In brace expansion, lists of alternatives in braces are expanded into multiple words. The brace expression {a,b} expands into two words, a and b. When a brace expression occurs in part of a word, the whole word is duplicated for each of the resulting words: a{b,c} expands to ab ac.

At first look, brace expansion looks a lot like a form of globbing, but there are several significant differences between brace expansion and globbing. The first is that brace expansion generates all specified names, whether or not any of them exist as files:

```
$ ls a{b,c}
ls: cannot access ab: No such file or directory
ls: cannot access ac: No such file or directory
```

Pathname globbing produces names sorted in order; by contrast, brace expansion always generates names in the order they were given:

```
$ echo X{h,e,l,l,o}
Xh Xe Xl Xl Xo
```

Brace expansions can be nested, as well. Nesting works from the inside out; inner groups are expanded to create more words, then those words are used for the next level of expansion. The following two examples are equivalent:

```
$ echo a{b{c,d},e{f,g}}
abc abd aef aeg
$ echo a{bc,bd,ef,eg}
abc abd aef aeg
```

Brace expansion occurs after parameter substitution, but before globbing. In zsh, if brace expansion results in glob patterns, the shell displays an error message instead of executing a command if any of the glob patterns do not match any files.

Brace expansion does not occur within double quotes. In shells that provide brace expansion, it occurs prior to other forms of expansion; thus you will not see brace expansion on the results of parameter substitution or globbing. Brace expansion only occurs if you explicitly include braces in your code, making it easy to avoid being affected by it unintentionally.

Brace expansion is available in ksh93, pdksh, bash, and zsh. In pdksh, bash, and zsh, brace expansion can be disabled. In zsh and pdksh, brace expansion is disabled by default in POSIX mode. In bash, it must be disabled separately by set +B. In practice, it is very rare for brace expansion to break a script that otherwise works, but it is possible. Brace expansion is often used to generate a list of file names, leading many users to assume that it is part of globbing. However, brace expansion can be used for many other purposes in a script. While this feature is not portable enough to rely on, it is powerful and expressive, and it is good to be aware of it.

BRACE EXPANSION IN CSH

In csh, brace expansion is sort of part of file name globbing. If there are no regular pattern characters in any of the words generated by brace expansion, it behaves the same as it does in the other shells. However, if there are pattern characters in any of those words, and any of those words match any files through regular globbing, then only the glob results are generated; the globs that didn't match anything are discarded. If there are pattern characters, but they don't match anything, they are generated normally.

This behavior leads to a lot of surprises when habitual csh users try to use brace expansion in ksh or bash.

Additional Parameter Expansion Features

A number of additional parameter expansion forms are provided by POSIX shells (see Table 7-1). These are additional variants similar in syntax to the ${param:-word} forms discussed in Chapter 4.

Table 7-1. *A Few More Parameter Expansions*

Pattern	Description
${#*parameter* }	Length of *parameter*. (0 if null or unset.)
${*parameter*#*pattern*}	Substitute *parameter*, removing the shortest match of *pattern* from the beginning.
${*parameter*##*pattern*}	Substitute *parameter*, removing the longest match of *pattern* from the beginning.
${*parameter*%*pattern*}	Substitute *parameter*, removing the shortest match of *pattern* from the end.
${*parameter*%%*pattern*}	Substitute *parameter*, removing the longest match of *pattern* from the end.

The ${#parameter} construct expands to the length of $parameter. It is sometimes used in expressions like test ${#parameter} -gt 0, which is another way of spelling test -n "${parameter}". The advantage of ${#parameter} is that it can be used without nearly as much worry about quoting; it expands into a plain integer value (sometimes zero), which never requires quoting.

The four pattern-based substitution rules all use a half-anchored pattern. Normally, a shell pattern must match all of the text it is being compared with; it is anchored at both ends of the text. In these rules, however, the pattern can match part of the text. The shell substitutes, not the matching text, but whatever text did not match. These are easiest to illustrate by example:

```
$ file=/home/seebs/shell/example.txt
$ echo "${file%/*}"
/home/seebs/shell
$ echo "${file%%/*}"

$ echo "${file#*/}"
home/seebs/shell/example.txt
$ echo "${file##*/}"
example.txt
```

The shortest-match forms are an exception to the general rule that pattern matching always matches the longest string it can. Instead, they look for the shortest possible substring that matches the given pattern. So, in the first example, the shortest substring (at the end of the whole file name) matching the pattern /* is /example.txt. The shell can't match any shorter pattern because that is the first slash (counting from the end); it doesn't match a longer pattern because it doesn't have to.

The longest match forms behave more like normal pattern matching but are only anchored on one side. Because the string starts with a /, followed by other characters, the whole string is matched by /* when looking for the longest match.

The rules that match at the beginning behave much the same way. The shortest match of */ just removes the leading /; remember that a * matches anything at all, including an empty string (this is why ${file#*} just substitutes $file). The longest match is the full path, leaving the file name.

The reason these rules remove the match, rather than leaving it, is that shell patterns are sometimes a little weak on complicated expressions. It is often useful to be able to obtain the name of a file with a file name suffix removed, but it is very hard to write a shell pattern to express "everything but a file name suffix." For instance, in a build script, you might have a list of source files and want to identify the corresponding object files. You can replace the suffix easily:

```
$ file=hello.c
$ echo "${file%.c}".o
hello.o
```

As with other parameter substitution rules, the word on the right-hand side is itself subject to parameter substitution. If you want to know what a pattern matched, you can use two of these rules to find out:

```
$ file=/home/seebs/shell/example.txt
$ echo "${file%/*}"
/home/seebs/shell
$ echo "${file#${file%/*}}"
/example.txt
```

In this example, the pattern used is the substitution of ${file%/*}, or /home/seebs/shell. Removing this from the beginning of $file shows /example.txt, which is the exact pattern matched by the /* in the first substitution. This does not always work if the inner substitution yields pattern characters:

```
$ file=[0-9]/hello
$ echo "${file%/*}"
[0-9]
$ echo "${file#${file%/*}}"
[0-9]/hello
```

The shell interprets [0-9] as a pattern, not as a literal string, when substituting it on the right-hand side. However, you can prevent this using quoting:

```
$ file=[0-9]/hello
$ echo "${file%/*}"
[0-9]
$ echo "${file#"${file%/*}"}"
/hello
```

This latter behavior is documented in the POSIX standard, and pdksh, ksh93, and bash all do it; however, at least some ash derivatives ignore the quotes (for more information on quoting inside parameter substitution, see the detailed discussion in Chapter 6).

If you want the effect of this sort of substitution in a pre-POSIX shell, you can usually duplicate it using sed or expr. Remember that these utilities use regular expressions, not shell patterns. To strip the directory name off a file, you would use the regular expression .*/, not just */:

```
file=`expr "$file" : '.*/\(.*\)$'`
```

This feature is a significant performance advantage in general, although less so in shells that implement expr as a builtin. (If you are wondering why you shouldn't just use basename and dirname, the answer is that they are not as universally available as expr; see the discussion of utility portability in Chapter 8.)

Arithmetic Substitution

The POSIX spec provides for arithmetic substitution, using $((*expression*)). The shell evaluates *expression* and substitutes its result. This is substantially similar to $(expr *expression*), but there are three key differences. The first is that the syntax is different; arithmetic substitution does not need special shell syntax characters in *expression* quoted, but expr does. Furthermore, expr requires each operator to be a separate argument; arithmetic substitution can parse expressions where operators have not been separated out by spaces. The following examples are equivalent:

```
$ echo $(expr \( 3 + 1 \) \* 5 )
20
$ echo $(( (3+1)*5 ))
20
```

The parentheses and asterisk need to be quoted for expr but do not in an arithmetic substitution; similarly, arithmetic substitution doesn't need spaces around the operators. If (3+1)*5 were passed to expr as an argument, it would be interpreted as a string, and no arithmetic would be performed.

The second major difference is that the available operators vary widely. The length and : (regular expression match) operators of expr (see Chapter 2 for a discussion of regular expressions and expr; the length operator just yields the length of its argument) are not available; instead, all operations work on numeric values. However, arithmetic substitution provides many additional operators, such as bitwise operators. In expr, & and | are logical operators (similar to the && and || operators in the shell). In arithmetic substitution, they are bitwise operators:

```
$ echo $(( 1 | 2 ))
3
$ echo $(expr 1 \| 2)
1
```

In expr, the first operand of | is evaluated, and if it is neither zero nor an empty string, its value is the result of the expression; otherwise, the second operand is evaluated and is the result. So, 1 | 2 evaluates 1, finds out that it is not zero or an empty string, and results in that value. In arithmetic substitution, 1 | 2 is the bitwise union of the two numbers, so the result is 3.

Finally, the third difference is that the arithmetic substitution itself can (in most shells) assign values to shell variables. While idiomatically it is often clearer to write x=$((x+1)), you can also write $((x=x+1)). This feature is not available in some implementations of ash. Note that the final result is still substituted, so $((x=1)) expands to 1; if it is on a line by itself, the shell tries to find a program named 1 to run.

Arithmetic expressions have a number of shorthands. A variable name is implicitly expanded when encountered without a leading $. Thus $((x)) is the same as $(($x)). Shell arithmetic may be limited to a signed 32-bit value. However, many shells provide additional functionality; some shells support floating point operations in arithmetic substitution, or provide C-style increment (++) and decrement (--) operators.

In portable scripts (assuming you're willing to rely on arithmetic substitution at all), you can count on basic C-style integer math, including bitwise operations. Don't rely on assignment to variables, the increment or decrement operators, or floating-point math.

Even if you don't plan to use arithmetic substitution, you have to be aware of it if you are using $()-style command substitution and subshells. In shells that support arithmetic substitution, $((and)) are tokens. To be on the safe side (and to avoid possible bugs), separate parentheses when nesting them. This comes back to the maximal munch rule described in Chapter 4; when $((is a token, then $(($((foo)|bar) is a syntax error because there is no corresponding)) token.

Globbing Extensions

The ksh, zsh, and bash shells offer additional globbing options. These are not particularly portable to other shells. There are two major sets to consider. One is the pattern grouping operators, introduced originally in ksh. These are available in ksh and pdksh; they are available in bash if the extglob shell option has been set and in zsh if the KSH_GLOB option has been set. These operators all work on grouped sets of patterns, called *pattern lists*. A pattern list consists of one or more patterns; if there are multiple patterns, they are separated by pipes (|) as they would be in a case statement. A special character followed by a pattern list in parentheses becomes a special glob operator. There are five such operators, as shown in Table 7-2.

Table 7-2. *Extra KSH GLOB Operators*

Pattern	Description
@(*pattern-list*)	Exactly one of the patterns in *pattern-list*.
?(*pattern-list*)	Zero or one of the patterns in *pattern-list*.
*(*pattern-list*)	Zero or more of the patterns in *pattern-list*.
+(*pattern-list*)	One or more of the patterns in *pattern-list*.
!(*pattern-list*)	None of the patterns in *pattern-list*.

There are a number of additional variants possible in ksh93, but this subset is available in bash, pdksh, and zsh as well.

The @, ?, *, and + variants are reasonably intuitive if you have worked with regular expressions. The @ pattern operator functions a bit like a character class, only matching larger patterns. The pattern *.@(tar.gz|tar.bz2|tgz|tbz2) matches any file name ending in one of the four suggested suffixes, which are common names for compressed tar archives. Note that while the @ operator itself matches only one of the provided patterns, this pattern quite happily matches x.tgz.tbz2.tar.gz; the @ operator matches the trailing suffix, the period matches the period before that suffix, and the whole rest of the pattern matches the initial *. The @ operator is similar to a regular expression using \{1,1\}; it is used only to introduce the pattern list. The ?, *, and + operators perform the same function as their equivalents in an extended regular expression (although they come before the pattern list, rather than following it).

The ! operator can be a lot more confusing to use. The pattern *!(foo)* can still match a file name containing the word foo because the foo can match one of the asterisks. In fact, even the pattern !(foo) can match a file name containing the word foo, as long as the file name contains something else as well. To match any file name without the word foo in it, use !(*foo*). Getting used to the way in which the generally greedy behavior of pattern expressions mingles with a negation operator can take time. Similarly, the expression !(foo)?(bar) can match a file named foobar; the initial !(foo) matches the string foobar, and the ?(bar) matches zero repetitions of the pattern bar.

Another globbing feature is recursive expansion, available primarily in zsh. The Z shell recognizes a special pattern rule of (*word*/)# as matching zero or more subdirectories matching *word*. As a particular shorthand, **/ is equivalent to (*/)# and can match both anything in the current directory and anything in any subdirectory of the current directory (or their subdirectories; it's recursive). With the -G option, ksh93 also recognizes **/, and also recognizes ** as a shorthand for every file or directory in the current directory or its subdirectories. This feature is moderately dangerous; it can easily do surprising or unwanted things, and it is not especially portable. If you want to find files in subdirectories, look into the find command.

Alias Substitution

Aliases allow a command name to be replaced with some other command name or code. Unlike other kinds of substitution, aliases can result in shell control structures. (However, it is not remotely portable to try to alias shell reserved words.) An alias typically takes the following form:

alias *text=replacement*

In general, aliases should be valid command names. Aliases are never substituted when quoted. This can offer a workaround for concerns about aliases interfering with the behavior of a script, as the name "ls" (including the quotes) is not subject to alias substitution. However, it is subject to confusing anyone trying to read your code.

The behavior of aliases varies noticeably between shells, and not all shells provide this feature. I do not recommend relying on this except in cases where you are quite sure what shell will execute a given piece of code. Some shells allow arbitrarily complicated alias expressions, whereas others can alias only simple command names.

The real problem with aliases in scripts, however, is not the portability problem; it is the maintainability problem. Just as C code that relies heavily on preprocessor behavior can be extremely difficult to understand or debug, shell code that uses aliases often becomes unmaintainable quickly. The primary use of aliases in historical code has been developing shorthands or abbreviations for common tasks. Use shell functions instead.

Syntax Extensions

A few shells offer additional syntactic features that do not fit well in other categories. This section reviews three of particular and common interest: additional forms of redirection, support for arrays, and the [[*expr*]] syntax for built-in test functionality, similar to the test program.

Redirections

There are a handful of additional redirection syntax features available in some shells. Both ksh and bash offer a rich selection of additional redirections. There are a few features unique to ksh93 and others found also in pdksh.

The >|*file* redirection operator opens and truncates *file*. This is the normal behavior for > redirection. However, in ksh and bash, the shell option noclobber prevents redirecting to existing files; this redirection overrides that option.

The bash-only <<<*word* operator operates a little like a here document, but instead of sending following lines of the shell script to a command as standard input, it expands *word* and uses that as the command's standard input. So, cat <<<$foo is similar to echo $foo. This is useful for commands that need only a small amount of input directed to them.

Another bash extension is the >&*N*- redirection operator (and the corresponding <&*N*-). These operators move one file descriptor to another, closing the original. The shell command exec 3>&2- is equivalent to running first exec 3>&2, then exec 2>&-.

Both bash and ksh support the <> operator, which opens a file for both reading and writing. If no descriptor number is provided, <> opens a file as standard input.

The final three operators are found only in ksh. The first is the coprocess operator (|&), which opens a special process in the background. This is only sort of a redirection; it is in some ways more like a command separator, and it occupies the same basic function as a pipe. When a program is run with |& as a redirection, the program is run in the background, with input and output attached to a special file descriptor maintained by the shell. You can write data to the coprocess by running commands >&p and read by running commands <&p. The coprocess continues until it exits, but you can close its input stream (which will typically cause most filter programs to exit) by redirecting its input stream to another file descriptor, and then closing it, as in the following code:

```
exec 3>&p
exec 3>&-
```

The first line duplicates the coprocess's input to file descriptor 3, and the second closes it. (Remember that the shell's output to the coprocess is the coprocess's input.)

The coprocess feature is moderately difficult to duplicate in any other shell; it may not be practical to rework a program that depends on it, so avoid depending on this feature in portable scripts.

Finally, ksh93 provides two additional redirection forms that are available only on systems that provide the /dev/fd directory containing special files that represent the standard file descriptors (so /dev/fd/2 is standard error). On these systems, you can specify input to, or output from, a command as though it were a file argument using the syntax <(*list*) to refer to the output of *list*, and >(*list*) to refer to its input. The shell runs the command in the background, with its output connected to a particular file descriptor; then the shell provides the name of that file descriptor's special file as an argument to a command. This is only useful with programs that expect their arguments to be file names:

```
$ echo <(ls)
/dev/fd/4
```

All of these redirection options are a bit specialized, and I do not recommend relying on any of them in portable scripts. Still, forewarned is forearmed. I have often wished that the coprocess feature had made it into the POSIX shell; it is one of the most persuasive arguments for writing a script that requires ksh.

Arrays

One of the most significant weaknesses of the shell as a general programming language is the lack of arrays. Arrays are available in ksh, zsh, and bash. All shells that support arrays support integer array subscripts. Additionally, zsh and ksh93 support associative arrays, which use text keys rather than integer values. Array subscripts (for regular arrays) are treated as arithmetic expressions, according to the rules described previously for arithmetic substitution. The number of elements in an array may be limited; pdksh restricts array subscripts to the range 0–1023.

In general, arrays are created either using the set command or by direct assignment. The expression x=(a b c) creates x as an array variable holding three values: ${x[0]} is a, ${x[1]} is b, and ${x[2]} is c. (In zsh, the indexes start at 1 unless the KSH_ARRAYS option has been set.)

In ksh93 and zsh, associative arrays are declared using the typeset -A command:

```
typeset -A foo
foo[a]=hello,
foo[b]=world
echo ${foo[a]} ${foo[b]}
```

```
hello, world
```

The associative array feature is probably familiar to programmers who have worked in just about any modern language; it first became commonly known to UNIX users through the awk utility.

Arrays are not portable to most shells. In practice, portable shell scripts must use the positional parameters as an array or engage in elaborate constructions using eval to create variable names dynamically (see the examples in Chapter 5). If you only need one array, it is fairly practical to use the positional parameters as that array (although, if you need more than nine items, you will have to get clever in traditional shells). If you need more than one, you can store long strings using delimiter characters (typically colons or spaces), then use the set command to extract them into an array. If your delimiter character is spaces, this is easy; the following code extracts the members of an array into the positional parameters:

```
set -- $array
```

Similarly, you can store the positional parameters into a variable using $*:

```
array=$*
```

If you need to use a different delimiter, you have to set (and restore) $IFS:

```
save_IFS=$IFS
IFS=:
set -- $array
IFS=$save_IFS
```

When substituted, $* delimits the positional parameters with the first character of $IFS, providing symmetry. Remember that there is no field splitting in assignment; you do not need to quote $* to assign from it.

Another array-handling option is to switch to m4sh, which gives you some limited "compile-time" array functionality; you can use m4 arrays to develop scripts that act somewhat as though the shell had arrays. Finally, depending on the data you need to work with, you may be able to use a temporary file and a tool like awk or sed to extract and modify values. This is pretty high overhead, though; I prefer to just use eval.

Built-In Tests

The ksh, bash, and zsh shells support a more flexible conditional test expression using double brackets. This is somewhat different syntactically from the [synonym for the test command, much as arithmetic substitution differs from expr. The syntax is [[*expression*]], and the rules for evaluating *expression* are somewhat simpler than the rules for the test utility. As with arithmetic substitution, *expression* is not subject to some of the normal shell features, such as field splitting. The exact set of tests supported varies somewhat from one shell to another, but in general this form handles most of the same expressions as the test program. As an additional feature, the shell recognizes && and || operators in these expressions (although some shells do not recognize -a and -o in these expressions).

Of particular note is that all three shells recognize file names of the form /dev/fd/N as referring to file descriptor N while processing these expressions. Thus even if the special /dev/fd files do not exist on a particular system, [[-t /dev/fd/0]] succeeds if standard input is considered to be a terminal device.

Unlike the regular test program (whether it is implemented as a builtin or not), the [[*expression*]] form does not recognize operators that were quoted, and operators are never optional. This eliminates the two common problems that require special treatment of values in conditional expressions; there is never any ambiguity over what is, or is not, an operator, so tricks like prefixing values with X are unneeded.

The [[*expression*]] syntax is not described by POSIX, although POSIX does reserve the [[and]] tokens as potentially having special meaning to the shell.

The select Loop

One of the really interesting features introduced in ksh is the select loop, which allows the user to pick an item from a list in an unambiguous manner:

```
echo "Where would you like to go for your vacation?"
select answer in Oz Detroit
do
  echo $answer
  break
done
```

The output of this script in ksh looks like this:

```
$ ksh vacation
Where would you like to go for your vacation?
1) Oz
2) Detroit
#? 1
Oz
$
```

This can be used to select items from lists. As with a for loop, parameter substitution or command substitution on the list is subject to field splitting, so you can build a list and then let the user pick a word from it. This feature is available in ksh, bash, and zsh; it is not present in ash, however, and is not in the POSIX standard.

The select control structure loops until the loop is explicitly terminated. Because select is implemented as a control structure, a script using it is always a syntax error in another shell. However, you can come surprisingly close; a detailed discussion of this is included at the end of this chapter in the section "Emulating Features."

Common Omissions

It is not always obvious what ought to count as a standard feature that has been omitted and what ought to count as an extension that has not been provided. The pattern-matching parameter substitution forms previously listed are defined by POSIX but are a little more esoteric than more basic features, such as the use of ! to negate the exit status of a command.

Stripped-down shells usually start by omitting interactive features (such as command history, expansion of parameters in prompts, and so on). Some shells omitted shell functions in the distant past, but no one's seen a shell without shell functions in years.

Another common way to strip a shell down is to omit built-in commands. As long as the commands also exist as separate programs, this may hurt performance slightly but has no other impact. However, some shells omit builtins that cannot be run as external commands, such as getopts. (In fact, every modern POSIX-like system seems to have this, with the obvious caveat that the default shell on Solaris is still pre-POSIX.)

In general, the biggest impact of a stripped-down system will be in utility programs, rather than in the core shell language itself. For instance, many embedded systems lack sed, awk, or the printf utility. Utility portability issues are discussed at greater length in Chapter 8.

Common Shells and Their Features

This section introduces some of the most common shells you are likely to encounter, giving a brief overview for each of where it fits in the shell family tree, what sorts of features it has or lacks, and how to invoke it for maximal POSIX compliance if you need that. These shells are introduced in alphabetical order by name; for example, dash is under the section "Debian Almquist Shell." Shells specific to a given system are prefixed with the system's name, as in the "Solaris /usr/xpg4/bin/sh" section.

You can sometimes guess which shell you are in by checking the value of $SHELL, but this is useless in determining which shell has been used as /bin/sh.

Almquist Shell

The Almquist shell (ash)) was developed by Kenneth Almquist as a compatible replacement for the Bourne shell shipped with SVR4 UNIX, plus POSIX features. Modern variants are POSIX-compliant by default. You can also find ash on many other systems; a variant of it is included in busybox, and it is also used in Cygwin and Minix. This is also the ancestor of the Debian ash (called dash), described in the "Debian Almquist Shell" section later in this chapter. The big strength of ash is that it is small, reasonably efficient, and fast. Some versions of ash are a little light on features like command-line editing, variable expansion in prompts, and other interactive features, but it is fine for scripting.

How to Identify

There is no simple way to figure out that you are running under ash. There is no standard predefined magic variable provided by the shell. Because ash is often used as /bin/sh, you can't check the shell's name, either. Luckily, there are relatively few version-specific quirks. The closest way I have found to identify ash is to check for everything else. If a shell is not a variety of ksh, bash, or zsh and does not seem to be a pre-POSIX shell, it may very well be ash.

Version Information

There is no formal numbering of ash versions. The initial release was in 1989, and since then ash has been in continuous development on the various BSD systems. Particular versions have been extracted from NetBSD (most often) and imported into Linux or other systems, but there are not usually version strings to identify them.

Major Compatibility Notes

There are two major bugs in early versions of ash that could affect portability, both involving command substitution. Probably the most significant is that in older versions of ash, command substitution of a single built-in command does not spawn a subshell, so the built-in command can modify the parent shell's environment. The other is that command substitution inside variable expansion did not work in one of the early versions migrated to Linux systems; ${FOO=`echo hello`} did not work as expected.

Getting POSIX Behavior

Conveniently simple, ash is by design a fairly closely matched POSIX shell. Very early versions were missing a few features, but the versions being distributed today are unlikely to hold many surprises.

Bourne-Again Shell

The GNU Bourne-again shell is probably one of the largest and most feature-filled variants. It has been in development since 1987. Unlike most of the other shells described as Bourne shell derivatives, bash incorporates a couple of features from csh. There are a lot of similarities between the extensions in bash and the extensions in ksh.

How to Identify

Check the environment variable $BASH_VERSION. This variable is set even when the shell is running in POSIX mode and contains the version number of the current shell.

Version Information

Early versions of bash (1.x) had a number of surprising behaviors that are mostly gone now. The 2.x and later versions use a new syntax for the output of set; older versions of bash, and other shells, may not be able to read this output. Finally, the 3.x versions introduced the support needed for the bash debugger; this is not available for older versions.

Major Compatibility Notes

Early versions of bash provided !-style history expansion, as used in csh. This only affects interactive use but is a major surprise in that it is one of the only cases where something inside single quotes can be expanded. In modern versions, this feature must be explicitly enabled. Also, bash introduces source as a synonym for the . command. In most cases, the compatibility problem is not that bash cannot run scripts written for other shells, but that other shells cannot run scripts written for bash. The bash shell provides a broad variety of builtins, often with extensions and added features, and the same caveats apply to these. The general caveats of modern POSIX-like shells, such as arithmetic substitution, apply to bash as well.

Getting POSIX Behavior

To force POSIX behavior, invoke bash with the --posix option or run set -o posix in the shell. The environment variable $POSIXLY_CORRECT also forces this behavior when set; setting it during the operation of a script takes effect immediately. Finally, if the bash program has the name sh, it goes into POSIX mode once it has read its startup files. You must also separately disable brace expansion (set +B) if you want better conformance; the feature is left on because it is very rare for a script that does not intend to use it to get affected accidentally.

Debian Almquist Shell

The Debian branch of the Almquist shell is an import of ash to use as a standard system shell. It was adopted because it is smaller and faster than bash and also with an eye to reducing the tendency for Linux scripts to be unportable to other UNIX-like systems. It was ported to Linux in 1997 by Herbert Xu and renamed to dash in 2002. It first showed up as /bin/sh on desktop Ubuntu around version 6.10, and is expected to be /bin/sh in Debian Lenny (frozen, but not shipped, as of this writing).

How to Identify

As with other ash variants, there is no obvious way to tell that you are running in dash. For instance, on a modern desktop Ubuntu system, /bin/sh is a symlink to /etc/alternatives/sh, which is a symlink to the selected shell, usually /bin/dash by default.

Version Information

On a desktop system, the package management system will usually have a version number available:

```
$ dpkg -l | grep dash
ii  dash                    0.5.4-8ubuntu1      POSIX-compliant shell
```

The exact way to extract this information varies from one system to another. However, the version number here does not necessarily correlate to a particular version of the ash shell. In general, a system providing dash provides a version modern enough to ignore the historical early quirks and lets you just write for the POSIX shell spec.

Major Compatibility Notes

There are no major surprises with dash, but be aware that many scripts on Linux systems may behave surprisingly in a non-bash shell. As a result, you may find that a system administrator has changed the default shell back to bash, so you have to watch out for bash extensions even if you think the shell should be dash.

Getting POSIX Behavior

As with ash, POSIX behavior is the default.

Korn Shell

The Korn shell was developed at Bell Labs by David Korn. It has been in use internally in various forms since 1982. An early version from 1986 has been distributed some, but widespread external use started with the 1988 releases. A variant of ksh was around in SVR4, and many System V–derived commercial UNIX systems have provided it. The current versions are available under an open source license, but earlier versions were not.

How to Identify

There is no simple way to identify whether you are in ksh, let alone what version. In ksh93, the special shell parameter ${.sh.version} contains the shell's version string; in ksh93t (June 2008) and later, this can also be accessed as $KSH_VERSION. Some systems provide a utility called what for identifying the versions of commands:

```
$ what $(which ksh93)
/usr/pkg/bin/ksh93
        [. . .]
        $Id: Version M 1993-12-28 q $
```

At a prompt, if you set the shell for its emacs-style command-line editing mode (set -o emacs), typing Ctrl-V displays the version information.

If you are willing to do some extra work, you can detect ksh by testing for the select control structure and then excluding other shells that offer simpler tests. The following script determines whether a shell has the select primitive and runs the last command of a pipeline in the parent shell:

```
eval "echo 1 | select no_select in false; do break; done" > /dev/null 2>&1
if $no_select; then
  echo "no select"
else
  echo "select"
fi
```

This script incorrectly indicates that there is no select control structure in pdksh or bash (because they run the select in a subshell). However, you can check for them using $KSH_VERSION and $BASH_VERSION, respectively. This script detects the select structure in zsh, ksh88, and ksh93; if this test determines that select is available, you can check $ZSH_VERSION to determine whether or not you are in zsh, and if you are not, you must be in some variety of ksh.

You cannot simply check ${.sh.version} because the invalid (for any other shell) parameter name causes a script to abort. Even eval is not enough to protect you from this in some shells, but a subshell can come to the rescue:

```
if ( test -n "${.sh.version}" ) 2>/dev/null ; then
  echo "ksh93"
else
  echo "not ksh93"
fi
```

You have to use a subshell here; ksh88, ash, and traditional sh all abort when trying to expand that variable.

Version Information

There are three major revisions of ksh: ksh86, ksh88, and ksh93. You are unlikely to encounter ksh86 in the wild. The ksh88 version is still used in some commercial UNIX systems as an implementation of the POSIX shell. There are a number of new features in ksh93, such as associative arrays and floating-point arithmetic, as well as a variable namespace feature using parameter names containing periods. Brace expansion is found in ksh93, but not in ksh88.

Major Compatibility Notes

The only compatibility problems you are likely to encounter with ksh are with scripts that happen to match some of the ksh syntax extensions. Brace and tilde expansion are both performed by ksh93; ksh88 performs tilde expansion, but not brace expansion.

Unlike most other shells (including pdksh), ksh runs the last command of a pipeline that runs in the parent shell; in ksh, echo hello | read greeting sets $greeting in the shell. This rarely breaks programs that were not expecting it, but it can be a source of portability problems if you rely on it.

Getting POSIX Behavior

There is no switch to make ksh behave more like a POSIX shell than it usually does. However, its features are mostly extensions, and all of the modern POSIX features are available by default. A POSIX script will, with rare exceptions, execute without difficulty in ksh.

Public Domain Korn Shell

The public domain Korn shell is a clone of ksh. It was written because ksh was not open source, and many systems lacked a POSIX shell. Since then, ksh has become open source, POSIX shells have become much more common, and bash has become much better for scripting. However, pdksh is still found on a number of systems. There are a few features in pdksh not found in ksh88 or ksh93, and pdksh has acquired some of the new ksh93 features.

How to Identify

The special shell parameter $KSH_VERSION contains the version information of the shell. Most versions of ksh do not, but ksh93t (June 2008) adds $KSH_VERSION as a synonym for ${.sh.version}.

Version Information

Every installation of pdksh I've seen over the last fifteen years has been version 5.2.14. The mainline ksh shell became more widely available, and pdksh hasn't been substantially upgraded since 2001. While it has some quirks, pdksh is stable.

Major Compatibility Notes

Unlike ksh, pdksh runs the last command of a pipeline in a subshell. There are other subtle differences between ksh and pdksh, described in the pdksh documentation, but most scripts written for ksh88 will run in pdksh.

Getting POSIX Behavior

Like bash, pdksh supports a POSIX mode in which it deviates from ksh behavior in favor of the POSIX specification; this can be controlled through set -o posix or the $POSIXLY_CORRECT environment variable.

Solaris /usr/xpg4/bin/sh

The /usr/xpg4/bin/sh program, when it has been installed, is a ksh88 shell modified a little to be a bit more like a POSIX shell. The name comes from the *X/Open Portability Guide*, Issue 4 (X/Open Company, 1992), which is one of the precursors to modern UNIX standards.

How to Identify

As with other ksh88 shells, there is no way to identify this shell from within a script (but see the previous "Korn Shell" section for some workarounds).

Version Information

This is a late, fairly well bug-fixed ksh88. It does not come in multiple versions.

Major Compatibility Notes

The only compatibility problems you are likely to encounter with this ksh variant are with scripts that happen to match some of the ksh syntax extensions. Being based on ksh88, this shell does not have brace expansion. Unlike most other shells (including pdksh), ksh runs the last command of a pipeline that runs in the parent shell; in ksh, echo hello | read greeting sets $greeting in the shell. This rarely breaks programs that were not expecting it, but it can be a source of portability problems if you rely on it.

Getting POSIX Behavior

This shell is already configured to offer POSIX shell functionality. It has no configuration choices to change this.

SVR2 Bourne Shell

The SVR2 Bourne shell, or derivatives of it, are the oldest shells I know of that are still in use today. Specifically, the Tru64 UNIX shell is an SVR2 derivative. (The documentation claims it is an SVR3.2 shell, but it has characteristic behaviors of older shells.)

How to Identify

The SVR2 Bourne shell is the only shell I am aware of in which the historical behavior survives of expanding "$@" to an empty quoted string when there are no parameters. It also lacks the getopts builtin. The following code identifies a shell with the old "$@" behavior:

```
( set dummy; shift; set dummy "$@"; shift; echo $# )
```

In an SVR3 or later shell, this should consistently print 0; in the SVR2 shell, it prints 1.

Version Information

There were a couple of variants of this, but most are now gone. The 8th Edition UNIX shell was a derivative, but it added modern "$@".

Major Compatibility Notes

In theory, the SVR2 Bourne shell wipes out the positional parameters when calling a shell function. However, the only known living version of this shell includes the SVR3 fix for this bug, and the positional parameters are restored after calling a shell function. This is the only shell lacking getopts or modern "$@" semantics.

This shell lacks the ! modifier to invert the status of a command, and it recognizes ^ as a synonym for | as a command separator. See also "Major Compatibility Notes" under the "SVR4 Bourne Shell" section; this shell has all of the quirks of the later shell.

Getting POSIX Behavior

You can't, but you can look for another shell on the system. A Korn shell is available on most variants. If you need to target this system, you may want to use an execution preamble to switch to that.

SVR4 Bourne Shell

The SVR4 Bourne shell program is extraordinarily stable, offering essentially a stable feature set since 1988, with occasional bug fixes or small updates in some systems. It is not a POSIX shell. For most modern users, this is the only non-POSIX shell you will find in regular use. This is the shell used by Solaris and Irix systems as /bin/sh.

How to Identify

While the SVR4 shell has no direct identifying cues as to its version, you can detect that you are probably running in it by running eval "! false" and checking $?. Most other shells will consider this to succeed, yielding 0; the SVR4 shell reports failure because there is no command named !.

Version Information

The SVR4 shell has only minor bug fixes and enhancements between the original SVR4 releases and the current version. The shell's version is determined by the system version; use uname to find that.

Major Compatibility Notes

This shell is included in Solaris and Irix, even today, and that is the reason to worry about the portability of POSIX-specified features. While there are other systems with pre-POSIX shells installed, these are by far the most common. Many systems seem to have migrated to the POSIX shell sometime in the last ten years or so, but these vendors have stayed with the old one for compatibility with older scripts, some of which might have their semantics changed by an update.

The SVR4 shell lacks the ! modifier used to reverse the return status of a command. It cannot access positional variables past $9; ${10} is an invalid construct in it. It supports backtick command substitution, but not $() command substitution. In the SVR4 shell, ^ is equivalent to a pipe on the command line; it must be quoted to be used in normal words or arguments to other commands.

The SVR4 shell provides getopts, unset, and modern "$@" behavior. (In fact, these were all introduced in SVR3 or so.)

A particular surprise is that, while set -- *args* sets the positional parameters, set -- does not clear them.

Getting POSIX Behavior

You can't; if you need POSIX behavior, you have to use another shell. Luckily, Solaris ships with several shells. Some of them are optional, but zsh appears to be installed by default on every remotely recent system and can be used as a POSIX shell. See the following section, "Execution Preambles," for information about getting into a more modern shell.

Traditional Shell

The V7 shell (the shell of 7th Edition UNIX) is generally regarded as the starting point of the modern Bourne shell. It can be identified as much by what it lacks as by what it provides. In practice, every shell has since evolved, but it is worth considering this shell simply for contrast. Table 7-3 gives a brief overview of major features that were not found in the V7 shell and when they were added.

Table 7-3. *Shell Features and Their Arrival*

Feature	First Available	Notes
Functions	SVR2	Shell functions did not support local positional parameters at first.
unset	SVR2	Not always found on small or specialized shells.
Function arguments	SVR3	Positional parameters can be used safely after a function call.
getopts	SVR3	Replaces the getopt utility.
8-bit support	SVR3	Previous shells used 8th bit for quoting information.
Symbolic signal names	SVR4	Previous shells allowed only numeric signal numbers.

Z Shell

The Z shell is an interesting offshoot or variant; it has been around for a long time, but by default is noticeably incompatible with the Bourne shell derivatives. However, it is also extremely configurable. Just as bash can emulate a POSIX shell, zsh can do a pretty good job of emulating ksh88 or a POSIX shell. This is important for portable code because zsh may be the closest thing to a POSIX shell available on some systems. The Z shell has been in development since 1990.

How to Identify

The special shell parameter $ZSH_VERSION indicates the version of zsh being run.

Version Information

You will rarely see versions prior to the 3.x version series in the wild. 4.x is more common now, and 4.2 is considered stable as of this writing.

Major Compatibility Notes

The most surprising change for users is that variable expansions are not subject to field splitting in zsh. The Z shell documentation describes this as a bug in other shells. (They are not alone in this view; Plan 9's rc shell went the same way.) You can override this behavior by setting the shell compatibility option or explicitly with setopt shwordsplit. There is an important exception: "$@" works as expected.

However, when emulating plain sh, zsh performs too much word splitting on the common idiom ${1+"$@"}. You can work around this using zsh's fairly powerful aliasing feature:

```
alias -g '${1+"$@"}'='"$@"'
```

It may be simpler to use "$@" without qualification; it works even on nearly all traditional shells still in use today.

Getting POSIX Behavior

In modern zsh, you can issue the command emulate sh or emulate ksh to set the shell into an emulation mode, primarily useful for running scripts. If zsh is invoked with the name sh or ksh, it automatically uses the corresponding emulation mode. (There is also a csh emulation mode, but it is of no use for POSIX shell scripting.)

Execution Preambles

Portable shell scripts face the common problem that sometimes a crucial feature is not available in a given shell. In some cases, the feature is important enough to justify going to some lengths to obtain a more standard shell environment. Sometimes, the goal is just to have predictable behavior. The configure scripts generated by autoconf use a great deal of startup code to ensure predictable behavior across a broad range of platforms. The following sample illustrates code to do this for a few shells:

```
# Be Bourne compatible
if test -n "${ZSH_VERSION+set}" && (emulate sh) >/dev/null 2>&1; then
  emulate sh
  NULLCMD=:
  # Zsh 3.x and 4.x performs word splitting on ${1+"$@"}, which
  # is contrary to our usage.  Disable this feature.
  alias -g '${1+"$@"}'='"$@"'
elif test -n "${BASH_VERSION+set}" && (set -o posix) >/dev/null 2>&1; then
  set -o posix
fi
DUALCASE=1; export DUALCASE # for MKS sh
```

This preamble causes three common shells (zsh, bash, and the MKS Toolkit sh used on some Windows systems) to behave more like a standard POSIX shell than they otherwise might.

There are three primary things you can do with an execution preamble. The first is simply to set shell options or variables that you use later in a script to simplify your code. The second is to feed the script into a shell that has a particular feature you need. Finally, the third option is to actually modify the script before executing it (whether through the same shell or a different one). This section discusses the general principles of developing and using execution preambles. For more information, look into the m4sh utility, which is used to build more portable shell scripts. As an m4sh script, the preceding sample preamble code (and a great deal more) would be written as follows:

```
AS_SHELL_SANITIZE
$as_unset CDPATH
```

This provides a fairly predictable and standardized environment, with a number of utility features and functions defined in a fairly portable way. While m4sh scripts are somewhat different from conventional shell scripts, they are extremely good at running in a variety of outright hostile environments. If you need bulletproofing, this may be the way to go.

Setting Options and Variables

In many cases, merely tweaking a couple of shell options will get you behavior that is standard enough to be useful. The "Common Shells and Their Features" section covers some of these. Another technique is to use variables to hold command option flags, command names, or other values that vary from one system to another. If a command is available only on some machines, and possibly optional on others, you can use a variable to hold the command's name. A historic example of this is the use of a RANLIB variable in makefiles. On some systems, the ranlib utility had to be run on archives; on other systems, it was not only unnecessary but unavailable. The solution is to store the name of the utility to run after creating an archive in a variable. You can do this in shell scripts, too:

```
save_IFS=$IFS
IFS=:
ranlib=:
for dir in $PATH; do
  if test -x "$dir"/ranlib; then
    ranlib="$dir"/ranlib
    break
  fi
done
IFS=$save_IFS
$ranlib archive
```

If there is a ranlib utility in the user's path, it is identified by the loop and stored in the $ranlib variable. The quotes around $dir are there because someone's path could contain directories containing spaces. If there is no ranlib utility available, the script continues anyway, running the : command (which ignores its arguments). Using variables to hold command names can simplify a lot of shell development.

This technique only works for commands, not for shell syntax. Some shells provide better semantics for shell functions when they are declared as function name() { . . . } rather than just as name() { . . . }. However, you cannot set a variable to expand to function and use it in this context because function is a keyword to those shells, and the result of substitution is not a keyword.

You can also use similar techniques to hold particular command-line arguments or other values that affect the behavior of a program. Imagine that you want to display a line of text without a trailing new line; there is no consistently portable way to do this, unfortunately (the flaws with echo are discussed in more detail in Chapter 8, which discusses utility portability). However, there are two very common ways to deal with this problem, and a script can test whether either of them is available:

```
case `echo -n "\c"` in
-n*c) func_echo_n() { echo "$@"; } ;;
*c) func_echo_n() { echo -n "$@"; } ;;
*) func_echo_n() { echo "$@\c"; } ;;
```

```
esac
func_echo_n Testing...
echo "Ok."
```

```
Testing...Ok.
```

This script defines a function called func_echo_n that will echo without a trailing new line if either of the common mechanisms works. (If neither does, the script just displays its output with a new line.) System V systems often supported a \c suffix to do this, while BSD systems tended to recognize the -n flag. If neither works, the output of the trial command begins with -n and ends with a c. If the output ends with a c but did not begin with -n, then the -n flag is accepted and presumably works. If the output does not end with a c, then the \c worked. This does not guarantee success, but it does prevent printing extraneous output; in the worst case, there will be new lines but no stray -n or \c strings floating around. (Outside of embedded systems, though, you should probably just use printf.)

Picking a Better Shell

Sometimes access to a particular feature is sufficiently crucial to make it necessary to run a script in a shell that provides it. Some of the POSIX features are extremely useful in shell programming, and it is quite possible to be surprised when you find yourself compelled to add support for a target you were sure was never going to come up.

One workaround is to find a shell providing the needed features and ensure that your script is always run in that shell. For a script full of bash-isms, the following preamble ensures execution in bash or warns the user as to what has gone wrong:

```
if test -z "$BASH_VERSION"; then
  save_IFS=$IFS
  IFS=:
  for dir in /bin /usr/bin /usr/local/bin /usr/pkg/bin /sw/bin $PATH; do
    bash="$dir/bash"
    if test -x "$bash" && test -n `"$bash" -c 'echo $BASH_VERSION'`
    2>/dev/null; then
      IFS=$save_IFS
      exec "$bash" "$0" "$@"
    fi
  done
  echo >&2 "Help!  I must be executed in bash."
  exit 1
fi
echo $BASH_VERSION
```

This preamble searches $PATH for a bash shell, and it exits if it cannot find one. A few points are of interest. One is the use of a common set of likely directories to search before $PATH, in case the user has an ill-considered search path. The test running bash to ensure it

is something that produces output when asked to expand $BASH_VERSION is in single quotes
because, if it used double quotes, it would require an unusually large number of backslashes.
The expansion has to be done in the target shell, so the command to pass to it should be
"echo \$BASH_VERSION". However, this quoted string occurs inside backticks, and the shell's
initial scan of the command substitution also consumes backslashes (which it doesn't inside
single quotes). So, to pass \$ to the bash called by the subshell, you would have to write \\\$:

```
if test -x "$bash" && test -n `"$bash" -c "echo \\\$BASH_VERSION"` 2>/dev/null; then
```

This is a great example of a case where selecting the right quoting mechanism makes your
life easier.

It is possible to base this kind of testing on a feature test, as well. For instance, if you are
fairly confident that the only target system you have with a pre-POSIX shell is Solaris, the following preamble gets you a fairly good POSIX shell:

```
if eval "! false" > /dev/null; then
  true
else
  exec /usr/bin/zsh "$0" "$@"
fi
if test -n "$ZSH_VERSION"; then
  emulate sh
  NULLCMD=:
fi
```

If the shell executing this does not know about the ! command prefix, the eval operation
fails, and the else branch is taken, executing the script with zsh (which supports that syntax).

The second test causes zsh to run in its standard shell mode, which is usually a good
choice for a script (and has no effect in other shells). There is a lot more you can do for an
execution preamble, but a simple preamble like this may be enough to get your script running
quickly on the targets you need it on. The combination of switching to a different shell, and
then configuring that shell to behave the way you want it to, is quite powerful. If you are thinking about more than one possible system, of course, the preamble gets longer. You would want
to search for multiple shells, not just zsh, and search a reasonable path. Because every step of
this is a new opportunity to make mistakes, you should probably not write an execution preamble much longer than the previous example; if you need more, this is where tools like m4sh
become really useful. As with most tools, using an existing tool is generally better than writing
your own. In particular, since much of the benefit of shell programming is ease of development, if you start getting bogged down in details someone else has already slogged through,
you are probably not getting a good return on your time.

Self-Modifying Code

If the feature you need is simple enough, it may be possible to emulate it in the current shell.
The standard configure scripts generated by autoconf use this technique to emulate the special shell variable $LINENO in shells that don't provide it. Doing this correctly is fairly hard,
and doing it portably requires a great deal of attention to additional special cases; if you write
a sed script, and one of the systems you need to run on has a buggy sed, you haven't gained
anything.

Don't be too hasty to use this; it has very limited applicability for most cases, and in general, you are better off with a generic execution preamble. Still, it is an option worth considering. The following fragment of the configure script shows how $LINENO can be replaced. (This is a small fraction of the code involved, dealing only with the actual substitution.)

```
sed '=' <$as_myself |
  sed '
    N
    s,$,-,
    : loop
    s,^\(['$as_cr_digits']*\)\(.*\)[$]LINENO\([^'$as_cr_alnum'_]\),\1\2\1\3,
    t loop
    s,-$,,
    s,^['$as_cr_digits']*\n,,
  ' >$as_me.lineno &&
chmod +x $as_me.lineno ||
  { echo "$as_me: error: cannot create $as_me.lineno; rerun with a POSIX shell
" >&2
  { (exit 1); exit 1; }; }
. ./$as_me.lineno
exit
```

This script, like much of autoconf, shows attention to a number of portability details commonly overlooked. The first line runs the script (the file name is stored in $as_myself) through sed, using the = command to print the line number before each line. (The default behavior of sed is to print every line after executing all commands, so the lines are printed after their line numbers.) The next sed script (explained in detail in Chapter 11) replaces each instance of $LINENO with the current line number; the output of this is stored in $as_me.lineno.

This script fragment highlights something that can be visually confusing in long blocks of quoted code for another language (in this case, sed). In this line, it looks at first as though variable names are being quoted for some reason:

```
s,^\(['$as_cr_digits']*\)\(.*\)[$]LINENO\([^'$as_cr_alnum'_]\),\1\2\1\3,
```

In fact, the variable names are outside the quotes, and everything else is in them. The single quote immediately preceding $as_cr_digits is the end of a quoted string starting on the second line (the line containing only sed '). The variables $as_cr_digits and $as_cr_alnum hold strings of standard ASCII digits and letters. This preserves behavior even on systems with unusual character sets or with defective character range handling. These variables in question are known to contain no spaces, so they don't cause the argument to sed to get broken into multiple words. If this were ambiguous, they might have been placed in double quotes:

```
s,^\(['"$as_cr_digits"']*\)\(.*\)[$]LINENO\([^'"$as_cr_alnum"'_]\),\1\2\1\3,
```

Another interesting choice is illustrated here; the . command is used to read and execute the created script. If the original script had used exec, the shell would have executed the created script, using its name for $0, and error messages would be from configure.lineno rather than configure. Furthermore, the positional parameters would need to be passed in again; this way, the script environment is preserved. A bare exit command exits with the return code of the previous command, and the return code of the . command is the return code of the executed code (assuming it was successful in finding and reading that code at all).

Emulating Features

In many cases, it is impossible to replace a shell feature. However, in a few cases, it may be possible to come surprisingly close. The following shell function can be used to replace select in most cases, replacing the select keyword with while func_select:

```
func_select () {
  func_select_args=0
  case $1 in
    [!_a-zA-Z]* | *[!_a-zA-Z0-9]* )
      echo >&2 "func_select: '$1' is not a valid variable name."
      return 1
      ;;
  esac
  func_select_var=$1
  shift
  case $1 in
    in) shift;;
    *) echo >&2 "func_select: usage: func_select var in ..."; return 1;;
  esac
  case $# in
    0) echo >&2 "func_select: usage: func_select var in ..."; return 1;;
  esac
  for func_select_arg
  do
    func_select_args=`expr $func_select_args + 1`
    eval func_select_a_$func_select_args=\$func_select_arg
  done
  REPLY=""
  while :
  do
    if test -z "$REPLY"; then
      func_select_i=1
      while test $func_select_i -le $func_select_args
      do
        eval echo "\"\$func_select_i) \$func_select_a_$func_select_i\""
        func_select_i=`expr $func_select_i + 1`
      done
    fi
    echo >&2 "${PS3:-#? }"
```

```
    if read REPLY; then
      if test -n "${REPLY}"; then
        case $REPLY in
          0* | *[!0-9]* )
            eval $func_select_var=
            ;;
          *)
            if test "$REPLY" -ge 1 && test "$REPLY" -le $func_select_args; then
              eval $func_select_var=\$func_select_a_$REPLY
            else
              eval $func_select_var=
            fi
            ;;
        esac
        return 0
      fi
    else
      eval $func_select_var=
      return 1
    fi
  done
}
```

Of course, if you've been following along, this function hardly requires comment. This is a large enough block of code, however, that it may be worth a bit of exploration. While none of the features used here are new, the combinations merit some discussion.

The first section of the function simply sets up variables. All variables are prefixed with func_select_, except for $REPLY (which is part of the normal behavior this function is supposed to emulate). The function validates its arguments minimally, insisting that the result variable have a valid identifier name and that at least one additional argument was provided. After this validation, the function builds an emulated array (see the in-depth discussion in Chapter 5) storing each of the choices in a numbered variable.

The main loop begins by setting $REPLY to an empty string. On each pass of the loop, if $REPLY is empty, the list is printed; this ensures that the list is printed the first time through. After that, the script prints a prompt and attempts to read a new value. If it fails, the output variable is emptied and the function returns. If a value is read, the function always returns; the only way to repeat the loop is if $REPLY is empty.

The test for a valid $REPLY value accepts only strings of digits, starting with a non-zero digit; this is accomplished by rejecting any pattern containing nondigits or starting with a zero. It would also be possible to strip leading zeroes. (In fact, one of the bugs of this implementation is that it does not strip leading and trailing spaces, which the real select does.) If a valid digit string is found, and it is between 1 and $func_select_args inclusive, the output variable is given the corresponding stored value.

Even this function has a few design choices reflecting a desire for portability. If you could safely assume you did not need to run in pre-POSIX shells, the $func_select_a_*N* variables would not be needed; you could use the positional parameters. When targeting a specific system, there might well be a better way to print the prompt; for instance, the printf command might be usable. (This example didn't use it because it was developed for use on an embedded system.) So one weakness of this is that the prompt is echoed with a trailing new line, which changes the output of the program slightly.

For purposes of getting a script that uses select running quickly on a shell other than ksh or bash, however, this is probably good enough. It works on shells as old as the traditional Bourne shell used in Solaris, and it also runs in modern shells. Be wary of that last part; it is important to check a portability feature like this against new shells, not just the older shells that originally needed it.

In fact, this emulation can be even closer in some shells; in ash, for instance, following the function declaration with an alias can give you essentially complete compatibility:

```
alias select='while func_select'
```

While this may look like a significant improvement, I do not recommend it. Aliasing behavior is a bit quirky and fairly unportable. Although aliases are now standard in POSIX shells, they are not universally available, and they are a rich source of unexpected errors. They are a wonderful interactive feature, but you should avoid them in scripting even when using a shell that supports them.

What's Next?

Chapter 8 takes a look at the major portability issues you are likely to encounter with common utility programs. While these programs are technically not part of the shell, they are essential to most shell programs. Chapter 8 also gives you information about what the common versions are, how to find good versions of a utility on a system, and what common features are not as portable as you might think.

CHAPTER 8

■ ■ ■

Utility Portability

This chapter discusses the portability of programs external to the shell. Most shell scripts need to use a number of programs other than the shell itself to achieve their ends. Compared to the divergence in the functions and options offered by utilities, the variance of all the shell languages is relatively trivial.

This chapter does not attempt to provide a complete or comprehensive list of differences between different utilities; such a list would be much larger than this book. A shell script may have access to hundreds, or even thousands, of distinct programs. Many programs exist in three or more distinct variants with different sets of options, different names for the same options, and other sources of confusion. Utilities can acquire, or lose, features between one version of a system and another. Keeping track of every detail specifically is impractical, amplifying the need to stick with standard features most of the time. The autoconf documentation has a particularly good list of issues you are likely to run into. This chapter gives a somewhat narrower list, but it also goes into general principles of portability and explores some of the ways to go about finding out what will be portable.

This chapter begins with an overview of common families of utilities, such as BSD and System V. Following this is a section on avoiding unnecessary dependencies, and ways to check to ensure that your code will be portable. The third section discusses a number of specific examples of common utility portability issues. Finally, I close with a discussion of how to cope when something you thought was portable enough turns out not to be.

Common Variations

While there are dozens of specific variants of many commands with particular local features added, there are broad categories into which many utility programs fall. The famous historical distinction in UNIX utilities is System V and BSD, with BSD utilities often offering radically different semantics and options than System V utilities. Often, if you recognize one utility on a system as favoring a particular heritage, it will turn out that many other utilities on the same system have the same background.

Many utilities on modern systems are more explicit about which of their features are standard and which are extensions. Start with the online manuals, called the *man pages* (they are accessed using a command called man). When reading the man page for a utility, check to see whether it has a "Standards" heading; if it does, this will give you guidance on where to look for information about what that utility might do on other systems. With that in mind, it's time to look into some of the heritage of the UNIX utility environment.

Days of Yore: System V and BSD

The first major portability problems from UNIX arose, unsurprisingly, when there started being more than one kind of UNIX. When students at the University of California, Berkeley, started distributing their own modified versions of UNIX, one of the most noticeable changes was a huge upswing in the number of utilities and the number of options for those utilities. As AT&T turned UNIX into a commercial product (System III, and then System V), some of these ideas were adopted and others were not. Meanwhile, AT&T's new features often didn't make it into BSD. The result was that, while the core features that had been present in the original code base were usually portable, features added by one group or the other tended not to be. Even worse, both groups showed some tendency to reject things they had not developed locally, a syndrome often referred to as "not invented here" (NIH) syndrome.

A general trend was for Berkeley systems to add a lot more features and options, sometimes changing a utility from a fairly specialized program into a much more general one. The love of special cases and options led to a famous quip:

Stop! Whoever crosseth the bridge of Death, must answer first these questions three, ere the other side he see:

"What is your name?"

"Sir Brian of Bell."

"What is your quest?"

"I seek the Holy Grail."

"What are four lowercase letters that are not legal flag arguments to the Berkeley UNIX version of 'ls'?"

"I, er. . . AIIIEEEEEE!"

—Mark-Jason Dominus

Of course, he's joking; in fact, there are five (e, j, v, y, and z).

Berkeley and System V UNIX continued to diverge in many respects, with subtle differences in the C library as well as their utilities. Going from one to the other could be quite confusing; the basic selection of utilities available differed widely, and even the utilities that existed on both might have radically different behaviors. This is also where the difficulties with echo originated (see the section "Common Utility Issues" later in this chapter).

Modern systems often support many of the idioms from both BSD and System V utilities. For instance, some versions of ps accept Berkeley options without hyphens and System V options with hyphens; on Mac OS X, you can use either ps aux or ps -ef, but ps ef complains that the f option is not valid. (The original Berkeley ps did not use hyphens to introduce its options, making this behavior moderately idiomatic for users of either system.)

GNU Arrives

The GNU project began in 1984, when Richard Stallman began to work on developing free utilities. It is important to note the distinction; he means "free" as in speech, not "free" as in beer. That is to say, the emphasis is not on cost; you may sell GNU software if you want to. Rather, the emphasis is on privileges or rights; if you have GNU software, you may sell it to other people, modify it, or otherwise use it pretty much as you wish. However, you must offer these same freedoms to others in any derivative works. So while you are free to acquire GNU make, modify it in any way you want, and use it, if you begin to pass on modified copies, you must make the source for the modifications available under equally nonrestrictive terms. (A more detailed discussion of the licensing implications is beyond the scope of this book, but if you write much code, you should make a point of being familiar with the common open source licenses.)

As time went on, the GNU project began to develop mostly compatible versions of a number of core UNIX utilities, such as grep. With many concerns in the air about software litigation, the GNU project adopted a philosophy that went beyond writing utilities from scratch to implementing them in ways that were expected to make it very unlikely that their internals were even similar to those of other implementations. This is how the GNU coding standards put it:

> For example, UNIX utilities were generally optimized to minimize memory use; if you go for speed instead, your program will be very different. You could keep the entire input file in memory and scan it there instead of using studio. Use a smarter algorithm discovered more recently than the UNIX program. Eliminate use of temporary files. Do it in one pass instead of two (we did this in the assembler).

—GNU Coding Standards, Section 2.1

GNU utilities often mixed and matched pieces of both System V and Berkeley functionality, as well as introduced many interesting new options. Some of these options later made it back into other systems, but not quickly.

GNU utilities frequently have exceptionally broad feature sets. Information about standards conformance is often kept in a separate set of documentation to be browsed with the GNU info reader, rather than put into man pages. For a long time, the GNU project advocated putting only incomplete summary documentation into man pages; while the info format is arguably better at many things, this results in users having to use more than one documentation reader, and many users remain unaware of the much greater documentation detail in the info pages.

GNU utilities introduced a new convention of option flags, which were whole words rather than single letters; these are called *long options*. The most commonly used options will also have single-letter abbreviations, but sometimes the long form is easier to remember. Long options are introduced with a double hyphen (--*option*). This behavior has shown up widely in other utilities but has not been formally standardized.

The GNU utilities are fairly widely portable, and in many cases you can arrange to install them even on a non-GNU system if you need a particular feature they offer. However, be careful when doing this, as other scripts may be depending on the behavior of the system's non-native utilities. Typically, a system that has both GNU and non-GNU versions of a utility prefixes the names of GNU utilities with g, as in gmake, gfind, or gtar.

Standardization

The POSIX standard is one of many UNIX standards that have come along; it is neither the first standard to come out nor the most recent. UNIX users found the difficulty of porting between systems frustrating, and standards and portability work began showing up. From the early Uniform Draft Standard (UDS) and System V Interface Definition (SVID) guides came POSIX and the X/Open Portability Guides. In many cases, these standards tended to track AT&T more closely than BSD, but both systems had some decisions adopted and ratified.

The POSIX and X/Open work has gradually converged on more recent standards, such as the Single UNIX Specification. Unfortunately, these standards have become gigantic, and conformance testing is large, complicated, and not always adequate. This is not to say the standards are not useful; they are excellent, but very few systems are fully conformant. If you are developing a system, you should pursue conformance, and scripts that do not need to be portable to older systems gain a lot of benefit from increased standardization.

You will find two central problems in trying to rely heavily on standardized features in portable scripting. The first is that many systems, especially open source systems, lack the funding to pursue every last nook and cranny of the gigantic specifications. The second is that many of the behaviors required need not be defaults. So, while POSIX does require a broad range of basic shell functionality, it may not be the case that /bin/sh is the shell that provides that functionality. In practice, NetBSD's /bin/sh is much closer to POSIX compliance than Solaris's /bin/sh, but the /usr/xpg4/bin/sh on Solaris might be more compliant than NetBSD's ash derivative. (As a disclaimer, I must admit that I have not done comprehensive testing of either; neither of them has ever failed to run a POSIX script for me, though.) A third, more subtle problem is that POSIX does not specify nearly as much as most people expect it to. The shebang notation (#! at the beginning of scripts) is not mandated or defined by POSIX, even though I have never personally seen a system that didn't use it.

Similar issues apply throughout the utilities used by the shell. Commands often continue to accept nonstandard options by default, converting to standard behavior only when you take special effort to obtain that behavior.

A number of utilities, especially GNU utilities, will adhere somewhat more closely to the POSIX specification if the environment variable $POSIXLY_CORRECT has been set.

In short, while standardization does help some, and your chances of getting a reasonable selection of basic utilities with standard features are much higher than they were in the early 80s, you still can't just code for the standard and forget about the details if you want your code to be portable. Unlike shell language portability, where preambles can generally fix things up well enough, utility programs are extremely difficult to replace on the fly in most cases; however, there are some cases where it may be practical to build a portable shell or C version of a utility and use that.

busybox

The busybox program, used heavily in embedded Linux systems, offers customized (and stripped-down) versions of a number of standard UNIX utilities. You may be wondering whether busybox is a shell or a utility; in fact, it is a combined binary that performs different functions depending on the name it is called with. Typically, a single binary containing a shell and a number of basic utilities is installed in a root file system, with most of the standard utilities as symbolic links to the busybox binary.

Porting to a system that uses busybox for most of its utilities can be a challenge. Not all busybox systems offer the same utilities; individual utilities may be removed from the busybox package to reduce space usage, and some systems install other utilities. While there is a busybox variant of grep, a vendor could also install a standard grep on a busybox system.

In general, if you are expecting to run on embedded systems, you need to know that before you start writing any code. You are no longer targeting a standard UNIX desktop environment, and there are a number of surprises. The biggest, though, is how many programs work just fine on busybox.

Shell Builtins

There are two significant aspects to shell builtins that affect utility portability. The first is the question of which standard utilities, such as test or expr, a given shell may have chosen to implement as built-in commands. The second question is this: Which of the features are provided that must be implemented as built-ins to work? The second question is better viewed as a shell language portability question, but the first question is significant when considering portability.

In many cases, the risk of shell builtins is that they will hide an underlying portability issue. For instance, the exceptionally useful printf utility is not universally available. It is provided as a builtin by ksh93 and bash, though, so it is quite possible to run a quick test in your preferred login shell on a target system and conclude that the command is provided by the system. (In fact, in the particular case of printf, it turns out that no system I can find lacks it in /bin/sh using the default path, whether as an external utility or a built-in command.) Even worse, a built-in command may have different behaviors in some cases than the external command or may offer additional features that you might accidentally use, thinking they are provided as part of the standard behavior of the command.

In most cases, the solution is simple: Rely on the common behavior rather than on extensions. However, you may want to ensure the use of an external command in some cases; specify the path to the command you want to execute. By contrast, if you know that you want a feature provided by the shell's built-in command, and that the external utility lacks it, do not specify the path.

Unfortunately, shells do not always document exactly which commands are built in or provide a standard way to check. You can, however, determine this indirectly by temporarily setting the $PATH environment variable to an empty string:

```
$ PATH="" ls; echo $?
ls: not found
127
$ PATH="" echo hello; echo $?
hello
0
```

The shell searches $PATH for a command (containing no slashes) that is not a builtin but does not search the path for built-in commands. This allows you to at least find out whether a shell is providing its own version of a command. The which utility can tell you whether a command is in your current path, but it does not tell you whether the shell has a builtin of the same name. Some shells offer useful additional features to let you find out whether a command is a function, alias, built-in command, or external command, but these are not portable or consistent between shells.

The question of whether a command is a builtin is not the only question; on some systems, there may be multiple versions of the same external command with different behaviors; see the section "Multiple Different Versions" later in this chapter for more information on that problem.

A third aspect of builtins and their impact on portability is more subtle; in some cases, a shell builtin has nothing to do with a command-line utility of the same name. For instance, some old systems had a FORTRAN compiler named fc. The POSIX history editing mechanism uses a shell builtin named fc. This kind of thing can be a bit surprising. Luckily, it is also fairly rare; developers tend to try to avoid clashing names, so it is atypical for two commands with the same name to come into widespread use.

Avoiding Unnecessary Dependencies

A program often has requirements or assumptions about its operating environment. In general, the things that must be true for a program to work are called its *dependencies*. When developing a script, you should aim to eliminate as many dependencies as possible in order to increase the number of systems your script will work on.

Determining whether a dependency is optional is not always easy. Be sure to distinguish between the particular programs you have available and the functions for which you are using them. For example, consider a script that uses a small Perl program to sort lines by their length:

```
#!/bin/sh
perl -e 'print sort { length $a <=> length $b } <>;' "$@"
```

This script (which could also be implemented easily enough as a pure Perl script) obviously requires the perl program to run. You might conclude that, to port this script, you must have perl installed on your target system. However, it is possible to duplicate this script's functionality without perl:

```
#!/bin/sh
cat "$@" | while read i
do
  echo "${#i} $i"
done | sort -n | sed -e 's/[0-9]* //'
```

This script is probably less efficient than the original script. However, it produces the same effect; each line is sorted by its length. The only external programs used are cat, sort, and sed (and possibly echo in a shell that does not provide it as a built-in command). None of these commands are rare, and none of the features used are rare or even particularly new. The result is almost certainly a great deal slower, but it is quite portable.

The cat `"$@"` idiom bears a moment's examination. In general, the cat command is not very useful in pipes; you can always just redirect something from a file or omit cat in the case where input should just be standard input. However, in this case, it performs the useful service of either concatenating all of the command-line arguments or simply passing standard input into the while loop. (Remember that `"$@"` does not expand to an empty string when there are no arguments, at least in recent shells; instead, it expands to nothing at all. In a very few older shells, you may need to use `${1+"$@"}`; this issue was discussed in more detail in Chapter 7.)

The hardest part of avoiding dependencies is usually identifying them. Most dependencies are possible to work around, but it can be very easy to mistakenly rely on something without realizing that it is not portable.

Relying on Extensions Considered Harmful

With all the material you've seen so far on portable programming, you might reasonably wonder why there are so many features that are not portable. While some portability problems are the result of a developer not completely implementing something, many more are the result of a developer choosing to implement something additional. Many system utilities have shortcomings that may be frustrating enough that a developer would correct for them.

With that in mind, understand that one of the limitations of portable shell programming is that it may be harder to write something portably than it would have been to write it relying on an extension. So why bother? The answer is that the payoff in portability is usually worth it. Often, a special option streamlines or simplifies something that you can do by a slightly longer route. For instance, some versions of cat have a line-numbering option, but this is easy enough to implement without using cat. While the option might be convenient, it is hardly necessary. It may save you a minute while writing the script—and cost you an hour when trying to use the script on another system.

Two major difficulties may arise when you try to run a script that relied on extensions on a new system. The first is that the new system, lacking the extensions, will probably have no documentation to tell you what they did. This can make it very difficult to determine what to use to replace the nonworking code. The second is that there is a chance that the new system may have different extensions using the same utility name or option flag; in this case, you get no warning as to what has gone wrong.

This leads to a piece of advice you may not expect in a book advocating portable programming: Learn to use the extensions available on the systems you use. Understand them because they will save you a lot of time and effort in one-off scripts. Keep in mind that they are extensions, but don't be afraid to learn them and use them when they are appropriate. Despite the apparent contradiction, I have generally found that familiarity with extensions makes it easier to avoid them. It also makes it easier to understand scripts that were not written portably.

Try to ensure that any features you rely on beyond the basic standards are clearly identified and are genuinely necessary. You will find it easier to keep your scripts running, and you will also find it easier to write new scripts if you have formed good habits.

During development, you may find it rewarding to use shell function wrappers that warn you about nonportable options rather than accepting them. This can make it easier to develop portable code during testing. If you wrote a number of these, you could put a directory containing them early in your $PATH while developing. (I am not aware of an existing collection of these, but it sounds really useful.)

Test with More Than One Shell on More Than One System

For some reason, authors love to advise people to try things and see what happens. This is excellent advice if you keep in mind that what happens today on a particular system may not be what happens tomorrow on a different system. When writing portable code, you should start by looking at documentation, standards, and other things that will be less ephemeral than a particular implementation's combination of bugs and extensions. However, sooner or later you will probably need to test some things out.

When this time comes, test on multiple targets. Run your code in several shells. Run your code on several systems. Developers sometimes refer to the set of possible combinations as the "matrix of pain" because it can be very difficult to keep multiple combinations working all at once. Luckily, portable shell code is not nearly as painful to maintain as some things are (such as combinations of kernel options across multiple architectures). The purpose of tests like these is to maximize the chance that you find out sooner, rather than later, about a prospective portability problem.

If you are writing for the plain POSIX shell, it may seem counterintuitive to intentionally seek out shells with additional features and extensions to test with. However, these additional features and extensions might, in some rare cases, cause a nonobvious bug. Furthermore, in many cases, differences are merely implementation choices, where any of several possible outcomes is permissible. You want to find out whether you are relying on any of these as soon as possible.

If you are writing significant production code, set up a test environment with all the target systems available. It may be impossible to catch every possible target environment, but for production code, it is reasonable to set up five or six target systems for testing. Be sure that your test code is run in the default environment for each system, not just in your personal shell. Most shell programmers have a number of changes in their environment that may create surprises, such as an unusual path, special environment variables, and more. (Note that you must also test your scripts in these environments, not just in the default environment.)

In fact, you may wish to steal an idea from developers who work in compiled languages and set up regular and automated testing of scripts across a variety of systems. Automated tests are more likely to be run than manual tests. In my experience, the times when I break the portability of my code are not the times when I am worried that I am about to do something nonportable, but rather the times when I am not thinking about it. Because of this, manual testing is surprisingly unlikely to catch the real errors; the times when I think to run the tests are the times when I've probably gotten the code right to begin with.

Document Your Assumptions

It is quite possible that, after reviewing your target environment, you will conclude that a particular dependency is simply too important. If you have a clear notion of what target systems you need to worry about, and you are quite sure they all provide a utility or a particular extension, you can go ahead and use it. Do yourself (and everyone else) a favor, though, and identify what the assumption was you made. A script that only runs in bash can be annoying. A script that only runs in bash, but presents itself as a generic shell script, is maddening.

If your script requires particular utilities, especially if they are not very widely installed, comment on them, or even check for them and warn the user if they are not available. A few comment lines at the beginning of a script, or near the line where you do something risky, could save a future developer (possibly you) hours or days of work. The quilt patch utility is excellent but relies heavily on GNU utility extensions. This is particularly difficult when targeting Mac OS X, as simply building GNU utilities for that system does not always produce desirable results; the file system has some unusual features not found in other UNIX systems, which are supported by special code unique to the OS X versions of some core utilities. Gary V. Vaughan, the technical reviewer for this book, spent a number of working days getting quilt working on Mac OS X a couple of years back. I've personally spent as much as a day on a single smallish script trying to make it work on a different version of UNIX; it can be very hard to track down portability bugs, especially undocumented ones.

Good documentation can help a lot. If a script clearly indicates what it is relying on, this makes it easier to understand the intended behavior. The biggest problem is often being unable to figure out what the writer intended the program to do in the first place.

Common Utility Issues

While it is impractical to give a list of all the variances you will encounter in the wild while writing shell scripts, there are a few issues so utterly persistent and pernicious that I want to call special attention to them. These are the programs that have bitten me repeatedly across a number of projects, have haunted me for years, and have otherwise caused more than their fair share of grief.

Public Enemy #1: echo

The echo utility is in a class by itself. While other programs may vary more widely in their behavior, none vary more widely per feature provided. The initial issue that started this all is quite simple; it is very common to wish to display some text without going to a new line immediately. This allows long lines of text or output to be assembled by bits and pieces and often dramatically improves the user interface of a script. Unfortunately, it cannot be done. The reason is that the Berkeley people added a feature to implement this using an option flag; the -n option suppresses the trailing new line. The System V people also added a feature to implement this; they added support for escape sequences and text ending with \c causes echo to suppress a line ending.

Neither of these is a good choice for a fundamental utility like echo. The key function of echo is to reproduce its arguments precisely. As soon as you create special cases, you have made things hard for the user. How should a user of Berkeley echo cause it to produce the string -n followed by a new line? Causing echo to interpret backslash escape sequences creates an additional nightmare. Depending on the version (and different versions, of course, do it differently), you not only have to deal with the shell's usual quoting rules, but take care to handle possibly differing versions of the quoting rules for echo. For instance, the command echo '\\' produces two backslashes in ksh but only one in zsh. You can mitigate this by calling /bin/echo explicitly, but it may not always have the behavior you want.

The blunt reality is that it is not portable to use echo when either the first argument begins with a hyphen or any argument contains a backslash. What's worse, there may not always be a portable alternative. Many modern systems provide an extremely flexible utility called printf. When it is available, this solves the problem by allowing you to specify both data and format, as well as providing for a number of other useful features, such as alignment, significant digits, and so on. In fact, I know of no desktop or server systems lacking `printf`; unfortunately, it is still sometimes omitted from embedded systems.

The Korn shell introduced a `print` built-in command to alleviate this problem, but it is portable only to `ksh` and `pdksh`. The Bourne-again shell provides a `printf` builtin, reasonably compatible with the common external utility.

The closest I have found to a remotely acceptable portable solution is to take advantage of other commands to filter the output of `echo`:

```
func_echo_noline () {
  /bin/echo X"$@" | awk '
{
  if (lastline != "") print lastline;
  else sub("X", "");
  lastline = $0;
}
END { printf "%s", lastline; }
'
}
```

Instead of trying to coerce the `echo` command into doing something useful, you can filter its output using the `awk` command. This small `awk` script strips the leading X (which is used to prevent `echo` from interpreting a `-n` argument as an option), then prints every line it receives, suppressing the new line after the last line. This is the simplest solution I've found to the "no new line" problem. (This `awk` script is explained in more detail in Chapter 11.)

None of this gets into a much more fundamentally awful decision; some versions of `echo` process backslash escapes and generally discard backslashes. This breaks the conventional idiom for escaping backslashes:

```
foo=`echo "$foo" | sed -e 's/\\/\\\\/g'`
```

A complete solution to this is large (around 140 lines of shell code in recent `configure` scripts). In short, it is extremely hard; this is a case where, if you can avoid embedded systems, the shortest path is to switch to `printf` or use a preamble to reexecute in a shell that has a built-in `echo` without the bug. (I am aware that the bug in question was implemented that way on purpose; it's still a bug.)

Multiple Different Versions

Some vendors helpfully provide more than one version of some common utilities. This can create a portability nightmare for scripts. For instance, on some older systems, utility programs might be found in /usr/bin, /usr/ucb, and /usr/5bin. The ucb directory would hold Berkeley versions of utilities, while 5bin would hold System V versions or programs designed to act mostly like them. Many modern systems have common programs stored in directories with names like /opt/package/bin, /usr/local/bin, or /usr/pkg/bin. Furthermore, users may have their own personal binaries in a directory in the path, and sometimes these binaries clash with standard system binaries.

Correcting for this is hard. If you provide your own setting for $PATH, you have to be sure you get it right on a broad variety of foreign systems. Even worse, in some cases, users may have chosen an unusual path value because they really do need your script to use different binaries. In general, your best bet is to test your scripts with multiple path settings but not to try to outsmart the user; use the provided path and hope for the best. However, do be aware that on systems with multiple binary directories, a change in the order of the path sometimes changes the behavior of utilities, even common and well-known utilities.

Archive Utilities

The UNIX environment provides a broad selection of archive utilities, but they are not as portable as you might hope. Archiving utilities are significant in many shell scripts because they are often a useful way to copy a large number of files while preserving *metadata*—attributes such as modification dates, permissions, or other traits beyond just the data in the file. Copying batches of files using an archive utility is frequently better than copying them using plain old cp. For network copying, there is often a substantial performance improvement from using archive files.

There are three primary archive utilities commonly used on UNIX systems: cpio, pax, and tar. Historically, cpio originated in AT&T, tar originated in BSD, and pax was introduced by POSIX. The tar utility is the least flexible but the most commonly available; it supports only its own native format. (Some versions may handle two or three variants of the tar format, but only variants within the format, not other formats.) The cpio and pax utilities support both the reading and writing of a variety of formats. The modern cpio format is probably the most comprehensive and flexible; it handles a variety of special cases (such as extracting only one of several hard links to the same file), which the others lack support for. There is an additional pax-only archive format (referred to as the pax format in the documentation) that is a superset of the POSIX tar format, which also supports hard links and very long pathnames.

All three produce uncompressed archives; if you want compression, you combine your archive utility with a compression utility. Some versions of the tar utility have options to do this automatically for you, but this is not portable. In general, all three are happy to work with archives on standard input or standard output, so you can use them in a pipeline with a compression utility. As an example, here are three roughly equivalent commands to create a compressed archive of the directory *files*:

```
tar cf - files | gzip > files.tar.gz
pax -w files | gzip > files.pax.gz
find files -print | cpio -o | gzip > files.cpio.gz
```

The tar and pax utilities implicitly recurse through named directories (this behavior can be disabled in pax). The cpio utility packs only those files explicitly named. Both cpio and pax can take file lists from standard input; tar only takes them on the command line. If you send the output of find into pax, be wary; it will generate multiple copies of files in a directory if you name both the files and the directory containing them. This all gets very complicated, and it is easier to see in tabular form, as shown in Table 8-1.

Table 8-1. *The Archive Utilities*

Utility	Recursive	Files on Input	Files on Command Line	Passthrough	Formats
tar	Yes	No	Yes	No	tar, POSIX tar
cpio	No	Yes	No	Yes	tar, POSIX tar, cpio
pax	Option	Yes	Yes	Yes	tar, POSIX tar, cpio, pax

There are several common cpio archive formats; most modern cpio utilities (and most versions of pax) can read and write each others' archives.

Because the use of archive utilities to create an archive and immediately unpack it is so common, both cpio and pax have the option of running in a direct copy mode. In this mode, they are similar to cp -R, only much better at preserving metadata.

Finally, there are many sorts of metadata. While all three utilities can generally handle the metadata traditionally supported by UNIX systems, many systems have newer features. Access control lists (ACLs) are commonly supported on modern UNIX. Mac OS X can have additional data stored under the same name in a separate "fork," which no non-Mac utility can even describe, let alone refer to or copy. (The utilities included with Mac OS X have, since Mac OS X version 10.4, generally handled this for you transparently.) Unfortunately, it is not portable to expect any of these utilities to copy such additional data. This is mitigated somewhat by the fact that the additional data themselves are not portable either.

For the most part, you can use the native archive utilities provided with a system and expect them to copy files well enough that they look the same to users. If metadata are lost, they are usually metadata that users would not have noticed in the first place. There are exceptions; on Mac OS X version 10.3, tar did not preserve resource forks. However, if you wanted to build a new version of GNU tar and use it on Mac OS X, it might not copy things correctly. (Luckily for you, the system's provided tar is a suitably modified GNU tar as of this writing.)

The implications of these differences for portable scripting are a bit of a pain. Nearly every system provides at least one of these utilities. Many provide two of them. Right now, tar is the most commonly available, but its limitations in dealing with long pathnames may make it impractical for some tasks. If you can find pax on the systems you need to work on, it is usually pretty good; it has a broader set of fundamental functionality than either of the others. However, if you need special features, such as reliable duplication of hard links in a copy, you may need cpio. Luckily, the GNU project provides a workable cpio program in fairly portable source.

Passing file names as standard input has one key limitation; file names containing new lines break it. This is not a specific bug in either pax or cpio, but a general limitation of the protocol. This bug does not necessarily result only in failures to archive files. If you are running as root and try to archive a user's home directory with find | cpio, think about what the archive ends up containing if the user has a directory named myroot<newline> containing files with the same relative paths as system files. A user who wanted a copy of /etc/passwd.master (the BSD convention for the file actually holding password data) could create a file called myroot<newline>/etc/passwd.master. Passed on standard input, this becomes two things: first, a directory named myroot (which does not exist and is not archived) and second, a file named /etc/passwd.master. You can pass file names as arguments to pax, but cpio does not have such an option.

WHAT ABOUT ZIP AND AR?

Many modern UNIX systems have one or more utilities to handle archives in the semi-standardized zip file format, which combines archiving and compression. Typically, these utilities would be named zip and unzip, with the former creating archives and the latter extracting files from archives or listing their contents. These formats may be a better choice if you have to share data files or output with Windows systems, but not all systems provide these utilities. While very many desktop systems do provide these utilities, some server-oriented systems omit them or make them optional packages.

Another archive utility only occasionally used is the classic ar archiver, used to combine object files into libraries. In fact, it can be used as a general-purpose archiver, but it lacks the flexibility of the other archivers, and many versions have punitively short name restrictions (such as 15 or 16 characters). In general, do not use this unless you are building libraries, and even then, more modern tools may be preferable.

Another common problem with archive utilities is their behavior when dealing with absolute paths. A few utilities, such as GNU tar, do not restore absolute file names by default; instead, they strip the leading slash and restore everything relative to the current directory. This behavior is wonderful, except when you get used to it and assume other programs will do it, too. Be very wary when unpacking archives that seem to have absolute paths, and be sure you know how your archiver of choice behaves before unpacking any archive containing an absolute path. Note that some variants may treat this differently; I have seen pax variants that automatically stripped leading slashes and others that didn't. Assuming that an archiver will safely restore only into the current directory can cause you a lot of trouble; I've lost a lot of data by assuming I could just extract a backup into a temporary directory, only to find that it restored over the data from which it had been backed up a week earlier.

The final problem often encountered in archives is long file names (including the path). The original tar header format allows the specification of file names up to 100 characters. This is not long enough. Modern POSIX archivers can usually handle up to 250 characters and should be able to handle each others' files; but older tar programs may choke on them, and they generally get file names wrong when extracting new archives containing files with names over 100 characters. To avoid these problems, use terse file names or use one of the cpio formats.

> ## LONG FILE NAMES
>
> We are not talking about the "innovation" of supporting file names longer than eight characters with more than a three-character extension. The early System V file system supported file names up to 14 characters. (Trivia point: This is why the semantics for `strncpy()` are inconsistent with all the other C library string functions. Early UNIX used 16-byte directory entries, which allowed 14 bytes for the file name; null terminating a 14-character string would have limited file names to 13 characters.) The original Mac OS HFS file system was limited to 31 and Berkeley UFS/FFS to 255. These limits are for each individual component in a directory path; paths may be much longer on some systems. A typical modern UNIX system will support at least 4096 total characters in a file's absolute pathname. Some will support relative paths of this length, even from deeply nested directories.
>
> In practice, most people never find out that `tar` can't portably handle names over 100 characters, or over 250 in modern `tar`. File names on UNIX are often typed; this imposes firm limits on how long most of them get. Still, be wary of these issues. File name portability is a special challenge because you can't always control a user's files.

Block Sizes

Many utilities give sizes or disk usage information in *blocks*. Most often, a block is 512 bytes, but it may also be 1024 bytes. Some utilities have (sadly, not always portable) options to specify other block sizes. The environment variable $BLOCKSIZE is not portable; there is no reliable expectation that `BLOCKSIZE=1m du` will give disk usage in megabytes rather than in kilobytes or half-kilobyte blocks. However, this variable does exist on many systems, especially BSD systems, and users may have set it. This can produce very surprising behavior; the typical failure mode is for an installer to query for free space on a disk, apply a scaling factor to the reported number of blocks, and conclude that your disk does not have enough space free. If you are using any utilities that rely on a block size, be sure to check what block size they use and verify that you know what units they are using. With larger disks, users may have set $BLOCKSIZE to something large; a megabyte is not uncommon, and gigabytes are starting to show up.

This has no impact on the block sizes used by dd.

Other Common Problems

For a comprehensive and often-updated list of issues with common utilities, check out the autoconf manual, which discusses issues you may face in writing portable shell scripts. This section gives a brief overview of some of the general problems you might encounter, as well as a few highlights from the larger list. Many of the issues described in the autoconf manual are rare on modern systems.

Avoiding these problems can be tricky. As the size of this list suggests, it is difficult to learn all the nooks and crannies of hundreds of utilities. A few basic techniques are available to you. The first is to be aware of standards. Check standard documentation, such as The Open Group's online standards (found in their catalog at www.opengroup.org/products/publications/catalog/t_c.htm) showing the current state of the standard. Read the man pages, and look in particular for information about standard conformance and extensions.

When you see a new option you had not previously encountered, be sure to check the man pages on other systems as well.

Testing a feature quickly on several unrelated systems may also help. You have to have a representative sample of your target systems; if you are writing truly portable code, this can be very difficult to obtain. Portability to systems you don't yet have access to is where a list like the one in this chapter (or the longer one in the autoconf manual) comes in handy.

You cannot simply assume that the features of the oldest system you have available are universal; in some cases, newer systems remove features when implementing new ones. This can lead to a problem where two systems provide mutually exclusive ways to solve a given problem. For instance, the option used with sort when using a key other than the entire input line varies between systems, with some new systems no longer accepting the historical options (details are provided in the following alphabetized list of commands).

While the core functions of utilities like sed are reasonably stable, many more esoteric utilities are unique to particular systems. Many systems provide the column command to convert input lines into columns (although not all do); only a few provide the rs command (a more general program that reshapes input data).

Case-insensitive file systems can occasionally create an extra utility portability problem; for instance, one common Perl module can provide aliases with names like GET and HEAD. If you install this on a machine with a case-insensitive (or case-preserving) file system, your path now determines whether the head command is a convenient utility to obtain results from a web server or a standard utility to display the first few lines of a file.

When trying to guess how portable a program will be, check the man page for "Standards" and "History" sections. A command that complies with POSIX is probably more portable than one with no listed provenance or that claims to have been introduced in 4.4BSD.

awk

In general, every system ought to have some variety of awk. Check for variants; there may also be nawk, gawk, or mawk. Any of these variants may be installed under the name awk. A few systems provide an old pre-POSIX awk by default, so check for others. If there is an oawk command, it is quite possible that plain awk is really nawk. If you have to use one of the old versions, it has a number of limitations, such as not supporting user-defined functions. The printf (or sprintf) function may have gratuitous smallish limits on format lengths in old versions.

If you are writing a significant amount of awk code, be sure to test it against at least a couple of variants. (See Chapter 11 for more information on awk.)

basename

Unfortunately, this is not universally available. You can use expr, or you can use ${var%%*/} constructs. The latter are marginally less portable, but if you find yourself committed to a POSIX shell, they're available.

cat

There are no options to the cat command in portable code. The things that some variants provide as options must be done using other programs or utilities.

chmod

Do not rely on the behavior of chmod when you don't specify which users a permission change applies to; use chmod a-w, not chmod -w.

cmp

On systems that distinguish between text and binary files, cmp compares binary files; for instance, on DOS systems, it will report differences in line endings and differences in content. The diff utility treats files as text files.

cp

There is no portable -r option, and even when there was, its behavior was often undesirable. Use -R or look at archive utilities as another option. The -p option may lose subsecond time-stamps on file systems that provide them.

cpio

See the "Archive Utilities" section earlier in the chapter. Some versions have options (usually -s and -S) to swap bytes of input data, which are useful when processing old binary archives; but these are not universal and may be unimplemented on modern systems.

cut

Most systems now distinguish between characters (-c) and bytes (-b). Some older systems may have only -c; these systems usually mean "bytes" when they say characters and are not multibyte aware.

date

The use of specifiers similar to those of strftime() in date to format output is fairly standard, but some systems may not implement all the standard specifiers. There is no portable way to specify a time other than the present to format or display, and not all systems provide one. BSD systems typically recognize -r *seconds*, where *seconds* is a number of seconds since the epoch. GNU systems typically recognize -d *date*, where *date* is any of a number of common date formats. One particular date format recognized by GNU date is @*seconds*, where *seconds* is the number of seconds since the epoch. SVR4 date has neither.

While the GNU date utility does have a -r option, it is -r *file* to report the last modification time of *file*; there is no corresponding option in BSD date. This is an example of a case where the error message you get using a construct on a different system might be surprising; if a script written on a BSD system uses date -r, the error message on the GNU system will not indicate an invalid argument, but rather complain about a nonexistent file.

diff

A few rare versions do not compare /dev/null to any file correctly. The unified patch format (-u option) is not completely portable. Patches in the "context diff" format (-c option) are not as easy to read, but they are more portable.

dirname

Not universally available. As with `basename`, you can use `expr` or the POSIX parameter substitution rules.

ditroff

See `nroff`.

dos2unix

Many systems include a program named `dos2unix` (and often another named `unix2dos`) to translate line endings. This is not portable; many other systems lack it. The general difficulty is that there are three common choices about line endings; new line only (UNIX), carriage return followed by new line (DOS and Windows), and carriage return only (classic Mac OS). Translating between these generically is slightly difficult because line-oriented UNIX utilities do not lend themselves well to translating line endings. You can use `tr` to remove trailing carriage returns from files known to be in the carriage return followed by new line (CRLF) format.

Removing or adding carriage returns is easy. Translating carriage returns to new lines is also easy. However, handling all three input formats generically is a bit hard. Even worse, some files genuinely contain both carriage returns and new lines, such as captured output from some programs. Be cautious when trying to translate line endings. (I know of no completely general solution. Sometimes you just have to know what the format is.)

echo

Not very portable. Avoid any backslashes in arguments to `echo`, and avoid first arguments starting with hyphens. Sadly, this is still often all there is, but see the previous discussion under the "Public Enemy #1: echo" section of this chapter. It may be better to just use `printf`, if you do not need to target embedded systems.

egrep

Not quite universally available, but neither is `grep -E`. Modern systems are more likely to support `grep -E`, and older systems are more likely to provide `egrep`. You can test for this:

```
if echo foo | grep -E '(f)oo' >/dev/null 2>&1; then
  EGREP='grep -E'
elif echo foo | egrep '(f)oo' >/dev/null 2>&1; then
  EGREP='egrep'
else
  echo >&2 "Cannot find viable egrep/grep -E!"
  exit 1
fi
```

The pattern `(f)oo` matches the string `foo` only if it is an extended regex. While I have never seen a system that provided an `egrep` (or `grep -E`) that did not work on extended regular expressions, I am also deeply distrustful of vendors at this stage in my career.

expect

The expect program is not a standard utility, although many systems install a variant of it.

expr

Prefix both strings and regular expressions (for the : operator) with X to avoid possible confusion or misparsing. While other characters might work, X is idiomatic. Many implementations offer extensions that are not portable; be careful. There are a number of quirks in regular expression handling in some systems; be careful. For additional information on regular expression matching and expr, see Chapter 2.

fgrep

As with egrep, POSIX specifies a new grep -F usage, which is not universally supported. Old systems may have fgrep, new systems may have grep -F. Unlike other grep variants, fgrep does not check for regular expressions; it checks for fixed strings. Contrary to various rumors, the "f" does not stand for "fast" or "file."

find

The replacement of {} with a file name in -exec is portable only when {} is an argument by itself. The -print0 option, which uses ASCII NUL characters instead of new lines to separate file names, is unfortunately not universal. See the discussion of xargs.

Older implementations of find used special predicates such as -depth, -follow, and -xdev to change searching behavior; newer implementations use corresponding -d, -h, and -x options, which precede the pathname. Neither solution is completely portable now. The -regex option is not portable either; the only portable name matching is the standard shell globbing used by -name. Different versions of find that support -regex may not use the same regex rules; GNU find defaults to the emacs regex rules (described in Chapter 2), for instance. Remember that the glob matching is done within find, so switching shells does not change which glob rules are used.

grep

Do not rely on options other than -clnv. There is no portable option to completely suppress output and yield only a return code; instead, redirect the output (and error) from grep to /dev/null. Some implementations of grep may behave surprisingly on binary files, and the behavior is not portable. Do not pass non-text data to grep in portable scripts.

groff

See nroff.

info

The GNU info documentation system is not universally available. It offers a number of very useful documentation tools, but info documentation tends to be underused because users prefer to read man pages. Do not rely on the availability of any of the tools usually used with this.

killall

This is not particularly portable. Even worse, different systems offer wildly different semantics for some common and likely command lines. Avoid this.

ldd

The ldd utility examines an executable file and tells you which shared libraries it uses. If you are writing an installation utility or something similar, this is exactly the tool you are likely to look at to see whether suitable shared libraries are available. Unfortunately, this utility is not universal. In particular, Mac OS X does not provide any program named ldd; the closest equivalent is otool -L, which is unique to Mac OS X. Some embedded systems will lack this, or have a version that does not function, as the version distributed with glibc is a bash script, and many embedded systems lack bash.

ln

Symbolic links are not totally portable, although they are pretty close these days; exceptions will usually be Windows machines running one of the UNIX emulation layers. The -f option is not portable. You may want to write a wrapper function that removes the destination file before linking when called with -f. The question of what to do if you need symbolic links and they are not available is difficult. In some cases, creating a hard link might be a workable alternative; in others, it could be a disaster (or simply not work). Copying files may be viable, but in some cases won't be. I do not think it is practical to try to develop a one-size-fits-all replacement for ln -s if you need to target Windows machines. Instead, for each use, think about what behavior you really want, and use it explicitly.

lp/lpr

The two most common printer commands, lp and lpr, are not quite compatible. The simplest cases are fairly stable, but many of the options and control features vary widely, and some historic options are unimplemented in some modern systems. If you need to do printing, you have to know a lot about the specific host systems you need to print on; there is nothing even approximating a portable way to guess at printer selection, printer options, and so on. Not all systems will react gracefully to all inputs to the print command, either. Behavior such as automatically converting input files to desired output formats is not portable. Do not pass large binary files to the lpr command unless you are quite sure about your target system doing what you want, or you will get a lot of scratch paper.

If there is a correctly configured printer at all, you should get consistently acceptable results from sending plain text files to either lp or lpr as standard input. To do more printing than this, you will have to accept that there is some lack of portability in your code. (Of course, any printing at all is at least a little unportable; not every system has a printer.) You can do quite well writing a small wrapper function that targets each of a handful of known systems, though. A representative code fragment might look something like this:

```
case `hostname` in
  server*)
    LP_TEXT='lpr -P line'
    LP_PS='lp -P postscript -o media=letter'
    ;;
  ...
esac
case $file in
  *.txt) $LP_TEXT "$file";;
  *.ps) $LP_PS "$file";;
  *) echo >&2 "Unknown file type for '$file'.";;
esac
```

This might be a good candidate for a separate wrapper script, which other scripts use for printing.

m4

The m4 macro processing language is extremely common, and I have never seen a nonembedded system without it. However, some programs may rely on additional features of GNU m4, which may be installed as gm4 on some systems. (The name shares the counting etymology of the term i18n for internationalization.) This program is especially useful if you decide to work with m4sh, which is (of course) written in very portable m4, but it is of some general utility for writing code to generate more code.

make

There is no portable way to include other files in a makefile. The good news is, if you are using make from a shell script, you can assemble the makefiles yourself. While many of the more elaborate make features are unique to a particular variant (usually GNU or BSD make, the two most elaborate members of the family), you can do a great deal with a few simple rules.

If you need inclusion or similar features, you can look at tools like automake or autoconf, which generate makefiles automatically. In simple cases, it may be sufficient to generate makefiles using a preprocessing tool, such as m4, or even create them using a simple shell script. Interestingly, while there is no single standard way to include other files in a makefile, it seems to be quite consistent that every variant of make supports some variant of include *file* or -include *file*. (See chapter 11 for information on how make uses the shell to execute commands.)

makeinfo

See info.

mkdir

Do not rely on the -p option. If you ignore that advice, do not combine -p and -m; the modes of intermediate directories are ambiguous. Some versions can fail if an intermediate directory is created while mkdir -p is running. You can use the widely available mkdirhier and mkinstalldirs shell code. You can also write your own wrapper for mkdir, which handles the -p option:

```
func_mkdir_p() {
  for dir in "$@"; do
    save_IFS=$IFS
    IFS=/
    set -- $dir
    IFS=$save_IFS
    (
      case $dir in
      /*) cd /; shift;;
      esac
      for subdir in "$@"; do
        test -z "$subdir" && continue
        if test -d "$subdir" || mkdir "$subdir"; then
          if cd "$subdir"; then
            :
          else
            echo >&2 "func_mkdir_p: Can't enter $subdir while creating $dir."
            exit 1
          fi
        else
          exit 1
        fi
      done
    )
  done
}
```

This function preserves the normal behavior of mkdir -p, including succeeding without comment if a given directory or subdirectory already exists. A leading / creates an empty $1, which is discarded using shift. The subshell is used to avoid having to keep track of the current directory. Empty subdirectories are ignored by standard UNIX convention. Finally, note the setting of the positional parameters inside a loop iterating over them. This works because the loop is not executed until the shell has already expanded "$@".

mktemp

The mktemp utility is not universally available. If you need temporary files, create a directory with mode 700, then create files in it. (To do this, create a directory after running umask 077; you may want to use a subshell for this to restore the previous umask). There is an excellent wrapper function for this (func_mktempdir) in libtoolize.

mv

Only the -f and -i options are portable. Do not try to move directories across file systems, as this is not portable; use archive utilities or cp and rm. There is no easy way to check whether a move is across file systems, but in general, it is safe to rename a directory without changing its parent directory; anything else you should probably do by copying in some way. The "Archive Utilities" section earlier in this chapter covers some of the issues you may face in copying files; there is no completely portable good answer.

Moving individual files is portable, although very old versions might have a brief window during which neither file exists. Windows- or DOS-based hosts do not allow you to rename an open file.

nroff

The roff utilities (nroff, troff, groff, and so on) are fairly widely supported. However, they do not always produce identical output; do not expect page layout or line break choices to be identical between versions. Not every system has these installed, although they are usually available.

pax

The pax utility is the POSIX "portable archiver," which is a cleaned-up interface for a program similar in functionality to tar. See the section "Archive Utilities" earlier in the chapter. pax is widely available, but not completely universal. If you can verify its availability on the systems you need to target, this may be the best choice.

perl

The perl program is the interpreter for the Perl programming language. Some systems use perl for a Perl 4 interpreter, and perl5 for a Perl 5 interpreter. Others use perl4 and perl, respectively. Do not count on perl being installed in /usr/bin, and do not count on the version without testing it. In fact, do not count on perl being installed at all; but if you must, remember that it may be somewhere unusual. Some systems may have multiple installations, some older and some newer. Many users like to use #!/usr/bin/env perl, but this prevents you from specifying the -w option on many systems. (And you should always, always use the -w option.)

pkill

As with killall, pkill is not universally available. Do not rely on this.

printf

The printf utility is found on SVR4-derived systems, on BSD systems, and on Linux systems; in fact, it is essentially universal outside of embedded systems. If you can be sure this is available on all the systems you need, this is infinitely superior to echo. Check your target systems, but this should be considered reasonably portable now. Avoid using options; there are no portable options. Avoid using format strings that begin with hyphens, as they might be taken as options. Most versions should handle a first argument of -- as a nonprinting sign that there are no options coming, but there is really no need for this. If you want to start a format string with a variable of some sort, begin it with %s and specify the variable as the first argument.

Note that printf is not a direct replacement for echo. It is actually a much nicer command, but you cannot simply change echo to printf and expect scripts to work. The most noticeable change is that printf does not provide a trailing new line automatically. The escape sequences used by printf all use backslashes, so it is simplest to use single quotes around format strings.

You can implement much of this functionality through clever use of a one-line awk script because the awk programming language has a standard printf function:

```
awk 'BEGIN { printf("%s", "foo") }'
```

Some very old awk implementations may only provide sprintf, requiring you to write print sprintf(...) and making it impossible to omit the trailing new line.

Some printf implementations(...) have fairly short limits on total length of formatted output or total length of individual conversions. The lowest limits I have encountered are a bit over 2000 characters for zero-padded numeric values. (Space-padded values did not have the same problem.) If you stay under that limit, you should have no problems.

ps

Predicting the option flags available for the ps command is an exercise in futility. I planned to write about how systems generally now support the modern POSIX (and historic System V) flags, but the first system I tested doesn't. On Berkeley systems, ps -ax will usually get you a list of all running processes; on other systems, it is ps -ef. It is very hard to write anything portable using ps output, but a partial example is provided in Chapter 10.

python

The python binary is the interpreter for Python. As with perl, you may have to look around a bit to find a particular version. Conventionally, specific versions are installed as python*X.Y*, so you can tell which version you have. One of my test systems has python2.4 but not python; do not assume that a system with Python installed will have a binary without a version number.

ranlib

The ranlib utility is used to create headers for archives created by the ar archiver. It is only rarely still needed on modern systems. Today, its primary function is illustrating examples of how to choose a utility on the fly by pointing out the use of true as a substitute on systems that no longer provide or require ranlib.

rm

Both the -f and -r options are portable. There is no guarantee that a silent rm -f has succeeded, and there are circumstances under which it can fail. It is not portable to call rm without any file arguments.

rpm2cpio

The rpm utility is not available for all systems. The rpm2cpio utility is also not available on all systems, but many systems provide it as a way to extract files from RPM packages without using the RPM database. Try not to depend on this in a script, but be aware that there is a way to get files out of an RPM package even without the rpm utility. However, rpm2cpio does not report the ownership of files in the package.

rs

The rs utility "reshapes" input; for instance, it can convert lines of data with one word to a line into columns of data. It is not universally available, being most common on BSD systems. Many of the things rs would be used for can be handled by some combination of cut, paste, or join; failing that, you can do just about anything in awk.

sed

The character used to separate patterns (like / in s/*from*/*to*/) may not portably appear in patterns, even in a character class. Use a separator that does not occur in these strings. There are a number of special case bugs with sed on older systems. On modern systems, you get the best portability writing a sed script as a single argument using new lines to separate commands and without the -e option. If you use ! on a command, do not leave a trailing space after the !. Some versions of sed strip leading whitespace from arguments to the a, c, and i commands. You can use a backslash at the beginning of a line to create an escaped space that suppresses this obnoxious behavior. (See Chapter 11 for more information about sed.)

sh

It would take a book (this one, by preference) to describe all the portability issues you may see in variants on the sh program. Remember that there is no guarantee that a shell script is actually running in /bin/sh; if you call a script with sh, it may behave differently than it would if you read it in with the . command or invoked $SHELL on it. If you call it with $SHELL, and your script is being run by a csh or tcsh user, it could be even worse. Your best bet is usually to make sure that all of your scripts either run correctly in /bin/sh or know how to reexecute themselves if they have to, and then always use sh to invoke them.

In general, avoid options other than -c and -x. It is fine to pass commands to a shell through a pipe, but you might be better off using some combination of eval and subshells.

sort

Pre-POSIX systems used +*N* to indicate an *N*-column offset in each line as the search key. POSIX uses -k *N* to indicate the *N*th column. So, sort +4 is the same as sort -k 5. The -k option is available on all modern systems, so use it; you are much more likely to encounter a system that does not handle the +*N* notation than a system that does not handle the -k notation. Behavior when handling complicated keys (such as numeric sorting by multiple keys, or even just numeric sorting by anything but the beginning of the line) is occasionally buggy, although most common cases work. Behavior when sorting nonnumeric keys numerically can be unpredictable. Bugs are much more common when inputs are large enough to require temporary files to hold intermediate results; try not to sort more data than can fit in memory.

stat

The stat utility (usually a wrapper around the stat(2) system call) is not portable. Many GNU and BSD systems provide utilities of this name, with comparable functionality, but they have wildly different invocations and outputs. You can use the test command to answer many questions about files and the ls command for others.

tar

See the section "Archive Utilities" earlier in the chapter. Remember to keep an eye out also for GNU tar (sometimes named gtar) and Jörg Schilling's "Schily tar," usually named star. You cannot safely assume that a particular version is available.

touch

On systems where the file system can represent subsecond timestamps, touch may not store information more precise than the second; this can actually change a file's timestamp to be up to one second in the past. On fast machines, this can be a problem.

troff

See nroff.

tsort

The tsort utility performs topological sorts. The most common use of it is to identify the order in which to specify object files to a linker that has to receive files in a sorted order. However, this program can be used for just about any kind of dependency checking. A typical usage would be to make a list of relationships between activities that must be performed in order. For example, if you were writing a script to raid and terrorize coastal villages, you might begin with a list of observations; you have to loot before you can pillage, and you must pillage before you burn. Furthermore, you must defeat all who oppose you before you can loot. You would express this to tsort as a file (or standard input stream) containing pairs of words. Idiomatically, there is one pair to a line:

```
$ tsort <<EOF
loot pillage
pillage burn
defeat loot
EOF
defeat
loot
pillage
burn
$
```

This utility is available on most systems, but sometimes outside the standard path; on Solaris, for instance, it is in /usr/ccs/bin.

unix2dos

See `dos2unix`.

unzip

See `zip`.

xargs

The `-0` option, which uses ASCII NUL characters instead of new lines to separate file arguments, is not totally portable. Unfortunately, its absence creates a serious problem that is at the very least a bug magnet and can create serious security holes. If you cannot ensure that your script will generally be run on systems that provide this option, avoid `xargs` with file lists that contain files you did not create. Note that this is no worse than the behavior you get passing a list into a `while read` *var* loop. It is a potential security hole if you aren't alert to it, but it may be livable. If you can be sure of systems where `find` and `xargs` support NUL character separators, use those options.

zip

This is an archive utility, usually paired with `unzip`. It is not universally available, although it's quite common on desktop systems.

What to Do When Something Is Unavailable

Sooner or later, you will find yourself in the uncomfortable circumstance of having guessed wrong on utility portability. The field is too large to keep track of; there are too many utilities to learn, and there are too many systems with local variants and surprises.

But all is not lost. You can generally work around the absence of a utility one way or another, and this section goes into some of the techniques used to handle these circumstances. There are several possible solutions to the problem of a missing utility. You can develop your own clone of it, if it is small, and include it with your script (or even implement it as a shell function in your script). You may be able to get the utility added to your target system, if you have any influence over it. In some cases, you can patch other utilities together to obtain the results you need. Sometimes, you can settle for something nearly good enough. If a system simply does not have symbolic links, you may be able to make do with hard links, or with copies.

One other resolution is on the table: Sometimes, you may find that the best you can do is insist on a more complete or modern system. This is a rare choice and should never be your first response to a problem, but keep it in mind.

Roll Your Own

Sometimes the best way to be sure you can rely on a utility or feature being available is to develop your own. Many common utility programs can be implemented (sometimes more tediously, or more slowly) in terms of other existing utility programs. There are a few ways to approach this. You can write separate utility programs, whether as shell scripts or in another language. However, this leaves you with an additional problem at installation time, which is ensuring that your helper programs also get installed. Many simpler utilities can be implemented as shell functions, which allows you to embed them in a program. You can even use your own script as multiple different programs by defining special command-line options to tell your script to do something special; for instance, the standard autoconf configure script behaves very differently when run with the --fallback-echo argument.

This technique is of limited and specialized applicability, but as long as the programs you need are simple enough to duplicate, it can work. It is also sometimes your only option.

Add a Missing Utility

You can require the user to install additional software or install it yourself. This presumes an environment with some control of the target system; for instance, a script to be run on machines on a corporate network may be able to simply impose a requirement that particular packages must be installed for the script to work. If you are shipping a product and want to rely on particular utilities, you can document them as requirements; this does not work as well because users never read documentation, but it is better than not documenting the requirement.

The weakness of this strategy is that there are times when it is simply impossible for the user to comply. While most scripts do not need to run on embedded systems today, there is a rapidly increasing pool of small portable devices that contain some variety of UNIX and a somewhat stripped-down environment.

Use Something Else

If it turns out that a utility you thought was universal isn't, use something else. The UNIX shell environment is a fairly full-featured programming language, and you can do just about anything in it with enough time and attention. Often, the problem is not that there is no portable solution, but that the portable solution requires you to make effective use of a utility you've never even heard of. This is a great time to go browsing around documentation, trying to think of other key words to search for, and so on.

Demand a Real System

This is sort of the antithesis of portable code, but it may apply. In the case where other requirements, such as performance or development time, are simply too crucial, and a particular system is causing you grief, you may want to see whether that system can be removed from the project definition. As is often the case, 10% of the time does 90% of the work. If you can establish that your code is fine except on systems with a particular flaw, but working around it is going to be difficult and time-consuming, this may be the course to pursue.

Do not do this merely because a system lacks an extension it would be neat to have. Reserve this for cases where the offending system is clearly wrong. Obviously, this never applies when a particular target system is central to the problem specification. If you are trying to write a script that will be used exclusively on an embedded system, you have to work with what that system provides. On the other hand, if you have a script aimed at full-featured desktop systems, it may be impractical to expect you to make it run also on an embedded system with only a stripped-down busybox.

In some cases, after further discussion, this can become the friendlier case of adding a missing utility (see the previous section). If the problem is just that a particular program is absent or buggy, a replacement can perhaps be found and stated as an explicit requirement.

A Few Examples

The first example I ever saw of a common problem along these lines was a little script called install.sh, which was common in free software packages. Because Berkeley and other systems had, in their typical fashion, all disagreed on how to write a program to copy a file to a given location with particular ownership and permissions, many programmers took to writing a portable script that performed the expected functions. The full functionality of the script can be quite complicated; some versions check to ensure they are not copying a file onto itself, strip binaries of debugging symbols, and otherwise do things that are commonly needed or useful when installing a file, but that are tedious to get right. Variants of this script are still found in many systems (as are dozens of totally unrelated files named install.sh).

The portability problems of echo have been solved (or at least worked around) in several different ways, illustrating some of the previously described strategies. Many scripts test for common behaviors and define two variables (nearly always named $C and $N, or $ECHO_C and $ECHO_N), which allow commands like echo $N No newline:$C. This is moderately idiomatic, and most shell programmers will recognize it. The following variant of an example from Chapter 7 illustrates this:

```
case `echo -n "\c"` in
-n*c) ECHO_N='' ECHO_C='' ;;
*c) ECHO_N='-n' ECHO_C='' ;;
*) ECHO_N='' ECHO_C='\c' ;;
esac
echo $ECHO_N Testing...$ECHO_C
echo "Ok."
```

```
Testing...Ok.
```

The AC_PROG_LIBTOOL macro in configure.in scripts (implemented by the libtool.m4 macro file distributed with libtool) provides a particularly complete workaround for a much more insidious problem: working around echo implementations that interpret backslashes. This code is about 250 lines of fairly complicated shell scripting. It is too much to reproduce here, but this is a fairly typical sample:

```
if test "X$echo" = Xecho; then
    # We didn't find a better echo, so look for alternatives.
    if test "X`(print -r '\t') 2>/dev/null`" = 'X\t' &&
        echo_testing_string=`(print -r "$echo_test_string") 2>/dev/null` &&
        test "X$echo_testing_string" = "X$echo_test_string"; then
        # This shell has a builtin print -r that does the trick.
        echo='print -r'
```

```
    elif (test -f /bin/ksh || test -f /bin/ksh$ac_exeext) &&
        test "X$CONFIG_SHELL" != X/bin/ksh; then
[...]
```

One of the cases used is to define a special argument, --fallback-echo, which causes the script to try to display its own arguments. The implementation is excellent:

```
if test "X$1" = X--fallback-echo; then
  # used as fallback echo
  shift
  cat <<EOF
$*
EOF
  exit 0
fi
```

This does not handle the case where you want to produce output without a new line, but it does eliminate the common problem of shells stripping backslashes.

Some users do something like any of the options previously discussed, but they create a shell function to wrap the desired behavior; this has been the solution I've generally encouraged (as in the original version of the $ECHO_N example, which was in Chapter 7). Some programmers simply rely on the printf command or on shell builtins like ksh's print. Any of these can provide consistent behavior, and some allow reliable production of unterminated lines. And, finally, a last option exists: Avoid starting the arguments to echo with a hyphen, avoid backslashes, and just accept the lack of a portable way to produce output with no new line at the end. This limits your output options, but it is completely portable.

A couple of counterexamples are also worth considering. A number of application installers for Linux systems have been pretty awful. The most obvious and recurring theme is the assumption that sh is always bash. A number of install scripts I have tried to use have choked badly because I usually have $BLOCKSIZE set to 1m in my environment; this resulted in naive install scripts declaring that a disk with 5GB free (5000 one-megabyte blocks) is not large enough to support an installation that requires 10MB because they interpreted 5000 blocks of reported free space as 2.5MB (5000 half-kilobyte blocks). Another common failure mode is assumptions about the stat utility, which I've seen several times in different installers.

What's Next?

This is just about it for the fiddly little details. What comes next is a bit of a higher-level perspective of portability. Chapter 9 talks about how to design scripts so that they will be easier to write portably and how to identify a good candidate for development as a shell script in the first place. Portability is important for reusability and value out of code, but there are other things you should consider as well. A portable script that is only useful once does you little good; next up is the question of how to make a script you will *want* to reuse on other systems.

CHAPTER 9

■ ■ ■

Bringing It All Together

So far, this book has focused mostly on technical details of the portability of the shell. Good portable code, however, requires additional skills. It is impossible to successfully test on everything; sooner or later, a script you write will be used on a system that didn't even exist when you wrote it. New standards will come out, new extensions will be defined, and new bugs will sneak into production releases. This chapter discusses some of the ways in which you can write scripts that are more likely to survive new systems.

It is not usually enough to have a script that will run on the existing systems you are targeting. Furthermore, it may not be enough to have a script that runs everywhere. If your script is confusing or unmaintainable as a result of your portability efforts, you will end up with more bugs; this makes your script useless to you.

Robustness

A program is called robust when it works despite unexpected failures. Robustness is useful on many levels. A robust program is more likely to work when something minor goes wrong; it is more likely to give useful diagnostics when something major goes wrong. Robust programs are more likely to detect and correct for bugs, to handle unexpected circumstances, and to survive transitions or changes in their working environment.

Robustness matters a little more in portable code than in other code because there are more things that might go unexpectedly wrong. Programs may provide multiple incompatible versions of a utility, but if you try to specify a particular one by path, your code may not survive a transition to other systems.

Computer security and reliability people often advocate a strategy of having multiple redundant layers of protection against errors; this is called *defense in depth*. You should design your code to detect, and protect against, errors at multiple points. Verify that file names are valid; check that operations succeed. There will be bugs sooner or later, even in your error-handling code. Test your assumptions early on, but test them later, too. Sanity-check values. If you think you've gotten the absolute path to a file, it had better have a path separator in it; if it doesn't, something went wrong.

Handling Failure

The essence of robust code is that it handles failure. You cannot ensure that nothing will ever fail; all you can do is check for failure and handle it. Handling an error need not mean correcting it. Sometimes, all you can do is diagnose that something went wrong and possibly abort execution before things get worse.

Handling Is Not Always Correction

In some cases, you can correct an error. That's great. In some cases, it is not possible to correct an error. At this point, you should emit a diagnostic explaining what went wrong, clean up, and abort. It is rarely beneficial to try to continue after a problem, although in some cases it can be. As a general rule, if future operations are not dependent on previous operations, try them all, reporting errors for the ones that fail. If operations are in a logical sequence, abort execution once something has gone wrong.

If You Can't, Don't

Let me start with the most important lesson of all in failure handling: *If you cannot do anything about an error, it is useless to check for it.* This doesn't mean you shouldn't check for errors that you can't completely correct; only errors you can't do anything about. For instance, consider the following code fragment:

```
func_die() {
  if echo "$@" >&2
  then :
  else # what goes here?
  fi
  exit 1
}
```

This function tries to display a message and then exit unsuccessfully, much like the standard Perl function die. It tests to ensure that the echo command succeeded, and if it doesn't . . . well, now what? If you can't write to standard error, you can't display a message on standard error saying that you can't write to standard error. The script was already going to exit with an abnormal exit code, so it can't use that to communicate that something has gone horribly wrong. While being unable to display error messages is perhaps a problem, it is not a problem you can solve. There is nothing that can be done to correct this error, or accommodate it, or work around it. If you are thinking, "Well, you could try to write a message to standard output," you get bonus points for creativity. But this is a very bad idea. If there is one thing worse than an undiagnosed error, it's an error diagnostic making it into what should have been a pure data stream.

There is another potential problem with this proposed function. If your script was expecting to do cleanup after a problem, that cleanup code may not get run, leaving temporary files or other objects in limbo, possibly cluttering things or causing errors on future runs. If you have cleanup code, run it before calling any function that is designed to exit the script (or use trap *cleanup_code* 0; see Chapter 6).

When You Find Yourself in a Hole, Stop Digging

The great disasters of my script programming career have usually been code that worked perfectly running after code that failed. Here is a sample of the sort of thing I have done wrong:

```
for i in $names
do
  mkdir $i
  cd $i
  [... do stuff ...]
  cd ..
  rm -rf $i
done
```

Nice, simple script, right? Here's my advice: Do not try this script when there is a possibility that one of the names in $names will be something like . (the current directory), will have a space in it, or anything else weird. Here's what happens with the word . in $names:

```
mkdir .              # fails
cd .                 # succeeds, but I'm still in the directory I started in
[... do stuff ...]   # might or might not work
cd ..                # oops, I'm now above the directory I started in
rm -rf .             # and now I remove the new working directory
```

Nicely catastrophic for a seemingly harmless chunk of code. Now, imagine that I'd written this with even minimal error checking:

```
for i in $names
do
  mkdir $i || continue
  ( cd $i || exit
  [... do stuff ...]
  )
  rm -rf $i
done
```

In this case, if the initial `mkdir` fails, nothing gets done at all. (No diagnostic message, which is bad style, but nothing happens, so at least I don't have to go looking for backups.) Putting the `cd` command in a subshell ensures that the next command after the subshell is in the directory I started in, no matter what happens. Whether I create or change directories during "do stuff," whatever happens is in a subshell and does not affect the calling code. There is still a lot of room for cleaning up this code and fixing it, but the two most common errors are now prevented.

Do not omit error checking. For readability and brevity, this book omits a large amount of error checking in many examples. Be more careful than that in production code.

One possibility to consider is using set -e to cause the shell to abort if an error occurs. When the -e option is set, the shell exits immediately after executing any complete command that yields a non-zero exit status. Commands that are in explicit tests, such as the control statements of if or while loops, do not cause the shell to exit, but individual commands in the body of a loop will cause an exit. If you use set -e, any command that could fail must be explicitly tested, or the script will abort without comment. For instance, the following fragment would not be safe:

```
diff -u file.old file.new > file.diffs
```

The `diff` command, in addition to writing differences between two files to standard output, returns a non-zero status if it encounters any differences. In cases where you simply do not care about the exit status of a command, you can follow it by `|| true`, ensuring that the command as a whole yields a successful return status, as in the following example:

```
diff -u file.old file.new > file.diffs || true
```

I do not recommend using `set -e`; it is uncomfortably vulnerable to overlooking boundary conditions that are genuinely harmless. Furthermore, the lack of any diagnostic message from the shell makes it hard to figure out what went wrong. (You can use a `trap` to print some kind of diagnostic, but there is still no way to say what went wrong.)

Temporary Files and Cleanup

In previous chapters, passing reference was made to using the `trap` command to handle cleanup of temporary files. The first thing you must know is that you cannot ensure that cleanup will be run successfully. If someone sends your script a `SIGKILL` command, execution ceases and nothing more gets done. If you need to ensure that data are never exposed, do not put them in temporary files.

The first stage of implementing good cleanup is simply to perform cleanup. If you create temporary files, delete them when you are done with them. However, there are a number of additional subtleties to the creation and use of temporary files. First, it is hard to create a temporary file securely, ensuring that other programs cannot create problems for your script's temporary file, whether maliciously or accidentally. Secondly, cleaning up temporary files can be complicated, especially if you create a number of them.

Creating Temporary Files

There are a number of issues you need to consider when creating a temporary file. First, you must ensure that there are no clashes. You want to make sure that other programs will not inadvertently end up using the same files you do. This applies both to instances of other programs and to multiple instances of the same script running at the same time. As a general rule, a good starting place is to use the process ID as one component of a file name. This generally provides reasonable protection against accidents. The only major caveat to keep in mind is that a long-running system will eventually recycle process IDs, so be sure to empty or truncate temporary files before using them even when using a process ID. Since two processes running at the same time cannot have the same pid, this may be enough.

However, there are a few limitations. If the location in which your temporary files are created is shared storage, there may be two programs running on different computers with the same pid, leading to clashes. Subshells have the same $$ value as their parent process, so a subshell trying to generate a unique name might clash. Finally, there is the most serious problem: Not all clashes are accidents. Malicious users often use the semi-predictable naming of temporary files as a way to attack vulnerable programs.

It is not sufficient to check whether a file exists before creating it; the window between the existence check and the creation of the file is plenty of time for an attacker to create a file your script can open, giving the attacker access to your temporary file. (Do not rely on the notion that this is too rare to occur; the attacker only has to get lucky once, but you have to get lucky every time.)

Quite simply, you cannot portably avoid this problem in shell. It isn't even entirely portable to work around this in C. The good solutions are not as widely standardized as you might hope. When you open a file, it is possible that it already existed; if it did, your script is compromised.

So, here is the secret to creating temporary files safely: Don't. If you really need a temporary file, you have to be in control not just of the file, but of the directory it is created in.

Creating Temporary Directories

While file creation is prone to risks, directory creation has a significant advantage: If you try to create a directory that already exists, mkdir fails. This allows you to be sure that the directory you finally create is actually owned by you. The only hard part is ensuring that the directory is not writeable by other users; otherwise, any attempt to create files in the directory is vulnerable to the problems previously described for temporary files. Ensure that the directory's mode is restrictive by using umask or using the -m mode option to mkdir. The following two examples are functionally equivalent:

```
(umask 077; mkdir $tmpdir)
mkdir -m 0700 $tmpdir
```

The -m *mode* option is portable to modern systems but avoids use of a subshell. If you need to target Windows systems, you might prefer it. To use this in a script, be sure to check whether mkdir succeeded. It is not sufficient to check whether the directory exists; if an attacker created the directory already, it will exist but will not be under your control. A typical usage might look like this:

```
if mkdir -m 0700 "$tmpdir" 2>/dev/null; then
  echo "Successful creation of temporary directory." >&2
else
  echo "Could not create temporary directory." >&2
fi
```

You might want to wrap this in a loop to try to generate likely directory names. For a more complete solution, look at the func_mktempdir function in libtool. There are a number of additional utilities, such as mktemp, that might help you out but are not universally available. Know your target systems. If mktemp is not available, at least try to make your temporary file names a little unpredictable. Using your pid ($$) alone is not very good at protecting against attackers; in shells that have the $RANDOM variable, you can use that, as in the following example (extracted from libtool):

```
my_tmpdir="${my_template}-${RANDOM-0}$$"
```

In a shell that has no special $RANDOM parameter, ${RANDOM-0} expands to 0 (or whatever a user may have set it to).

Once you have succeeded in creating a directory, you can use it to hold temporary files. Because the directory is owned by you and has a restrictive mode, you do not need to worry about race conditions or attackers, as long as the temporary directory itself is reasonably secure. (Of course, a user with root privileges can override this, but a user with root privileges always wins a security fight.)

Do not use the -p option with mkdir in this circumstance. First, it is nonportable. Second, mkdir -p silently succeeds if the target directory already exists. This eliminates the security benefit of using mkdir instead of just creating individual temporary files. If you wish to make an arbitrarily nested directory, you can do so by looping through making the directories one at a time. For a more detailed example, examine the func_mkdir_p implementation in libtoolize.

Removing Temporary Files

When you are done with temporary files, delete them. (For debugging, you may wish to have an option to your script that suppresses this normally desired behavior.) If you are using a temporary directory, and you should be, this is made much easier by the fact that you can simply delete the whole directory and its contents.

In general, you should be aggressive about deleting files as soon as you can; this reduces the amount of junk left around the system if a script is killed unexpectedly. Try to avoid relying on exit traps (see the discussion in the next section, "Handling Interrupts"); instead, ensure that files are deleted as soon as you are done with them. It may make sense to store a list of files to remove when done, or you can remove a whole temporary directory at once. In general, though, leaving all the files until the end is careless and may result in unwanted surprises.

UNLINKED FILES

There is a clever trick known to a fair number of UNIX users that helps eliminate the scourge of temporary files: Delete them before you are done using them. On a UNIX system, in general, if you open a file, then use rm to delete it, the file still exists. The file has been unlinked, and does not exist in the directory hierarchy anymore, but the system does not actually clear the file out from the disk until the file has been closed. Some programs make clever use of this to create files that are then used to store or share data. When the program ends, the file descriptor is automatically closed, and the file ceases to exist. This works no matter how the program terminates; even a SIGKILL doesn't change it.

This is an exceptionally cool trick, which you can use to do all sorts of magic. It does have one tiny little flaw—it is not portable. (It is also less useful in shell scripts than it would be in C because the shell has no easy way to look around in an open file.) In particular, this is not available at all on Windows-like systems, but even UNIX systems might sometimes use a file system that does not allow an open file to be deleted. Be aware of the technique, but don't use it in scripts.

Handling Interrupts

The shell does not have a real exception handling mechanism in the sense that some more recent programming languages do. However, the trap command can provide for some simple emergency recovery after errors. In particular, you can use the special signal 0 to perform cleanup tasks whenever the script exits, assuming it exits cleanly (rather than being killed by another signal, for instance). The following script fragment creates a temporary directory (using an admittedly insecure name for brevity), then registers a handler to remove it on exit:

```
mkdir /tmp/example.$$
trap "rm -rf /tmp/example.$$" 0
```

This example works as designed, but it is vulnerable to a subtle bug. Imagine that two pieces of code in your script do the same thing:

```
mkdir /tmp/example_a.$$
trap "rm -rf /tmp/example_a.$$" 0
mkdir /tmp/example_b.$$
trap "rm -rf /tmp/example_b.$$" 0
```

This script removes the example_b directory, but not the example_a directory; the second exit trap replaces the first.

While this provides for last-minute cleanup for normal script exits, it doesn't do anything when a signal is caught by another handler. If the shell exits from an interrupt handler, it is likely to run an exit trap handler (though zsh does not).

There is no definite rule as to whether or not you should trap interrupts. In general, it is nice to clean up any temporary files you are creating, although you may want an option to suppress this behavior; it can be maddening to debug a script that deletes all the evidence when it screws up. Leave that strategy to the politicians. The case where it's most important to start trapping interrupts is code with critical sections where a system's intermediate states are unusable. If you are modifying system files in a script, it may make sense to trap interrupts to prevent accidents. Most scripts have no reason to trap most signals.

Startup Files and Environment Variables

The entire environment in which you write scripts is potentially subject to user interference. Executing commands relies on the $PATH environment variable, but there's more. Many utilities have behavior that can be influenced by environment variables. The $BLOCKSIZE environment variable can, on some systems, alter the output of many common utilities.

In some shells, there are startup scripts that may be processed even when running a shell script. For instance, pdksh and ash run the $ENV setup script at the start of execution even when running a script. Because shell functions and aliases both take priority over external commands, it is possible that a user's startup environment will substantially alter the behavior of a script.

There is very little you can do to be sure that none of this has happened to you. You can set the $BLOCKSIZE variable to an empty string while you are using utilities that rely on it. But be sure to set it back later; users probably set it for a reason. By the time your code is executing, however, it is too late to try to prevent $ENV from being run.

Ultimately, this is an unwinnable fight. Take a few reasonable precautions, but apart from that, if users run in a sufficiently misconfigured shell, scripts will fail. This is a good reason for users not to configure their environment badly. There are clever tricks (quoting the names of aliased commands, trying to reexecute the script with $ENV set to an empty string), but ultimately it is not worth the hassle. It is up to the user not to give you a hopelessly misconfigured environment.

Documentation and Comments

In general, the shell does not care about comments. You should.

The concept of defense in depth extends beyond just the question of how you try to ensure that there are no bugs. There will be bugs. You will need to maintain this code, or someone else will. (And don't get careless about that; you'll be the "someone else" for other peoples' code some day.) When you have to debug a script that you or someone else wrote long ago, you will need to understand how it works to identify the bugs. Good comments are a big part of successful debugging.

Furthermore, beyond the mere question of individual code comments explaining code fragments, be sure to have some top-level documentation. What is this script? What does it do? What arguments does it take? What arguments are valid? What systems has it been tested on? What assumptions does it make? Every one of those questions could, quite easily, turn out to be the source of a major problem somewhere down the road. Answer them early on, ideally in comments within your script.

When you validate arguments (and you should always do this), be sure you give a clear error message (to standard error, not standard output) showing your script's usage options. Stick to the normal UNIX conventions to express options and arguments.

What to Document

Describe the basic purpose and design of your script. Explain what job it does, and how it should be invoked. Here's a sample:

```
# errno: Explain error names or numbers
# usage: errno error...
# e.g., errno ENOENT
# output:
# ENOENT [2]:            No such file or directory
# inputs should be integers or symbolic errno values.
# relies on /usr/include/sys/errno.h
```

This small chunk of text tells you pretty much what you need to know to maintain this program, and if you're an experienced C programmer who's used a number of platforms, it even gives you a pretty good idea of what's likely to go wrong. Different systems use different files to hold the error definitions, here described as existing in /usr/include/sys/errno.h. If this utility gives cryptic error messages (other than those intended) on a new system, it is quite likely that the problem has to do with the choice of header file. If I had taken the two minutes it took to write that back in 1994 when I wrote this script, I would have saved myself about ten minutes of staring at a script I no longer remembered anything much about in 2008. (This was the one shell script from my previous work that needed modification when I started doing more Linux work.)

What to Comment

Not everything. There is no code so unreadable as code that has been commented by someone who thinks everything needs comments. Avoid commenting on common and well-known idioms; use such idioms frequently so that you need fewer comments. Your goal is not to comment lots; it is to comment well and clearly. A reader only needs to see this once to lose all hope that the program in question is going to work:

```
count=`expr $count + 1` # add 1 to count
```

In general, comments should tell the reader something that might not be obvious. Go ahead and assume that your reader knows what basic UNIX commands do. The subject of comments should be an explanation of *why* you are doing something, rather than just a simple description of *what* you are doing. Compare these two comments:

```
args="$args $i" # append $i to $args
args="$args $i" # build list of files
```

The former comment is useless; the latter comment at least tells you what the purpose or goal of the code is.

Any function you define should have at least a brief comment explaining its arguments, behaviors, and any outputs. Distinguish between return code, output, and side effects (such as file modification). This description should be in addition to any comments needed on the function's actual code.

Comment mechanisms sparingly, but there are times when this is appropriate. If it takes you a while to get a very small piece of code right, go ahead and explain it. I have rarely seen a shell using eval in a way that could not have benefited from an explanatory comment.

Stylistically, feel free to put small comments on the same line as the code they explain, although I recommend a bit of extra space to make them visually distinct. If you have several commented lines in a row, aligning the comments can make them easier to read. Longer comments or comments on whole blocks of code tend to look better above the code they explain. Some programs are obliged to process options, even if they occur later in the command line. The following script fragment does this and explains what it is doing:

```
# sort arguments into options and file names
files=""
opts=""
for i
do
  case $i in
  -*) opts="$opts $i";;    # name starting with - is an option
  *) files="$files $i";;
  esac
done
```

The comment at the top of the fragment explains the purpose of the code; the inline comment explains a particular convention to the reader. Of course, you would do better to use something more flexible, such as the command processing code illustrated in Chapter 6.

The most common problem with comments in old code, and one of the key arguments against over-commenting, is that comments tend to become inaccurate over time. When you update code, be sure to update the comments as well. This is more work in code with more comments, especially trivial comments. It is common for tiny details of a script to change; it is rare for fundamental algorithms or designs to change. This suggests a good guideline in commenting; your comments should explain the code, not repeat it. Otherwise, you end up with comments that start out useless, and eventually become wrong. Imagine encountering the following line in a script you are debugging:

```
BLOCK=4096      # use one-kilobyte BLOCKSIZE
```

Is this a bug? If it is, is the bug that the comment is wrong or that the definition of BLOCK is wrong? Is the name of the variable wrong? This comment creates more questions than it answers. It is also, distressingly, not a particularly atypical comment. In this case, the best guess is that the code originally read BLOCKSIZE=1024, and that the code has changed and the comment hasn't. If you are looking for a bug, especially a bug involving handling of block sizes, it is quite possible that this is it. (This example is based on real code I saw, although it was not in a shell script.)

Degrade Gracefully

Programs that do the best they can, correctly, rather than failing dismally, are said to *degrade gracefully*. It is quite reasonable to try to provide extra features when possible, but if those features impact portability, it is often better to provide an alternative, even if it may be less functional. For instance, some installation scripts that need root privileges try to use the sudo utility to gain them. When the utility is installed, and when the user has access to it, this can be quite convenient. However, if the sudo utility is missing, such a script may fail unconditionally, even when run as root. That makes the script less useful to users who have root access but lack the sudo utility. A better choice would be to try to use sudo only if it is installed. If the utility is unavailable, check for permissions instead. If you need additional privileges, tell the user what privileges you need, and exit gracefully without doing anything else; if you already have the needed privileges, just run normally.

If there is some check you must make in a fairly frequent operation, make it into a shell function. There is no reason to write your test for a given utility, or even just a conditional operation, dozens of times. You might want to use the system's install utility if it is available, but fall back on manual copying. (A disclaimer: There are differences between traditional BSD and System V install programs. You may not want to use either.) First, you would determine the path to the system utility, if it's in $PATH:

```
found_install=` IFS=':';
  for dir in $PATH; do
    test -x "$dir"/install && { echo "$dir"/install; exit 0; }
  done `
```

This mildly elaborate chunk of code checks each directory in $PATH for an executable named install; if it finds one, it echoes the name and the subshell exits. (The exit is needed in case of a system on which there is more than one such program in $PATH.) Given this, you could write code like the following to install a program in $HOME/bin:

```
if test -n "$found_install"; then
  "$found_install" -m 755 newscript "$HOME/bin"
else
  rm -f "$HOME/bin/newscript"
  cp newscript "$HOME/bin"
  chmod 755 "$HOME/bin/newscript"
fi
```

While this works fine for a single file, it quickly becomes awkward. The first step in correcting this is to move it into a function:

```
func_install() {
  for file
  do
    if test -n "$found_install"; then
      "$found_install" -m 755 "$file" "$HOME/bin"
    else
      rm -f "$HOME/bin/$file"
      cp newscript "$HOME/bin"
      chmod 755 "$HOME/bin/$file"
    fi
  done
}
```

Now, calls to this function are much briefer, and easier to write, than the longer if-else construct was. However, there is another improvement possible. In general, the value of $found_install should never change. So why test it all the time?

```
if test -n "$found_install"; then
  func_install() {
    for file
    do
      "$found_install" -m 755 "$file" "$HOME/bin"
    done
  }
else
  func_install() {
    for file
    do
      rm -f "$HOME/bin/$file"
      cp newscript "$HOME/bin"
      chmod 755 "$HOME/bin/$file"
    done
  }
fi
```

Now, the function definition depends on the results of the initial test, and each function call omits the separate test. While in this case the behaviors are fairly similar (though not identical), this works even when the net result is a noticeable difference in provided functionality.

Of course, this assumes that all the `install` utilities are compatible; they are not, and this is why many programs ship with an external `install-sh` script, which tries to provide a reasonably stable set of options and semantics. The tricky part is that the conventional System V `install` utility has completely different semantics for the `-c` option. The BSD semantics are probably better; this is why people tend to specify it or provide wrappers (such as the portable `install-sh` distributed with many configure scripts).

Specify, and Test For, Requirements

Whenever possible, test for the preconditions your script requires rather than just failing dismally. A script that needs root privileges should test for them first and give an informative error message if it doesn't have them. Trying to run with a genuine requirement absent is crazy. It is not just that your script may not work; it is that it may work partially. A few pages full of "Permission denied" messages are bad enough, but the commands that don't fail may have surprising effects (see "When You Find Yourself in a Hole, Stop Digging" earlier in this chapter).

As a general rule, once you have a list of requirements for your script (inputs, valid arguments, privileges, programs you depend on), you should check for them all before starting to do anything substantial. (This can impose a substantial performance cost; see the next section, "Scripts That Write Scripts.")

As you write the documentation describing your requirements, write tests for any that you can figure out a way to test for. Be as cautious and thorough as you have time for; the frequency with which surprising things go wrong is itself surprising.

Finally, if you come up with an elegant test for a requirement, and it implies a workaround, feel free to remove the requirement and just write the script to be more portable in the first place. It will save you time later.

Scripts That Write Scripts

Sometimes the best way to develop a portable script is to use another utility to create the final script. There are two major ways to pursue this. One is to use a tool like `m4sh` to build a very carefully tuned portable script while hiding most of the hard work from you. Another is to write a script that creates as output a less portable script tuned for a given system.

M4SH, AUTOCONF, AND AUTOMAKE

There are a lot of tasks for which m4sh might be a particularly good choice. The weaknesses of m4sh are that it imposes additional syntax constraints and that the generated scripts can be a bit hard to read. On the other hand, with careful use, it can produce exceptionally portable scripts, complete with fairly full-featured execution preambles.

The choice of whether to write a relatively simple script without these features or to use these features is not one with an unambiguous and universal right answer. If you need to run on a very broad range of target systems, tools like m4sh are probably quite valuable in keeping on top of a variety of systems with strange and unpredictable limitations. If you have the luxury of assuming POSIX systems and shells, such tools may be overkill. If you have to target extremely specialized systems (such as small embedded systems lacking many common utilities), m4sh will not help you very much.

If you are interested in using m4sh, you should look at a recent autoconf release for the basic utility. For additional insights, get a recent release of libtool to see how m4sh is used to build flexible and powerful scripts. Of particular interest is that you can add your own portability shims; for instance, standard autoconf does not test for the buggy echo implementations that strip backslashes, but libtool has code to do this.

Building a Script for a Specific Target

If it is practical to ensure that a script is always recreated for each target system, you can run another program (often a script) on each target that performs all the usual tests and builds the script correctly for a particular target. The result is an output file that is not portable, but is built in a way that allows it to target multiple systems. People who have worked in compiled languages will find this oddly familiar. This can noticeably improve the runtime performance of a script on a given system, but it does leave you with a problem: If you fix bugs on a given system, you have to do extra work to propagate them to other systems. This is usually only useful if performance is very important for a given script. A few milliseconds of startup time are usually a nonissue.

The simplest way to do this is to run something similar to an execution preamble; however, instead of executing the variable definitions and function definitions, write them into a file that becomes a header for a script. The remainder of the script code can be appended to this preamble to create a working script. For instance, the following header might work on a POSIX standard system with no special requirements:

```
#!/bin/sh
```

A system where the default shell is pre-POSIX might need a more elaborate header:

```
#!/bin/zsh
emulate sh
NULLCMD=:
```

In each case, the idea is to replace ten or 20 lines of execution preamble with the special case code needed for a particular system. The "script file" appended to these would lack the shebang line and be written with the assumption that the shell is always a standard POSIX shell. The preceding headers could be generated by a simple script:

```
#!/bin/sh
if eval '! false' 2>/dev/null; then
  func_script() {
    for i
    do
      ( echo "#!/bin/sh"; cat $i ) > $i.out
    done
  }
else
  func_script() {
    for i
    do
      ( echo "#!/bin/zsh"; echo "emulate sh"; echo "NULLCMD=:"; cat $i ) > $i.out
    done
  }
fi
func_script "$@"
```

Given the names of input script files, this creates new files (with .out appended to their names) with suitable execution preambles. There is plenty more you could usefully do in such a script; this is a minimal example to illustrate the technique. (More complete examples may be found in Chapter 7.)

Mixing with Other Languages

It is not necessary that a program used to create shell scripts be itself a shell script; the m4sh language uses m4, and some people have done reasonably well using make to create shell scripts. In particular, you should be comfortable with using both sed and awk, which are excellent candidates for textual manipulation (such as rewriting or modifying shell scripts). It is also useful to learn m4. Chapter 11 comes back to the question of how to mix shell code with other languages.

There are very few targets for which Perl is not available, but there are a fair number on which it is not installed out of the box (most notably, NetBSD). Although Perl is undoubtedly a more powerful and convenient language than the Bourne shell for many tasks, I continue to write many scripts primarily in shell.

What's Next?

Chapter 10 gets even farther away from the fiddly details and explores the question of what makes a shell script work well in a broader environment: conventions your scripts should follow, ways to be sure your script will stay useful on new systems and in new circumstances, and more.

CHAPTER 10

■ ■ ■

Shell Script Design

Many portability problems are made more approachable through good design. Good design makes it easier to isolate dependencies and reduces the chance that a portability issue with a tangentially related feature will prevent a script from performing its primary function. This chapter introduces some of the general principles of shell script design. There are other books that go into much more detail on shell script design and on program design in general. I focus primarily on issues applicable to shell scripts and, in particular, to portable shell scripts.

This chapter is full of guidelines, some of which are not always rules. The important thing is not to follow every guideline exactly in all cases; your goal should be to understand the purpose of each guideline, as well as understand when to follow it and when not to. As with many things, you have to know the rules before you can understand when to break them.

Because UNIX has largely accreted and evolved through the work of hundreds of people at many different companies over a period of decades, there is not total consistency. The mere fact that an existing utility does something a given way does not mean you should consider it a good example. For instance, no one should ever emulate the command-line argument parsing of dd; its *param=value* options are arcane, error-prone, and hard to remember. If `dd if=/dev/zero of=image bs=1m count=16` had been spelled `dd -i /dev/zero -o image -b 1m -n 16`, more people would be able to use it successfully without keeping the man page open. Of course, a more modern dd might support `--blocksize 1m --count 16`, which is pretty close, but then your code is no longer as portable as it used to be. (It's also reasonable to observe that redirection is probably better than the `if=/of=` arguments.)

This chapter uses an example of a hypothetical utility design—a small program called pids, developed to provide a scriptable alternative to the ps command.

Do One Thing Well

Why does portable `tar` not compress its archives? Why is there no built-in sort functionality in vi? In general, a program that does exactly one thing is much simpler to use than a program that does many things, and it can be mixed with programs that do other things. The UNIX convention that archive utilities do not worry about compression, and compression utilities do not worry about file hierarchies, has resulted in typically better performance of both tasks. Rob Pike's presentation "UNIX Style, or cat -v Considered Harmful" (USENIX Summer Conference Proceedings, 1983) made this case rather more sternly, but quite well. (See also the companion paper to the presentation, "Program Design in the UNIX Environment," co-written with Brian W. Kernighan: `http://harmful.cat-v.org/cat-v/unix_prog_design.pdf`.)

This is not to say no program should ever have a bit of additional functionality. The ls command does sort its output. This is not just for convenience, though; it is because some of the sorting options sort the output according to information that ls does not display. For instance, ls -t sorts files by modification time, but it does not display the modification time. It makes sense for ls to pay attention to file modification times because they are part of the information it extracts when doing long listings. Even when ls displays modification times, the display format is not something that sort could easily use as a sorting key, while the time-stamps ls obtains from the file system are integer values that can be sorted easily and quickly.

There are a number of utilities that allow you to kill processes by name; no two are the same. These are, I think, a bad design. The correct design, which I have adopted for pids, would be a program that lets you list processes by name, which can be combined easily with the existing kill utility.

Separate Functionality

One of the great strengths of the shell is its use as glue code. Often, a script that has become difficult to maintain or port would be better implemented as multiple programs, with a single top-level script combining the function of other programs. Just as a script using grep is much clearer to read than a script that implements it inline using while loops, it is often clearer to separate out some functionality and make it into a separate script. Describe your program carefully and see whether it would make sense to describe it in terms of other scripts; if so, you may be better off writing them separately. In some cases, shell functions can give you some of the same organizational benefit. Often, though, the greatest benefits come from complete separation.

When you separate a script into components, you make it easier to maintain the script. Each component is simpler and better focused. A problem with one does not necessarily affect the others. In general, this pays off substantially. Furthermore, the components are likely to get reused in other scripts, and additional development on them will pay greater dividends. The sort utility is much more powerful than the built-in sorting features many non-UNIX tools have acquired because it is used everywhere. When every application developer has to write a completely redundant sorting implementation, every application gets whatever mini-mal sorting functionality is good enough to get it out the door. Shared functionality tends to be a lot better. So if there's a task you need to perform for your script, think about ways in which you could use it again in other programs; if you can think of two cases where you'd use it, it is probably worth separating out.

Often, an application can be implemented very nicely as a wrapper around a simple fil-ter that performs some interesting task; write the filter, and you can experiment with ways to make its functionality available. A spelling checker could be nothing more than a simple pro-gram that identifies likely misspelled words, leaving it up to other programs to decide how to use this functionality.

The pids utility does nothing but obtain and display the pids of processes.

Isolate Dependencies

Sometimes, there is no way to prevent a script from depending on something you simply can-not do portably. However, if nearly every system provides a way to do it, and the problem is only that these ways are different, writing a generic utility to solve that specific problem makes it easy to write an otherwise portable script relying on that utility. In some cases, this could be implemented as a simple shell function in your main script, but if it is useful enough on its own, it may be worth creating the separate program as well.

For instance, you could possibly write a program that reliably extracts the current pid of a process by name, even though no one call to ps can portably give you that information. This is what gave me the idea for the pids utility; while it is very hard to solve the complete problem generally, it is easy to solve the important part on any given system. With this utility in place, adding functionality on a new system should take only a few minutes.

Be Cooperative

There is a corollary to the guidance to do one thing well—make it easy for other programs to use your script to do that one thing. Whatever your script does, try to write it so it will be easy for other scripts to use as a component. Thinking about how other scripts might use yours may give you key insights into what you ought to do. Try to stick with standard and well-understood formats; data that can be represented as lines of text generally should be because many UNIX utilities work very well on lines of text. If you need to work with binary data, be flexible about file names. If it makes sense to run your script on multiple files at a time, allow it; don't require repeated invocations. Be sure to give a meaningful exit status.

Be sure that incorrect or invalid command invocations yield an informative usage message. This will help someone actually make use of your script, rather than abandoning it in disgust because it doesn't seem to do anything.

If your script produces output that another program could possibly take as input, make sure that error messages are not set to standard output. Error messages being mistaken for real program output can be a problem for other programs.

The -n ("not really") option, known as --dry-run in some GNU software, displays output describing what a program would do rather than doing it. For any program that could ever damage or alter data, especially one whose behavior is not absolutely consistent and trivial, this option is a very good idea. (It is understandable that rm lacks it because its behavior is so simple. For more complicated programs, such as make, it is extremely useful to be able to ask the following question: "So, hypothetically, if I ran this program with these options, just how far up which creek would I end up, and where would the paddle be?"

The pids utility should produce simple output describing a mapping of process IDs to process names. My initial plan is to have the default be to print both the pid and the process name, in case it is called with multiple process names, and have an option to print only pids. Output is one entry per line to make it easier for other programs to further filter or manipulate output. Exit status is success if at least one matching program was found and failure otherwise.

Filters, File Manipulation, and Program Manipulation

In general, most scripts can be described as falling into one of these three categories. There are powerful UNIX conventions for how programs in each category should be designed; adhering to these conventions will make your script more useful to other users. Each of these types of programs has unique traits that influence how it should be designed; this section introduces some of the key design goals of each type.

Designing a Filter

In nearly every case, a filter should work like cat; it should take an arbitrary selection of files as inputs, or simply pass through standard input if no files are provided. Most filters treat a selection of files as though they had been concatenated as a single input file, except when diagnosing errors. (Whenever possible, a program should identify the specific input file and line on which an error occurred.)

Some filters offer options for operating in place. This is often a wonderful feature, but it should never be an implicit default. Users are expecting your program to produce its results on standard output; overwriting files without an explicit request is almost always wrong. A common idiom is to recognize a -i option for in-place operations; some programs, such as sed or perl, extend this to allow specification of a suffix to append to the original version of the file. If you are offering only one of these choices, though, always write output to standard output rather than operating in place. It is a trivial matter to wrap a standard filter on files in place; it is somewhat harder to wrap an in-place program and create a usable filter. (See the sidebar "Destructive and Reversible" for more thoughts on this.)

FILTERS IN PLACE

Of course, the correct solution is not *filter < file > file*. The file is truncated before the filter is even started, and the filter then reads an empty file, processes no data, and writes its output back into the file. There are two common idioms for this; first, you could run the filter into a new temporary file, then rename it over the original:

```
filter < file > file.new
mv file.new file
```

The alternative is to first rename the file, then run the filter directed into the original file. For instance, you might use this instead:

```
mv file file.orig
filter < file.orig > file
rm file.orig
```

If you do this, do not delete the original file unless the filter succeeded; even then, provide an option to leave the original file around as a backup.

Given a program that operates in place, you can do the same thing backward to create a filter:

```
cp file file.new
in_place file.new
cat file.new
rm file.new
```

In both cases, the usual caveats about temporary files and security apply.

In most cases, there is no reason for a filter to perform any sorting on its inputs or out-puts. Emulate uniq, which simply specifies that input must be sorted. A filter is, by definition, designed to work well in a pipeline; don't feel bad about a usage pattern where people might need to merge your script with others.

The exit status of a filter should normally be success if it did anything and failure other-wise. For instance, grep succeeds when it matches at least one line and fails when it matches no lines. In some cases, it may make more sense to report failure if any operation fails; for instance, ls reports failure if any operation failed, even if it listed some files.

You might not think pids is a filter, but data sources are a special case of a filter; they just prefer to go on the left end of a pipeline. You could even modify pids to take a list of names on standard input, although I did not implement this.

Designing a File Manipulator

Commands that manipulate files but don't take file names on the command line are annoying. Taking command names on standard input can be a great feature for programs to offer, but it should never be the only choice. If you use new line separators, there is no way to submit some file names; if you use NUL characters, many programs cannot interact with you. Support it as an option, but take command-line arguments, too.

Recursion is generally a good option but only sometimes a good default. Archive utili-ties and the like may want to recurse into directories by default. Others should not. Do not overthink your selection of files; unless the kinds of operations you describe are unique and specific to your application, you are better off providing an interface making it easy for users to feed your script arguments using find. If you want to provide a recursion option, use -r or -R; if you want an option to prevent recursion, you might use -d (by analogy with ls) or a long option with a name like --no-recurse.

If your utility performs tests on files, look closely at the behavior of grep -l; it has gener-ally stood the test of time. The default behavior of showing only file contents when processing a single file (or standard input), but showing file names and contents when processing mul-tiple files, is usually correct. The -l option (list only file names) is well known and fairly useful. Keep in mind the opportunity for optimization that this affords; once you find a successful match, you can show the file name and skip on to the next file. You don't have to finish reading a large file to find more matches.

A file manipulator should report failure if any manipulation fails. If operations on each file are logically distinct, try on every file even if some have failed. If operations on a given file are logically sequential, though, stop after the first one that fails.

Designing a Program Manipulator

Program manipulation is a general description of the astounding variety of scripts most com-monly written by system administrators; these are scripts that automate common tasks. Every such script should support a -v option to display information about what it is doing. You will kick yourself if your script doesn't provide more verbose output; your script will misbehave, and you will have to add this feature before you can even start debugging it. I often go a step further and support a -x option, which does nothing more elaborate than set -x. The output isn't pretty or user-friendly, but it tells you what happened.

Study other similar programs and try to keep a similar interface. The apachectl utility offers an excellent example of how to make a single, reasonably well-contained utility that handles a variety of closely related tasks. When possible, try to think through a whole process and build a script that automates it. Include lots of error checking in automated tasks; one of the key weaknesses such scripts often start with is not knowing when something has gone wrong, which a user would have noticed right away when performing the task interactively.

Programs that manipulate other programs or perform complicated operations often use an idiom of taking general options followed by a subcommand, which can then take additional options or arguments. Examples include the git and cvs commands, which take a number of verbs describing the intended operation—for instance, git pull or git push. Additional options specified after the verb may differ from one verb to another. Options specified before the verb have general meanings; in some cases (at least with cvs), the same option is valid both before and after a given verb, but with very different meanings. This is annoying; don't do it.

A verb-based interface like this is mostly useful when all of the verbs are closely related; for instance, they all work with the same source code system. Some programs go the other way, installing a large number of programs with simple names; for example, the nmh mail client installed 39 separate programs on one of my machines. The disadvantage of separate commands like this is the greatly increased risk of clashes, amplified by the risk that the names chosen will be likely and usable ones, which other people are more likely to want to use as well. It is easy to imagine other developers wanting to use names like scan, mark, or refile. Given a choice, I would say I prefer the single command with many verbs. In fact, this can be implemented as a wrapper script, which uses a private directory full of specific commands; the goal is just to keep $PATH clean.

The exit status of a program manipulator should simply indicate whether or not it succeeded. If you try to start another program, and fail, report the failure and indicate it in your exit status.

Command-Line Options and Arguments

The choice of how to invoke a script is a significant factor in whether it will ever be any use to you. In general, try to avoid relying on environment variables to control behavior; favor command-line options to set flags. Try to make sure that the most common behavior is the default to keep command lines short. If you find that you always want to specify an option, make it the default and provide the opposite choice. A script designed for interactive use might originally be designed to operate quietly, with a -v flag to cause more verbose output; if users consistently specify this flag, make it the default and provide a -q flag to suppress the output instead.

Be aware of the convention of combining command-line options; -ab should be synonymous with -a -b. GNU sed accepts the option -i to operate in place (though this option is not portable). The argument -i.bak instructs sed to keep the original file, with .bak appended to its name. Having forgotten about that special case, I once shortened sed -i -e *expr* to `sed -ie` *expr*. This did not do what I meant; it saved the original file under the name *filee*. (The default with no `-e` arguments is to treat the first argument as an expression, so the output was otherwise correct.)

There are two key distinctions here. The first is between options that always take an argument and options that optionally take an argument. The latter are more confusing. If an option always takes an argument, it is usually reasonable to treat the rest of the word as being an argument to that option. Asking friends who write shell scripts, I have come to the conclusion that many script programmers do not consistently agree on what they expect to happen when options that take arguments are combined into words. From a user interface standpoint, the best thing may be to try to avoid the question. For instance, were I to design a `-i` option for `sed`, I would probably have a separate option for the suffix. This way, the boolean option has predictable and simple syntax, and the non-boolean option also has unambiguous syntax. The boilerplate option-processing code presented in Chapter 6 implements semantics that are unlikely to surprise most experienced users.

All programs should recognize `--` as indicating the end of options. Programs which accept file names should generally treat `-` as a synonym for standard input.

It may seem that the proliferation of options contradicts the advice to do one thing well. It does not. Doing something well often implies doing it under a variety of different circumstances and in a number of different ways. Allowing users to sort on arbitrary keys, numerically, reversing some keys but not others, offers a great deal of flexibility but does not change the fundamental purpose of the `sort` program. The e-mail reader option in GNU `hello` is an intentionally awful example of completely unrelated functionality. The many UNIX programs that display or set a particular value (such as `hostname` or `date`) are questionable designs. It is, however, almost certainly a design flaw that `date` does not use an option to indicate the semantic shift from setting to displaying the date.

Try to avoid relying on long options. While they are easy to remember, they are bulky and annoying to type. Common options should always have a single-character spelling, and it is fine, even preferable, to have no long options at all.

When specifying sizes, be flexible about input. At the very least, you should recognize KB/MB as size units. Defaults should use 1024-byte blocks as "KB," even though they are strictly considered KiB (see the sidebar "What's a Mebibyte?"); the same goes for MB, GB, and even TB.

WHAT'S A MEBIBYTE?

For years, users have been posting on forums, writing to customer support departments, and otherwise complaining that their hard drives are not as large as advertised. The reason is that computers like to do things in powers of two (32, 64, 128, and so on), and 1024 is a much more natural number for a computer to work with than 1000. As a result, a "kilobyte" of data is nearly always understood to mean 1,024 bytes of data. Similarly, a megabyte is usually 1,048,576 bytes. However, a long time ago, drive manufacturers realized that they could gain about 5% capacity instantly by using the standard metric prefixes, calling each 1,000,000 bytes a "megabyte." (With gigabytes, the ratio is a bit over 7%.) Of course, this usage makes some sense; it is quirky at best to have a prefix that always, consistently, across any unit of measure, means "one million" except, when referring to data, it means "1.048576 million."

The solution, of course, is to introduce new terms; *kibibyte*, *mebibyte*, and so on ("bi" being short for "binary"). One KiB (kibibyte) is exactly 1,024 bytes. With this usage in place, it is more reasonable to use the standard K prefix to mean 1,000 exactly.

Unfortunately, this just means that it is now even less clear to users what KB and MB mean. To add to the confusion, many users (as well as many developers and many product packaging designers) are not aware that B and b are different; B is bytes (in context, this means 8 bits), while b is bits. So 8Mb of data are 1MB of data, unless one of them was using the metric prefixes. . . .

If you are interpreting user-specified sizes, such as block sizes, default to bytes, ignore bits, and support both the K and Ki prefixes. If you support only the K prefix, use it for 1024; this is what users will mean, for now. When reporting output, use the Ki and Mi prefixes so users get used to them and learn about them, reducing future confusion.

Designing Options

The most common options should be easy-to-remember lowercase letters. There are a number of conventions in UNIX command-line arguments (see Table 10-1). In general, the most common arguments should just be plain arguments, not command-line options. For instance, the file arguments to most commands are just specified as any file names after the last option; by contrast, a script file to run from is usually specified with a particular option (often -f).

If you have several closely related options, it may make more sense to implement them as a single option that takes an argument to distinguish between cases. However, most of the time an option with an argument is a string or file name.

The Table 10-1 introduces a few common options that users are likely to guess at or remember easily. The list is not exhaustive. Some letters have multiple traditional uses, which are listed separately. The GNU coding standards have a similar list of long option names that have been used in GNU utilities.

Table 10-1. *Common Options*

Option	Mnemonic	Meaning
--	(none)	End of options; following arguments are not options, even if they have hyphens.
-0	zero	Use NUL instead of new line as a record separator.
-1	one	Process one record or item at a time (suppresses columnar output, for instance).
-a	all	Display/process things that might otherwise be skipped over.
-a	and	Join two arguments (when arguments form an expression).
-A	absolute	Use absolute paths rather than relative paths (for instance, in an archive program).
-b	blank	Ignore blank characters.
-c	cat	Force use of standard output; used by compress, gzip, and other utilities that usually operate in place.
-c	command	Run a specific command (as in sh -c).
-c	count	Display counts of output instead of output.
-C	columns	Display output in columns.
-d	debug	Display debugging output; see also -x.
-e	expression	Argument is an expression to process; used in languages like sed or Perl.
-f	file	Specify a file from which to read commands or configuration
-f	force	Go ahead (presumably without asking the user for confirmation), even if there are problems; see also -i.
-f	field	Specify a field separator or specify fields; see also -t.
-h	human	Human-readable output; for instance, display sizes in MiB/GiB (see the sidebar "What's a Mebibyte?") as appropriate.
-i	in-place	Operate in place (used with filters).
-i	interactive	Ask user about operations; see also -n/-y, or -f.
-i	input	Input file name or input mode.
-l	list	Display a list of names or matches, as in grep -l.
-l	long	Display things in a longer or more verbose format; see also -v.
-m	max	Maximum value or limit.
-m	min	Minimum value or limit.
-n	number	A number, such as number of lines to print or number of commands to run.
-n	no	Assume negative answers to all questions, making an interactive program non-interactive; see also -i/-y.
-n	dry run	Do not actually do anything; just indicate what the program would do if it were doing something.
-o	or	Allow either of two arguments (when arguments form an expression).

Continued

Table 10-1. *Continued*

Option	Mnemonic	Meaning
-o	output	Name of output file name (instead of standard output).
-r,-R	recursive	Process all files in directories and their subdirectories.
-r	reverse	Reverse order of sorted output.
-q	quiet	Suppress output; see also -s.
-s	silent	Suppress output; see also -q.
-s	suffix	Specify a file name suffix used by the script.
-t	tab	Specify a field separator; mnemonic is that some programs use a tab character by default.
-u	user	As an option, display information about users; as an option with an argument, name a user to restrict the scope of a display.
-x	eXecution trace	Display trace of execution; see also -d.
-x, -X	eXclude	Exclude some files or data from processing.
-x	cross	Do not cross file system boundaries while recursing (from find's historical but no longer portable -xdev primitive, now spelled as the -x option).
-v	verbose	Display additional information or output, such as names of files as they are processed.
-V	version	Display version information.
-y	yes	Assume positive answers to all questions, making an interactive program noninteractive; see also -i/-n.

If you can find a likely English word to use as a mnemonic to pick the letter to use for a given option, do so. Users find options easier to learn with a mnemonic. Try to favor idiomatic choices whenever possible. It is often permissible to use the second letter of a word; for instance, some tar implementations use -X to denote a list of files to eXclude.

If you have a pair of related options, it is often helpful to use the same letter for both, using a capital letter for the less common option.

The pids utility takes several options. The -u option (user) restricts it to displaying only processes owned by the named user; the -t option (tty) restricts it to displaying only processes that have a given terminal device. The -p option (in this case, the mnemonic is "pid") displays only the pid, rather than both pid and process name. Finally, the -a option is an alternative to giving program names on the command line and requests all processes.

Options and Inputs

In general, things that change the behavior of a program should be command-line options, but some programs, most noticeably program manipulators, will have good reason to use or refer to a configuration file. Generally, input files specified on the command line or as standard input should be data to process rather than configuration or setup.

Options should determine how your script processes its inputs. Information about what you will do, changes to algorithms, or changes to user interaction should be options. Actual data to be processed should be inputs or specified as names on the command line. There are a few conventional exceptions; the expr utility operates on its arguments, for instance.

A number of programming languages, such as sed, awk, Perl, and Ruby, take small programs on the command line rather than as input files, as a convenience.

The pids utility has no stream inputs, but it takes names of programs to look for on the command line.

Set Reasonable Limits

A shell script is not always a good place to try to expand the bounds of computer science or win an argument about artificial intelligence. It is great for a program to try to do what the user intends; it is bad for a program to be totally unpredictable. "Smart" interfaces are often plagued by personal idiosyncrasies; they may seem wonderfully intuitive to the author and utterly random to everyone else. Conventions and predictable behavior are generally more useful than trying to guess what the user wants. In particular, be extremely careful with destructive operations; a program that lists files might reasonably try to guess at which file the user wanted, but a program that deletes them had better not.

DESTRUCTIVE AND REVERSIBLE

An action that can be undone is called a *reversible* operation. An action that destroys or overwrites data is called a *destructive* operation. In general, you should be careful with operations that are destructive or irreversible, and be exceptionally careful with operations that are both. However, the UNIX convention is not to put up barriers to operation. Do not prevent a user from deleting a file; just avoid deleting files casually or broadly.

Note that not all destructive operations are irreversible, and not all irreversible operations are destructive. In-place operations are usually destructive, but some may be easily reversed; for instance, the patch utility can nearly always reverse any patch it can apply, so it is usually safe to apply them in place without worrying too much. The behavior is reversible because the patch set is separate from the files operated on.

Perhaps paradoxically, many data losses are caused by programs where destructive behaviors usually warn the user. Experienced UNIX users are usually careful with the rm command. Some systems "helpfully" alias it to rm -i, requiring confirmation of each file. This causes two problems. The first is that users may become careless about running rm, assuming that the safety net is there. The other is that users may acquire the habit of typing rm -f to override this behavior. This can override cases where the normal rm command would have asked for confirmation, resulting in worse safety than the user would have had with neither -i nor -f in the picture. Do not do this. If you ask a lot of questions to which the answer is always yes, the user will be trained to always answer yes without reading. Ask questions only when there is real doubt.

Define Your Functional Scope

The quick and easy nature of scripting often causes people to start writing a script without a clear idea of exactly what the script will do. This often leads to problems. Figure out what you are and are not trying to do early on; this will save you a lot of trouble later as you try to figure out what your script is supposed to do. Defining your functional scope early on helps you make sure your script is going to do one thing well, not several things poorly. If you really do need to do several things, defining your scope helps you separate them out into multiple tasks that you can handle separately.

Feel free to throw together a prototype while you think through your interface, but be sure your work environment will give you the time you need to redevelop the script completely once the prototype reveals your initial design mistakes. Otherwise, you will be stuck with something unmaintainable. Never let anyone convince you that a prototype is a final product. Rapid prototyping is only a strength if you do not get stuck with the resulting prototype as a production product.

Be ready to limit your allowed inputs. Most programs should not try to magically do the right thing with all possible inputs; rather, they should try to handle reasonable inputs and expect callers to sanitize inputs as necessary. The netpbm utility suite does a good job of standardizing on an internal format, using conversion utilities to get data in and out; this provides a model where most programs can ignore most of the hard work of dealing with formats and stay focused on simple tasks.

The scope of the pids utility is not as obvious as you might think. What do we mean by the "name" of a process? For instance, should I be able to distinguish between /usr/bin/perl and /usr/local/bin/perl? My solution is to mostly leave this up to the user. The pids utility tries to find processes with matching names but uses shell patterns, so the user can specify a pattern that might match multiple names.

Define Your Target Scope

From a portability standpoint, this is perhaps the most important step. Try very hard to avoid narrowing your scope unreasonably. POSIX shells may be a reasonable target; bash is probably not. If you are planning to narrow your target scope, be sure you have a good reason to do so. (See the sidebar, "Requirements Done Wrong," for an example of when not to.) For a famous example, consider quilt, which is a selection of bash scripts relying heavily on GNU extensions to a number of utilities. Is that a good choice? Given the number of people I know who have spent days or weeks trying to get quilt working on other systems, I'd guess it isn't. However, quilt does its job well enough that people put up with the portability hassle. (The interesting question, of course, is how hard it would have been to write it more portably? I can't say.)

REQUIREMENTS DONE WRONG

I recently had occasion to try to run a script (the `ldd` utility distributed with the GNU C library) on an embedded system. It failed; it turned out to have a firm dependency on `bash`. In fact, the functional extent of the dependency on `bash` was a test for whether the `pipefail` option (specific to `bash` version 3) was available. Removing the test allowed the script to function perfectly well in other shells. (It still displayed extra dollar signs occasionally because the script relies on the localized string extension in `bash`, but it performed its expected function correctly and reliably.)

Browsing around, I discovered that other users had discovered the same thing. One had submitted a one-line patch to make the script work correctly both in `bash` and in other shells. The maintainer responded with a derisive comment about how widely available `bash` is, and how everyone should just install it. While this might make sense for desktop systems, it is a very bad strategy for a fundamental system component. Some of the target systems involved are small enough that `bash` would be a very noticeable cost and could deny users the space for real features they need.

It is one thing to depend on extra features, such as the array features that some shells offer. That may be justifiable, although it is usually better not to go there. However, gratuitous incompatibilities are nearly always a bad choice.

Don't forget embedded systems. For all the differences between desktop UNIX systems, the big gap is between full-featured conventional UNIX and the tiny stripped-down subsets used in embedded systems. The environments used during bootstrapping or installation of a system are also often extremely restrictive, although you usually don't have to code for them unless you are an OS vendor. Think carefully about embedded systems; you may find the answer is that you do not want to support them or that your script makes no sense in an embedded environment. Deciding to avoid embedded systems can be perfectly reasonable, but think it through.

In some cases, context may imply requirements of your target systems. The installer for a video card driver can make a few more assumptions about its target system than a network configuration utility could. Commercial applications can often specify requirements for their target systems, but don't be too quick to rely on these requirements; changing market conditions might change your target systems abruptly. Users may also surprise you; a number of installers written for one UNIX system have been used on another in conjunction with emulation support.

Finally, remember that the availability of a feature does not obligate you to depend on it. Write more portably than you think you have to; it is much more likely for you to be unhappy later because a script is not portable enough than because it is too portable.

In the case of `pids`, the underlying task is not exactly portable, but it is possible to do two important things. The first is to handle the most common cases; the second is to make sure that cases not handled are diagnosed immediately to the user.

Case Study: pids

The pids utility is small and fairly simple. I wrote it using a Solaris system, running a single ps command on a BSD system to guess at the right values for the BSD code case. It worked on the BSD system without modification; for Linux, I had to add an entry to a table.

Here's the first chunk of the program:

```
#!/bin/sh
func_usage () {
  echo >&2 "usage: pids [-u user] [-t tty] [-p] -a | progname [...]"
  exit 1
}
case `uname -sr` in
  SunOS*5*)
    sys=sysv;;
  Darwin*|*BSD*)
    sys=bsd;;
  Linux*)
    sys=bsd;;
  *)
    echo >&2 "Unknown system type: `uname -sr`"
    exit 1
    ;;
esac
```

The func_usage function serves as a catch-all for displaying diagnostics and exiting. There are several points in the program where it might turn out that the invocation is incorrect; this lets me write the message in only one place.

The next section is the guts of the "portability" (I use the term loosely) of this program. In practice, the systems available to me generally honor either the traditional BSD options to ps or the traditional System V options. (Interestingly, the Linux system I tried honors both; if you change the Linux case to sys=sysv, the script works identically.) The uname command gives you two key pieces of information: the system's name and the version number. You need the version number because modern Solaris is known as SunOS 5 and is fairly incompatible with the previous release, which is known as SunOS 4. (In fact, SunOS 4 was discontinued around 2000, but it does still exist in some environments.) It might be wiser to check by feature rather than system type; in the case of ps, though, it is much easier to identify two common types rather than trying to parse headers.

The decision I made to error out rather than guessing is based on a history of programs guessing badly for me. I wanted the program to tell the user immediately what went wrong. It is easy enough to guess at how to adapt to a new system, but the program can't do it.

Next up, processing arguments (using getopts for brevity):

```
opt_a=false
opt_p=false
opt_u=
opt_t=
```

```
while getopts 'apu:t' o
do
  case $o in
    a) opt_a=true;;
    p) opt_p=true;;
    u) opt_u=$OPTARG;;
    t) opt_t=$OPTARG;;
    \?) func_usage;;
  esac
done
shift `expr $OPTIND - 1`

# require program name
$opt_a || test $# -ne 0 || func_usage
found_any=false
```

Again, nothing here is particularly surprising. This program does very little sanity check-ing of its arguments, but it does require that either the -a option was given or at least one program name was given. (Any arguments past the options are assumed to be program names.) The found_any variable is used to determine the final exit status of the program.

The next section of code is the actual work of extracting data from the output of ps. It is a fairly simple code fragment:

```
case $sys in
  bsd) ps auxww | awk '$2 != "PID" { print $1, $2, $7, $11 }' ;;
  sysv) ps -ef | awk '$2 != "PID" { print $1, $2, $6, $8 }' ;;
  *) echo >&2 "unknown system $sys."; exit 1 ;;
esac | while read uid pid tty cmd
```

I'll get to the loop body in just a moment, but this part merits separate discussion. There are two issues in trying to extract the data I want. The first is that BSD and System V variants use different arguments to control the display of ps. The second is that the display formats are different. In each case, an awk script is used to display four fields: the user ID, process ID, ter-minal name, and command name. (Only the first word of the first word (the command name) of the command line is given, not any arguments.)

The BSD arguments specify listing processes owned by (a)ll users (the default is only the current user), in a format displaying (u)ser information, including processes with no control-ling terminal (the x option, for which there is no mnemonic), on a (w)ide display. The w option is specified twice. The default for Berkeley ps is to limit all lines to 80 characters; the w option specifies a wide display (132) characters, and specifying it again removes the limit. This is necessary because the name of the command could quite easily exceed the available width otherwise, resulting in a truncated display. The missing hyphen is intentional; one convention some systems have adopted is to use traditional Berkeley semantics when the hyphen before the options is omitted, and System V semantics when the hyphen is provided.

The System V options are easier; it displays (e)very process (the equivalent of BSD's ax options), and gives a (f)ull listing. The full listing format implies arbitrarily long lines and pro-vides the additional information (user and terminal) the script wants.

The entire `case` statement is redirected into a `while` loop, using the `read` command to extract data from lines. The `read` command divides input (performing word splitting) until it reaches the last variable, at which point any remaining text is combined into that variable. In this case, because I know that the fields (uid, pid, and terminal) are consistently free of space characters, I do not have to worry about that splitting. It does the right thing.

The remaining code is the body of the `while` loop, which displays matching lines:

```
do
  if test -n "$opt_u" && test "$opt_u" != $uid; then
    continue
  fi
  if test -n "$opt_t" && test "$opt_t" != $tty; then
    continue
  fi
  if $opt_a; then
    found=true
  else
    found=false
    for prog
    do
      case $cmd in
      $prog|*/$prog) found=true; break;;
      esac
    done
  fi
  if $found; then
    found_any=true
    if $opt_p; then
      printf "%d\n" "$pid" || exit 0
    else
      printf "%d %s\n" "$pid" "$cmd" || exit 0
    fi
  fi
done
$found_any
```

The tests for $opt_u and $opt_t are straightforward. The next section of code determines whether the program matches. If the -a option was specified, all programs are considered to match. Otherwise, each remaining positional parameter is checked against the command name. Specifying the full path would be annoying, so the script accepts any leading path in front of the program name, or just the unqualified program name. Remember that shell patterns are implicitly anchored; if $prog is perl, this will not match perl5, local_perl, or any other such variant.

If a match was found, the script displays either the process ID alone (if the -p option was given) or the process ID and the matching command name. It might be better to display $prog than $cmd here; a caller who is checking which of several program names matched might be surprised.

Finally, $found_any is expanded and executed. If no matches were ever found, $found_any is false, and the script indicates failure to the caller. Otherwise, it indicates success. Be sure to think about exit status when designing a script, as callers will expect it to be meaningful.

What's Next?

Chapter 11 takes a closer look at a few of the most common programs, other than the shell, that shell programs have to interact with: make, which calls the shell for everything it does, and sed and awk, which are used heavily by many larger shell scripts. Chapter 11 also discusses some general issues of mixing code written in multiple languages.

■ ■ ■

Mixing and Matching

The shell is a powerful language, but it does not do everything. Some other languages are heavily used by shell scripts to perform tasks that the shell itself is not very well suited for; similarly, programs in some other languages use the shell to do some of their heavy lifting. This chapter discusses a few of the issues you may encounter when using other languages from the shell, or the shell from other languages.

This chapter starts with some general information about embedding code in one language within code in another language. Following that are sections on embedding shell code in specific other languages and on embedding code in other languages in shell code. These sections briefly discuss the reasons for which you would use each combination, but they do not attempt to completely explain other languages.

Mixing Quoting Rules

The most fundamental problem of mixing shell and other code is that other languages typically have different quoting rules than the shell. For instance, both Perl and Ruby allow \' to occur in single-quoted strings to include single quotes in them. This is useful because they do not share the shell's implicit concatenation of adjacent quoted strings, so the shell idiom wouldn't work, but it is often surprising to shell programmers. While very few large shell scripts are typically embedded in either Perl or Ruby programs, both have convenient syntax for embedding small scripts, including command substitution.

Nested quoting is complicated and easy to get wrong. Conflicting quoting rules are also easy to get wrong. Nested quoting using different rules can be a real hassle, and no one gets it right on the first try every time. It's most effective to separate scripts out, and this tends to produce other benefits, as you'll be able to generalize and make more use of each component. However, there are cases where a small embedded script is really too specialized, and not large enough, to justify a separate executable.

In general, your best bet with languages that do not require single quotes very often is to use single quotes in the shell to pass code into other languages. Here documents are only occasionally useful; many scripting languages read scripts from files, not standard input, and the most common programs to write this way are filters, which need to be able to use standard input for data anyway.

To get nested quoting correct, start by writing the embedded program correctly as a separate file with correct quoting. Once you have done this, you can look at how to quote this string in the outer scripting language. You may find it practical to bypass the first step with experience, but if something goes wrong, try a separate program first; it is a lot easier to debug.

As an example, the following awk script extracts information from C header files. Many headers defining symbolic names for constants use the following convention to describe the meanings of each constant:

```
#define NAME 23 /* Description of name */
```

For instance, somewhere under most implementations of <errno.h>, there is a file containing lines like this:

```
#define ENOMEM           12                  /* Cannot allocate memory */
```

This format lends itself well to extraction in a simple awk script:

```
/^#define/ && $2 == "ENOMEM" {
  for (i = 5; i < NF; ++i) {
    foo = foo " " $i;
  }
  printf("%-22s%s\n", $2 " [" $3 "]:", foo);
  foo = ""
}
```

This script could be passed in as a single argument to the awk command (using single quotes in a shell script) or saved as a file and invoked with awk -f *file*. This script combines a number of awk's features somewhat awkwardly to produce output such as this:

```
ENOMEM [12]:            Cannot allocate memory
```

The output format is a bit elaborate and bears a little explanation; the output looks better if the error name is left-aligned and the numbers are immediately next to it. First constructing the string ENOMEM [12]:, then printing it left-adjusted in a field, provides an interface where the descriptive text is also aligned, making it easier to read larger blocks of output (such as multiple lines in sequence).

This program can be easily wrapped in a simple shell script. Because the script uses only double quotes, it can be wrapped using a single pair of single quotes, except for embedding a value. Here's a way you might do it:

```
for arg
do
  awk '/^#define/ && $2 == "'"$arg"'" {
    for (i = 5; i < NF; ++i) {
      foo = foo " " $i;
    }
    printf("%-22s%s\n", $2 " [" $3 "]:", foo);
    foo = ""
  }' < /usr/include/sys/errno.h
done
```

This scriptlet (assuming that your system's <errno.h> is structured like a BSD one, which it may not be) prints similar output for each matched argument. The interesting part is the argument embedding; "'"$arg"'" is a simple case of handling nested quoting. This awk script is composed from three adjacent strings; the first single-quoted string ends with a double quote, then there is a double-quoted string containing only $arg, and then the next single-quoted string starts with a double quote. If $arg contains the string ENOMEM, this expands to "ENOMEM" in the awk program. This is not necessarily the best way to pass data to awk. You might do better to use awk's -v option to assign variables:

```
for arg
do
  awk -v arg="$arg" '/^#define/ && $2 == arg {
    for (i = 5; i < NF; ++i) {
      foo = foo " " $i;
    }
    printf("%-22s%s\n", $2 " [" $3 "]:", foo);
    foo = ""
  }' < /usr/include/sys/errno.h
done
```

When you have to embed multiple kinds of quotes, it gets trickier. Just remember that you can always switch quoting styles to combine different rules. Be especially careful when trying to get backslashes into embedded code; this is one of the big arguments for using single quotes as much as possible.

For a more extreme example, m4's quoting rules are totally different from the shell's (although arguably superior). By default, m4 quotes start with ` and end with '. Obviously, this is vastly superior in terms of unambiguous nesting. Just as obviously, it is not a good fit for shell code. To resolve this, m4sh uses the m4 language's built-in (and thoroughly sanity-destroying) changequote primitive to change the quoting mechanism; in m4sh, quotes are [ ]. These were selected, not because they are uncommonly used, but because they are almost always balanced. By contrast, an unmatched ending parenthesis is often seen in case statements. This is the real reason the examples in this book have preferred test to [.

Embedding Shell Scripts in Code

Shell code can be embedded in other programs. Many UNIX programs have some limited shell-out functionality, allowing them to run single commands; these commands are almost always passed to the shell. Quoting rules vary widely between languages; be sure you know which quoting rules apply. Editors that allow you to run shell commands may have their own special quoting and input rules; check the documentation.

By far the most common program in which shell code is included is make, and it deserves a bit of discussion.

Shell and make

The shell is heavily used by most implementations of make because it is the canonical command interpreter and is used to execute commands. In general, each individual command (a single line in a make rule) is run in a separate shell. However, you can join lines together using backslashes at the end of each line, and it is possible to write many shell scripts on a single line by using semicolons instead of new lines as line terminators. This section discusses the use of shell commands embedded as make rules, but it does not try to explain the rest of make; there are wonderful books and tutorials available on the topic, and it is beyond the scope of this book.

USE TABS

In the 20 years or so I have been using make, I have never gone a full year without at least one error caused by using spaces rather than tabs as the indentation for the rules in a makefile. When you get a cryptic message like "need an operator" or "missing separator," it usually means you have forgotten to use tabs.

As with any language, make has its own quoting rules. Like the shell, make also substitutes variables. These expansions occur before the command is passed to the shell; unfortunately, they may also be confusingly similar to shell expressions. To pass a dollar sign to the shell, use the make variable $$. To substitute a make variable, use parentheses around its name, as in $(CFLAGS). This is confusingly similar to shell command substitution, but it is unrelated; think of $(CFLAGS) as being the equivalent of a shell program's ${CFLAGS}. The extra punctuation is much less optional in make, however. You should use it always, not just when there are other words nearby.

Anything that make passes to the shell is a single line. The behavior of comments in a makefile is thus not what you would expect for the same text occurring in a shell script. For instance, the following script is a two-line shell script:

```
echo hello # \
echo world
```

```
hello
world
```

The line continuation character is ignored because it is in a comment. However, if you specified the same text as a rule in a makefile, it would behave differently:

```
$ cat test.mk
default:
        echo hello # \
        echo world
$ make -f test.mk
echo hello #  echo world
hello
```

The rule is joined into a single line by make; the lines are joined, and the resulting rule is echo hello # echo world. Although make recognizes lines starting with # as comments, it does nothing special with a comment character in the middle of the line, so the whole line is passed to the shell as is. The shell comment extends to the end of the whole command because the whole command is a single line; the second command is not executed. This is a common mistake. There is a more subtle additional mistake; even if the comment character weren't there, the output would be `hello echo world` because there is no statement separator. To write multi-line scripts as single commands in a makefile, you must use semicolons between statements.

Be extremely careful about shell portability in `make` rules. There is no portable or safe way to cause a different shell to be used, so you are generally stuck with whatever shell the `make` program chooses. Users developing on some Linux systems sometimes produce `make` rules that only work if `/bin/sh` is actually `bash`. Don't do that.

Embedding shell code in `make` is not especially risky. Just remember that the code you write in the makefile is subject to processing, substitution, and quoting in `make` before it is passed to the shell. With that in mind, the shell gives `make` the flow control features (such as iteration through loops) it has always lacked. When writing longer sections of code, remember that `make` determines success or failure the same way the shell does, and it usually aborts whenever any build rule fails. If you write a build rule as an embedded shell script, be sure its return code is correct. For example, the following build rule has a serious problem:

```
timestamps:
        ( date; $(MAKE) build; date ) > build.log 2>&1
```

This rule appears to run a build with timestamps before and after the build, storing the output in a log file. In fact, it does this. However, the exit status of the shell command will always be the exit status of the second `date` command, which is unlikely to fail. If the build fails, `make` will not know about it or stop processing additional rules. To fix this, store the exit status and provide it to the caller:

```
timestamps:
        ( date; $(MAKE) build; x=$?; date; exit $x ) > build.log 2>&1
```

This rule passes back the status of the significant command rather than the status of another command. Another choice you might consider is to use `&&` to join commands:

```
timestamps:
        ( date && $(MAKE) build && date ) > build.log 2>&1
```

This does preserve exit status, but it deprives you of the second timestamp if a build fails.

Shell and C

On UNIX-like systems, the `system()` library call usually passes its argument to the shell for processing. On non-UNIX systems, the command processor may be a different shell or may be absent entirely; relying on the UNIX shell makes C code less portable than it would be otherwise. The C language has relatively simple quoting rules inside double quotes; you can pass new lines (written \n), single quotes (no special treatment needed), and double quotes (written \"). Line continuation in C, as in `make`, happens before data are passed to the shell, so do not rely on it. If you really want to write a long multi-line script in C, the most idiomatic way is to rely on C's automatic string concatenation and use new lines:

```
system("if true; then\n"
       "   echo hello\n"
       "fi");
```

This produces a string equivalent to `"if true; then\n   echo hello\nfi"`, but it is easier to read. Some C compilers offer extensions to accept embedded new lines in strings; do not rely on this. It is not portable, and it is also not especially useful.

This, of course, begs the question of whether it makes sense to embed non-trivial script code in C at all. In general, it does not. If you want to run external commands from C, you should normally restrict yourself to calling out to external programs using `fork()` and `exec()`. If you want to run a script, it is usually better to have an external script program rather than trying to embed it.

Embedding Code in Shell Scripts

Code in other languages is usually embedded in shell scripts when the languages lend themselves well to being used as filters. Two of the most famous examples are `sed` and `awk`, which are discussed in detail in the rest of this chapter.

Once you are comfortable with the shell's quoting mechanisms, embedding programs in your shell scripts is usually easy. Most of the time, single quotes will do everything you want, except for shell variables substituted into the embedded program.

Embedding shell variables in programs can range from relatively simple to fairly difficult, depending on the context in the embedded code. If you can be sure that the variable never has a value that would require special quoting in the embedded language, it is pretty easy:

```
cmd -e 'code '"$var"' more code'
```

This embeds the shell variable `$var` between `code` and `more code`. It is not quoted in the embedded code, though. If it needs quoting, you have to ensure that the shell variable's value is correctly quoted before embedding it. File names and user-supplied input can require a great deal of work to sanitize correctly for embedded code. In some cases, it is better to truncate or remove invalid inputs rather than try to preserve them through quoting.

Shell and sed

The sed utility provides a generalized editing facility that can be used as a filter (the `-i` option for editing in place is not universal). It is most heavily used to perform simple substitutions using regular expression patterns, but it is substantially more powerful than this. The sed utility uses basic regular expressions—mostly. Some versions support additional features, such as alternation (`\|`) or the `\?` and `\+` extensions; others do not. Do not use these. In general, do not escape anything with a backslash in sed unless it is a character that has special meaning when escaped with a backslash or is the expression delimiter. A few versions of sed do not support using asterisks on subexpressions, only on single character atoms (including character classes).

Mostly, sed is used for cases where you want to perform reasonably simple translations of files—for instance, replacing special marker text with string values. Like many utilities, sed is built around the assumptions of a shell script. Given no other instructions, it reads from standard input and writes to standard output. By default, it performs any instructions given to it, then prints each line.

One of the major uses of sed is to work around shells that lack the POSIX parameter substitution operators, such as ${*var#pattern*}. (You can also usually do this with expr.) For instance, one idiomatic usage would be to grab a directory name from a pathname:

```
$ dir=`printf "%s" "$path" | sed -e 's,.*/,,'`
```

While this usage is idiomatic, it is probably better to use expr for simple cases like this. If all you want to do is display part of a string, use expr.

While the s// command in sed is usually illustrated with slashes, it is portable to use other characters instead. When working with path names, it is even preferable. Commas are a common choice. Exclamation points are popular, too, but cause problems in shells (csh, very old bash), which use ! for history expansion. In general, sed commands that use delimiters let you pick a delimiter.

Even a small sed command can do very useful things. You have previously seen the common convention of prefixing strings with X to prevent them from being taken as options. This leads to a handy idiom:

```
Xsed="sed -e 's,^X,,'"
func_echo () {
  echo X"$@" | $Xsed
}
```

Even if the first argument is -n, this function can display it reliably. Unfortunately, this is not enough to work around the versions of echo that strip backslashes. You might wonder why this example doesn't just use expr, as previously suggested. The reason is that sed can take multiple -e arguments, and this provides a useful idiom:

```
echo X"$var" | $Xsed -e s/foo/bar/
```

This replaces foo with bar in the contents of $var, even if $var happens to start with a hyphen. Since piping small strings into sed is a fairly common task (and to be fair, there are many substitutions expr cannot make), and many versions of echo are obnoxious, this is a great way to magically hide the problem. On modern systems (or even moderately old ones, as long as they're not stripped-down embedded systems), printf may be better. Still, it's a good idiom to know. You never know when you'll suddenly need it.

sed scripts do not need quoting beyond backslashes, and those only in limited circumstances, such as when a regular expression contains the delimiter character used for the command. When writing a sed command with multiple separate commands, you have several options. You can use multiple -e arguments or separate commands with semicolons, but if you want to write a longer script, it is often better to write a single script using embedded new lines. It is usually easier to read multiple commands on multiple lines than squished together on one. Long single-quoted strings are your best friend here. Use the standard concatenation trick to embed variable substitutions in sed scripts; the following trivial example shows how you might emulate grep using sed:

```
sed -n -e '/'"$regex"'/p'
```

This prints every line matching $regex, unless it contains forward slashes. The sed command ends up being */regex*/p, which prints lines matching *regex*. The -n option prevents sed from printing every line automatically, so only lines explicitly printed are displayed. A common mistake is to omit the -n:

```
sed -e '/'"$regex"'/p'
```

This command prints every input line and prints lines matching $regex twice.

Solving the delimiter problem is a bit tricky. In general, you want to escape delimiter characters with backslashes, but the backslash itself is special to sed. Luckily, this is easier than it sounds:

```
pat=`printf "%s\n" "$pat" | sed -e 's,/,\\/,g'`
```

This causes the variable $pat to have every slash replaced with a backslash followed by a slash. If you then expand $pat in a sed script, the backslashes protect the forward slashes and cause them not to be interpreted as delimiters. It is important to use single quotes to quote the sed script; otherwise, you need twice as many backslashes because each pair of backslashes becomes a single backslash in the argument passed to sed, which then simply protects the following character and disappears. Be sure to sanitize variables you plan to embed in sed scripts; otherwise, you may get unpleasant surprises.

■Caution You will also see this idiom using echo, but some versions of echo strip backslashes. If you try to use this to escape backslashes, or if your string happens to contain backslashes for any other reason, it may not work portably with echo. You can find examples of how to work around this in libtool. Some of them have a lot of backslashes.

Longer sed scripts can do truly amazing things. This makes a good time to review the configure script code, which replaces $LINENO with the line number of a script:

```
sed '=' <$as_myself |
  sed '
    N
    s,$,-,
    : loop
    s,^\(['$as_cr_digits']*\)\(.*\)[$]LINENO\([^'$as_cr_alnum'_]\),\1\2\1\3,
    t loop
    s,-$,,
    s,^['$as_cr_digits']*\n,,
  ' >$as_me.lineno
```

The first script prints the line number of each line, then prints the line. So the output at the top of the script might be this:

```
1
#!/bin/sh
2
# Guess values for system-dependent variables and create Makefiles.
```

The body of the script is impressive, impressive enough, in fact, that the script gives credit to the inventors (plural):

```
# (Raja R Harinath suggested sed '=', and Paul Eggert wrote the
# second 'sed' script.  Blame Lee E. McMahon for sed's syntax.  :-)
```

To understand what this script does, first have a look at what it comes out to when the autoconf $as_cr values have been filled in. I've used character ranges for expressiveness; the actual variables are completely spelled out.

```
N
s,$,-,
: loop
s,^\([0-9]*\)\(.*\)[$]LINENO\([^0-9A-Za-z_]\),\1\2\1\3,
t loop
s,-$,,
s,^[0-9]*\n,,
```

For each line, sed begins by merging it with the next line (the N command). A hyphen is appended to the line. This is a trick reminiscent of the case ,$list, in trick introduced in Chapter 2; the purpose is to ensure that $LINENO never occurs at the end of the line, so you can always check the following character to see whether it could be part of an identifier.

Next, there is a small loop. The : command in sed introduces a label, which can be branched to later. (Yes, sed has flow control.) Each iteration of the loop performs a replacement. It replaces the text $LINENO (the dollar sign is in a character class, so it matches a literal dollar sign rather than the end of the string) with an initial string of digits. This idiom is extremely important to understand; it forms the basis of all sorts of things you can do with regular expressions that you cannot do without them.

The key is the use of grouped matches and the ability to refer back to them. (Since the reference back is not part of the matching regular expression, this is not technically a backreference; the same technique is available even in extended regular expression implementations lacking backreference support.)

When this substitute pattern is reached, a typical input buffer might be this:

```
124
echo "configure: $LINENO: I am an example code fragment."
```

Table 11-1 shows how this line matches the regular expression.

Table 11-1. *Matching a Complicated Regular Expression*

Pattern	Text
^\([0-9]*\)	124
\(.*\)	<newline>echo "configure:<space>
[$]LINENO	$LINENO
\([^A-Za-z0-9_]\)	:

The rest of the line is not matched; the regular expression matches only up through the colon after $LINENO. Because there is a successful match, this is replaced. The first chunk (containing the line number) is replaced by \1; since it was this text that formed \1, nothing changes. The second part is replaced by \2; again, nothing changes. After \2, the script inserts \1 again. Finally, \3 is replaced by itself. Because $LINENO was not in any group, it is not kept; instead, it is replaced by \1. So, $LINENO is replaced by 124, and nothing else happens.

This idiom is important because it means that you can do a replacement operation where you match on surrounding context that you do not wish to replace or modify; you can use groups around the material you need to match on, and then use \N references to replace those groups with their original text.

After the replacement, there is a branch; the t command branches back to the label if any substitutions have been made. (This is necessary because the regular expression in question can't be repeated with the /g modifier.) Once all instances of $LINENO on a line have been replaced, the t does not branch, and the script continues.

The last two commands remove the trailing hyphen from the line and remove the line number from the beginning of the buffer. The N command joined the lines, preserving the trailing new line; the last command replaces any initial string of digits followed by a new line, leaving the original line (before the = script) with only the $LINENO changes.

You may be surprised to find that, to an experienced sed user, this is fairly obvious. It's a powerful language and worth learning.

Shell and awk

The awk language (named after its creators, Aho, Weinberger, and Kernighan) fills a number of roles in shell scripts. While it is overkill for many simple substitution or pattern-matching operations, it offers a great deal of flexibility in performing more elaborate computations and generating interesting reports. In general, an awk script consists of a series of conditions and associated actions; a condition determines which actions to perform, and actions do things like calculating and printing values. Unlike sed, awk uses extended regular expressions. This section introduces the basic features of awk and the many variants of awk you are likely to encounter.

Why Use awk?

There are several key features awk provides that make it useful in shell scripts. The first, and most obvious, is associative arrays (also called *hashes*). In awk, a variable can be an array in which the indices are arbitrary strings rather than just numbers. This is an exceedingly flexible data type, allowing for the creation of lookup tables with keys, such as file names or other arbitrary strings. In many cases, it is desirable to accumulate data as you process input, and then do something with the accumulated data only after all the input has been processed. Finally, awk's implicit splitting of input into fields and flexible operations on fields make it easy to express a lot of common operations without a lot of additional setup work.

While sed scripts tend to be short and terse, often only a single short line, many awk scripts run across multiple lines. Resist the temptation to cram a whole complicated awk script onto a single line; go ahead and write a longer script over multiple lines.

In awk, strings should be quoted (using double quotes). An unquoted word is interpreted as a variable, not a literal string. There is no shell-like distinction between assignment and substitution; variable names are always given as plain words. Operators and literal numbers need no quoting or special markers.

While processing each line, awk automatically splits it into *fields*; usually these are the words of a line, delimited by whitespace, but you can specify a different delimiter. Fields are numbered starting at 1, with field 0 referring to the whole line. To get the value of a field, you use a dollar sign: $0 is the whole line, $1 is the first field, and so on. The built-in variable NF holds the number of fields on the current line; you can refer to the last field as $NF. In general, any variable can be used this way. This can be a bit of a shock for shell programmers, who expect $var to be the value of *var*.

Like the shell, awk treats uninitialized variables as empty. However, awk can perform both numeric and string operations; in a numeric context, an uninitialized variable is treated as a zero. Strings of digits and numbers are mostly interchangeable; if you try to add a number to a string of digits, the string is converted to a number and added. The transparent conversion between strings and numbers, and the implicit initialization of fields, make awk a very friendly language for writing reports. Associative arrays in particular are a wonderful feature. Many of the behaviors you see in awk are also common in Perl scripts.

Basic Concepts

The central concept of awk is the *rule*, also called a *pattern-action statement*. A rule is a condition (called the pattern) and a block of code (called the action). Conditions are just awk expressions, typically referring to the fields of the current line. The expression /regex/ implicitly matches the extended regular expression *regex* against $0. If the expression is true for a given input line, the block is executed for that line. An empty expression is always true. An empty action is interpreted as print, which implicitly prints $0. The following fragment of awk code prints the last word of each line of input containing the text hello:

```
/hello/ {
  print $NF
}
```

You can also perform matches on a particular field (the ~ operator is the explicit regex match operator).

```
$1 ~ /hello/ {
  print "goodbye, " $2
}
```

The special conditions BEGIN and END define rules that are executed once only; BEGIN rules before any input is read, and END rules after all input has been read. If you want to change the special variables RS and FS (record separator and field separator), you must use a BEGIN rule. Older code sometimes uses a BEGIN rule to insert shell variables into awk variables:

```
awk 'BEGIN { x='"$x"' } ...'
```

In "new awk" (1986 or so and later), you can use the -v option instead:

```
awk -v x="$x" '...'
```

Typically, END rules are used to provide summaries or reports after processing and interpreting a data file. The following example reads the output of an ls -l command:

```
/\.h$/ { h += $5 }
/\.c$/ { c += $5 }
END { print "C source: ", c; print "Headers: ", h }
```

Saved as a file named codesize, this could be used from the command line:

```
$ ls -l | awk -f codesize
C source:  98093
Headers:  14001
```

The lack of initialization and setup code is one of the reasons awk is popular.

If you provide two expressions separated by commas for a rule, the rule is considered to match every line between one where the first expression matches and one where the second expression matches. The lines matching the first and second expressions are included, as shown in the following example (using the implicit print $0 action):

```
$ awk '/a/,/b/' << EOF
> 1
> a
> 2
> b
> 3
> EOF
a
2
b
```

Expressions can use variables defined by the user, not just the predefined variables and the fields from the current line. Of particular interest to shell programmers, because the shell has no native equivalent, are awk's arrays. An array in awk is a collection of values indexed by strings. You can use just about any expression as the index for an array. Members that did not exist, like variables that did not exist, are treated as zero or empty. The following script prints a list of the first words of its input line, with the count of occurrences of each word:

```
$ awk '{ count[$1]++ }
> END { for (val in count) print val ": " count[val]; }' <<EOF
> example
> test
> example
> script
> awk
> program
> EOF
program: 1
script: 1
awk: 1
example: 2
test: 1
```

The order of output is not deterministic in this case; arrays are not stored in any particular order in awk. You can, of course, use sort on your output. You can also do your own sorting of output, although this is a bit more complicated (there is no built-in sort function).

In addition to the basic operators, awk has functions. A function takes an argument list (which may be empty for some functions) and returns a value. For instance, the tolower() function returns its argument converted to lowercase:

```
$ echo "WHAT CAPS LOCK KEY?" | awk '{ print tolower($0) }'
what caps lock key?
```

Functions can be used anywhere in an expression; the following awk script prints only input containing lowercase letters:

```
$0 != toupper($0)
```

Since the rule has no specified action, the implicit print is used. Note that the input is not modified by the function call; normal values passed to functions are passed by value (meaning that the function can change the copy passed to it, but not the original object). This is different for arrays.

Furthermore, in addition to the built-in functions awk provides, you can define your own functions. A user-defined function looks a little like a rule:

```
function greet(who) {
  print "Hello, " who
}
```

The parameters a function is declared with are local variables, assigned from any parameters passed to it when the function is called. Functions are declared at the top level of the awk program, not inside rules. Functions in awk may be recursive; each function gets its own local copy of the parameters.

Variants

The original awk language was quite popular, but it had some limitations. A newer version, called nawk, was developed starting around 1985, and was the basis of the 1988 book *The Awk Programming Language* (by Alfred V. Aho, Brian W. Kernighan, and Peter J. Weinberger; Addison Wesley). Since then, the GNU project has contributed another version (gawk), and Mike Brennan introduced another version called mawk. In practice, nearly every system in use today provides something roughly compatible with nawk, although some variants provide many more features. There is also a small awk implementation available in busybox; it seems to be nawk-compatible. The most substantial upgrade of "new awk" is user-defined functions and is essentially universally available now. However, a few systems provide a "traditional" awk, usually the same systems that provide a "traditional" shell.

If you are doing a great deal of awk programming, it makes sense to search around for the best available awk implementation. In fact, even if a program is otherwise pure awk, it may be better to embed it in a shell script that can do some initial command-line argument parsing and pick a good awk interpreter. The following snippet looks for a good version of awk, preferring the faster and more powerful interpreters:

```
if test -z "$AWK"; then
  for variant in mawk gawk nawk awk
  do
    save_IFS=$IFS
    IFS=:
    for dir in $PATH
    do
      IFS=$save_IFS
      if test -x "$dir/$variant"; then
        AWK="$dir/$variant"
        break
      fi
    done
    IFS=$save_IFS
    test -n "$AWK" && break
  done
fi
```

As always, trust the user; a user is unlikely to specify $AWK without good reason. Combining this with command-line parsing, whether using getopts or something like the boilerplate introduced in Chapter 6, allows you to write powerful and fairly portable awk scripts that handle arguments much more gracefully than traditional awk. Note that there are two points at which this script restores $IFS. The line at the top of the inner loop ensures that following commands will execute with $IFS restored; the line after the loop ensures that $IFS gets restored even if $PATH is empty and the loop never executes. In this particular case, neither of these boundary conditions is likely to come up, but it is good to develop careful habits.

Portability Concerns

Essentially every system since the late 80s has provided some variant of "new awk." This section covers the key portability notes among the new awk variants (including gawk and mawk). Special thanks are due to the autoconf portability notes, which caught a number of quirks I had never run into.

Do not put spaces in front of the parentheses in a function declaration; this is not portable. Function declarations in awk do need the function keyword, unlike shell functions:

```
function foo() { print "Please give your function a more creative name." }
```

The order of operations when iterating over an array is not deterministic; do not assume it is any order (not "order of insertion" or "sorted," for instance). It is not even guaranteed that the order is the same on successive iterations! A single for (*var* in *array*) will hit every member of the array, but there is no guarantee at all about order.

The last semicolon in a block is probably optional. Some people use them based on vague recollections that there was an awk implementation somewhere that required them. (Shell { } blocks definitely require a trailing semicolon or new line; awk may not.) I have omitted them because I cannot find an awk implementation that needs them.

If an awk script is not supposed to process any lines of input, run it with /dev/null (or any empty file) as input; some implementations may try to read input even when the POSIX spec says they shouldn't.

At least one awk mishandles anchors in alternating expressions, such as /^foo|bar/. If you have to use such expressions, put them inside a group—for instance, /^(foo|.*bar)/.

Several implementations reset NF and the field variables before executing an END block; if you need to refer to their last values, save them in regular user-defined variables.

Features you can use portably across new awk implementations include user-defined functions: the ?: operator, the getline function, the exponentiation operator (^), and a number of string and math functions. Variable assignment using -v is universal in new awk, but not found in traditional awk. If you are using autoconf, AC_PROG_AWK can find a working new awk on every known system.

Only single-dimensional arrays are available in traditional awk. In fact, even in modern awk, what is really available is not multidimensional arrays, but a convenient syntactic shorthand for constructing array keys:

```
a[x,y,z] = 3
```

This syntax allows you to store data structures much like multidimensional arrays, but you cannot easily extract "every array member in column 1."

Embedding awk in Shell Scripts

There are two good pieces of advice to consider about embedding small awk scripts in your shell scripts. The first is that you should always think about whether what you want to do can be done better using tr, expr, cut, paste, or one of the other similar small and specialized tools UNIX provides. Many tasks can be performed more efficiently by sort and uniq -c than they can by an awk script building a table of values and printing them out. There is no need to use awk to display fields of output when cut can do the same thing.

The second piece of advice is that maybe you should use tiny little awk scripts for a lot of things like this anyway. It is true that a script often runs faster using smaller and more specialized utilities. However, it is often easier to write the correct code using awk, and this may be more important when you are in a hurry. For instance, if you want the process IDs of every process matching a pattern, it is easy to write:

```
$ ps ax | awk '/pattern/ { print $1 }'
```

However, there's no reason you couldn't do this just as well with grep and cut:

```
$ ps ax | grep -e 'pattern' | cut -f 1
```

Well, there's one. This doesn't work. By default, cut expects delimiters to be tabs, and ps doesn't normally use tabs, so the whole line is a single field. No problem! Just use spaces:

```
$ ps ax | grep -e 'pattern' | cut -f 1 -d ' '
```

Oops. Turns out this works only when the pid extends to the left of the display; the default right-aligned output puts spaces in front of shorter pids (on my system, those with 1–4 digit numbers), and cut treats those as fields.

What this means to you: For a script where performance matters, it is probably worth figuring out the right way to do something with other tools. Often they will be much faster. However, in the fairly common case where you're just writing something to get a result right now, it is worth being comfortable enough with awk to emit one-line scripts quickly and easily.

Slightly longer scripts can generally be embedded using single quotes, but if your script gets to be a screenful or full of text, it is worth considering making it a separate file and using awk -f *file*. If you need to pass variables into the awk script, use the -v option. Even if you are embedding the script, it may be easier to follow it if you use the -v option to pass in variables instead of messing around with quotes.

Utilities and Languages

Is sed a utility or a language? Really, it is both. One of the sources of the flexibility of many UNIX utilities is that they have substantial expressive power, and indeed, often implement complete (if simplistic) languages. There are programming languages whose expression parsers are not as flexible as those used by find or test. The downside of this is that, to program the shell effectively, you have to have at least basic familiarity with a handful of smaller languages that are used for particular purposes.

HAVING IT BOTH WAYS: APPLESCRIPT

AppleScript is hardly portable, but it offers an excellent example of the interesting case of a language that is both easy to embed in shell scripts and easy to embed shell scripts in. Shell scripts on an OS X system can run chunks of AppleScript code using the osascript command; AppleScripts can spawn shell scripts using the do shell script language command. Because many Mac OS applications can be controlled from AppleScript, but many common UNIX shell tasks are very difficult from AppleScript, this substantially enhances the functional range of both languages. If you use a Mac, you should make a point of learning both languages.

Because do shell script uses the shell (always /bin/sh, which is bash on current systems) to parse commands, shell commands run from AppleScript are subject to the full range of command parsing, substitutions, and so on. Quoting AppleScript variables for the shell can be done using the quoted form of command. Note that it can be a bit disconcerting to switch back and forth between AppleScript's astounding verbosity and the shell's surprising terseness.

You can also pass a script in on standard input to the osascript utility, either by default (if there are no file name arguments and no -e options) or by explicitly naming - as the script file. This allows the use of here documents in the shell to contain nicely indented and expressive AppleScript scripts.

AppleScript is fairly similar to the HyperTalk language used in HyperCard, and thus somewhat similar to Runtime Revolution, a third-party scripting language targeting Mac, Windows, and Linux systems. In Runtime Revolution, you can use shell command substitution using the syntax put the shell of (*command*) into *variable*.

In the end, the shell is just another utility. It is an extremely powerful one with a complex (sometimes regrettably so) command language, which uses other utilities, and even other programming languages, as its building blocks. You can develop new utilities using existing utilities and new programs relying on these new utilities. For many tasks, the shell's performance weaknesses have long since ceased to be a significant weakness on modern systems; many shell scripts operate many times faster than their human users can type.

Used carefully, with a bit of attention to detail and planning, the shell allows for extremely rapid development of programs with unusually high portability across a broad range of systems.

What's Next?

The appendices. By kind permission of The Open Group, this book includes the specification for the POSIX shell; while some of the features described are not perfectly portable (yet. . .), the POSIX shell spec offers a clear description of many core shell features.

Beyond that, what's next is up to you. I recommend making a point of reading existing shell scripts; you may find a number of interesting idioms in distributions like shtool (a collection of small but very useful and highly portable shell scripts). When looking at programs you've never used, check to see whether they might be shell scripts; of the 404 commands in /usr/bin on one of my home systems, 32 are shell scripts. Reading a script you've never seen before can be informative.

If you want to master the shell, read lots of scripts and write lots of scripts. Don't settle for merely being able to guess what a script does; understand it. Find out what other programs it uses, and find out what they do. Automate aggressively. Feel free to write something that just automates part of a task; it's a great way to get started. You may be surprised at how easy it is to fill in the rest. About halfway through writing this book, I decided to automate "just the easy part" of a task which usually took me about three or four hours. Six hours later, I had it *all* automated.

Test your code on multiple systems and with multiple shells. You will learn a lot by doing this, and it will save you a lot of trouble when you unexpectedly have to target a new machine. I say when, rather than if, because personal experience has taught me that it is so.

■■■

The Shell Command Language

The POSIX shell language spec is full of things you probably never knew about the shell. Unfortunately, many of them are not true of historic shells; if they were, this would have been a very short book.

There are a number of features formally specified by POSIX, which this book has described as unportable; not every shell complies with POSIX. You may be more disturbed to discover that there are a number of features that this book has described as portable, but which POSIX does not specify. The most noticeable example is the #! script header. Don't worry—while such features may not be portable to every POSIX machine, they are quite consistently available on anything that looks like, or even smells a little like, UNIX.

In general, where the POSIX specification has terminology, I've deferred to their choice. The one noticeable gap is the term *expansion*. I use the term *substitution* to refer to the replacement of variable expressions with variable values. The POSIX specification calls it expansion (except for commands, which they say are substituted). There is no semantic difference; I just like the term substitution better.

■**Note** All external documents referenced in this appendix are available at www.opengroup.org.

---

2. Shell Command Language

This chapter contains the definition of the Shell Command Language.

2.1 Shell Introduction

The shell is a command language interpreter. This chapter describes the syntax of that command language as it is used by the *sh* utility and the *system()* and *popen()* functions defined in the System Interfaces volume of IEEE Std 1003.1-2001.

The shell operates according to the following general overview of operations. The specific details are included in the cited sections of this chapter.

1. The shell reads its input from a file (see *sh*), from the **-c** option or from the *system*() and *popen*() functions defined in the System Interfaces volume of IEEE Std 1003.1-2001. If the first line of a file of shell commands starts with the characters "#!", the results are unspecified.

2. The shell breaks the input into tokens: words and operators; see Token Recognition.

3. The shell parses the input into simple commands (see Simple Commands) and compound commands (see Compound Commands).

4. The shell performs various expansions (separately) on different parts of each command, resulting in a list of pathnames and fields to be treated as a command and arguments; see Word Expansions.

5. The shell performs redirection (see Redirection) and removes redirection operators and their operands from the parameter list.

6. The shell executes a function (see Function Definition Command), built-in (see Special Built-In Utilities), executable file, or script, giving the names of the arguments as positional parameters numbered 1 to *n*, and the name of the command (or in the case of a function within a script, the name of the script) as the positional parameter numbered 0 (see Command Search and Execution).

7. The shell optionally waits for the command to complete and collects the exit status (see Exit Status for Commands).

2.2 Quoting

Quoting is used to remove the special meaning of certain characters or words to the shell. Quoting can be used to preserve the literal meaning of the special characters in the next paragraph, prevent reserved words from being recognized as such, and prevent parameter expansion and command substitution within here-document processing (see Here-Document).

The application shall quote the following characters if they are to represent themselves:

```
|  &  ;  <  >  (  )  $  `  \  "  '  <space>  <tab>  <newline>
```

and the following may need to be quoted under certain circumstances. That is, these characters may be special depending on conditions described elsewhere in this volume of IEEE Std 1003.1-2001:

```
*  ?  [  #  ˜  =  %
```

The various quoting mechanisms are the escape character, single-quotes, and double-quotes. The here-document represents another form of quoting; see Here-Document.

2.2.1 Escape Character (Backslash)

A backslash that is not quoted shall preserve the literal value of the following character, with the exception of a <newline>. If a <newline> follows the backslash, the shell shall interpret this as line continuation. The backslash and <newline>s shall be removed before splitting the input into tokens. Since the escaped <newline> is removed entirely from the input and is not replaced by any white space, it cannot serve as a token separator.

2.2.2 Single-Quotes

Enclosing characters in single-quotes (' ') shall preserve the literal value of each character within the single-quotes. A single-quote cannot occur within single-quotes.

2.2.3 Double-Quotes

Enclosing characters in double-quotes ("") shall preserve the literal value of all characters within the double-quotes, with the exception of the characters dollar sign, backquote, and backslash, as follows:

$

The dollar sign shall retain its special meaning introducing parameter expansion (see Parameter Expansion), a form of command substitution (see Command Substitution), and arithmetic expansion (see Arithmetic Expansion).

The input characters within the quoted string that are also enclosed between "$(" and the matching ')' shall not be affected by the double-quotes, but rather shall define that command whose output replaces the "$(...)" when the word is expanded. The tokenizing rules in Token Recognition, not including the alias substitutions in Alias Substitution, shall be applied recursively to find the matching ')'.

Within the string of characters from an enclosed "${" to the matching '}', an even number of unescaped double-quotes or single-quotes, if any, shall occur. A preceding backslash character shall be used to escape a literal '{' or '}'. The rule in Parameter Expansion shall be used to determine the matching '}'.

`

The backquote shall retain its special meaning introducing the other form of command substitution (see Command Substitution). The portion of the quoted string from the initial backquote and the characters up to the next backquote that is not preceded by a backslash, having escape characters removed, defines that command whose output replaces "` ... `" when the word is expanded. Either of the following cases produces undefined results:

- A single-quoted or double-quoted string that begins, but does not end, within the "` ... `" sequence

- A "` ... `" sequence that begins, but does not end, within the same double-quoted string

\

The backslash shall retain its special meaning as an escape character (see Escape Character (Backslash)) only when followed by one of the following characters when considered special:

```
$    `    "    \    <newline>
```

The application shall ensure that a double-quote is preceded by a backslash to be included within double-quotes. The parameter '@' has special meaning inside double-quotes and is described in Special Parameters.

2.3 Token Recognition

The shell shall read its input in terms of lines from a file, from a terminal in the case of an interactive shell, or from a string in the case of *sh* **-c** or *system*(). The input lines can be of unlimited length. These lines shall be parsed using two major modes: ordinary token recognition and processing of here-documents.

When an **io_here** token has been recognized by the grammar (see Shell Grammar), one or more of the subsequent lines immediately following the next **NEWLINE** token form the body of one or more here-documents and shall be parsed according to the rules of Here-Document.

When it is not processing an **io_here**, the shell shall break its input into tokens by applying the first applicable rule below to the next character in its input. The token shall be from the current position in the input until a token is delimited according to one of the rules below; the characters forming the token are exactly those in the input, including any quoting characters. If it is indicated that a token is delimited, and no characters have been included in a token, processing shall continue until an actual token is delimited.

1. If the end of input is recognized, the current token shall be delimited. If there is no current token, the end-of-input indicator shall be returned as the token.

2. If the previous character was used as part of an operator and the current character is not quoted and can be used with the current characters to form an operator, it shall be used as part of that (operator) token.

3. If the previous character was used as part of an operator and the current character cannot be used with the current characters to form an operator, the operator containing the previous character shall be delimited.

4. If the current character is backslash, single-quote, or double-quote ('\', ' ", or ')' and it is not quoted, it shall affect quoting for subsequent characters up to the end of the quoted text. The rules for quoting are as described in Quoting. During token recognition no substitutions shall be actually performed, and the result token shall contain exactly the characters that appear in the input (except for <newline> joining), unmodified, including any embedded or enclosing quotes or substitution operators, between the quote mark and the end of the quoted text. The token shall not be delimited by the end of the quoted field.

5. If the current character is an unquoted '$' or '`', the shell shall identify the start of any candidates for parameter expansion (Parameter Expansion), command substitution (Command Substitution), or arithmetic expansion (Arithmetic Expansion) from their introductory unquoted character sequences: '$' or "${", "$(" or '`', and "$((", respectively. The shell shall read sufficient input to determine the end of the unit to be expanded (as explained in the cited sections). While processing the characters, if instances of expansions or quoting are found nested within the substitution, the shell shall recursively process them in the manner specified for the construct that is found.

The characters found from the beginning of the substitution to its end, allowing for any recursion necessary to recognize embedded constructs, shall be included unmodified in the result token, including any embedded or enclosing substitution operators or quotes. The token shall not be delimited by the end of the substitution.

6. If the current character is not quoted and can be used as the first character of a new operator, the current token (if any) shall be delimited. The current character shall be used as the beginning of the next (operator) token.

7. If the current character is an unquoted <newline>, the current token shall be delimited.

8. If the current character is an unquoted <blank>, any token containing the previous character is delimited and the current character shall be discarded.

9. If the previous character was part of a word, the current character shall be appended to that word.

10. If the current character is a '#', it and all subsequent characters up to, but excluding, the next <newline> shall be discarded as a comment. The <newline> that ends the line is not considered part of the comment.

11. The current character is used as the start of a new word.

Once a token is delimited, it is categorized as required by the grammar in Shell Grammar.

2.3.1 Alias Substitution

The processing of aliases shall be supported on all XSI-conformant systems or if the system supports the User Portability Utilities option (and the rest of this section is not further marked for these options).

After a token has been delimited, but before applying the grammatical rules in Shell Grammar, a resulting word that is identified to be the command name word of a simple command shall be examined to determine whether it is an unquoted, valid alias name. However, reserved words in correct grammatical context shall not be candidates for alias substitution. A valid alias name (see the Base Definitions volume of IEEE Std 1003.1-2001, Section 3.10, Alias Name) shall be one that has been defined by the *alias* utility and not subsequently undefined using *unalias*. Implementations also may provide predefined valid aliases that are in effect when the shell is invoked. To prevent infinite loops in recursive aliasing, if the shell is not currently processing an alias of the same name, the word shall be replaced by the value of the alias; otherwise, it shall not be replaced.

If the value of the alias replacing the word ends in a <blank>, the shell shall check the next command word for alias substitution; this process shall continue until a word is found that is not a valid alias or an alias value does not end in a <blank>.

When used as specified by this volume of IEEE Std 1003.1-2001, alias definitions shall not be inherited by separate invocations of the shell or by the utility execution environments invoked by the shell; see Shell Execution Environment.

2.4 Reserved Words

Reserved words are words that have special meaning to the shell; see Shell Commands. The following words shall be recognized as reserved words:

```
!         do      esac    in
{         done    fi      then
}         elif    for     until
case      else    if      while
```

This recognition shall only occur when none of the characters is quoted and when the word is used as:

- The first word of a command

- The first word following one of the reserved words other than **case**, **for**, or **in**

- The third word in a **case** command (only **in** is valid in this case)

- The third word in a **for** command (only **in** and **do** are valid in this case)

See the grammar in Shell Grammar.

The following words may be recognized as reserved words on some implementations (when none of the characters are quoted), causing unspecified results:

```
[[
```

```
]]
```

```
function
```

```
select
```

Words that are the concatenation of a name and a colon (':') are reserved; their use produces unspecified results.

2.5 Parameters and Variables

A parameter can be denoted by a name, a number, or one of the special characters listed in Special Parameters. A variable is a parameter denoted by a name.

A parameter is set if it has an assigned value (null is a valid value). Once a variable is set, it can only be unset by using the *unset* special built-in command.

2.5.1 Positional Parameters

A positional parameter is a parameter denoted by the decimal value represented by one or more digits, other than the single digit 0. The digits denoting the positional parameters shall always be interpreted as a decimal value, even if there is a leading zero. When a positional parameter with more than one digit is specified, the application shall enclose the digits in braces (see Parameter Expansion). Positional parameters are initially assigned when the shell is invoked (see *sh*), temporarily replaced when a shell function is invoked (see Function Definition Command), and can be reassigned with the *set* special built-in command.

2.5.2 Special Parameters

Listed below are the special parameters and the values to which they shall expand. Only the values of the special parameters are listed; see Word Expansions for a detailed summary of all the stages involved in expanding words.

@

Expands to the positional parameters, starting from one. When the expansion occurs within double-quotes, and where field splitting (see Field Splitting) is performed, each positional parameter shall expand as a separate field, with the provision that the expansion of the first parameter shall still be joined with the beginning part of the original word (assuming that the expanded parameter was embedded within a word), and the expansion of the last parameter shall still be joined with the last part of the original word. If there are no positional parameters, the expansion of '@' shall generate zero fields, even when '@' is double-quoted.

*

Expands to the positional parameters, starting from one. When the expansion occurs within a double-quoted string (see Double-Quotes), it shall expand to a single field with the value of each parameter separated by the first character of the *IFS* variable, or by a <space> if *IFS* is unset. If *IFS* is set to a null string, this is not equivalent to unsetting it; its first character does not exist, so the parameter values are concatenated.

#

Expands to the decimal number of positional parameters. The command name (parameter 0) shall not be counted in the number given by '#' because it is a special parameter, not a positional parameter.

?

Expands to the decimal exit status of the most recent pipeline (see Pipelines).

-

(Hyphen.) Expands to the current option flags (the single-letter option names concatenated into a string) as specified on invocation, by the *set* special built-in command, or implicitly by the shell.

$

Expands to the decimal process ID of the invoked shell. In a subshell (see Shell Execution Environment), '$' shall expand to the same value as that of the current shell.

!

Expands to the decimal process ID of the most recent background command (see Lists) executed from the current shell. (For example, background commands executed from subshells do not affect the value of "$!" in the current shell environment.) For a pipeline, the process ID is that of the last command in the pipeline.

0

(Zero.) Expands to the name of the shell or shell script. See *sh* for a detailed description of how this name is derived.

See the description of the *IFS* variable in Shell Variables.

2.5.3 Shell Variables

Variables shall be initialized from the environment (as defined by the Base Definitions volume of IEEE Std 1003.1-2001, Chapter 8, Environment Variables and the *exec* function in the System Interfaces volume of IEEE Std 1003.1-2001) and can be given new values with variable assignment commands. If a variable is initialized from the environment, it shall be marked for export immediately; see the *export* special built-in. New variables can be defined and initialized with variable assignments, with the *read* or *getopts* utilities, with the *name* parameter in a **for** loop, with the ${ *name= word*} expansion, or with other mechanisms provided as implementation extensions.

The following variables shall affect the execution of the shell:

ENV

The processing of the ENV shell variable shall be supported on all XSI-conformant systems or if the system supports the User Portability Utilities option.

This variable, when and only when an interactive shell is invoked, shall be subjected to parameter expansion (see Parameter Expansion) by the shell and the resulting value shall be used as a pathname of a file containing shell commands to execute in the current environment. The file need not be executable. If the expanded value of ENV is not an absolute pathname, the results are unspecified. ENV shall be ignored if the user's real and effective user IDs or real and effective group IDs are different.

HOME

The pathname of the user's home directory. The contents of HOME are used in tilde expansion (see Tilde Expansion).

IFS

(Input Field Separators.) A string treated as a list of characters that is used for field splitting and to split lines into fields with the read command. If IFS is not set, the shell shall behave as if the value of IFS is <space>, <tab>, and <newline>; see Field Splitting. Implementations may ignore the value of IFS in the environment at the time the shell is invoked, treating IFS as if it were not set.

LANG

Provide a default value for the internationalization variables that are unset or null. (See the Base Definitions volume of IEEE Std 1003.1-2001, Section 8.2, Internationalization Variables for the precedence of internationalization variables used to determine the values of locale categories.)

LC_ALL

The value of this variable overrides the LC_* variables and LANG, as described in the Base Definitions volume of IEEE Std 1003.1-2001, Chapter 8, Environment Variables.

LC_COLLATE

Determine the behavior of range expressions, equivalence classes, and multi-character collating elements within pattern matching.

LC_CTYPE

Determine the interpretation of sequences of bytes of text data as characters (for example, single-byte as opposed to multi-byte characters), which characters are defined as letters (character class **alpha**) and <blank>s (character class **blank**), and the behavior of character classes within pattern matching. Changing the value of LC_CTYPE after the shell has started shall not affect the lexical processing of shell commands in the current shell execution environment or its subshells. Invoking a shell script or performing exec sh subjects the new shell to the changes in LC_CTYPE .

LC_MESSAGES

Determine the language in which messages should be written.

LINENO

Set by the shell to a decimal number representing the current sequential line number (numbered starting with 1) within a script or function before it executes each command. If the user unsets or resets LINENO, the variable may lose its special meaning for the life of the shell. If the shell is not currently executing a script or function, the value of LINENO is unspecified. This volume of IEEE Std 1003.1-2001 specifies the effects of the variable only for systems supporting the User Portability Utilities option.

NLSPATH

Determine the location of message catalogs for the processing of LC_MESSAGES.

PATH

A string formatted as described in the Base Definitions volume of IEEE Std 1003.1-2001, Chapter 8, Environment Variables, used to effect command interpretation; see Command Search and Execution.

PPID

Set by the shell to the decimal process ID of the process that invoked this shell. In a subshell (see Shell Execution Environment), PPID shall be set to the same value as that of the parent of the current shell. For example, echo $ PPID and (echo $ PPID) would produce the same value. This volume of IEEE Std 1003.1-2001 specifies the effects of the variable only for systems supporting the User Portability Utilities option.

PS1

Each time an interactive shell is ready to read a command, the value of this variable shall be subjected to parameter expansion and written to standard error. The default value shall be "$ ". For users who have specific additional implementation-defined privileges, the default may be another, implementation-defined value. The shell shall replace each instance of the character '!' in PS1 with the history file number of the next command to be typed. Escaping the '!' with another '!' (that is, "!!") shall place the literal character '!' in the prompt. This volume of IEEE Std 1003.1-2001 specifies the effects of the variable only for systems supporting the User Portability Utilities option.

PS2

Each time the user enters a <newline> prior to completing a command line in an interactive shell, the value of this variable shall be subjected to parameter expansion and written to standard error. The default value is "> ". This volume of IEEE Std 1003.1-2001 specifies the effects of the variable only for systems supporting the User Portability Utilities option.

PS4

When an execution trace (set -x) is being performed in an interactive shell, before each line in the execution trace, the value of this variable shall be subjected to parameter expansion and written to standard error. The default value is "+ ". This volume of IEEE Std 1003.1-2001 specifies the effects of the variable only for systems supporting the User Portability Utilities option.

PWD

Set by the shell to be an absolute pathname of the current working directory, containing no components of type symbolic link, no components that are dot, and no components that are dot-dot when the shell is initialized. If an application sets or unsets the value of PWD, the behaviors of the cd and pwd utilities are unspecified.

2.6 Word Expansions

This section describes the various expansions that are performed on words. Not all expansions are performed on every word, as explained in the following sections.

Tilde expansions, parameter expansions, command substitutions, arithmetic expansions, and quote removals that occur within a single word expand to a single field. It is only field splitting or pathname expansion that can create multiple fields from a single word. The single exception to this rule is the expansion of the special parameter '@' within double-quotes, as described in Special Parameters.

The order of word expansion shall be as follows:

1. Tilde expansion (see Tilde Expansion), parameter expansion (see Parameter Expansion), command substitution (see Command Substitution), and arithmetic expansion (see Arithmetic Expansion) shall be performed, beginning to end. See item 5 in Token Recognition.

2. Field splitting (see Field Splitting) shall be performed on the portions of the fields generated by step 1, unless *IFS* is null.

3. Pathname expansion (see Pathname Expansion) shall be performed, unless *set* -**f** is in effect.

4. Quote removal (see Quote Removal) shall always be performed last.

The expansions described in this section shall occur in the same shell environment as that in which the command is executed.

If the complete expansion appropriate for a word results in an empty field, that empty field shall be deleted from the list of fields that form the completely expanded command, unless the original word contained single-quote or double-quote characters.

The '$' character is used to introduce parameter expansion, command substitution, or arithmetic evaluation. If an unquoted '$' is followed by a character that is either not numeric, the name of one of the special parameters (see Special Parameters), a valid first character of a variable name, a left curly brace ('{') or a left parenthesis, the result is unspecified.

2.6.1 Tilde Expansion

A "tilde-prefix" consists of an unquoted tilde character at the beginning of a word, followed by all of the characters preceding the first unquoted slash in the word, or all the characters in the word if there is no slash. In an assignment (see the Base Definitions volume of IEEE Std 1003.1-2001, Section 4.21, Variable Assignment), multiple tilde-prefixes can be used: at the beginning of the word (that is, following the equal sign of the assignment), following any unquoted colon, or both. A tilde-prefix in an assignment is terminated by the first unquoted colon or slash. If none of the characters in the tilde-prefix are quoted, the characters in the tilde-prefix following the tilde are treated as a possible login name from the user database. A portable login name cannot contain characters outside the set given in the description of the *LOGNAME* environment variable in the Base Definitions volume of IEEE Std 1003.1-2001, Section 8.3, Other Environment Variables. If the login name is null (that is, the tilde-prefix contains only the tilde), the tilde-prefix is replaced by the value of the variable *HOME*. If *HOME* is unset, the results are unspecified. Otherwise, the tilde-prefix shall be replaced by a pathname of the initial working directory associated with the login name obtained using the *getpwnam*() function as defined in the System Interfaces volume of IEEE Std 1003.1-2001. If the system does not recognize the login name, the results are undefined.

2.6.2 Parameter Expansion

The format for parameter expansion is as follows:

```
${expression}
```

where *expression* consists of all characters until the matching '}'. Any '}' escaped by a backslash or within a quoted string, and characters in embedded arithmetic expansions, command substitutions, and variable expansions, shall not be examined in determining the matching '}'.

The simplest form for parameter expansion is:

```
${parameter}
```

The value, if any, of *parameter* shall be substituted.

The parameter name or symbol can be enclosed in braces, which are optional except for positional parameters with more than one digit or when *parameter* is followed by a character that could be interpreted as part of the name. The matching closing brace shall be determined by counting brace levels, skipping over enclosed quoted strings, and command substitutions.

If the parameter name or symbol is not enclosed in braces, the expansion shall use the longest valid name (see the Base Definitions volume of IEEE Std 1003.1-2001, Section 3.230, Name), whether or not the symbol represented by that name exists.

If a parameter expansion occurs inside double-quotes:

- Pathname expansion shall not be performed on the results of the expansion.

- Field splitting shall not be performed on the results of the expansion, with the exception of '@'; see Special Parameters.

In addition, a parameter expansion can be modified by using one of the following formats. In each case that a value of *word* is needed (based on the state of *parameter*, as described below), *word* shall be subjected to tilde expansion, parameter expansion, command substitution, and arithmetic expansion. If *word* is not needed, it shall not be expanded. The '}' character that delimits the following parameter expansion modifications shall be determined as described previously in this section and in Double-Quotes. (For example, ${ **foo-bar} xyz}** would result in the expansion of **foo** followed by the string **xyz}** if **foo** is set, else the string "barxyz}").

${*parameter:-word*}

Use Default Values. If *parameter* is unset or null, the expansion of *word* shall be substituted; otherwise, the value of *parameter* shall be substituted.

${*parameter:=word*}

Assign Default Values. If *parameter* is unset or null, the expansion of *word* shall be assigned to *parameter*. In all cases, the final value of *parameter* shall be substituted. Only variables, not positional parameters or special parameters, can be assigned in this way.

${*parameter:?[word]*}

Indicate Error if Null or Unset. If *parameter* is unset or null, the expansion of *word* (or a message indicating it is unset if *word* is omitted) shall be written to standard error and the shell exits with a non-zero exit status. Otherwise, the value of *parameter* shall be substituted. An interactive shell need not exit.

${*parameter:+word*}

Use Alternative Value. If *parameter* is unset or null, null shall be substituted; otherwise, the expansion of *word* shall be substituted.

In the parameter expansions shown previously, use of the colon in the format shall result in a test for a parameter that is unset or null; omission of the colon shall result in a test for a parameter that is only unset. The following table summarizes the effect of the colon:

	parameter	parameter	parameter
	Set and Not Null	Set But Null	Unset
${parameter:-word}	substitute parameter	substitute word	substitute word
${parameter-word}	substitute parameter	substitute null	substitute word
${parameter:=word}	substitute parameter	assign word	assign word
${parameter=word}	substitute parameter	substitute null	assign word
${parameter:?word}	substitute parameter	error, exit	error, exit
${parameter?word}	substitute parameter	substitute null	error, exit
${parameter:+word}	substitute word	substitute null	substitute null
${parameter+word}	substitute word	substitute word	substitute null

In all cases shown with "substitute", the expression is replaced with the value shown. In all cases shown with "assign", *parameter* is assigned that value, which also replaces the expression.

${#parameter}

String Length. The length in characters of the value of *parameter* shall be substituted. If *parameter* is '*' or '@', the result of the expansion is unspecified.

The following four varieties of parameter expansion provide for substring processing. In each case, pattern matching notation (see Pattern Matching Notation), rather than regular expression notation, shall be used to evaluate the patterns. If *parameter* is '*' or '@', the result of the expansion is unspecified. Enclosing the full parameter expansion string in double-quotes shall not cause the following four varieties of pattern characters to be quoted, whereas quoting characters within the braces shall have this effect.

${parameter%word}

Remove Smallest Suffix Pattern. The *word* shall be expanded to produce a pattern. The parameter expansion shall then result in *parameter*, with the smallest portion of the suffix matched by the *pattern* deleted.

${parameter%%word}

Remove Largest Suffix Pattern. The *word* shall be expanded to produce a pattern. The parameter expansion shall then result in *parameter*, with the largest portion of the suffix matched by the *pattern* deleted.

${parameter#word}

Remove Smallest Prefix Pattern. The *word* shall be expanded to produce a pattern. The parameter expansion shall then result in *parameter*, with the smallest portion of the prefix matched by the *pattern* deleted.

${parameter##word}

Remove Largest Prefix Pattern. The *word* shall be expanded to produce a pattern. The parameter expansion shall then result in *parameter*, with the largest portion of the prefix matched by the *pattern* deleted.

The following sections are informative.

${*parameter:-word*}

In this example, *ls* is executed only if *x* is null or unset. (The $(*ls*) command substitution notation is explained in Command Substitution.)

${x:-$(ls)}

${*parameter:=word*}

```
unset X
echo ${X:=abc}
```
abc

${*parameter:?word*}

```
unset posix
echo ${posix:?}
```
sh: posix: parameter null or not set

${*parameter:+word*}

```
set a b c
echo ${3:+posix}
```
posix

${*#parameter*}

```
HOME=/usr/posix
echo ${#HOME}
```
10

${*parameter%word*}

```
x=file.c
echo ${x%.c}.o
```
file.o

${*parameter%%word*}

```
x=posix/src/std
echo ${x%%/*}
```
posix

${*parameter#word*}

```
x=$HOME/src/cmd
echo ${x#$HOME}
```
/src/cmd

${*parameter##word*}

```
x=/one/two/three
echo ${x##*/}
```
three

The double-quoting of patterns is different depending on where the double-quotes are placed:

```
"${x#*}"
```

The asterisk is a pattern character.

```
${x#"*"}
```

The literal asterisk is quoted and not special.
End of informative text.

2.6.3 Command Substitution

Command substitution allows the output of a command to be substituted in place of the command name itself. Command substitution shall occur when the command is enclosed as follows:

```
$(command)
```

or (backquoted version):

```
`command`
```

The shell shall expand the command substitution by executing *command* in a subshell environment (see Shell Execution Environment) and replacing the command substitution (the text of *command* plus the enclosing "$()" or backquotes) with the standard output of the command, removing sequences of one or more <newline>s at the end of the substitution. Embedded <newline>s before the end of the output shall not be removed; however, they may be treated as field delimiters and eliminated during field splitting, depending on the value of *IFS* and quoting that is in effect.

Within the backquoted style of command substitution, backslash shall retain its literal meaning, except when followed by: '$', '`', or '\' (dollar sign, backquote, backslash). The search for the matching backquote shall be satisfied by the first backquote found without a preceding backslash; during this search, if a non-escaped backquote is encountered within a shell comment, a here-document, an embedded command substitution of the $(*command*) form, or a quoted string, undefined results occur. A single-quoted or double-quoted string that begins, but does not end, within the "` ...`" sequence produces undefined results.

With the $(*command*) form, all characters following the open parenthesis to the matching closing parenthesis constitute the *command*. Any valid shell script can be used for *command*, except a script consisting solely of redirections which produces unspecified results.

The results of command substitution shall not be processed for further tilde expansion, parameter expansion, command substitution, or arithmetic expansion. If a command substitution occurs inside double-quotes, field splitting and pathname expansion shall not be performed on the results of the substitution.

Command substitution can be nested. To specify nesting within the backquoted version, the application shall precede the inner backquotes with backslashes, for example:

```
\`command\`
```

If the command substitution consists of a single subshell, such as:

```
$( (command) )
```

a conforming application shall separate the "$(" and '(' into two tokens (that is, separate them with white space). This is required to avoid any ambiguities with arithmetic expansion.

2.6.4 Arithmetic Expansion

Arithmetic expansion provides a mechanism for evaluating an arithmetic expression and substituting its value. The format for arithmetic expansion shall be as follows:

```
$((expression))
```

The expression shall be treated as if it were in double-quotes, except that a double-quote inside the expression is not treated specially. The shell shall expand all tokens in the expression for parameter expansion, command substitution, and quote removal.

Next, the shell shall treat this as an arithmetic expression and substitute the value of the expression. The arithmetic expression shall be processed according to the rules given in *Arithmetic Precision and Operations*, with the following exceptions:

- Only signed long integer arithmetic is required.

- Only the decimal-constant, octal-constant, and hexadecimal-constant constants specified in the ISO C standard, Section 6.4.4.1 are required to be recognized as constants.

- The *sizeof()* operator and the prefix and postfix "++" and "--" operators are not required.

- Selection, iteration, and jump statements are not supported.

All changes to variables in an arithmetic expression shall be in effect after the arithmetic expansion, as in the parameter expansion "${x=value}".

If the shell variable x contains a value that forms a valid integer constant, then the arithmetic expansions "$((x))" and "$(($x))" shall return the same value.

As an extension, the shell may recognize arithmetic expressions beyond those listed. The shell may use a signed integer type with a rank larger than the rank of **signed long**. The shell may use a real-floating type instead of **signed long** as long as it does not affect the results in cases where there is no overflow. If the expression is invalid, the expansion fails and the shell shall write a message to standard error indicating the failure.

The following sections are informative.

EXAMPLES

A simple example using arithmetic expansion:

```
# repeat a command 100 times
x=100
while [ $x -gt 0 ]
do
```

```
    command    x=$(($x-1))
done
```

End of informative text.

2.6.5 Field Splitting

After parameter expansion (Parameter Expansion), command substitution (Command Substitution), and arithmetic expansion (Arithmetic Expansion), the shell shall scan the results of expansions and substitutions that did not occur in double-quotes for field splitting and multiple fields can result.

The shell shall treat each character of the *IFS* as a delimiter and use the delimiters to split the results of parameter expansion and command substitution into fields.

1. If the value of *IFS* is a <space>, <tab>, and <newline>, or if it is unset, any sequence of <space>s, <tab>s, or <newline>s at the beginning or end of the input shall be ignored and any sequence of those characters within the input shall delimit a field. For example, the input:

   ```
   <newline><space><tab>foo<tab><tab>bar<space>
   ```

   yields two fields, **foo** and **bar**.

2. If the value of *IFS* is null, no field splitting shall be performed.

3. Otherwise, the following rules shall be applied in sequence. The term "*IFS* white space" is used to mean any sequence (zero or more instances) of white space characters that are in the *IFS* value (for example, if *IFS* contains <space>/ <comma>/ <tab>, any sequence of <space>s and <tab>s is considered *IFS* white space).

   a. *IFS* white space shall be ignored at the beginning and end of the input.

   b. Each occurrence in the input of an *IFS* character that is not *IFS* white space, along with any adjacent *IFS* white space, shall delimit a field, as described previously.

   c. Non-zero-length *IFS* white space shall delimit a field.

2.6.6 Pathname Expansion

After field splitting, if *set* **-f** is not in effect, each field in the resulting command line shall be expanded using the algorithm described in Pattern Matching Notation, qualified by the rules in Patterns Used for Filename Expansion.

2.6.7 Quote Removal

The quote characters: '\', '"', and '' (backslash, single-quote, double-quote) that were present in the original word shall be removed unless they have themselves been quoted.

2.7 Redirection

Redirection is used to open and close files for the current shell execution environment (see Shell Execution Environment) or for any command. Redirection operators can be used with numbers representing file descriptors (see the Base Definitions volume of IEEE Std 1003.1-2001, Section 3.165, File Descriptor) as described below.

The overall format used for redirection is:

```
[n]redir-op word
```

The number *n* is an optional decimal number designating the file descriptor number; the application shall ensure it is delimited from any preceding text and immediately precede the redirection operator *redir-op*. If *n* is quoted, the number shall not be recognized as part of the redirection expression. For example:

```
echo \2>a
```

writes the character 2 into file **a**. If any part of *redir-op* is quoted, no redirection expression is recognized. For example:

```
echo 2\>a
```

writes the characters 2>*a* to standard output. The optional number, redirection operator, and *word* shall not appear in the arguments provided to the command to be executed (if any).

Open files are represented by decimal numbers starting with zero. The largest possible value is implementation-defined; however, all implementations shall support at least 0 to 9, inclusive, for use by the application. These numbers are called "file descriptors". The values 0, 1, and 2 have special meaning and conventional uses and are implied by certain redirection operations; they are referred to as *standard input*, *standard output*, and *standard error*, respectively. Programs usually take their input from standard input, and write output on standard output. Error messages are usually written on standard error. The redirection operators can be preceded by one or more digits (with no intervening <blank>s allowed) to designate the file descriptor number.

If the redirection operator is "<<" or "<<-", the word that follows the redirection operator shall be subjected to quote removal; it is unspecified whether any of the other expansions occur. For the other redirection operators, the word that follows the redirection operator shall be subjected to tilde expansion, parameter expansion, command substitution, arithmetic expansion, and quote removal. Pathname expansion shall not be performed on the word by a non-interactive shell; an interactive shell may perform it, but shall do so only when the expansion would result in one word.

If more than one redirection operator is specified with a command, the order of evaluation is from beginning to end.

A failure to open or create a file shall cause a redirection to fail.

2.7.1 Redirecting Input

Input redirection shall cause the file whose name results from the expansion of *word* to be opened for reading on the designated file descriptor, or standard input if the file descriptor is not specified.

The general format for redirecting input is:

```
[n]<word
```

where the optional *n* represents the file descriptor number. If the number is omitted, the redirection shall refer to standard input (file descriptor 0).

2.7.2 Redirecting Output

The two general formats for redirecting output are:

```
[n]>word
[n]>|word
```

where the optional *n* represents the file descriptor number. If the number is omitted, the redirection shall refer to standard output (file descriptor 1).

Output redirection using the '>' format shall fail if the *noclobber* option is set (see the description of *set* -**C**) and the file named by the expansion of *word* exists and is a regular file. Otherwise, redirection using the '>' or ">|" formats shall cause the file whose name results from the expansion of *word* to be created and opened for output on the designated file descriptor, or standard output if none is specified. If the file does not exist, it shall be created; otherwise, it shall be truncated to be an empty file after being opened.

2.7.3 Appending Redirected Output

Appended output redirection shall cause the file whose name results from the expansion of word to be opened for output on the designated file descriptor. The file is opened as if the *open()* function as defined in the System Interfaces volume of IEEE Std 1003.1-2001 was called with the O_APPEND flag. If the file does not exist, it shall be created.

The general format for appending redirected output is as follows:

```
[n]>>word
```

where the optional *n* represents the file descriptor number. If the number is omitted, the redirection refers to standard output (file descriptor 1).

2.7.4 Here-Document

The redirection operators "<<" and "<<-" both allow redirection of lines contained in a shell input file, known as a "here-document", to the input of a command.

The here-document shall be treated as a single word that begins after the next <newline> and continues until there is a line containing only the delimiter and a <newline>, with no <blank>s in between. Then the next here-document starts, if there is one. The format is as follows:

```
[n]<<word
    here-document
delimiter
```

where the optional *n* represents the file descriptor number. If the number is omitted, the here-document refers to standard input (file descriptor 0).

If any character in *word* is quoted, the delimiter shall be formed by performing quote removal on *word*, and the here-document lines shall not be expanded. Otherwise, the delimiter shall be the *word* itself.

If no characters in *word* are quoted, all lines of the here-document shall be expanded for parameter expansion, command substitution, and arithmetic expansion. In this case, the backslash in the input behaves as the backslash inside double-quotes (see Double-Quotes).

However, the double-quote character ('"') shall not be treated specially within a here-document, except when the double-quote appears within "$()", "` `", or "${}".

If the redirection symbol is "<<-", all leading <tab>s shall be stripped from input lines and the line containing the trailing delimiter. If more than one "<<" or "<<-" operator is specified on a line, the here-document associated with the first operator shall be supplied first by the application and shall be read first by the shell.

The following sections are informative.

EXAMPLES

An example of a here-document follows:

```
cat <<eof1; cat <<eof2
Hi,
eof1
Helene.
eof2
```

End of informative text.

2.7.5 Duplicating an Input File Descriptor

The redirection operator:

[*n*]<&*word*

shall duplicate one input file descriptor from another, or shall close one. If *word* evaluates to one or more digits, the file descriptor denoted by *n*, or standard input if *n* is not specified, shall be made to be a copy of the file descriptor denoted by *word*; if the digits in *word* do not represent a file descriptor already open for input, a redirection error shall result; see Consequences of Shell Errors. If *word* evaluates to '-', file descriptor *n*, or standard input if *n* is not specified, shall be closed. Attempts to close a file descriptor that is not open shall not constitute an error. If *word* evaluates to something else, the behavior is unspecified.

2.7.6 Duplicating an Output File Descriptor

The redirection operator:

[*n*]>&*word*

shall duplicate one output file descriptor from another, or shall close one. If *word* evaluates to one or more digits, the file descriptor denoted by *n*, or standard output if *n* is not specified, shall be made to be a copy of the file descriptor denoted by *word*; if the digits in *word* do not represent a file descriptor already open for output, a redirection error shall result; see Consequences of Shell Errors. If *word* evaluates to '-', file descriptor *n*, or standard output if *n* is not specified, is closed. Attempts to close a file descriptor that is not open shall not constitute an error. If *word* evaluates to something else, the behavior is unspecified.

2.7.7 Open File Descriptors for Reading and Writing

The redirection operator:

[*n*]<>*word*

shall cause the file whose name is the expansion of *word* to be opened for both reading and writing on the file descriptor denoted by *n*, or standard input if *n* is not specified. If the file does not exist, it shall be created.

2.8 Exit Status and Errors

2.8.1 Consequences of Shell Errors

For a non-interactive shell, an error condition encountered by a special built-in (see Special Built-In Utilities) or other type of utility shall cause the shell to write a diagnostic message to standard error and exit as shown in the following table:

Error	Special Built-In	Other Utilities
Shell language syntax error	Shall exit	Shall exit
Utility syntax error (option or operand error)	Shall exit	Shall not exit
Redirection error	Shall exit	Shall not exit
Variable assignment error	Shall exit	Shall not exit
Expansion error	Shall exit	Shall exit
Command not found	N/A	May exit
Dot script not found	Shall exit	N/A

An expansion error is one that occurs when the shell expansions defined in Word Expansions are carried out (for example, "${x!y}", because '!' is not a valid operator); an implementation may treat these as syntax errors if it is able to detect them during tokenization, rather than during expansion.

If any of the errors shown as "shall exit" or "(may) exit" occur in a subshell, the subshell shall (respectively may) exit with a non-zero status, but the script containing the subshell shall not exit because of the error.

In all of the cases shown in the table, an interactive shell shall write a diagnostic message to standard error without exiting.

2.8.2 Exit Status for Commands

Each command has an exit status that can influence the behavior of other shell commands. The exit status of commands that are not utilities is documented in this section. The exit status of the standard utilities is documented in their respective sections.

If a command is not found, the exit status shall be 127. If the command name is found, but it is not an executable utility, the exit status shall be 126. Applications that invoke utilities without using the shell should use these exit status values to report similar errors.

If a command fails during word expansion or redirection, its exit status shall be greater than zero.

Internally, for purposes of deciding whether a command exits with a non-zero exit status, the shell shall recognize the entire status value retrieved for the command by the equivalent of the *wait()* function WEXITSTATUS macro (as defined in the System Interfaces volume of IEEE Std 1003.1-2001). When reporting the exit status with the special parameter '?', the shell shall report the full eight bits of exit status available. The exit status of a command that terminated because it received a signal shall be reported as greater than 128.

2.9 Shell Commands

This section describes the basic structure of shell commands. The following command descriptions each describe a format of the command that is only used to aid the reader in recognizing the command type, and does not formally represent the syntax. Each description discusses the semantics of the command; for a formal definition of the command language, consult Shell Grammar.

A *command* is one of the following:

- Simple command (see Simple Commands)

- Pipeline (see Pipelines)

- List compound-list (see Lists)

- Compound command (see Compound Commands)

- Function definition (see Function Definition Command)

Unless otherwise stated, the exit status of a command shall be that of the last simple command executed by the command. There shall be no limit on the size of any shell command other than that imposed by the underlying system (memory constraints, {ARG_MAX}, and so on).

2.9.1 Simple Commands

A "simple command" is a sequence of optional variable assignments and redirections, in any sequence, optionally followed by words and redirections, terminated by a control operator.

When a given simple command is required to be executed (that is, when any conditional construct such as an AND-OR list or a **case** statement has not bypassed the simple command), the following expansions, assignments, and redirections shall all be performed from the beginning of the command text to the end:

1. The words that are recognized as variable assignments or redirections according to Shell Grammar Rules are saved for processing in steps 3 and 4.

2. The words that are not variable assignments or redirections shall be expanded. If any fields remain following their expansion, the first field shall be considered the command name and remaining fields are the arguments for the command.

3. Redirections shall be performed as described in Redirection.

4. Each variable assignment shall be expanded for tilde expansion, parameter expansion, command substitution, arithmetic expansion, and quote removal prior to assigning the value.

In the preceding list, the order of steps 3 and 4 may be reversed for the processing of special built-in utilities; see Special Built-In Utilities.

If no command name results, variable assignments shall affect the current execution environment. Otherwise, the variable assignments shall be exported for the execution environment of the command and shall not affect the current execution environment (except for special built-ins). If any of the variable assignments attempt to assign a value to a read-only variable, a variable assignment error shall occur. See Consequences of Shell Errors for the consequences of these errors.

If there is no command name, any redirections shall be performed in a subshell environment; it is unspecified whether this subshell environment is the same one as that used for a command substitution within the command. (To affect the current execution environment, see the *exec()* special built-in.) If any of the redirections performed in the current shell execution environment fail, the command shall immediately fail with an exit status greater than zero, and the shell shall write an error message indicating the failure. See Consequences of Shell Errors for the consequences of these failures on interactive and non-interactive shells.

If there is a command name, execution shall continue as described in Command Search and Execution. If there is no command name, but the command contained a command substitution, the command shall complete with the exit status of the last command substitution performed. Otherwise, the command shall complete with a zero exit status.

Command Search and Execution

If a simple command results in a command name and an optional list of arguments, the following actions shall be performed:

1. If the command name does not contain any slashes, the first successful step in the following sequence shall occur:

   a. If the command name matches the name of a special built-in utility, that special built-in utility shall be invoked.

   b. If the command name matches the name of a function known to this shell, the function shall be invoked as described in Function Definition Command. If the implementation has provided a standard utility in the form of a function, it shall not be recognized at this point. It shall be invoked in conjunction with the path search in step 1d.

   c. If the command name matches the name of a utility listed in the following table, that utility shall be invoked.

Alias	false	jobs	read	wait
bg	fc	kill	true	
cd	fg	newgrp	umask	
command	getopts	pwd	unalias	

d. Otherwise, the command shall be searched for using the *PATH* environment variable as described in the Base Definitions volume of IEEE Std 1003.1-2001, Chapter 8, Environment Variables:

  i. If the search is successful:

   a. If the system has implemented the utility as a regular built-in or as a shell function, it shall be invoked at this point in the path search.

   b. Otherwise, the shell executes the utility in a separate utility environment (see Shell Execution Environment) with actions equivalent to calling the *execve()* function as defined in the System Interfaces volume of IEEE Std 1003.1-2001 with the *path* argument set to the pathname resulting from the search, *arg0* set to the command name, and the remaining arguments set to the operands, if any.

   If the *execve()* function fails due to an error equivalent to the [ENOEXEC] error defined in the System Interfaces volume of IEEE Std 1003.1-2001, the shell shall execute a command equivalent to having a shell invoked with the pathname resulting from the search as its first operand, with any remaining arguments passed to the new shell, except that the value of "$0" in the new shell may be set to the command name. If the executable file is not a text file, the shell may bypass this command execution. In this case, it shall write an error message, and shall return an exit status of 126.

  ii. Once a utility has been searched for and found (either as a result of this specific search or as part of an unspecified shell start-up activity), an implementation may remember its location and need not search for the utility again unless the *PATH* variable has been the subject of an assignment. If the remembered location fails for a subsequent invocation, the shell shall repeat the search to find the new location for the utility, if any.

  iii. If the search is unsuccessful, the command shall fail with an exit status of 127 and the shell shall write an error message.

2. If the command name contains at least one slash, the shell shall execute the utility in a separate utility environment with actions equivalent to calling the *execve()* function defined in the System Interfaces volume of IEEE Std 1003.1-2001 with the *path* and *arg0* arguments set to the command name, and the remaining arguments set to the operands, if any.

If the *execve()* function fails due to an error equivalent to the [ENOEXEC] error, the shell shall execute a command equivalent to having a shell invoked with the command name as its first operand, with any remaining arguments passed to the new shell. If the executable file is not a text file, the shell may bypass this command execution. In this case, it shall write an error message and shall return an exit status of 126.

2.9.2 Pipelines

A *pipeline* is a sequence of one or more commands separated by the control operator ' | '. The standard output of all but the last command shall be connected to the standard input of the next command.

The format for a pipeline is:

```
[!] command1 [ | command2 ...]
```

The standard output of *command1* shall be connected to the standard input of *command2*. The standard input, standard output, or both of a command shall be considered to be assigned by the pipeline before any redirection specified by redirection operators that are part of the command (see Redirection).

If the pipeline is not in the background (see Asynchronous Lists), the shell shall wait for the last command specified in the pipeline to complete, and may also wait for all commands to complete.

Exit Status

If the reserved word ! does not precede the pipeline, the exit status shall be the exit status of the last command specified in the pipeline. Otherwise, the exit status shall be the logical NOT of the exit status of the last command. That is, if the last command returns zero, the exit status shall be 1; if the last command returns greater than zero, the exit status shall be zero.

2.9.3 Lists

An *AND-OR list* is a sequence of one or more pipelines separated by the operators "&&" and " | | ".

A *list* is a sequence of one or more AND-OR lists separated by the operators ' ; ' and '&' and optionally terminated by ' ; ', '&', or <newline>.

The operators "&&" and " | | " shall have equal precedence and shall be evaluated with left associativity. For example, both of the following commands write solely **bar** to standard output:

```
false && echo foo || echo bar
true || echo foo && echo bar
```

A ' ; ' or <newline> terminator shall cause the preceding AND-OR list to be executed sequentially; an '&' shall cause asynchronous execution of the preceding AND-OR list.

The term "compound-list" is derived from the grammar in Shell Grammar; it is equivalent to a sequence of *lists*, separated by <newline>s, that can be preceded or followed by an arbitrary number of <newline>s.

The following sections are informative.

The following is an example that illustrates <newline>s in compound-lists:

```
while
    # a couple of <newline>s


    # a list
    date && who || ls; cat file
    # a couple of <newline>s


    # another list
    wc file > output & true


do
    # 2 lists
    ls
    cat file
done
```

End of informative text.

Asynchronous Lists

If a command is terminated by the control operator ampersand ('&'), the shell shall execute the command asynchronously in a subshell. This means that the shell shall not wait for the command to finish before executing the next command.

The format for running a command in the background is:

command1 & [*command2* & ...]

The standard input for an asynchronous list, before any explicit redirections are performed, shall be considered to be assigned to a file that has the same properties as **/dev/null**. If it is an interactive shell, this need not happen. In all cases, explicit redirection of standard input shall override this activity.

When an element of an asynchronous list (the portion of the list ended by an ampersand, such as *command1*, above) is started by the shell, the process ID of the last command in the asynchronous list element shall become known in the current shell execution environment; see Shell Execution Environment. This process ID shall remain known until:

1. The command terminates and the application waits for the process ID.

2. Another asynchronous list invoked before "$!" (corresponding to the previous asynchronous list) is expanded in the current execution environment.

The implementation need not retain more than the {CHILD_MAX} most recent entries in its list of known process IDs in the current shell execution environment.

Exit Status

The exit status of an asynchronous list shall be zero.

Sequential Lists

Commands that are separated by a semicolon (';') shall be executed sequentially.
The format for executing commands sequentially shall be:

command1 `[; command2]` ...

Each command shall be expanded and executed in the order specified.

Exit Status

The exit status of a sequential list shall be the exit status of the last command in the list.

AND Lists

The control operator "&&" denotes an AND list. The format shall be:

command1 `[ && command2]` ...

First *command1* shall be executed. If its exit status is zero, *command2* shall be executed, and so on, until a command has a non-zero exit status or there are no more commands left to execute. The commands are expanded only if they are executed.

Exit Status

The exit status of an AND list shall be the exit status of the last command that is executed in the list.

OR Lists

The control operator "||" denotes an OR List. The format shall be:

command1 `[ || command2]` ...

First, *command1* shall be executed. If its exit status is non-zero, *command2* shall be executed, and so on, until a command has a zero exit status or there are no more commands left to execute.

Exit Status

The exit status of an OR list shall be the exit status of the last command that is executed in the list.

2.9.4 Compound Commands

The shell has several programming constructs that are "compound commands", which provide control flow for commands. Each of these compound commands has a reserved word or control operator at the beginning, and a corresponding terminator reserved word or operator at the end. In addition, each can be followed by redirections on the same line as the terminator. Each redirection shall apply to all the commands within the compound command that do not explicitly override that redirection.

Grouping Commands

The format for grouping commands is as follows:

(*compound-list*)

Execute *compound-list* in a subshell environment; see Shell Execution Environment. Variable assignments and built-in commands that affect the environment shall not remain in effect after the list finishes.

{ *compound-list*;}

Execute *compound-list* in the current process environment. The semicolon shown here is an example of a control operator delimiting the } reserved word. Other delimiters are possible, as shown in Shell Grammar; a <newline> is frequently used.

Exit Status

The exit status of a grouping command shall be the exit status of *compound-list*.

The for Loop

The **for** loop shall execute a sequence of commands for each member in a list of *items*. The **for** loop requires that the reserved words **do** and **done** be used to delimit the sequence of commands.

The format for the **for** loop is as follows:

```
for name [ in [word ... ]]do
    compound-list


done
```

First, the list of words following **in** shall be expanded to generate a list of items. Then, the variable *name* shall be set to each item, in turn, and the *compound-list* executed each time. If no items result from the expansion, the *compound-list* shall not be executed. Omitting:

```
in word ...
```

shall be equivalent to:

```
in "$@"
```

Exit Status

The exit status of a **for** command shall be the exit status of the last command that executes. If there are no items, the exit status shall be zero.

Case Conditional Construct

The conditional construct **case** shall execute the *compound-list* corresponding to the first one of several *patterns* (see Pattern Matching Notation) that is matched by the string resulting from the tilde expansion, parameter expansion, command substitution, arithmetic expansion, and quote removal of the given word. The reserved word **in** shall denote the beginning of the patterns to be matched. Multiple patterns with the same *compound-list* shall be delimited by the '|' symbol. The control operator ')' terminates a list of patterns corresponding to a given action. The *compound-list* for each list of patterns, with the possible exception of the last, shall be terminated with ";;". The **case** construct terminates with the reserved word **esac** (**case** reversed).

The format for the **case** construct is as follows:

```
case word in
    [(]pattern1) compound-list;;
    [[(]pattern[ | pattern] ... ) compound-list;;] ...
    [[(]pattern[ | pattern] ... ) compound-list]
```


```
esac
```

The ";;" is optional for the last *compound-list*.

In order from the beginning to the end of the **case** statement, each *pattern* that labels a *compound-list* shall be subjected to tilde expansion, parameter expansion, command substitution, and arithmetic expansion, and the result of these expansions shall be compared against the expansion of *word*, according to the rules described in Pattern Matching Notation (which also describes the effect of quoting parts of the pattern). After the first match, no more patterns shall be expanded, and the *compound-list* shall be executed. The order of expansion and comparison of multiple *patterns* that label a *compound-list* statement is unspecified.

Exit Status

The exit status of **case** shall be zero if no patterns are matched. Otherwise, the exit status shall be the exit status of the last command executed in the *compound-list*.

The if Conditional Construct

The **if** command shall execute a *compound-list* and use its exit status to determine whether to execute another *compound-list*.

The format for the **if** construct is as follows:

```
if compound-listthen
    compound-list[elif compound-listthen
    compound-list] ...
[else
    compound-list]
```


```
fi
```

The **if** *compound-list* shall be executed; if its exit status is zero, the **then** *compound-list* shall be executed and the command shall complete. Otherwise, each **elif** *compound-list* shall be executed, in turn, and if its exit status is zero, the **then** *compound-list* shall be executed and the command shall complete. Otherwise, the **else** *compound-list* shall be executed.

Exit Status

The exit status of the **if** command shall be the exit status of the **then** or **else** *compound-list* that was executed, or zero, if none was executed.

The while Loop

The **while** loop shall continuously execute one *compound-list* as long as another *compound-list* has a zero exit status.

The format of the **while** loop is as follows:

```
while compound-list-1do
    compound-list-2


done
```

The *compound-list-1* shall be executed, and if it has a non-zero exit status, the **while** command shall complete. Otherwise, the *compound-list-2* shall be executed, and the process shall repeat.

Exit Status

The exit status of the **while** loop shall be the exit status of the last *compound-list-2* executed, or zero if none was executed.

The until Loop

The **until** loop shall continuously execute one *compound-list* as long as another *compound-list* has a non-zero exit status.

The format of the **until** loop is as follows:

```
until compound-list-1do
    compound-list-2


done
```

The *compound-list-1* shall be executed, and if it has a zero exit status, the **until** command completes. Otherwise, the *compound-list-2* shall be executed, and the process repeats.

Exit Status

The exit status of the **until** loop shall be the exit status of the last *compound-list-2* executed, or zero if none was executed.

2.9.5 Function Definition Command

A function is a user-defined name that is used as a simple command to call a compound command with new positional parameters. A function is defined with a "function definition command".

The format of a function definition command is as follows:

fname() *compound-command*[*io-redirect* ...]

The function is named *fname*; the application shall ensure that it is a name (see the Base Definitions volume of IEEE Std 1003.1-2001, Section 3.230, Name). An implementation may allow other characters in a function name as an extension. The implementation shall maintain separate name spaces for functions and variables.

The argument *compound-command* represents a compound command, as described in Compound Commands.

When the function is declared, none of the expansions in Word Expansions shall be performed on the text in *compound-command* or *io-redirect*; all expansions shall be performed as normal each time the function is called. Similarly, the optional *io-redirect* redirections and any variable assignments within *compound-command* shall be performed during the execution of the function itself, not the function definition. See Consequences of Shell Errors for the consequences of failures of these operations on interactive and non-interactive shells.

When a function is executed, it shall have the syntax-error and variable-assignment properties described for special built-in utilities in the enumerated list at the beginning of Special Built-In Utilities.

The *compound-command* shall be executed whenever the function name is specified as the name of a simple command (see Command Search and Execution). The operands to the command temporarily shall become the positional parameters during the execution of the *compound-command*; the special parameter '#' also shall be changed to reflect the number of operands. The special parameter 0 shall be unchanged. When the function completes, the values of the positional parameters and the special parameter '#' shall be restored to the values they had before the function was executed. If the special built-in *return* is executed in the *compound-command*, the function completes and execution shall resume with the next command after the function call.

Exit Status

The exit status of a function definition shall be zero if the function was declared successfully; otherwise, it shall be greater than zero. The exit status of a function invocation shall be the exit status of the last command executed by the function.

2.10 Shell Grammar

The following grammar defines the Shell Command Language. This formal syntax shall take precedence over the preceding text syntax description.

2.10.1 Shell Grammar Lexical Conventions

The input language to the shell must be first recognized at the character level. The resulting tokens shall be classified by their immediate context according to the following rules (applied in order). These rules shall be used to determine what a "token" is that is subject to parsing at the token level. The rules for token recognition in Token Recognition shall apply.

1. A <newline> shall be returned as the token identifier **NEWLINE**.

2. If the token is an operator, the token identifier for that operator shall result.

3. If the string consists solely of digits and the delimiter character is one of '<' or '>', the token identifier **IO_NUMBER** shall be returned.

4. Otherwise, the token identifier **TOKEN** results.

Further distinction on **TOKEN** is context-dependent. It may be that the same **TOKEN** yields **WORD**, a **NAME**, an **ASSIGNMENT**, or one of the reserved words below, dependent upon the context. Some of the productions in the grammar below are annotated with a rule number from the following list. When a **TOKEN** is seen where one of those annotated productions could be used to reduce the symbol, the applicable rule shall be applied to convert the token identifier type of the **TOKEN** to a token identifier acceptable at that point in the grammar. The reduction shall then proceed based upon the token identifier type yielded by the rule applied. When more than one rule applies, the highest numbered rule shall apply (which in turn may refer to another rule). (Note that except in rule 7, the presence of an '=' in the token has no effect.)

The **WORD** tokens shall have the word expansion rules applied to them immediately before the associated command is executed, not at the time the command is parsed.

2.10.2 Shell Grammar Rules

1. [Command Name]

   When the **TOKEN** is exactly a reserved word, the token identifier for that reserved word shall result. Otherwise, the token **WORD** shall be returned. Also, if the parser is in any state where only a reserved word could be the next correct token, proceed as above.

■**Note** Because at this point quote marks are retained in the token, quoted strings cannot be recognized as reserved words. This rule also implies that reserved words are not recognized except in certain positions in the input, such as after a <newline> or semicolon; the grammar presumes that if the reserved word is intended, it is properly delimited by the user, and does not attempt to reflect that requirement directly. Also note that line joining is done before tokenization, as described in Escape Character (Backslash), so escaped <newline>s are already removed at this point.

   Rule 1 is not directly referenced in the grammar, but is referred to by other rules, or applies globally.

2. [Redirection to or from filename]

   The expansions specified in Redirection shall occur. As specified there, exactly one field can result (or the result is unspecified), and there are additional requirements on pathname expansion.

3. [Redirection from here-document]

Quote removal shall be applied to the word to determine the delimiter that is used to find the end of the here-document that begins after the next <newline>.

4. [Case statement termination]

When the **TOKEN** is exactly the reserved word **esac**, the token identifier for **esac** shall result. Otherwise, the token **WORD** shall be returned.

5. [**NAME** in **for**]

When the **TOKEN** meets the requirements for a name (see the Base Definitions volume of IEEE Std 1003.1-2001, Section 3.230, Name), the token identifier **NAME** shall result. Otherwise, the token **WORD** shall be returned.

6. [Third word of **for** and **case**]

    a. [**case** only]

    When the **TOKEN** is exactly the reserved word **in**, the token identifier for **in** shall result. Otherwise, the token **WORD** shall be returned.

    b. [**for** only]

    When the **TOKEN** is exactly the reserved word **in** or **do**, the token identifier for **in** or **do** shall result, respectively. Otherwise, the token **WORD** shall be returned.

7. (For a. and b.: As indicated in the grammar, a *linebreak* precedes the tokens **in** and **do**. If <newline>s are present at the indicated location, it is the token after them that is treated in this fashion.)

8. [Assignment preceding command name]

    a. [When the first word]

    If the **TOKEN** does not contain the character '=', rule 1 is applied. Otherwise, 7b shall be applied.

    b. [Not the first word]

    If the **TOKEN** contains the equal sign character:

- If it begins with '=', the token **WORD** shall be returned.

- If all the characters preceding '=' form a valid name (see the Base Definitions volume of IEEE Std 1003.1-2001, Section 3.230, Name), the token **ASSIGNMENT_WORD** shall be returned. (Quoted characters cannot participate in forming a valid name.)

- Otherwise, it is unspecified whether it is **ASSIGNMENT_WORD** or **WORD** that is returned.

Assignment to the **NAME** shall occur as specified in Simple Commands.

9. [**NAME** in function]

When the **TOKEN** is exactly a reserved word, the token identifier for that reserved word shall result. Otherwise, when the **TOKEN** meets the requirements for a name, the token identifier **NAME** shall result. Otherwise, rule 7 applies.

10. [Body of function]

Word expansion and assignment shall never occur, even when required by the rules above, when this rule is being parsed. Each **TOKEN** that might either be expanded or have assignment applied to it shall instead be returned as a single **WORD** consisting only of characters that are exactly the token described in Token Recognition.

```
/* -----------------------------------------------------------
The grammar symbols
------------------------------------------------------ */


%token  WORD
%token  ASSIGNMENT_WORD
%token  NAME
%token  NEWLINE
%token  IO_NUMBER


/* The following are the operators mentioned above. */


%token  AND_IF    OR_IF    DSEMI
/*       '&&'      '||'     ';;'     */


%token  DLESS  DGREAT  LESSAND  GREATAND  LESSGREAT  DLESSDASH
/*       '<<'   '>>'    '<&'     '>&'      '<>'       '<<-'     */


%token  CLOBBER
/*        '>|'   */


/* The following are the reserved words. */


%token  If    Then   Else   Elif   Fi   Do   Done
/*       'if'  'then' 'else' 'elif' 'fi' 'do' 'done'   */


%token  Case   Esac   While   Until   For
/*       'case' 'esac' 'while' 'until' 'for'   */
```

```
/* These are reserved words, not operator tokens, and are
   recognized when reserved words are recognized. */


%token  Lbrace    Rbrace    Bang
/*       '{'       '}'        '!'    */


%token  In
/*       'in'    */


/* --------------------------------------------------------
   The Grammar
   ----------------------------------------------------- */


%start  complete_command
%%
complete_command : list separator
                 | list
                 ;
list               : list separator_op and_or
                   |                    and_or
                   ;
and_or             :                          pipeline
                   | and_or AND_IF linebreak pipeline
                   | and_or OR_IF  linebreak pipeline
                   ;
pipeline           :      pipe_sequence
                   | Bang pipe_sequence
                   ;
pipe_sequence      :                          command
                   | pipe_sequence '|' linebreak command
                   ;
command            : simple_command
                   | compound_command
                   | compound_command redirect_list
                   | function_definition
                   ;
compound_command : brace_group
                 | subshell
                 | for_clause
                 | case_clause
                 | if_clause
                 | while_clause
                 | until_clause
                 ;
```

```
subshell        : '(' compound_list ')'
                ;
compound_list   :                  term
                | newline_list term
                |                  term separator
                | newline_list term separator
                ;
term            : term separator and_or
                |               and_or
                ;
for_clause      : For name linebreak                            do_group
                | For name linebreak in          sequential_sep do_group
                | For name linebreak in wordlist sequential_sep do_group
                ;
name            : NAME                    /* Apply rule 5 */
                ;
in              : In                      /* Apply rule 6 */
                ;
wordlist        : wordlist WORD
                |          WORD
                ;
case_clause     : Case WORD linebreak in linebreak case_list    Esac
                | Case WORD linebreak in linebreak case_list_ns Esac
                | Case WORD linebreak in linebreak              Esac
                ;
case_list_ns    : case_list case_item_ns
                |           case_item_ns
                ;
case_list       : case_list case_item
                |           case_item
                ;
case_item_ns    :     pattern ')'                linebreak
                |     pattern ')' compound_list linebreak
                | '(' pattern ')'                linebreak
                | '(' pattern ')' compound_list linebreak
                ;
case_item       :     pattern ')' linebreak    DSEMI linebreak
                |     pattern ')' compound_list DSEMI linebreak
                | '(' pattern ')' linebreak    DSEMI linebreak
                | '(' pattern ')' compound_list DSEMI linebreak
                ;
pattern         :             WORD         /* Apply rule 4 */
                | pattern '|' WORD         /* Do not apply rule 4 */
                ;
if_clause       : If compound_list Then compound_list else_part Fi
                | If compound_list Then compound_list          Fi
                ;
```

```
else_part           : Elif compound_list Then else_part
                    | Else compound_list
                    ;
while_clause        : While compound_list do_group
                    ;
until_clause        : Until compound_list do_group
                    ;
function_definition : fname '(' ')' linebreak function_body
                    ;
function_body       : compound_command                  /* Apply rule 9 */
                    | compound_command redirect_list    /* Apply rule 9 */
                    ;
fname               : NAME                               /* Apply rule 8 */
                    ;
brace_group         : Lbrace compound_list Rbrace
                    ;
do_group            : Do compound_list Done             /* Apply rule 6 */
                    ;
simple_command      : cmd_prefix cmd_word cmd_suffix
                    | cmd_prefix cmd_word
                    | cmd_prefix
                    | cmd_name cmd_suffix
                    | cmd_name
                    ;
cmd_name            : WORD                   /* Apply rule 7a */
                    ;
cmd_word            : WORD                   /* Apply rule 7b */
                    ;
cmd_prefix          :                   io_redirect
                    | cmd_prefix io_redirect
                    |                   ASSIGNMENT_WORD
                    | cmd_prefix ASSIGNMENT_WORD
                    ;
cmd_suffix          :                   io_redirect
                    | cmd_suffix io_redirect
                    |                   WORD
                    | cmd_suffix WORD
                    ;
redirect_list       :                   io_redirect
                    | redirect_list io_redirect
                    ;
io_redirect         :                   io_file
                    | IO_NUMBER io_file
                    |                   io_here
                    | IO_NUMBER io_here
                    ;
```

```
io_file        : '<'        filename
               | LESSAND    filename
               | '>'        filename
               | GREATAND   filename
               | DGREAT     filename
               | LESSGREAT  filename
               | CLOBBER    filename
               ;
filename       : WORD                     /* Apply rule 2 */
               ;
io_here        : DLESS      here_end
               | DLESSDASH  here_end
               ;
here_end       : WORD                     /* Apply rule 3 */
               ;
newline_list   :                NEWLINE
               | newline_list NEWLINE
               ;
linebreak      : newline_list
               | /* empty */
               ;
separator_op   : '&'
               | ';'
               ;
separator      : separator_op linebreak
               | newline_list
               ;
sequential_sep : ';' linebreak
               | newline_list
               ;
```

2.11 Signals and Error Handling

When a command is in an asynchronous list, the shell shall prevent SIGQUIT and SIGINT signals from the keyboard from interrupting the command. Otherwise, signals shall have the values inherited by the shell from its parent (see also the *trap* special built-in).

When a signal for which a trap has been set is received while the shell is waiting for the completion of a utility executing a foreground command, the trap associated with that signal shall not be executed until after the foreground command has completed. When the shell is waiting, by means of the *wait* utility, for asynchronous commands to complete, the reception of a signal for which a trap has been set shall cause the *wait* utility to return immediately with an exit status >128, immediately after which the trap associated with that signal shall be taken.

If multiple signals are pending for the shell for which there are associated trap actions, the order of execution of trap actions is unspecified.

2.12 Shell Execution Environment

A shell execution environment consists of the following:

- Open files inherited upon invocation of the shell, plus open files controlled by *exec*

- Working directory as set by *cd*

- File creation mask set by *umask*

- Current traps set by *trap*

- Shell parameters that are set by variable assignment (see the *set* special built-in) or from the System Interfaces volume of IEEE Std 1003.1-2001 environment inherited by the shell when it begins (see the *export* special built-in)

- Shell functions; see Function Definition Command

- Options turned on at invocation or by *set*

- Process IDs of the last commands in asynchronous lists known to this shell environment; see Asynchronous Lists

- Shell aliases; see Alias Substitution

Utilities other than the special built-ins (see Special Built-In Utilities) shall be invoked in a separate environment that consists of the following. The initial value of these objects shall be the same as that for the parent shell, except as noted below.

- Open files inherited on invocation of the shell, open files controlled by the *exec* special built-in plus any modifications, and additions specified by any redirections to the utility

- Current working directory

- File creation mask

- If the utility is a shell script, traps caught by the shell shall be set to the default values and traps ignored by the shell shall be set to be ignored by the utility; if the utility is not a shell script, the trap actions (default or ignore) shall be mapped into the appropriate signal handling actions for the utility

- Variables with the *export* attribute, along with those explicitly exported for the duration of the command, shall be passed to the utility environment variables

The environment of the shell process shall not be changed by the utility unless explicitly specified by the utility description (for example, *cd* and *umask*).

A subshell environment shall be created as a duplicate of the shell environment, except that signal traps set by that shell environment shall be set to the default values. Changes made to the subshell environment shall not affect the shell environment. Command substitution, commands that are grouped with parentheses, and asynchronous lists shall be executed in a subshell environment. Additionally, each command of a multi-command pipeline is in a subshell environment; as an extension, however, any or all commands in a pipeline may be executed in the current environment. All other commands shall be executed in the current shell environment.

2.13 Pattern Matching Notation

The pattern matching notation described in this section is used to specify patterns for matching strings in the shell. Historically, pattern matching notation is related to, but slightly different from, the regular expression notation described in the Base Definitions volume of IEEE Std 1003.1-2001, Chapter 9, Regular Expressions. For this reason, the description of the rules for this pattern matching notation are based on the description of regular expression notation, modified to include backslash escape processing.

2.13.1 Patterns Matching a Single Character

The following patterns matching a single character shall match a single character: ordinary characters, special pattern characters, and pattern bracket expressions. The pattern bracket expression also shall match a single collating element. A backslash character shall escape the following character. The escaping backslash shall be discarded.

An ordinary character is a pattern that shall match itself. It can be any character in the supported character set except for NUL, those special shell characters in Quoting that require quoting, and the following three special pattern characters. Matching shall be based on the bit pattern used for encoding the character, not on the graphic representation of the character. If any character (ordinary, shell special, or pattern special) is quoted, that pattern shall match the character itself. The shell special characters always require quoting.

When unquoted and outside a bracket expression, the following three characters shall have special meaning in the specification of patterns:

? - A question-mark is a pattern that shall match any character.

* - An asterisk is a pattern that shall match multiple characters, as described in Patterns Matching Multiple Characters.

[- The open bracket shall introduce a pattern bracket expression.

The description of basic regular expression bracket expressions in the Base Definitions volume of IEEE Std 1003.1-2001, Section 9.3.5, RE Bracket Expression shall also apply to the pattern bracket expression, except that the exclamation mark character ('!') shall replace the circumflex character ('^') in its role in a "non-matching list" in the regular expression notation. A bracket expression starting with an unquoted circumflex character produces unspecified results.

When pattern matching is used where shell quote removal is not performed (such as in the argument to the *find - name* primary when *find* is being called using one of the *exec* functions as defined in the System Interfaces volume of IEEE Std 1003.1-2001, or in the *pattern* argument to the *fnmatch()* function), special characters can be escaped to remove their special meaning by preceding them with a backslash character. This escaping backslash is discarded. The sequence "\\" represents one literal backslash. All of the requirements and effects of quoting on ordinary, shell special, and special pattern characters shall apply to escaping in this context.

2.13.2 Patterns Matching Multiple Characters

The following rules are used to construct patterns matching multiple characters from patterns matching a single character:

1. The asterisk ('*') is a pattern that shall match any string, including the null string.

2. The concatenation of patterns matching a single character is a valid pattern that shall match the concatenation of the single characters or collating elements matched by each of the concatenated patterns.

3. The concatenation of one or more patterns matching a single character with one or more asterisks is a valid pattern. In such patterns, each asterisk shall match a string of zero or more characters, matching the greatest possible number of characters that still allows the remainder of the pattern to match the string.

2.13.3 Patterns Used for Filename Expansion

The rules described so far in Patterns Matching a Single Character and Patterns Matching Multiple Characters are qualified by the following rules that apply when pattern matching notation is used for filename expansion:

1. The slash character in a pathname shall be explicitly matched by using one or more slashes in the pattern; it shall neither be matched by the asterisk or question-mark special characters nor by a bracket expression. Slashes in the pattern shall be identified before bracket expressions; thus, a slash cannot be included in a pattern bracket expression used for filename expansion. If a slash character is found following an unescaped open square bracket character before a corresponding closing square bracket is found, the open bracket shall be treated as an ordinary character. For example, the pattern "a[b/c]d" does not match such pathnames as **abd** or **a/d**. It only matches a pathname of literally **a[b/c]d**.

2. If a filename begins with a period ('.'), the period shall be explicitly matched by using a period as the first character of the pattern or immediately following a slash character. The leading period shall not be matched by:

   - The asterisk or question-mark special characters
   - A bracket expression containing a non-matching list, such as "[!a]", a range expression, such as "[%-0]", or a character class expression, such as "[[:punct:]]"

   It is unspecified whether an explicit period in a bracket expression matching list, such as "[.abc]", can match a leading period in a filename.

3. Specified patterns shall be matched against existing filenames and pathnames, as appropriate. Each component that contains a pattern character shall require read permission in the directory containing that component. Any component, except the last, that does not contain a pattern character shall require search permission. For example, given the pattern:

   `/foo/bar/x*/bam`

search permission is needed for directories **/** and **foo**, search and read permissions are needed for directory **bar**, and search permission is needed for each **x*** directory. If the pattern matches any existing filenames or pathnames, the pattern shall be replaced with those filenames and pathnames, sorted according to the collating sequence in effect in the current locale. If the pattern contains an invalid bracket expression or does not match any existing filenames or pathnames, the pattern string shall be left unchanged.

2.14 Special Built-In Utilities

The following "special built-in" utilities shall be supported in the shell command language. The output of each command, if any, shall be written to standard output, subject to the normal redirection and piping possible with all commands.

The term "built-in" implies that the shell can execute the utility directly and does not need to search for it. An implementation may choose to make any utility a built-in; however, the special built-in utilities described here differ from regular built-in utilities in two respects:

1. A syntax error in a special built-in utility may cause a shell executing that utility to abort, while a syntax error in a regular built-in utility shall not cause a shell executing that utility to abort. (See Consequences of Shell Errors for the consequences of errors on interactive and non-interactive shells.) If a special built-in utility encountering a syntax error does not abort the shell, its exit value shall be non-zero.

2. Variable assignments specified with special built-in utilities remain in effect after the built-in completes; this shall not be the case with a regular built-in or other utility.

The special built-in utilities in this section need not be provided in a manner accessible via the *exec* family of functions defined in the System Interfaces volume of IEEE Std 1003.1-2001.

Some of the special built-ins are described as conforming to the Base Definitions volume of IEEE Std 1003.1-2001, Section 12.2, Utility Syntax Guidelines. For those that are not, the requirement in *Utility Description Defaults* that "--" be recognized as a first argument to be discarded does not apply and a conforming application shall not use that argument.

■■■

The *sh* Utility

The description of the *sh* utility includes a number of features not found in some traditional shells, but it gives a good summary of basic usage. Much of this specifies interactive features (which are not universal among shells), but the basic invocation material is a handy reference.

■**Note** All external documents referenced in this appendix are available at www.opengroup.org.

Name

sh - shell, the standard command language interpreter

Synopsis

```
sh [-abCefhimnuvx][-o option][+abCefhimnuvx][+o option]
      [command_file [argument...]]

sh -c[-abCefhimnuvx][-o option][+abCefhimnuvx][+o option]command_string
      [command_name [argument...]]

sh -s[-abCefhimnuvx][-o option][+abCefhimnuvx][+o option][argument]
```

Description

The *sh* utility is a command language interpreter that shall execute commands read from a command line string, the standard input, or a specified file. The application shall ensure that the commands to be executed are expressed in the language described in *Shell Command Language*.

Pathname expansion shall not fail due to the size of a file.

Shell input and output redirections have an implementation-defined offset maximum that is established in the open file description.

Options

The *sh* utility shall conform to the Base Definitions volume of IEEE Std 1003.1-2001, Section 12.2, Utility Syntax Guidelines, with an extension for support of a leading plus sign ('+') as noted below.

The **-a**, **-b**, **-C**, **-e**, **-f**, **-m**, **-n**, **-o** *option*, **-u**, **-v**, and **-x** options are described as part of the *set* utility in *Special Built-In Utilities*. The option letters derived from the *set* special built-in shall also be accepted with a leading plus sign ('+') instead of a leading hyphen (meaning the reverse case of the option as described in this volume of IEEE Std 1003.1-2001).

The following additional options shall be supported:

-c

Read commands from the *command_string* operand. Set the value of special parameter 0 (see *Special Parameters*) from the value of the *command_name* operand and the positional parameters ($1, $2, and so on) in sequence from the remaining *argument* operands. No commands shall be read from the standard input.

-i

Specify that the shell is *interactive*; see below. An implementation may treat specifying the **-i** option as an error if the real user ID of the calling process does not equal the effective user ID or if the real group ID does not equal the effective group ID.

-s

Read commands from the standard input.

If there are no operands and the **-c** option is not specified, the **-s** option shall be assumed.

If the **-i** option is present, or if there are no operands and the shell's standard input and standard error are attached to a terminal, the shell is considered to be *interactive*.

Operands

The following operands shall be supported:

-

A single hyphen shall be treated as the first operand and then ignored. If both '-' and "--" are given as arguments, or if other operands precede the single hyphen, the results are undefined.

argument

The positional parameters ($1, $2, and so on) shall be set to *arguments*, if any.

command_file

The pathname of a file containing commands. If the pathname contains one or more slash characters, the implementation attempts to read that file; the file need not be executable. If the pathname does not contain a slash character:

- The implementation shall attempt to read that file from the current working directory; the file need not be executable.

- If the file is not in the current working directory, the implementation may perform a search for an executable file using the value of *PATH* , as described in *Command Search and Execution*.

Special parameter 0 (see *Special Parameters*) shall be set to the value of *command_file*. If *sh* is called using a synopsis form that omits *command_file*, special parameter 0 shall be set to the value of the first argument passed to *sh* from its parent (for example, *argv*[0] for a C program), which is normally a pathname used to execute the *sh* utility.

command_name

A string assigned to special parameter 0 when executing the commands in *command_string*. If *command_name* is not specified, special parameter 0 shall be set to the value of the first argument passed to *sh* from its parent (for example, *argv*[0] for a C program), which is normally a pathname used to execute the *sh* utility.

command_string

A string that shall be interpreted by the shell as one or more commands, as if the string were the argument to the *system*() function defined in the System Interfaces volume of IEEE Std 1003.1-2001. If the *command_string* operand is an empty string, *sh* shall exit with a zero exit status.

Stdin

The standard input shall be used only if one of the following is true:

- The **-s** option is specified.

- The **-c** option is not specified and no operands are specified.

- The script executes one or more commands that require input from standard input (such as a *read* command that does not redirect its input).

See the INPUT FILES section.

When the shell is using standard input and it invokes a command that also uses standard input, the shell shall ensure that the standard input file pointer points directly after the command it has read when the command begins execution. It shall not read ahead in such a manner that any characters intended to be read by the invoked command are consumed by the shell (whether interpreted by the shell or not) or that characters that are not read by the invoked command are not seen by the shell. When the command expecting to read standard input is started asynchronously by an interactive shell, it is unspecified whether characters are read by the command or interpreted by the shell.

If the standard input to *sh* is a FIFO or terminal device and is set to non-blocking reads, then *sh* shall enable blocking reads on standard input. This shall remain in effect when the command completes.

Input Files

The input file shall be a text file, except that line lengths shall be unlimited. If the input file is empty or consists solely of blank lines or comments, or both, *sh* shall exit with a zero exit status.

Environment Variables

The following environment variables shall affect the execution of *sh*:

ENV

This variable, when and only when an interactive shell is invoked, shall be subjected to parameter expansion (see *Parameter Expansion*) by the shell, and the resulting value shall be used as a pathname of a file containing shell commands to execute in the current environment. The file need not be executable. If the expanded value of *ENV* is not an absolute pathname, the results are unspecified. *ENV* shall be ignored if the real and effective user IDs or real and effective group IDs of the process are different.

FCEDIT

This variable, when expanded by the shell, shall determine the default value for the **-e** *editor* option's *editor* option-argument. If *FCEDIT* is null or unset, *ed* shall be used as the editor. This volume of IEEE Std 1003.1-2001 specifies the effects of this variable only for systems supporting the User Portability Utilities option.

HISTFILE

Determine a pathname naming a command history file. If the *HISTFILE* variable is not set, the shell may attempt to access or create a file **.sh_history** in the directory referred to by the *HOME* environment variable. If the shell cannot obtain both read and write access to, or create, the history file, it shall use an unspecified mechanism that allows the history to operate properly. (References to history "file" in this section shall be understood to mean this unspecified mechanism in such cases.) An implementation may choose to access this variable only when initializing the history file; this initialization shall occur when *fc* or *sh* first attempt to retrieve entries from, or add entries to, the file, as the result of commands issued by the user, the file named by the *ENV* variable, or implementation-defined system start-up files. Implementations may choose to disable the history list mechanism for users with appropriate privileges who do not set *HISTFILE*; the specific circumstances under which this occurs are implementation-defined. If more than one instance of the shell is using the same history file, it is unspecified how updates to the history file from those shells interact. As entries are deleted from the history file, they shall be deleted oldest first. It is unspecified when history file entries are physically removed from the history file. This volume of IEEE Std 1003.1-2001 specifies the effects of this variable only for systems supporting the User Portability Utilities option.

HISTSIZE

Determine a decimal number representing the limit to the number of previous commands that are accessible. If this variable is unset, an unspecified default greater than or equal to 128 shall be used. The maximum number of commands in the history list is unspecified, but shall be at least 128. An implementation may choose to access this variable only when initializing the history file, as described under *HISTFILE* . Therefore, it is unspecified whether changes made to *HISTSIZE* after the history file has been initialized are effective.

HOME

Determine the pathname of the user's home directory. The contents of *HOME* are used in tilde expansion as described in *Tilde Expansion*. This volume of IEEE Std 1003.1-2001 specifies the effects of this variable only for systems supporting the User Portability Utilities option.

IFS

(Input Field Separators.) A string treated as a list of characters that shall be used for field splitting and to split lines into words with the *read* command. See *Field Splitting*. If *IFS* is not set, the shell shall behave as if the value of *IFS* were <space>, <tab>, and <newline>. Implementations may ignore the value of *IFS* in the environment at the time *sh* is invoked, treating *IFS* as if it were not set.

LANG

Provide a default value for the internationalization variables that are unset or null. (See the Base Definitions volume of IEEE Std 1003.1-2001, Section 8.2, Internationalization Variables for the precedence of internationalization variables used to determine the values of locale categories.)

LC_ALL

If set to a non-empty string value, override the values of all the other internationalization variables.

LC_COLLATE

Determine the behavior of range expressions, equivalence classes, and multi-character collating elements within pattern matching.

LC_CTYPE

Determine the locale for the interpretation of sequences of bytes of text data as characters (for example, single-byte as opposed to multi-byte characters in arguments and input files), which characters are defined as letters (character class **alpha**), and the behavior of character classes within pattern matching.

LC_MESSAGES

Determine the locale that should be used to affect the format and contents of diagnostic messages written to standard error.

MAIL

Determine a pathname of the user's mailbox file for purposes of incoming mail notification. If this variable is set, the shell shall inform the user if the file named by the variable is created or if its modification time has changed. Informing the user shall be accomplished by writing a string of unspecified format to standard error prior to the writing of the next primary prompt string. Such check shall be performed only after the completion of the interval defined by the *MAILCHECK* variable after the last such check. The user shall be informed only if *MAIL* is set and *MAILPATH* is not set. This volume of IEEE Std 1003.1-2001 specifies the effects of this variable only for systems supporting the User Portability Utilities option.

MAILCHECK

Establish a decimal integer value that specifies how often (in seconds) the shell shall check for the arrival of mail in the files specified by the *MAILPATH* or *MAIL* variables. The default value shall be 600 seconds. If set to zero, the shell shall check before issuing each primary prompt. This volume of IEEE Std 1003.1-2001 specifies the effects of this variable only for systems supporting the User Portability Utilities option.

MAILPATH

Provide a list of pathnames and optional messages separated by colons. If this variable is set, the shell shall inform the user if any of the files named by the variable are created or if any of their modification times change. (See the preceding entry for *MAIL* for descriptions of mail arrival and user informing.) Each pathname can be followed by '%' and a string that shall be subjected to parameter expansion and written to standard error when the modification time changes. If a '%' character in the pathname is preceded by a backslash, it shall be treated as a literal '%' in the pathname. The default message is unspecified.

The *MAILPATH* environment variable takes precedence over the *MAIL* variable. This volume of IEEE Std 1003.1-2001 specifies the effects of this variable only for systems supporting the User Portability Utilities option.

NLSPATH

Determine the location of message catalogs for the processing of *LC_MESSAGES*.

PATH

Establish a string formatted as described in the Base Definitions volume of IEEE Std 1003.1-2001, Chapter 8, Environment Variables, used to effect command interpretation; see *Command Search and Execution*.

PWD

This variable shall represent an absolute pathname of the current working directory. Assignments to this variable may be ignored unless the value is an absolute pathname of the current working directory and there are no filename components of dot or dot-dot.

Asynchronous Events

Default.

Stdout

See the STDERR section.

Stderr

Except as otherwise stated (by the descriptions of any invoked utilities or in interactive mode), standard error shall be used only for diagnostic messages.

Output Files

None.

Extended Description

See *Shell Command Language*. The following additional capabilities are supported on systems supporting the User Portability Utilities option.

Command History List

When the *sh* utility is being used interactively, it shall maintain a list of commands previously entered from the terminal in the file named by the *HISTFILE* environment variable. The type, size, and internal format of this file are unspecified. Multiple *sh* processes can share access to the file for a user, if file access permissions allow this; see the description of the *HISTFILE* environment variable.

Command Line Editing

When *sh* is being used interactively from a terminal, the current command and the command history (see *fc*) can be edited using *vi*-mode command line editing. This mode uses commands, described below, similar to a subset of those described in the *vi* utility. Implementations may offer other command line editing modes corresponding to other editing utilities.

The command *set* **-o** *vi* shall enable *vi*-mode editing and place *sh* into *vi* insert mode (see Command Line Editing (vi-mode)). This command also shall disable any other editing mode that the implementation may provide. The command *set* **+o** *vi* disables *vi*-mode editing.

Certain block-mode terminals may be unable to support shell command line editing. If a terminal is unable to provide either edit mode, it need not be possible to *set* **-o** *vi* when using the shell on this terminal.

In the following sections, the characters *erase, interrupt, kill,* and *end-of-file* are those set by the *stty* utility.

Command Line Editing (vi-mode)

In *vi* editing mode, there shall be a distinguished line, the edit line. All the editing operations which modify a line affect the edit line. The edit line is always the newest line in the command history buffer.

With *vi*-mode enabled, *sh* can be switched between insert mode and command mode.

When in insert mode, an entered character shall be inserted into the command line, except as noted in vi Line Editing Insert Mode. Upon entering *sh* and after termination of the previous command, *sh* shall be in insert mode.

Typing an escape character shall switch *sh* into command mode (see vi Line Editing Command Mode). In command mode, an entered character shall either invoke a defined operation, be used as part of a multi-character operation, or be treated as an error. A character that is not recognized as part of an editing command shall terminate any specific editing command and shall alert the terminal. Typing the *interrupt* character in command mode shall cause *sh* to terminate command line editing on the current command line, reissue the prompt on the next line of the terminal, and reset the command history (see *fc*) so that the most recently executed command is the previous command (that is, the command that was being edited when it was interrupted is not reentered into the history).

In the following sections, the phrase "move the cursor to the beginning of the word" shall mean "move the cursor to the first character of the current word" and the phrase "move the cursor to the end of the word" shall mean "move the cursor to the last character of the current word". The phrase "beginning of the command line" indicates the point between the end of the prompt string issued by the shell (or the beginning of the terminal line, if there is no prompt string) and the first character of the command text.

vi Line Editing Insert Mode

While in insert mode, any character typed shall be inserted in the current command line, unless it is from the following set.

<newline>

Execute the current command line. If the current command line is not empty, this line shall be entered into the command history (see *fc*).

erase

Delete the character previous to the current cursor position and move the current cursor position back one character. In insert mode, characters shall be erased from both the screen and the buffer when backspacing.

interrupt

Terminate command line editing with the same effects as described for interrupting command mode; see Command Line Editing (vi-mode).

kill

Clear all the characters from the input line.

<control>-V

Insert the next character input, even if the character is otherwise a special insert mode character.

<control>-W

Delete the characters from the one preceding the cursor to the preceding word boundary. The word boundary in this case is the closer to the cursor of either the beginning of the line or a character that is in neither the **blank** nor **punct** character classification of the current locale.

end-of-file

Interpreted as the end of input in *sh*. This interpretation shall occur only at the beginning of an input line. If *end-of-file* is entered other than at the beginning of the line, the results are unspecified.

<ESC>

Place *sh* into command mode.

vi Line Editing Command Mode

In command mode for the command line editing feature, decimal digits not beginning with 0 that precede a command letter shall be remembered. Some commands use these decimal digits as a count number that affects the operation.

The term *motion command* represents one of the commands:

<space> 0 b F l W ^ $; E f T w | , B e h t

If the current line is not the edit line, any command that modifies the current line shall cause the content of the current line to replace the content of the edit line, and the current line shall become the edit line. This replacement cannot be undone (see the **u** and **U** commands below). The modification requested shall then be performed to the edit line. When the current line is the edit line, the modification shall be done directly to the edit line.

Any command that is preceded by *count* shall take a count (the numeric value of any preceding decimal digits). Unless otherwise noted, this count shall cause the specified operation to repeat by the number of times specified by the count. Also unless otherwise noted, a *count* that is out of range is considered an error condition and shall alert the terminal, but neither the cursor position, nor the command line, shall change.

The terms *word* and *bigword* are used as defined in the *vi* description. The term *save buffer* corresponds to the term *unnamed buffer* in *vi*.

The following commands shall be recognized in command mode:

<newline>

Execute the current command line. If the current command line is not empty, this line shall be entered into the command history (see *fc*).

<control>-L

Redraw the current command line. Position the cursor at the same location on the redrawn line.

#

Insert the character '#' at the beginning of the current command line and treat the resulting edit line as a comment. This line shall be entered into the command history; see *fc*.

=

Display the possible shell word expansions (see *Word Expansions*) of the bigword at the current command line position.

Note This does not modify the content of the current line, and therefore does not cause the current line to become the edit line.

These expansions shall be displayed on subsequent terminal lines. If the bigword contains none of the characters '?', '*', or '[', an asterisk ('*') shall be implicitly assumed at the end. If any directories are matched, these expansions shall have a '/' character appended. After the expansion, the line shall be redrawn, the cursor repositioned at the current cursor position, and *sh* shall be placed in command mode.

\

Perform pathname expansion (see *Pathname Expansion*) on the current bigword, up to the largest set of characters that can be matched uniquely. If the bigword contains none of the characters '?', '*', or '[', an asterisk ('*') shall be implicitly assumed at the end. This maximal expansion then shall replace the original bigword in the command line, and the cursor shall be placed after this expansion. If the resulting bigword completely and uniquely matches a directory, a '/' character shall be inserted directly after the bigword. If some other file is completely matched, a single <space> shall be inserted after the bigword. After this operation, *sh* shall be placed in insert mode.

*

Perform pathname expansion on the current bigword and insert all expansions into the command to replace the current bigword, with each expansion separated by a single <space>. If at the end of the line, the current cursor position shall be moved to the first column position following the expansions and *sh* shall be placed in insert mode. Otherwise, the current cursor position shall be the last column position of the first character after the expansions and *sh* shall be placed in insert mode. If the current bigword contains none of the characters '?', '*', or '[', before the operation, an asterisk shall be implicitly assumed at the end.

@letter

Insert the value of the alias named *_letter*. The symbol *letter* represents a single alphabetic character from the portable character set; implementations may support additional characters as an extension. If the alias *_letter* contains other editing commands, these commands shall be performed as part of the insertion. If no alias *_letter* is enabled, this command shall have no effect.

[count]˜

Convert, if the current character is a lowercase letter, to the equivalent uppercase letter and *vice versa*, as prescribed by the current locale. The current cursor position then shall be advanced by one character. If the cursor was positioned on the last character of the line, the case conversion shall occur, but the cursor shall not advance. If the '˜' command is preceded by a *count*, that number of characters shall be converted, and the cursor shall be advanced to the character position after the last character converted. If the *count* is larger than the number of characters after the cursor, this shall not be considered an error; the cursor shall advance to the last character on the line.

[*count*].

Repeat the most recent non-motion command, even if it was executed on an earlier command line. If the previous command was preceded by a *count*, and no count is given on the '.' command, the count from the previous command shall be included as part of the repeated command. If the '.' command is preceded by a *count*, this shall override any *count* argument to the previous command. The *count* specified in the '.' command shall become the count for subsequent '.' commands issued without a count.

[*number*]**v**

Invoke the *vi* editor to edit the current command line in a temporary file. When the editor exits, the commands in the temporary file shall be executed and placed in the command history. If a *number* is included, it specifies the command number in the command history to be edited, rather than the current command line.

[*count*]**l** (ell)

[*count*]<space>

Move the current cursor position to the next character position. If the cursor was positioned on the last character of the line, the terminal shall be alerted and the cursor shall not be advanced. If the *count* is larger than the number of characters after the cursor, this shall not be considered an error; the cursor shall advance to the last character on the line.

[*count*]**h**

Move the current cursor position to the *count*th (default 1) previous character position. If the cursor was positioned on the first character of the line, the terminal shall be alerted and the cursor shall not be moved. If the count is larger than the number of characters before the cursor, this shall not be considered an error; the cursor shall move to the first character on the line.

[*count*]**w**

Move to the start of the next word. If the cursor was positioned on the last character of the line, the terminal shall be alerted and the cursor shall not be advanced. If the *count* is larger than the number of words after the cursor, this shall not be considered an error; the cursor shall advance to the last character on the line.

[*count*]**W**

Move to the start of the next bigword. If the cursor was positioned on the last character of the line, the terminal shall be alerted and the cursor shall not be advanced. If the *count* is larger than the number of bigwords after the cursor, this shall not be considered an error; the cursor shall advance to the last character on the line.

[*count*]**e**

Move to the end of the current word. If at the end of a word, move to the end of the next word. If the cursor was positioned on the last character of the line, the terminal shall be alerted and the cursor shall not be advanced. If the *count* is larger than the number of words after the cursor, this shall not be considered an error; the cursor shall advance to the last character on the line.

[*count*]**E**

Move to the end of the current bigword. If at the end of a bigword, move to the end of the next bigword. If the cursor was positioned on the last character of the line, the terminal shall be alerted and the cursor shall not be advanced. If the *count* is larger than the number of bigwords after the cursor, this shall not be considered an error; the cursor shall advance to the last character on the line.

[*count*]**b**

Move to the beginning of the current word. If at the beginning of a word, move to the beginning of the previous word. If the cursor was positioned on the first character of the line, the terminal shall be alerted and the cursor shall not be moved. If the *count* is larger than the number of words preceding the cursor, this shall not be considered an error; the cursor shall return to the first character on the line.

[*count*]**B**

Move to the beginning of the current bigword. If at the beginning of a bigword, move to the beginning of the previous bigword. If the cursor was positioned on the first character of the line, the terminal shall be alerted and the cursor shall not be moved. If the *count* is larger than the number of bigwords preceding the cursor, this shall not be considered an error; the cursor shall return to the first character on the line.

^

Move the current cursor position to the first character on the input line that is not a <blank>.

$

Move to the last character position on the current command line.

0

(Zero.) Move to the first character position on the current command line.

[*count*]|

Move to the *count*th character position on the current command line. If no number is specified, move to the first position. The first character position shall be numbered 1. If the count is larger than the number of characters on the line, this shall not be considered an error; the cursor shall be placed on the last character on the line.

[*count*]**f***c*

Move to the first occurrence of the character 'c' that occurs after the current cursor position. If the cursor was positioned on the last character of the line, the terminal shall be alerted and the cursor shall not be advanced. If the character 'c' does not occur in the line after the current cursor position, the terminal shall be alerted and the cursor shall not be moved.

[*count*]**F***c*

Move to the first occurrence of the character 'c' that occurs before the current cursor position. If the cursor was positioned on the first character of the line, the terminal shall be alerted and the cursor shall not be moved. If the character 'c' does not occur in the line before the current cursor position, the terminal shall be alerted and the cursor shall not be moved.

[*count*]**t***c*

Move to the character before the first occurrence of the character 'c' that occurs after the current cursor position. If the cursor was positioned on the last character of the line, the terminal shall be alerted and the cursor shall not be advanced. If the character 'c' does not occur in the line after the current cursor position, the terminal shall be alerted and the cursor shall not be moved.

[*count*]**T***c*

Move to the character after the first occurrence of the character 'c' that occurs before the current cursor position. If the cursor was positioned on the first character of the line, the terminal shall be alerted and the cursor shall not be moved. If the character 'c' does not occur in the line before the current cursor position, the terminal shall be alerted and the cursor shall not be moved.

[*count*]**;**

Repeat the most recent **f**, **F**, **t**, or **T** command. Any number argument on that previous command shall be ignored. Errors are those described for the repeated command.

[*count*]**,**

Repeat the most recent **f**, **F**, **t**, or **T** command. Any number argument on that previous command shall be ignored. However, reverse the direction of that command.

a

Enter insert mode after the current cursor position. Characters that are entered shall be inserted before the next character.

A

Enter insert mode after the end of the current command line.

i

Enter insert mode at the current cursor position. Characters that are entered shall be inserted before the current character.

I

Enter insert mode at the beginning of the current command line.

R

Enter insert mode, replacing characters from the command line beginning at the current cursor position.

[*count*]**c***motion*

Delete the characters between the current cursor position and the cursor position that would result from the specified motion command. Then enter insert mode before the first character following any deleted characters. If *count* is specified, it shall be applied to the motion command. A *count* shall be ignored for the following motion commands:

0   ^ $ c

If the motion command is the character 'c', the current command line shall be cleared and insert mode shall be entered. If the motion command would move the current cursor position toward the beginning of the command line, the character under the current cursor position shall not be deleted. If the motion command would move the current cursor position toward the end of the command line, the character under the current cursor position shall be deleted. If the *count* is larger than the number of characters between the current cursor position and the end of the command line toward which the motion command would move the cursor, this shall not be considered an error; all of the remaining characters in the aforementioned range shall be deleted and insert mode shall be entered. If the motion command is invalid, the terminal shall be alerted, the cursor shall not be moved, and no text shall be deleted.

C

Delete from the current character to the end of the line and enter insert mode at the new end-of-line.

S

Clear the entire edit line and enter insert mode.

[*count*]**r***c*

Replace the current character with the character 'c'. With a number *count*, replace the current and the following *count*-1 characters. After this command, the current cursor position shall be on the last character that was changed. If the *count* is larger than the number of characters after the cursor, this shall not be considered an error; all of the remaining characters shall be changed.

[*count*]_

Append a <space> after the current character position and then append the last bigword in the previous input line after the <space>. Then enter insert mode after the last character just appended. With a number *count*, append the *count*th bigword in the previous line.

[*count*]**x**

Delete the character at the current cursor position and place the deleted characters in the save buffer. If the cursor was positioned on the last character of the line, the character shall be deleted and the cursor position shall be moved to the previous character (the new last character). If the *count* is larger than the number of characters after the cursor, this shall not be considered an error; all the characters from the cursor to the end of the line shall be deleted.

[*count*]**X**

Delete the character before the current cursor position and place the deleted characters in the save buffer. The character under the current cursor position shall not change. If the cursor was positioned on the first character of the line, the terminal shall be alerted, and the **X** command shall have no effect. If the line contained a single character, the **X** command shall have no effect. If the line contained no characters, the terminal shall be alerted and the cursor shall not be moved. If the *count* is larger than the number of characters before the cursor, this shall not be considered an error; all the characters from before the cursor to the beginning of the line shall be deleted.

[*count*]**d***motion*

Delete the characters between the current cursor position and the character position that would result from the motion command. A number *count* repeats the motion command *count* times. If the motion command would move toward the beginning of the command line, the character under the current cursor position shall not be deleted. If the motion command is **d**, the entire current command line shall be cleared. If the *count* is larger than the number of characters between the current cursor position and the end of the command line toward which the motion command would move the cursor, this shall not be considered an error; all of the remaining characters in the aforementioned range shall be deleted. The deleted characters shall be placed in the save buffer.

D

Delete all characters from the current cursor position to the end of the line. The deleted characters shall be placed in the save buffer.

[*count*]**y***motion*

Yank (that is, copy) the characters from the current cursor position to the position resulting from the motion command into the save buffer. A number *count* shall be applied to the motion command. If the motion command would move toward the beginning of the command line, the character under the current cursor position shall not be included in the set of yanked characters. If the motion command is **y**, the entire current command line shall be yanked into the save buffer. The current cursor position shall be unchanged. If the *count* is larger than the number of characters between the current cursor position and the end of the command line toward which the motion command would move the cursor, this shall not be considered an error; all of the remaining characters in the aforementioned range shall be yanked.

Y

Yank the characters from the current cursor position to the end of the line into the save buffer. The current character position shall be unchanged.

[*count*]p

Put a copy of the current contents of the save buffer after the current cursor position. The current cursor position shall be advanced to the last character put from the save buffer. A *count* shall indicate how many copies of the save buffer shall be put.

[*count*]P

Put a copy of the current contents of the save buffer before the current cursor position. The current cursor position shall be moved to the last character put from the save buffer. A *count* shall indicate how many copies of the save buffer shall be put.

u

Undo the last command that changed the edit line. This operation shall not undo the copy of any command line to the edit line.

U

Undo all changes made to the edit line. This operation shall not undo the copy of any command line to the edit line.

[*count*]k

[*count*]-

Set the current command line to be the *count*th previous command line in the shell command history. If *count* is not specified, it shall default to 1. The cursor shall be positioned on the first character of the new command. If a **k** or **-** command would retreat past the maximum number of commands in effect for this shell (affected by the *HISTSIZE* environment variable), the terminal shall be alerted, and the command shall have no effect.

[*count*]j

[*count*]+

Set the current command line to be the *count*th next command line in the shell command history. If *count* is not specified, it shall default to 1. The cursor shall be positioned on the first character of the new command. If a **j** or **+** command advances past the edit line, the current command line shall be restored to the edit line and the terminal shall be alerted.

[*number*]G

Set the current command line to be the oldest command line stored in the shell command history. With a number *number*, set the current command line to be the command line *number* in the history. If command line *number* does not exist, the terminal shall be alerted and the command line shall not be changed.

/pattern<newline>

Move backwards through the command history, searching for the specified pattern, beginning with the previous command line. Patterns use the pattern matching notation described in *Pattern Matching Notation*, except that the '^' character shall have special meaning when it appears as the first character of *pattern*. In this case, the '^' is discarded and the characters after the '^' shall be matched only at the beginning of a line. Commands in the command history shall be treated as strings, not as filenames. If the pattern is not found, the current command line shall be unchanged and the terminal is alerted. If it is found in a previous line, the current command line shall be set to that line and the cursor shall be set to the first character of the new command line.

If *pattern* is empty, the last non-empty pattern provided to / or ? shall be used. If there is no previous non-empty pattern, the terminal shall be alerted and the current command line shall remain unchanged.

?pattern<newline>

Move forwards through the command history, searching for the specified pattern, beginning with the next command line. Patterns use the pattern matching notation described in *Pattern Matching Notation*, except that the '^' character shall have special meaning when it appears as the first character of *pattern*. In this case, the '^' is discarded and the characters after the '^' shall be matched only at the beginning of a line. Commands in the command history shall be treated as strings, not as filenames. If the pattern is not found, the current command line shall be unchanged and the terminal alerted. If it is found in a following line, the current command line shall be set to that line and the cursor shall be set to the fist character of the new command line.

If *pattern* is empty, the last non-empty pattern provided to / or ? shall be used. If there is no previous non-empty pattern, the terminal shall be alerted and the current command line shall remain unchanged.

n

Repeat the most recent / or ? command. If there is no previous / or ?, the terminal shall be alerted and the current command line shall remain unchanged.

N

Repeat the most recent / or ? command, reversing the direction of the search. If there is no previous / or ?, the terminal shall be alerted and the current command line shall remain unchanged.

Exit Status

The following exit values shall be returned:

0

The script to be executed consisted solely of zero or more blank lines or comments, or both.

1-125

A non-interactive shell detected a syntax, redirection, or variable assignment error.

127

A specified *command_file* could not be found by a non-interactive shell.

Otherwise, the shell shall return the exit status of the last command it invoked or attempted to invoke (see also the *exit* utility in *Special Built-In Utilities*).

Consequences Of Errors

See Consequences of Shell Errors.

The following sections are informative.

Application Usage

Standard input and standard error are the files that determine whether a shell is interactive when **-i** is not specified. For example:

```
sh > file
```

and:

```
sh 2> file
```

create interactive and non-interactive shells, respectively. Although both accept terminal input, the results of error conditions are different, as described in *Consequences of Shell Errors*; in the second example a redirection error encountered by a special built-in utility aborts the shell.

A conforming application must protect its first operand, if it starts with a plus sign, by preceding it with the "−" argument that denotes the end of the options.

Applications should note that the standard *PATH* to the shell cannot be assumed to be either **/bin/sh** or **/usr/bin/sh**, and should be determined by interrogation of the *PATH* returned by *getconf PATH*, ensuring that the returned pathname is an absolute pathname and not a shell built-in.

For example, to determine the location of the standard *sh* utility:

```
command -v sh
```

On some implementations this might return:

```
/usr/xpg4/bin/sh
```

Furthermore, on systems that support executable scripts (the "#!" construct), it is recommended that applications using executable scripts install them using *getconf* **-v** to determine the shell pathname and update the "#!" script appropriately as it is being installed (for example, with *sed*). For example:

```
#
# Installation time script to install correct POSIX shell pathname
#
# Get list of paths to check
#
Sifs=$IFS
IFS=:
set $(getconf PATH)
IFS=$Sifs
#
# Check each path for 'sh'
#
for i in $@
do
    if [ -f ${i}/sh ];
    then
        Pshell=${i}/sh
    fi
done
#
# This is the list of scripts to update. They should be of the
# form '${name}.source' and will be transformed to '${name}'.
# Each script should begin:
#
# !INSTALLSHELLPATH -p
#
scripts="a b c"
#
# Transform each script
#
for i in ${scripts}
do
    sed -e "s|INSTALLSHELLPATH|${Pshell}|" < ${i}.source > ${i}
done
```

Examples

1. Execute a shell command from a string:

```
sh -c "cat myfile"
```

2. Execute a shell script from a file in the current directory:

```
sh my_shell_cmds
```

Rationale

The *sh* utility and the *set* special built-in utility share a common set of options.

The KornShell ignores the contents of *IFS* upon entry to the script. A conforming application cannot rely on importing *IFS*. One justification for this, beyond security considerations, is to assist possible future shell compilers. Allowing *IFS* to be imported from the environment prevents many optimizations that might otherwise be performed via dataflow analysis of the script itself.

The text in the STDIN section about non-blocking reads concerns an instance of *sh* that has been invoked, probably by a C-language program, with standard input that has been opened using the O_NONBLOCK flag; see *open()* in the System Interfaces volume of IEEE Std 1003.1-2001. If the shell did not reset this flag, it would immediately terminate because no input data would be available yet and that would be considered the same as end-of-file.

The options associated with a *restricted shell* (command name *rsh* and the **-r** option) were excluded because the standard developers considered that the implied level of security could not be achieved and they did not want to raise false expectations.

On systems that support set-user-ID scripts, a historical trapdoor has been to link a script to the name **-i**. When it is called by a sequence such as:

```
sh -
```

or by:

```
#! usr/bin/sh -
```

the historical systems have assumed that no option letters follow. Thus, this volume of IEEE Std 1003.1-2001 allows the single hyphen to mark the end of the options, in addition to the use of the regular "--" argument, because it was considered that the older practice was so pervasive. An alternative approach is taken by the KornShell, where real and effective user/group IDs must match for an interactive shell; this behavior is specifically allowed by this volume of IEEE Std 1003.1-2001.

Note There are other problems with set-user-ID scripts that the two approaches described here do not resolve.

The initialization process for the history file can be dependent on the system start-up files, in that they may contain commands that effectively preempt the user's settings of *HISTFILE* and *HISTSIZE*. For example, function definition commands are recorded in the history file, unless the *set* **-o** *nolog* option is set. If the system administrator includes function definitions in some system start-up file called before the *ENV* file, the history file is initialized before the user gets a chance to influence its characteristics. In some historical shells, the history file is initialized just after the *ENV* file has been processed. Therefore, it is implementation-defined whether changes made to *HISTFILE* after the history file has been initialized are effective.

The default messages for the various *MAIL -related* messages are unspecified because they vary across implementations. Typical messages are:

`"you have mail\n"`

or:

`"you have new mail\n"`

It is important that the descriptions of command line editing refer to the same shell as that in IEEE Std 1003.1-2001 so that interactive users can also be application programmers without having to deal with programmatic differences in their two environments. It is also essential that the utility name *sh* be specified because this explicit utility name is too firmly rooted in historical practice of application programs for it to change.

Consideration was given to mandating a diagnostic message when attempting to set *vi*-mode on terminals that do not support command line editing. However, it is not historical practice for the shell to be cognizant of all terminal types and thus be able to detect inappropriate terminals in all cases. Implementations are encouraged to supply diagnostics in this case whenever possible, rather than leaving the user in a state where editing commands work incorrectly.

In early proposals, the KornShell-derived *emacs* mode of command line editing was included, even though the *emacs* editor itself was not. The community of *emacs* proponents was adamant that the full *emacs* editor not be standardized because they were concerned that an attempt to standardize this very powerful environment would encourage vendors to ship strictly conforming versions lacking the extensibility required by the community. The author of the original *emacs* program also expressed his desire to omit the program. Furthermore, there were a number of historical systems that did not include *emacs*, or included it without supporting it, but there were very few that did not include and support *vi*. The shell *emacs* command line editing mode was finally omitted because it became apparent that the Korn-Shell version and the editor being distributed with the GNU system had diverged in some respects. The author of *emacs* requested that the POSIX *emacs* mode either be deleted or have a significant number of unspecified conditions. Although the KornShell author agreed to consider changes to bring the shell into alignment, the standard developers decided to defer specification at that time. At the time, it was assumed that convergence on an acceptable definition would occur for a subsequent draft, but that has not happened, and there appears to be no impetus to do so. In any case, implementations are free to offer additional command line editing modes based on the exact models of editors their users are most comfortable with.

Early proposals had the following list entry in vi Line Editing Insert Mode :

\

If followed by the *erase* or *kill* character, that character shall be inserted into the input line. Otherwise, the backslash itself shall be inserted into the input line.

However, this is not actually a feature of *sh* command line editing insert mode, but one of some historical terminal line drivers. Some conforming implementations continue to do this when the *stty* **iexten** flag is set.

Future Directions

None.

See Also

Shell Command Language, cd, echo, exit(), fc, pwd, read(), set, stty, test, umask(), vi, the System Interfaces volume of IEEE Std 1003.1-2001, *dup(), exec, exit(), fork(), open(), pipe(), signal(), system(), ulimit(), umask(), wait()*

Change History

First released in Issue 2.

Issue 5

The FUTURE DIRECTIONS section is added.

Text is added to the DESCRIPTION for the Large File Summit proposal.

Issue 6

The Open Group Corrigendum U029/2 is applied, correcting the second SYNOPSIS.

The Open Group Corrigendum U027/3 is applied, correcting a typographical error.

The following new requirements on POSIX implementations derive from alignment with the Single UNIX Specification:

- The option letters derived from the *set* special built-in are also accepted with a leading plus sign ('+').

- Large file extensions are added:

  - Pathname expansion does not fail due to the size of a file.

  - Shell input and output redirections have an implementation-defined offset maximum that is established in the open file description.

In the ENVIRONMENT VARIABLES section, the text "user's home directory" is updated to "directory referred to by the *HOME* environment variable".

Descriptions for the *ENV* and *PWD* environment variables are included to align with the IEEE P1003.2b draft standard.

The normative text is reworded to avoid use of the term "must" for application requirements.

■■■

Regular Expressions

The POSIX specification defines two kinds of regular expressions: basic regular expressions, such as those used by historic sed and grep, and extended regular expressions, used by awk (and egrep). There are other kinds, but these two form the basis of what you need to know. While some documentation describes basic regular expressions as "obsolete," they are still in widespread use. (However, if you are developing software, please use extended regular expressions.)

This appendix is also significant because the shell pattern matching function (see Appendix A for the complete shell specification) is defined in terms of section 9.3.5, "RE Bracket Expression."

■Note All external documents referenced in this appendix are available at www.opengroup.org.

---

9. Regular Expressions

Regular Expressions (REs) provide a mechanism to select specific strings from a set of character strings.

Regular expressions are a context-independent syntax that can represent a wide variety of character sets and character set orderings, where these character sets are interpreted according to the current locale. While many regular expressions can be interpreted differently depending on the current locale, many features, such as character class expressions, provide for contextual invariance across locales.

The Basic Regular Expression (BRE) notation and construction rules in Basic Regular Expressions shall apply to most utilities supporting regular expressions. Some utilities, instead, support the Extended Regular Expressions (ERE) described in Extended Regular Expressions; any exceptions for both cases are noted in the descriptions of the specific utilities using regular expressions. Both BREs and EREs are supported by the Regular Expression Matching interface in the System Interfaces volume of IEEE Std 1003.1-2001 under *regcomp()*, *regexec()*, and related functions.

9.1 Regular Expression Definitions

For the purposes of this section, the following definitions shall apply:

entire regular expression

The concatenated set of one or more BREs or EREs that make up the pattern specified for string selection.

matched

A sequence of zero or more characters shall be said to be matched by a BRE or ERE when the characters in the sequence correspond to a sequence of characters defined by the pattern.

Matching shall be based on the bit pattern used for encoding the character, not on the graphic representation of the character. This means that if a character set contains two or more encodings for a graphic symbol, or if the strings searched contain text encoded in more than one codeset, no attempt is made to search for any other representation of the encoded symbol. If that is required, the user can specify equivalence classes containing all variations of the desired graphic symbol.

The search for a matching sequence starts at the beginning of a string and stops when the first sequence matching the expression is found, where "first" is defined to mean "begins earliest in the string". If the pattern permits a variable number of matching characters and thus there is more than one such sequence starting at that point, the longest such sequence is matched. For example, the BRE "bb*" matches the second to fourth characters of the string "abbbc", and the ERE "(wee|week)(knights|night)" matches all ten characters of the string "weeknights".

Consistent with the whole match being the longest of the leftmost matches, each sub-pattern, from left to right, shall match the longest possible string. For this purpose, a null string shall be considered to be longer than no match at all. For example, matching the BRE "\(.*\).*" against "abcdef", the subexpression "(\1)" is "abcdef", and matching the BRE "\(a*\)*" against "bc", the subexpression "(\1)" is the null string.

When a multi-character collating element in a bracket expression (see RE Bracket Expression) is involved, the longest sequence shall be measured in characters consumed from the string to be matched; that is, the collating element counts not as one element, but as the number of characters it matches.

BRE (ERE) matching a single character

A BRE or ERE that shall match either a single character or a single collating element.

Only a BRE or ERE of this type that includes a bracket expression (see RE Bracket Expression) can match a collating element.

BRE (ERE) matching multiple characters

A BRE or ERE that shall match a concatenation of single characters or collating elements.

Such a BRE or ERE is made up from a BRE (ERE) matching a single character and BRE (ERE) special characters.

invalid

This section uses the term "invalid" for certain constructs or conditions. Invalid REs shall cause the utility or function using the RE to generate an error condition. When invalid is not used, violations of the specified syntax or semantics for REs produce undefined results: this may entail an error, enabling an extended syntax for that RE, or using the construct in error as literal characters to be matched. For example, the BRE construct "\{1,2,3\}" does not comply with the grammar. A conforming application cannot rely on it producing an error nor matching the literal characters "\{1,2,3\}".

9.2 Regular Expression General Requirements

The requirements in this section shall apply to both basic and extended regular expressions.

The use of regular expressions is generally associated with text processing. REs (BREs and EREs) operate on text strings; that is, zero or more characters followed by an end-of-string delimiter (typically NUL). Some utilities employing regular expressions limit the processing to lines; that is, zero or more characters followed by a <newline>. In the regular expression processing described in IEEE Std 1003.1-2001, the <newline> is regarded as an ordinary character and both a period and a non-matching list can match one. The Shell and Utilities volume of IEEE Std 1003.1-2001 specifies within the individual descriptions of those standard utilities employing regular expressions whether they permit matching of <newline>s; if not stated otherwise, the use of literal <newline>s or any escape sequence equivalent produces undefined results. Those utilities (like *grep*) that do not allow <newline>s to match are responsible for eliminating any <newline> from strings before matching against the RE. The *regcomp*() function in the System Interfaces volume of IEEE Std 1003.1-2001, however, can provide support for such processing without violating the rules of this section.

The interfaces specified in IEEE Std 1003.1-2001 do not permit the inclusion of a NUL character in an RE or in the string to be matched. If during the operation of a standard utility a NUL is included in the text designated to be matched, that NUL may designate the end of the text string for the purposes of matching.

When a standard utility or function that uses regular expressions specifies that pattern matching shall be performed without regard to the case (uppercase or lowercase) of either data or patterns, then when each character in the string is matched against the pattern, not only the character, but also its case counterpart (if any), shall be matched. This definition of case-insensitive processing is intended to allow matching of multi-character collating elements as well as characters, as each character in the string is matched using both its cases. For example, in a locale where "Ch" is a multi-character collating element and where a matching list expression matches such elements, the RE "[[.Ch.]]" when matched against the string "char" is in reality matched against "ch", "Ch", "cH", and "CH".

The implementation shall support any regular expression that does not exceed 256 bytes in length.

9.3 Basic Regular Expressions

9.3.1 BREs Matching a Single Character or Collating Element

A BRE ordinary character, a special character preceded by a backslash, or a period shall match a single character. A bracket expression shall match a single character or a single collating element.

9.3.2 BRE Ordinary Characters

An ordinary character is a BRE that matches itself: any character in the supported character set, except for the BRE special characters listed in BRE Special Characters.

The interpretation of an ordinary character preceded by a backslash ('\') is undefined, except for:

- The characters ')', '(', '{', and '}'
- The digits 1 to 9 inclusive (see BREs Matching Multiple Characters)
- A character inside a bracket expression

9.3.3 BRE Special Characters

A BRE special character has special properties in certain contexts. Outside those contexts, or when preceded by a backslash, such a character is a BRE that matches the special character itself. The BRE special characters and the contexts in which they have their special meaning are as follows:

. [\

The period, left-bracket, and backslash shall be special except when used in a bracket expression (see RE Bracket Expression). An expression containing a '[' that is not preceded by a backslash and is not part of a bracket expression produces undefined results.

*

The asterisk shall be special except when used:

- In a bracket expression
- As the first character of an entire BRE (after an initial '^', if any)
- As the first character of a subexpression (after an initial '^', if any); see BREs Matching Multiple Characters

^

The circumflex shall be special when used as:

- An anchor (see BRE Expression Anchoring)
- The first character of a bracket expression (see RE Bracket Expression)

$

The dollar sign shall be special when used as an anchor.

9.3.4 Periods in BREs

A period ('.'), when used outside a bracket expression, is a BRE that shall match any character in the supported character set except NUL.

9.3.5 RE Bracket Expression

A bracket expression (an expression enclosed in square brackets, "[]") is an RE that shall match a single collating element contained in the non-empty set of collating elements represented by the bracket expression.

The following rules and definitions apply to bracket expressions:

1. A bracket expression is either a matching list expression or a non-matching list expression. It consists of one or more expressions: collating elements, collating symbols, equivalence classes, character classes, or range expressions. The right-bracket (']') shall lose its special meaning and represent itself in a bracket expression if it occurs first in the list (after an initial circumflex ('^'), if any). Otherwise, it shall terminate the bracket expression, unless it appears in a collating symbol (such as "[.].]") or is the ending right-bracket for a collating symbol, equivalence class, or character class. The special characters '.', '*', '[', and '\' (period, asterisk, left-bracket, and backslash, respectively) shall lose their special meaning within a bracket expression.

    The character sequences "[.", "[=", and "[:" (left-bracket followed by a period, equals-sign, or colon) shall be special inside a bracket expression and are used to delimit collating symbols, equivalence class expressions, and character class expressions. These symbols shall be followed by a valid expression and the matching terminating sequence ".]", "=]", or ":]", as described in the following items.

2. A matching list expression specifies a list that shall match any single-character collating element in any of the expressions represented in the list. The first character in the list shall not be the circumflex; for example, "[abc]" is an RE that matches any of the characters 'a', 'b', or 'c'. It is unspecified whether a matching list expression matches a multi-character collating element that is matched by one of the expressions.

3. A non-matching list expression begins with a circumflex ('^'), and specifies a list that shall match any single-character collating element except for the expressions represented in the list after the leading circumflex. For example, "[^abc]" is an RE that matches any character except the characters 'a', 'b', or 'c'. It is unspecified whether a non-matching list expression matches a multi-character collating element that is not matched by any of the expressions. The circumflex shall have this special meaning only when it occurs first in the list, immediately following the left-bracket.

4. A collating symbol is a collating element enclosed within bracket-period ("[." and ".]") delimiters. Collating elements are defined as described in *Collation Order*. Conforming applications shall represent multi-character collating elements as collating symbols when it is necessary to distinguish them from a list of the individual characters that make up the multi-character collating element. For example, if the string "ch" is a collating element defined using the line:

```
collating-element <ch-digraph> from "<c><h>"
```

in the locale definition, the expression "[[.ch.]]" shall be treated as an RE containing the collating symbol 'ch', while "[ch]" shall be treated as an RE matching 'c' or 'h'. Collating symbols are recognized only inside bracket expressions. If the string is not a collating element in the current locale, the expression is invalid.

5. An equivalence class expression shall represent the set of collating elements belonging to an equivalence class, as described in *Collation Order*. Only primary equivalence classes shall be recognized. The class shall be expressed by enclosing any one of the collating elements in the equivalence class within bracket-equal ("[=" and "=]") delimiters. For example, if 'a', 'à', and 'â' belong to the same equivalence class, then "[[=a=]b]", "[[=à=]b]", and "[[=â=]b]" are each equivalent to "[aàâb]". If the collating element does not belong to an equivalence class, the equivalence class expression shall be treated as a collating symbol.

6. A character class expression shall represent the union of two sets:

   a. The set of single-character collating elements whose characters belong to the character class, as defined in the *LC_CTYPE* category in the current locale.

   b. An unspecified set of multi-character collating elements.

   All character classes specified in the current locale shall be recognized. A character class expression is expressed as a character class name enclosed within bracket-colon ("[:" and ":]") delimiters.

   The following character class expressions shall be supported in all locales:

   ```
   [:alnum:]   [:cntrl:]   [:lower:]   [:space:]
   [:alpha:]   [:digit:]   [:print:]   [:upper:]
   [:blank:]   [:graph:]   [:punct:]   [:xdigit:]
   ```

   In addition, character class expressions of the form:

   ```
   [:name:]
   ```

   are recognized in those locales where the *name* keyword has been given a **charclass** definition in the *LC_CTYPE* category.

7. In the POSIX locale, a range expression represents the set of collating elements that fall between two elements in the collation sequence, inclusive. In other locales, a range expression has unspecified behavior: strictly conforming applications shall not rely on whether the range expression is valid, or on the set of collating elements matched. A range expression shall be expressed as the starting point and the ending point separated by a hyphen ('-').

   In the following, all examples assume the POSIX locale.

   The starting range point and the ending range point shall be a collating element or collating symbol. An equivalence class expression used as a starting or ending point of a range expression produces unspecified results. An equivalence class can be used portably within a bracket expression, but only outside the range. If the represented set of collating elements is empty, it is unspecified whether the expression matches nothing, or is treated as invalid.

The interpretation of range expressions where the ending range point is also the starting range point of a subsequent range expression (for example, "[a-m-o]") is undefined.

The hyphen character shall be treated as itself if it occurs first (after an initial '^', if any) or last in the list, or as an ending range point in a range expression. As examples, the expressions "[-ac]" and "[ac-]" are equivalent and match any of the characters 'a', 'c', or '-'; "[^-ac]" and "[^ac-]" are equivalent and match any characters except 'a', 'c', or '-'; the expression "[%--]" matches any of the characters between '%' and '-' inclusive; the expression "[--@]" matches any of the characters between '-' and '@' inclusive; and the expression "[a--@]" is either invalid or equivalent to '@', because the letter 'a' follows the symbol '-' in the POSIX locale. To use a hyphen as the starting range point, it shall either come first in the bracket expression or be specified as a collating symbol; for example, "[][.-.]-0]", which matches either a right bracket or any character or collating element that collates between hyphen and 0, inclusive.

If a bracket expression specifies both '-' and ']', the ']' shall be placed first (after the '^', if any) and the '-' last within the bracket expression.

9.3.6 BREs Matching Multiple Characters

The following rules can be used to construct BREs matching multiple characters from BREs matching a single character:

1. The concatenation of BREs shall match the concatenation of the strings matched by each component of the BRE.

2. A subexpression can be defined within a BRE by enclosing it between the character pairs "\(" and "\)". Such a subexpression shall match whatever it would have matched without the "\(" and "\)", except that anchoring within subexpressions is optional behavior; see BRE Expression Anchoring. Subexpressions can be arbitrarily nested.

3. The back-reference expression '\n' shall match the same (possibly empty) string of characters as was matched by a subexpression enclosed between "\(" and "\)" preceding the '\n'. The character 'n' shall be a digit from 1 through 9, specifying the nth subexpression (the one that begins with the nth "\(" from the beginning of the pattern and ends with the corresponding paired "\)"). The expression is invalid if less than n subexpressions precede the '\n'. For example, the expression "\(.*\)\1$" matches a line consisting of two adjacent appearances of the same string, and the expression "\(a\)*\1" fails to match 'a'. When the referenced subexpression matched more than one string, the back-referenced expression shall refer to the last matched string. If the subexpression referenced by the back-reference matches more than one string because of an asterisk ('*') or an interval expression (see item (5)), the back-reference shall match the last (rightmost) of these strings.

4. When a BRE matching a single character, a subexpression, or a back-reference is followed by the special character asterisk ('*'), together with that asterisk it shall match what zero or more consecutive occurrences of the BRE would match. For example, "[ab]*" and "[ab][ab]" are equivalent when matching the string "ab".

5. When a BRE matching a single character, a subexpression, or a back-reference is followed by an interval expression of the format "\{m\}", "\{m,\}", or "\{m,n\}", together with that interval expression it shall match what repeated consecutive occurrences of the BRE would match. The values of m and n are decimal integers in the range $0 <= m <= n <= \{RE\_DUP\_MAX\}$, where m specifies the exact or minimum number of occurrences and n specifies the maximum number of occurrences. The expression "\{m\}" shall match exactly m occurrences of the preceding BRE, "\{m,\}" shall match at least m occurrences, and "\{m,n\}" shall match any number of occurrences between m and n, inclusive.

For example, in the string "abababcccccccd" the BRE "c\{3\}" is matched by characters seven to nine, the BRE "\(ab\)\{4,\}" is not matched at all, and the BRE "c\{1,3\}d" is matched by characters ten to thirteen.

The behavior of multiple adjacent duplication symbols ('*' and intervals) produces undefined results.

A subexpression repeated by an asterisk ('*') or an interval expression shall not match a null expression unless this is the only match for the repetition or it is necessary to satisfy the exact or minimum number of occurrences for the interval expression.

9.3.7 BRE Precedence

The order of precedence shall be as shown in the following table:

BRE Precedence (from high to low)	
Collation-related bracket symbols	[==] [::] [..]
Escaped characters	\<special character>
Bracket expression	[]
Subexpressions/back-references	\(\) \n
Single-character-BRE duplication	* \{m,n\}
Concatenation	
Anchoring	^ $

9.3.8 BRE Expression Anchoring

A BRE can be limited to matching strings that begin or end a line; this is called "anchoring". The circumflex and dollar sign special characters shall be considered BRE anchors in the following contexts:

1. A circumflex ('^') shall be an anchor when used as the first character of an entire BRE. The implementation may treat the circumflex as an anchor when used as the first character of a subexpression. The circumflex shall anchor the expression (or optionally subexpression) to the beginning of a string; only sequences starting at the first character of a string shall be matched by the BRE. For example, the BRE "^ab" matches "ab" in the string "abcdef", but fails to match in the string "cdefab". The BRE "\(^ab\)" may match the former string. A portable BRE shall escape a leading circumflex in a subexpression to match a literal circumflex.

2. A dollar sign ('$') shall be an anchor when used as the last character of an entire BRE. The implementation may treat a dollar sign as an anchor when used as the last character of a subexpression. The dollar sign shall anchor the expression (or optionally subexpression) to the end of the string being matched; the dollar sign can be said to match the end-of-string following the last character.

3. A BRE anchored by both '^' and '$' shall match only an entire string. For example, the BRE "^abcdef$" matches strings consisting only of "abcdef".

9.4 Extended Regular Expressions

The extended regular expression (ERE) notation and construction rules shall apply to utilities defined as using extended regular expressions; any exceptions to the following rules are noted in the descriptions of the specific utilities using EREs.

9.4.1 EREs Matching a Single Character or Collating Element

An ERE ordinary character, a special character preceded by a backslash, or a period shall match a single character. A bracket expression shall match a single character or a single collating element. An ERE matching a single character enclosed in parentheses shall match the same as the ERE without parentheses would have matched.

9.4.2 ERE Ordinary Characters

An ordinary character is an ERE that matches itself. An ordinary character is any character in the supported character set, except for the ERE special characters listed in ERE Special Characters. The interpretation of an ordinary character preceded by a backslash ('\') is undefined.

9.4.3 ERE Special Characters

An ERE special character has special properties in certain contexts. Outside those contexts, or when preceded by a backslash, such a character shall be an ERE that matches the special character itself. The extended regular expression special characters and the contexts in which they shall have their special meaning are as follows:

.[\(

The period, left-bracket, backslash, and left-parenthesis shall be special except when used in a bracket expression (see RE Bracket Expression). Outside a bracket expression, a left-parenthesis immediately followed by a right-parenthesis produces undefined results.

)

The right-parenthesis shall be special when matched with a preceding left-parenthesis, both outside a bracket expression.

*+?{

The asterisk, plus-sign, question-mark, and left-brace shall be special except when used in a bracket expression (see RE Bracket Expression). Any of the following uses produce undefined results:

- If these characters appear first in an ERE, or immediately following a vertical-line, circumflex, or left-parenthesis

- If a left-brace is not part of a valid interval expression (see EREs Matching Multiple Characters)

|

The vertical-line is special except when used in a bracket expression (see RE Bracket Expression). A vertical-line appearing first or last in an ERE, or immediately following a vertical-line or a left-parenthesis, or immediately preceding a right-parenthesis, produces undefined results.

^

The circumflex shall be special when used as:

- An anchor (see ERE Expression Anchoring)

- The first character of a bracket expression (see RE Bracket Expression)

$

The dollar sign shall be special when used as an anchor.

9.4.4 Periods in EREs

A period ('.'), when used outside a bracket expression, is an ERE that shall match any character in the supported character set except NUL.

9.4.5 ERE Bracket Expression

The rules for ERE Bracket Expressions are the same as for Basic Regular Expressions; see RE Bracket Expression.

9.4.6 EREs Matching Multiple Characters

The following rules shall be used to construct EREs matching multiple characters from EREs matching a single character:

1. A concatenation of EREs shall match the concatenation of the character sequences matched by each component of the ERE. A concatenation of EREs enclosed in parentheses shall match whatever the concatenation without the parentheses matches. For example, both the ERE "cd" and the ERE "(cd)" are matched by the third and fourth character of the string "abcdefabcdef".

2. When an ERE matching a single character or an ERE enclosed in parentheses is followed by the special character plus-sign ('+'), together with that plus-sign it shall match what one or more consecutive occurrences of the ERE would match. For example, the ERE "b+(bc)" matches the fourth to seventh characters in the string "acabbbcde". And, "[ab]+" and "[ab][ab]*" are equivalent.

3. When an ERE matching a single character or an ERE enclosed in parentheses is followed by the special character asterisk ('*'), together with that asterisk it shall match what zero or more consecutive occurrences of the ERE would match. For example, the ERE "b*c" matches the first character in the string "cabbbcde", and the ERE "b*cd" matches the third to seventh characters in the string "cabbbcdebbbbbbcdbc". And, "[ab]*" and "[ab][ab]" are equivalent when matching the string "ab".

4. When an ERE matching a single character or an ERE enclosed in parentheses is followed by the special character question-mark ('?'), together with that question-mark it shall match what zero or one consecutive occurrences of the ERE would match. For example, the ERE "b?c" matches the second character in the string "acabbbcde".

5. When an ERE matching a single character or an ERE enclosed in parentheses is followed by an interval expression of the format "{m}", "{m,}", or "{m,n}", together with that interval expression it shall match what repeated consecutive occurrences of the ERE would match. The values of m and n are decimal integers in the range $0 <= m <= n <= $ {RE_DUP_MAX}, where m specifies the exact or minimum number of occurrences and n specifies the maximum number of occurrences. The expression "{m}" matches exactly m occurrences of the preceding ERE, "{m,}" matches at least m occurrences, and "{m,n}" matches any number of occurrences between m and n, inclusive.

   For example, in the string "ababababcccccccd" the ERE "c{3}" is matched by characters seven to nine and the ERE "(ab){2,}" is matched by characters one to six.

The behavior of multiple adjacent duplication symbols ('+', '*', '?', and intervals) produces undefined results.

An ERE matching a single character repeated by an '*', '?', or an interval expression shall not match a null expression unless this is the only match for the repetition or it is necessary to satisfy the exact or minimum number of occurrences for the interval expression.

9.4.7 ERE Alternation

Two EREs separated by the special character vertical-line ('|') shall match a string that is matched by either. For example, the ERE "a((bc)|d)" matches the string "abc" and the string "ad". Single characters, or expressions matching single characters, separated by the vertical bar and enclosed in parentheses, shall be treated as an ERE matching a single character.

9.4.8 ERE Precedence

The order of precedence shall be as shown in the following table:

ERE Precedence (from high to low)	
Collation-related bracket symbols	[==] [::] [..]
Escaped characters	\\<special character>
Bracket expression	[]
Grouping	()
Single-character-ERE duplication	* + ? {m,n}
Concatenation	
Anchoring	^ $
Alternation	|

For example, the ERE "abba|cde" matches either the string "abba" or the string "cde" (rather than the string "abbade" or "abbcde", because concatenation has a higher order of precedence than alternation).

9.4.9 ERE Expression Anchoring

An ERE can be limited to matching strings that begin or end a line; this is called "anchoring". The circumflex and dollar sign special characters shall be considered ERE anchors when used anywhere outside a bracket expression. This shall have the following effects:

1. A circumflex ('^') outside a bracket expression shall anchor the expression or subexpression it begins to the beginning of a string; such an expression or subexpression can match only a sequence starting at the first character of a string. For example, the EREs "^ab" and "(^ab)" match "ab" in the string "abcdef", but fail to match in the string "cdefab", and the ERE "a^b" is valid, but can never match because the 'a' prevents the expression "^b" from matching starting at the first character.

2. A dollar sign ('$') outside a bracket expression shall anchor the expression or subexpression it ends to the end of a string; such an expression or subexpression can match only a sequence ending at the last character of a string. For example, the EREs "ef$" and "(ef$)" match "ef" in the string "abcdef", but fail to match in the string "cdefab", and the ERE "e$f" is valid, but can never match because the 'f' prevents the expression "e$" from matching ending at the last character.

9.5 Regular Expression Grammar

Grammars describing the syntax of both basic and extended regular expressions are presented in this section. The grammar takes precedence over the text. See the Shell and Utilities volume of IEEE Std 1003.1-2001, Section 1.10, Grammar Conventions.

9.5.1 BRE/ERE Grammar Lexical Conventions

The lexical conventions for regular expressions are as described in this section.

Except as noted, the longest possible token or delimiter beginning at a given point is recognized.

The following tokens are processed (in addition to those string constants shown in the grammar):

COLL_ELEM_SINGLE

Any single-character collating element, unless it is a **META_CHAR**.

COLL_ELEM_MULTI

Any multi-character collating element.

BACKREF

Applicable only to basic regular expressions. The character string consisting of '\' followed by a single-digit numeral, '1' to '9'.

DUP_COUNT

Represents a numeric constant. It shall be an integer in the range 0 <= **DUP_COUNT** <= {RE_DUP_MAX}. This token is only recognized when the context of the grammar requires it. At all other times, digits not preceded by '\' are treated as **ORD_CHAR**.

META_CHAR

One of the characters:

^

When found first in a bracket expression

-

When found anywhere but first (after an initial '^', if any) or last in a bracket expression, or as the ending range point in a range expression

]

When found anywhere but first (after an initial '^', if any) in a bracket expression

L_ANCHOR

Applicable only to basic regular expressions. The character '^' when it appears as the first character of a basic regular expression and when not **QUOTED_CHAR**. The '^' may be recognized as an anchor elsewhere; see BRE Expression Anchoring.

ORD_CHAR

A character, other than one of the special characters in **SPEC_CHAR**.

QUOTED_CHAR

In a BRE, one of the character sequences:

\^   \.   *   \[\$ \\

In an ERE, one of the character sequences:

```
\^    \.    \[    \$    \(    \)    \|
\*    \+    \?    \{    \\
```

R_ANCHOR

(Applicable only to basic regular expressions.) The character '$' when it appears as the last character of a basic regular expression and when not QUOTED_CHAR. The '$' may be recognized as an anchor elsewhere; see BRE Expression Anchoring.

SPEC_CHAR

For basic regular expressions, one of the following special characters:

.

Anywhere outside bracket expressions

\

Anywhere outside bracket expressions

[

Anywhere outside bracket expressions

^

When used as an anchor (see BRE Expression Anchoring) or when first in a bracket expression

$

When used as an anchor

*

Anywhere except first in an entire RE, anywhere in a bracket expression, directly following "\(", directly following an anchoring '^'

For extended regular expressions, shall be one of the following special characters found anywhere outside bracket expressions:

```
^    .    [    $    (    )    |
*    +    ?    {    \
```

(The close-parenthesis shall be considered special in this context only if matched with a preceding open-parenthesis.)

9.5.2 RE and Bracket Expression Grammar

This section presents the grammar for basic regular expressions, including the bracket expression grammar that is common to both BREs and EREs.

```
%token      ORD_CHAR QUOTED_CHAR DUP_COUNT


%token      BACKREF L_ANCHOR R_ANCHOR


%token      Back_open_paren  Back_close_paren
/*             '\('               '\)'       */


%token      Back_open_brace  Back_close_brace
/*             '\{'               '\}'        */


/* The following tokens are for the Bracket Expression
   grammar common to both REs and EREs. */


%token      COLL_ELEM_SINGLE COLL_ELEM_MULTI META_CHAR


%token      Open_equal Equal_close Open_dot Dot_close Open_colon Colon_close
/*             '[='        '=]'       '[.'     '.]'       '[:'       ':]'  */


%token      class_name
/* class_name is a keyword to the LC_CTYPE locale category */
/* (representing a character class) in the current locale */
/* and is only recognized between [: and :] */


%start      basic_reg_exp
%%


/* ---------------------------------------------
   Basic Regular Expression
   ---------------------------------------------
*/
```

```
basic_reg_exp   :              RE_expression
                | L_ANCHOR
                |                           R_ANCHOR
                | L_ANCHOR                  R_ANCHOR
                | L_ANCHOR RE_expression
                |              RE_expression R_ANCHOR
                | L_ANCHOR RE_expression R_ANCHOR
                ;
RE_expression   :              simple_RE
                | RE_expression simple_RE
                ;
simple_RE       : nondupl_RE
                | nondupl_RE RE_dupl_symbol
                ;
nondupl_RE      : one_char_or_coll_elem_RE
                | Back_open_paren RE_expression Back_close_paren
                | BACKREF
                ;
one_char_or_coll_elem_RE : ORD_CHAR
                | QUOTED_CHAR
                | '.'
                | bracket_expression
                ;
RE_dupl_symbol : '*'
                | Back_open_brace DUP_COUNT                 Back_close_brace
                | Back_open_brace DUP_COUNT ','             Back_close_brace
                | Back_open_brace DUP_COUNT ',' DUP_COUNT Back_close_brace
                ;


/* --------------------------------------------
   Bracket Expression
   --------------------------------------------
*/
bracket_expression : '[' matching_list ']'
                | '[' nonmatching_list ']'
                ;
matching_list   : bracket_list
                ;
nonmatching_list : '^' bracket_list
                ;
bracket_list    : follow_list
                | follow_list '-'
                ;
```

```
follow_list      :                  expression_term
                 | follow_list expression_term
                 ;
expression_term : single_expression
                 | range_expression
                 ;
single_expression : end_range
                 | character_class
                 | equivalence_class
                 ;
range_expression : start_range end_range
                 | start_range '-'
                 ;
start_range      : end_range '-'
                 ;
end_range        : COLL_ELEM_SINGLE
                 | collating_symbol
                 ;
collating_symbol : Open_dot COLL_ELEM_SINGLE Dot_close
                 | Open_dot COLL_ELEM_MULTI Dot_close
                 | Open_dot META_CHAR Dot_close
                 ;
equivalence_class : Open_equal COLL_ELEM_SINGLE Equal_close
                 | Open_equal COLL_ELEM_MULTI Equal_close
                 ;
character_class : Open_colon class_name Colon_close
                 ;
```

The BRE grammar does not permit **L_ANCHOR** or **R_ANCHOR** inside "\(" and "\)" (which implies that '^' and '$' are ordinary characters). This reflects the semantic limits on the application, as noted in BRE Expression Anchoring. Implementations are permitted to extend the language to interpret '^' and '$' as anchors in these locations, and as such, conforming applications cannot use unescaped '^' and '$' in positions inside "\(" and "\)" that might be interpreted as anchors.

9.5.3 ERE Grammar

This section presents the grammar for extended regular expressions, excluding the bracket expression grammar.

Note The bracket expression grammar and the associated **%token** lines are identical between BREs and EREs. It has been omitted from the ERE section to avoid unnecessary editorial duplication.

```
%token   ORD_CHAR QUOTED_CHAR DUP_COUNT
%start   extended_reg_exp
%%

/* -----------------------------------------
   Extended Regular Expression
   -----------------------------------------
*/
extended_reg_exp     :                        ERE_branch
                     | extended_reg_exp '|' ERE_branch
                     ;
ERE_branch           :              ERE_expression
                     | ERE_branch ERE_expression
                     ;
ERE_expression       : one_char_or_coll_elem_ERE
                     | '^'
                     | '$'
                     | '(' extended_reg_exp ')'
                     | ERE_expression ERE_dupl_symbol
                     ;
one_char_or_coll_elem_ERE  : ORD_CHAR
                     | QUOTED_CHAR
                     | '.'
                     | bracket_expression
                     ;
ERE_dupl_symbol      : '*'
                     | '+'
                     | '?'
                     | '{' DUP_COUNT                '}'
                     | '{' DUP_COUNT ','            '}'
                     | '{' DUP_COUNT ',' DUP_COUNT '}'
                     ;
```

The ERE grammar does not permit several constructs that previous sections specify as having undefined results:

- **ORD_CHAR** preceded by '\'

- One or more *ERE_dupl_symbol*s appearing first in an ERE, or immediately following '|', '^', or '('

- '{' not part of a valid *ERE_dupl_symbol*

- '|' appearing first or last in an ERE, or immediately following '|' or '(', or immediately preceding ')'

Implementations are permitted to extend the language to allow these. Conforming applications cannot use such constructs.

Index

You Need the Companion eBook

Your purchase of this book entitles you to buy the companion PDF-version eBook for only $10. Take the weightless companion with you anywhere.

We believe this Apress title will prove so indispensable that you'll want to carry it with you everywhere, which is why we are offering the companion eBook (in PDF format) for $10 to customers who purchase this book now. Convenient and fully searchable, the PDF version of any content-rich, page-heavy Apress book makes a valuable addition to your programming library. You can easily find and copy code—or perform examples by quickly toggling between instructions and the application. Even simultaneously tackling a donut, diet soda, and complex code becomes simplified with hands-free eBooks!

Once you purchase your book, getting the $10 companion eBook is simple:

❶ Visit **www.apress.com/promo/tendollars/**.

❷ Complete a basic registration form to receive a randomly generated question about this title.

❸ Answer the question correctly in 60 seconds, and you will receive a promotional code to redeem for the $10.00 eBook.

THE EXPERT'S VOICE™

2855 TELEGRAPH AVENUE | SUITE 600 | BERKELEY, CA 94705

Offer valid through 5/17/09.